A CHURCH BY DAYLIGHT

'But reassurance is just what Christians should not be looking for at this point in their history ... The fragility of their religion is not due to the theologians but to its role in our social life.'
Alasdair MacIntyre in *Against the Self-Images of the Age*

'All I'm saying is that the Western world will either live by what it professes to believe in or it will cease to exist.'
James Baldwin in *A Rap on Race*

By the same author

On the Church
The Deployment and Payment of the Clergy
The Death and Resurrection of the Church

Philosophy
The Annihilation of Man
The Meaning of Human Existence
The English Philosophers
Nature into History
Persons and Perception
Alternatives to Christian Belief
Coming to Terms with Sex

Biography
Sir Thomas More
Son of Man

Autobiography
The Living Hedge
Angry Young Man
Boy down Kitchener Street

A CHURCH BY DAYLIGHT

A reappraisement of the Church
of England and its future

LESLIE PAUL

GEOFFREY CHAPMAN
LONDON   1973

Geoffrey Chapman
Cassell & Collier Macmillan Publishers Ltd, London
35 Red Lion Square, London WC1R 4SG
Sydney, Auckland, Toronto, Johannesburg

The Macmillan Publishing Co. Inc. New York

First published 1973
© 1973 Leslie Paul

ISBN 0 225 65979 4

Printed in Great Britain by A. Wheaton & Co., Exeter

Contents

for Eric James

'I have a good eye, uncle: I can see a church by daylight.'
                                    Much Ado About Nothing

Acknowledgements

I HAVE to acknowledge my great gratitude to John M. Turner of the Queen's College, Birmingham, for reading all the historical sections and for his fertile criticism and encouragement, and to W. H. Saumarez Smith for generously finding time to read the whole and making such careful comments: to Nicholas Molony for the expert drawing of the graphs and charts: to Archdeacon John Lewis and Group-Captain A. W. Caswell C.B.E., of Hereford Diocese, and to Brigadier P. R. Hemans C.B.E., and Mark Cornwall-Jones of the Southwark Diocese, and Ronald Neuss of the Statistical Unit of the Central Board of Finance for help with figures or for checking them. I am indebted to Professor Geoffrey Parrinder of King's College, Strand, for figures about world religions. My gratitude goes to Jean Nutter for checking MSS. and proofs and to Mrs Ruby Gordon for wrestling with so many drafts and revisions. My general indebtedness to the Institute for the Study of Worship and Religious Architecture, of which I am an Hon. fellow, is plain and acknowledged in parts III and IV. I have to thank Mrs Suzanne Chapman, Edward Carpenter, Paul Wilkinson and Eric James—and many others—for their enthusiasm and encouragement. I sent letters to the *Church Times* and *Church of England Newspaper* asking for information and help. The replies were overwhelming and I must thank all those who took the trouble to write to me and send me material. Much of it has been used in the book, and there acknowledged. All of it proved of value in filling in the background for me, and I am grateful: I have made new friends.

While this was 'a work in progress' some small part appeared in journals: 'The Role of the Clergy Today—An Organizational Approach: Problems of Deployment', *The Expository Times*, vol. LXXXVII, No. 7, April 1971; 'The Legal Straitjacket of the Church of England', *Contemporary Review*, vol. 220, No. 1276, May 1972; 'The Church: Aid or Obstacle?', *The Modern Churchman*, vol. XVI, No. 1, October 1972. The article in *The Expository Times* was published in *The Social Sciences and The Churches*, ed. C. L. Mitton, T. & T. Clark, Edinburgh, 1972. Some of the historical section was given as lectures in Eastern College, St David's, Pa, when I was Lilly Scholar-in-Residence there in the Fall of 1970: many of my students at the Queen's College, Birmingham, suffered these expositions too.

The Queen's College, Birmingham, 1969–70;   LESLIE PAUL
Madley, Hereford, 1970–73

Introduction

'The doctrine of the Church of England is grounded in the holy Scriptures, and in such teachings of the ancient Fathers and Councils of the Church as are agreeable to the said Scriptures. In particular such doctrine is to be found in the Thirty-nine Articles of Religion, The Book of Common Prayer, and the Ordinal.'

Canon A5

'God is decreeing to begin some new and great period in His Church, even to the reforming of Reformation itself. What does He then but reveal Himself to His servants, and as His manner is, first to His Englishmen?'

Milton, *Areopagitica*

WHAT is the Church of England? This is as daunting a question as asking what is the establishment, or a social class, or, even, what is time. It is something one is sure one knows until one is asked to describe or define it. Just to relate the tangle of law, tradition, proprietary rights, spiritual inheritance, pragmatic genius, theological nullity, democratic experiment and civilized antiquity which constitutes, but still neither describes nor defines, the Church of England, is task enough. To speak of its future is another matter altogether. It may be an impertinence to try. Perhaps it has none.

Yet there is something which is irreducibly the Church of England in the social experience of many of us. As I wrote the first sentence on this page there was a knock at the door and the vicar entered. He had come to bring comfort to an invalid, to offer help in a purely secular matter, to enquire of me, a reader, how the services I had been responsible for had gone. His three errands typify the most important roles of the vicar down the centuries. They create his social presence. As so many of his fellow-citizens have known him he has been the man of the cloth ready to bring help and comfort to those in need and to play a part in community affairs, and the man responsible for the acts of worship of the community or communities covered by his parish, dissenters notwithstanding. Though the community might not regard the last as his most important task, *he* probably would. Legally, they are the reason for his presence. Irreducibly, this is the Church of England, the priest or presbyter in the midst of his flock, serving them after his fashion from a nucleus of distinctive buildings appointed for the purpose—and so a fixed point of reference in a constantly changing social and political scene. And the same would be true of every European country served by a major Christian Church, whether established or not, and would constitute the felt presence of the Church. The existence of dissenting Churches would normally only underline that presence and its primacy.

This concreteness of parson and holy buildings in a community has to be understood as the Church's being-in-society, from which much follows. It is not all that the Church is, but while much else that it is may be hidden from the community, the primal impact remains. The priest is as archetypal as farmer or sailor, king or soldier. His church is more of an archetype than a school or a castle: it is as old an image as the home. Such powerful archetypes as schoolmaster or policeman are newcomers beside the priest: even more than they, he is the butt of popular humour.

What then of the role and presence of the bishop? The bishop is never the same universal figure as the priest. There is no instantaneous social recognition of his role: he is less familiar to folklore than a lord, but his place is seen to be with him in the nebulous grouping of unpopular ruling figures—certainly socially, and probably geographically, distant. For such reasons the bishop could not be seen as the Church's 'being-in-society' as the parish priest was. The bishop was understood as the man with authority over the priest, of whom the priest had to be wary, as the common man had to be wary of the king. He belonged like the king to the great of the land.

Still moving among archetypes—what of the laity? The impact of monasteries and nunneries upon medieval societies was enormous, and invariably corporate. It was not the individual monk, or a prior or abbot, however holy, who impressed, so much as the whole monastic body, a disciplined religious army, much of whose power came from its separation *within* society. Sects have sometimes achieved a powerful collective presence-to-society which made individuals within it anonymous, but lay congregations, in the Church of England at least, never did so in the modern world. If they achieved a corporate presence in the past it has gone unrecorded. It was not part of the contract of being-the-laity. The historic contract was to be loyal, to be docile, to be instructed, to give alms, and to have reservations and lines of retreat. The congregation was a listening presence on Sundays, and an important one, but only as an audience is a powerful presence at a performance. The same terms of being apply—that it fragments after the show. Individual lay people were esteemed, *within the congregation*, for their closeness to, influence upon the priest, or as a vehicle of his will, but this discriminating regard for a few is the negation of regard for, awe of, the congregational presence such as the Church of Scotland achieved in its Kirk sessions. The point is that the congregation is not in general in Churches seen as archetypal in the way that priest, Church, bishop, monastery are seen to be. The congregation is the grass 'the Church' grazes over and on which it gets fat. It is in part a legacy of the Middle Ages when the hierarchical structures of the prelatical Church stood in extreme separation from the worshippers. That 'Church' was felt as a presence apart, a power necessary but dangerous, with its own logic of action which was not the common man's. In such a situation the laity, the worshippers, could have no corporate identity within the Church: rather they would form the element in which the priestly fishes swam. Without the element the fishes would die. But nothing in nature would turn the sea itself into fish. It is easy in such a situation for the fish to think that without them the sea would not continue to exist.

And this is to ask, archetypes aside, what is the role and status of the laity in the being of the Church—universally, as well as specifically within the Church of England. It is a question the Reformation tried to answer. It is a question one fears might never have been asked so widely and urgently now were the Churches not standing with their backs to the wall. The estates of the realm in England were the crown, the nobility, the Church. The commons were just the commons. There is an irony in the situation that the king only summoned the Commons when he wanted money and war and could not do without them. And so the Commons acquired a corporate status over against the traditional occupants of the seats of power, with all sorts of unforeseen consequences.

It is not a triviality to ask about the role of the laity, for one is also asking *what is the being of the Church?* One way of answering this is to enquire where the authority lies to determine who is a member of the Church. And in an episcopal Church only one answer is possible —it is the bishop. All authority ultimately derives from him. The ordinary incumbent exercises his office for the bishop and with his licence. A bishop ordains him. A bishop inducts him to his living. A bishop is the only priest who is fully a priest in the sense that he can not only baptise, marry and celebrate the eucharist, but confirm, consecrate, ordain, license, condemn, suspend, excommunicate, defrock. In the earliest Churches he was the only one who said Masses. He received all the donations and decided the distribution of funds. He directed men and settled disputes on doctrine. He was the authoritarian leader of a team. He allotted roles and posts. As the numbers of clergy and of churches grew his power increased. In a foundational sense the ministry in the diocese was his and he delegated what parts of it he chose to whom he chose. The multiplication of parishes, the growth of their powers and even their present legal independence in the Church of England has never altered the theoretical sense of the parochial ministry as the episcopal ministry vicariously exercised.

As a recent Report[1] reminds us, the bishop as I have just described him is seen 'as receiving his authority direct from Christ through the existing episcopate and their predecessors. On this view, the bishop exercises the authority of Christ, delegated to him, over the Church. His authority derived from Christ, is in no sense derived from other members of the Church, though it is mediated through them. The Church chooses him to be a bishop: Christ, through the episcopate, makes him one.'[2]

---

[1] *Bishops and Dioceses, Report of the ACCM Ministry Committee Working Party on the Episcopate*, chaired by the Bishop of Derby, CIO, London 1971. I was a member of this working party.
[2] Op. cit. p. 9.

So high a doctrine of the episcopacy tends to reduce every other stratum of the Church to a nullity, particularly if bishops are chosen from their peers, or from above, by archbishops, the pope, or an authority standing outside, such as the crown, and not elected: of course such a doctrine maintains that sense of the Church in its apartness from the laity of which I have spoken. No one has the right to contend with the direct appointee of Christ, or to diminish Christ's power!

Outside the Roman Church this doctrine is seldom held in all its purity but something more nearly in accord with what the Report just quoted calls 'the second view', that the bishop receives his authority 'from Christ through the Church'. The authority is *analogous* to that which Christ exercises over the whole Church, rather than precisely that power. 'The Church chooses the man to exercise this authority, and he is answerable to God and the Church for the way in which he exercises it.'[3] Vague though this may be, it points to an important shift. The Church *corporately* is now the bearer of Christ's charisma: those to whom it delegates authority are in part responsible to it for the exercise of their power. There is not a Hobbesian surrender of all power to the sovereign bishop. It is a step from this to the doctrine that *episcope* (oversight) belongs to the whole Church corporately, the whole Church being the Body of Christ in the world. 'This authority is delegated by the Church to the Bishop, as other kinds of authority are delegated by the Church to other office holders in the Church. It is convenient for the bishops to exercise it, though this authoritative role could be exercised by others just as conveniently.'[4] And it is with this doctrine that we move towards the understanding of the Church as, finally, the community of all the faithful answerable corporately to God for the whole of its acts. It is true that Reformation Churches taught this and believed that they had accomplished it, though new presbyter turned out to be 'old priest writ large'. No matter. The doctrine now moves the bowels of the episcopal Churches of the world, particularly the Roman.

It is very hard to discover what the primitive Church was like institutionally. Jesus commissioned his twelve disciples. This was very much in a more ancient tradition of pupils gathering in blessed poverty round a wise teacher to learn from him and to go away and spread his way of life. It is a Greek conception rather than a Jewish one. The older prophets were often solitary. That the disciples stayed with Jesus throughout his campaign for the repentance of Israel hardly changes that concept: it was so extraordinarily brief. Moving about with him made them a tighter band, with a common purse, but not very much more. The Gospels paint them as fallible men, and do not exalt their status: often

---

[3] Op. cit. p. 9.
[4] Op. cit. p. 10.

their ambitions are rebuked. One betrayed him, all at the crisis forsook him. The sending-out of the seventy appears to be a true missionary enterprise but not with the aim of establishing new institutions in opposition to the synagogues, but principally to teach.

It is a sizeable group of followers to whom Jesus appears at the Resurrection, and geographically extended, but it only seems to take on organizational forms at the Ascension, when a successor was appointed to Judas by the drawing of lots. It is probably true that the early Church after the first persecution was over was two Churches, a small quietist group under Peter and James in Jerusalem, and the aggressive missionary Church under Paul at work (at first) among the synagogues of the diaspora in Asia Minor. The two Churches did not always agree. It certainly seems as though Paul felt himself the real head of that new Christian Church, Peter notwithstanding. Oversight of Paul's Church comes naturally from disciples, peripatetic missioners and such, but it works mostly to commend and command the new doctrine rather than to institute a particular ecclesiastical structure. Like Topsy, that just growed.

Dr William Neil writes, 'In the light of Luke's record in *Acts* there is nothing sacrosanct about the present form of the Church in any of its branches. It was launched into the world as the community of the Holy Spirit and it opened its doors to all and sundry on the simple basis of their acceptance of Jesus Christ as Saviour and Lord. Subsequently organization and discipline became necessary but none of this was of the essence of its origins, for the unity of the earliest Christians was based on quite a modest four-fold formula: faith in Christ in accordance with the apostolic teaching, the fellowship of all believers issuing in social action, regular sacramental observance, and common prayer.... It was on such an unpretentious basis of unity that the Church began.'[5]

It is easy to see the primitive Church as something makeshift, improvised and only growing to order, discipline, hierarchy as it expanded and its resources and its needs mounted. One can view it all sociologically and say that a process of routinization and professionalization inevitably took place and that this phase was marked by the emergence of a trained priestly élite. The Jesus whose authority the élite claimed could be viewed as the shepherd, the saviour of the flock of the parables of the pastoral mission, or as the rejected Messiah of Jewish tradition, or as the divine high priest interceding with the Father for the sins of the world on the sacrificial Jewish temple model. It was the last which more and more came to dominate. The concept of the rejected Messiah faded as the Church lost its Jewish foundations. The priestly

---

[5] *The Truth about the Early Church*, Hodder, London 1970 p. 124.

understanding triumphed when the Church became first the godchild of and then the heir to, the Roman Empire and took those prestigious powers, priestly, political, judicial, symbolized by the papal triple crown. What was created under Rome was terribly apposite to feudalism and was sealed by it. Probably these forms, the forms repeated with variations in the great Churches of the West, were necessary if the Church was to grow, consolidate and teach the world a coherent doctrine and endow it with common forms of worship. But they are not obligatory on the Churches for ever and ever. If we go back to the Jerusalem Church terrorized by the unconverted Saul and come down to our own times where we find it represented not only by great worldly Churches but by small underground groups under terrorist regimes we have to say that the forms of the Church have been protean. No one order is the legitimate one. The only compulsion is to seek the one that best serves the times. At the core of all of them have been two elements—the fellowship of the faithful and a commissioned presbyter serving them. One could risk a generalization and say that the Church was at its most charismatic and energetic when the two were so closely conjoined that each element could speak confidently for the other: at its most dominating and powerful when the priestly element was autocratically in control: at its weakest when the elements no longer understood each other and drifted apart, and away from the world to which they no longer knew how to speak.

In the high doctrine of the Church of England what the Church is, irreducibly, is its bishops and priests, that is, those held to be directly commissioned by Christ. Were there no laity, nevertheless a Church would be present in these dedicated men as it was present in the persons of Augustine and his mission priests at Canterbury in 597 AD or in Columbus, Patrick, Alban earlier. To a Church in this irreducible sense buildings are not indispensable. The earliest Masses and preachings were said under the village oak or before a cross of wood set up in some central place. One may also speak of what such a Church might irreducibly be liturgically. So long as there were those authorized episcopally to celebrate the eucharist, to preach the gospel and to baptise, the Church would be present liturgically and kerygmatically. It would create its own *koinonia* as the Salvation Army did at street corners. If such a stripped-down Church was recognized by people and rulers as the Christian presence required by society, one might even speak of it as established. But it could be without laws, without even stipends and with virtually no property.

Yet in the other, far less high doctrine, we may conceive of the Church as it must have been under Saul's persecution in Jerusalem, or in the days of the martyrdoms in Rome, or in Stalin's or Hitler's penal camps —a Church which is no more than the faithful meeting together in small, secret groups to witness and to pray, and being the Church in that place with or without the benefit of priest or bishop: indeed facing death and historical oblivion: a Church more self-effacing even than the Church of the catacombs was once supposed to be. If such a Church had its members commissioned to preside over the eucharist; if its members received baptism; if it remained as faithful as it could therefore to Dr Neil's four elements, here would be the indubitable Church reaching back to the small frightened gatherings praying in dark Jerusalem hovels at the time of Stephen's martyrdom when terror whirled like a storm through the streets.

Whether we look at a Church moved by the high doctrine, as finding its being through Christ's representatives, or in a doctrine of the utmost theological simplicity as the gathering of the faithful baptised, the *laos*, the people of God, without distinction of rank ('where two or three are gathered together in my name there am I in the midst of them') we can see what I may call the irreducible Church as something so much simpler, so much less uncluttered than any contemporary Church, that one stands amazed by the legal, administrative and propertied complexities of all great modern Churches and compelled to ask, are they Christ's work?

It is quite reasonable to conceive of a Church of England far simpler, far more primitive than the existing institution, yet competent to fulfil the tasks for which it was instituted: indeed releasing, out of its simplicity, a new charisma. Nothing in ecclesiastical history condemns this. All movements of renewal struggle to achieve it. A troubled longing for such an uncluttered Church is understandable and to be praised. Alas, the clutter is understandable too. It is part of the defence of the Church against the world and against the demands of God. In the perspective of history, as the Church settled and converted, as it created its disciplined communities, as its role on its own insistence became central to society and its presence ubiquitous, so the buildings rose, the uniforms multiplied.

The Church's buildings became themselves part of the witness to the permanence of the Church, and what it preached, in a world of flux. They stood up in every community as symbols. They lifted themselves up like lightning conductors to the flash of God. They attracted to themselves devotion, decoration, immense wealth. Before long the Church which had begun as a mission of devotion to the unworldliness of Christ, as a struggle against the dominance of 'the prince of the world', became itself enmeshed in the world, a source of the power and riches it began by condemning and despising. Enmeshed in the law too, and in government of societies. Once you have riches and power, the law becomes concerned with your proprietary rights, either to uphold them or to expropriate. Government becomes concerned with taxes and the right to tax; with the proper forms of the collection and disposal of properties and money; with the exercise of power, the punishment of offenders; with the liberties of the subject and the relationship of the civil power to ecclesiastical structures and aspirations. Both civil and ecclesiastical authorities become concerned with abuse, misappropriation of funds and the corruptions of individuals. Both camps must face the malevolence of bigotry and stupidity. Quite unchristian hatreds seethe. Christ himself becomes an instrument handy for the pursuit of ambition. The missionary dynamic which begins in innocence against the world, reforming the world, ends up by its very success an historic institution in the world, discovering in its bosom the very sins against which once, single-mindedly, it campaigned. It is compromised. Such is the situation of the Church of England, one which it shares with every other great Church. It is tempting to say, this has nothing to do with Christ, let it end, and let us start again. But starting again has its problems, particularly if it means the same old cycle, and it has been tried. It is unhistoric too. There are other things to be said. The struggle of the Churches for incorruptibility in the midst of corruption adds profoundly to our religious understanding of the tragedy and hope of man's situation, and what it means in the absence of hope to be the recipient of grace. What the Churches tried to be, and what they became, and what they sought to undo, has added a rich strain to our culture and every culture is a form of man's understanding of himself and his potentiality. We have to hold on to that understanding through the institutions which enshrine it, and remember that the Church is a sinning Church.

There is more besides. Within the Church (the Church of England in this instance), no matter how swathed in complexities and fustian legalities, lie the irreducible elements of the Christian ministry, priests and bishops, a sacred liturgy, a will to preach and baptise, the gathered faithful. If much of its worldliness can be attributed to the charge upon it to tangle with the world, something the secularizing theologians must approve, much of its appalling complexity has been accumulated in the double process of striving to preserve unbroken its primitive mandate and at the same time accommodating itself erastian fashion to the secular power prepared to give other ends a higher loyalty, and devoted to religion in the degree that it could serve the ends of government.

Can it ever be simplified?

Limits have to be recognized. In a process of stripping-down there must come a point where poverty of resources starves the mission itself. Equally, the accumulation of resources, the creation of an immense top-heavy institution ends up with an insupportable structure which nevertheless has to be supported. At that point support, or maintenance, tends to have a higher priority than mission. The wheels have to be kept turning. The artillerymen are so exhausted dragging their guns through the mud that they can never get around to firing them. The mission dies.

Of course, economic difficulties are already forcing a simplification, but it often appears to be a piecemeal simplification, a little cut here and a little reform there, not inspired by a theology of the Church but forced by the diocesan budgetary prospects. Of course, such effects are cumulative, and what could result from them would be a miniaturized Church of England quite unaware that the witch had turned it overnight into a dwarf. Whereas what is needed is a renewed Church responding to a Toynbee-like challenge with a clearheaded response.

It is part of the purpose of this book to discuss the possibilities of a renewal in simplicity among the many futures the Church may choose for itself or events press upon it.

PART ONE

The Church in History

'If you want to go forward from here, then the steps that got us here have to be incorporated into where we are going next.'

Margaret Mead in *A Rap on Race*

ONE
The Thousand Years

FROM the time of the landing of the mission of Augustine in Kent to the death of Queen Elizabeth I in 1603 is in the round a thousand years. During all that time a Church of England flourished which, even at the end, was hardly distinguishable from its catholic neighbours on the continent. By one tradition the date of Augustine's arrival has been identified as the coming of Christianity to England. Every schoolboy knows the story that the Abbot Gregory saw flaxen-haired boys exposed for sale in the slave market in Rome and said of them, 'Non sunt Angli, sed Angeli', and that this moved him to an interest in the Christianization of their country where it might have moved a modern prelate to a protest against slavery.

But Augustine was a late comer. His campaign was to win over the pagan kingdoms of the Anglo-Saxons who, in driving the Britons into Wales, Ireland and Brittany, had destroyed the remnants of Roman culture and social organization and with it a British Church which already boasted its martyrs, missionaries, bishops, monasteries and devout faithful. The names of St Patrick, St Columba, St Ninian, St Alban are associated with that earlier and strongly independent Christian enterprise. Certainly from the third century, perhaps even from the second century, a Christian Church existed in Britain. The span of life even of the pre-Augustinian Church could have been as much as four hundred years, which is about the time that has elapsed since the Elizabethan settlement. Henry VIII's Act of Supremacy and Elizabeth's settlement involved serious changes but no breach of continuity with the medieval Church.[1] Without too great an exaggeration we may speak of a Church of England coming down to us from fourteen hundred, perhaps eighteen hundred years ago. It is an impressive span of time. It makes the Church of England the oldest social institution in the land. One is tempted to qualify that, in the light of its sadly reduced social role. Is the Church even the same Church? In its modern setting one is

---

[1] For a view of continuity see B. L. Manning, *The Making of Modern English Religion*, London 1929.

compelled to recognize the Church of England as one Church among many in a fragmented and pluralistic society, and one among many social institutions. One sees the Churches themselves as socio-religious institutions, shorn of much of their historic power and influence, struggling to breathe amid a riot of secular enterprises—universities, schools, banks, political parties and institutions, newspapers, mass media, factories and production plants, bursting cities and booming air lines— and all the clutter, noise and confusion of an onward driving technological world out of control.

Against that picture one can speak of the Church of England as for many centuries, perhaps up to the end of the eighteenth century, *the* social institution of the land—the source of learning and of moral law, the fount of education and of help to the poor, the origin of much of the poetry of life and beauty of cities. Indeed, through its liturgy, preaching and Bible the creator of language and culture. But how poverty-stricken that tribute is! Not for want of trying on the part of the author but because he, like everyone else in our spiritually dessicated world, cannot easily grasp the role of the Church when the Church was all. It almost misses the point to speak of the Church as 'the creator of language and culture'. It *was* the culture. It was the centre of the drama of human existence. It was itself a cosmic event. It showed forth the expulsion of Adam and Eve from Eden, the consequent fall of man, the conquest of the promised land, the covenant with God, the entry of the Son of God into the world to redeem man, his rejection and passion on the cross, his triumph over death, the victorious march of his church as his instrument in the conversion and redemption of the world, the promised second coming. Every churchgoer, willing or unwilling, was caught up in his Saviour's will. His personal participation was inescapable for *he* would be judged as the first man was judged and pay through all eternity for his degree of faithfulness on earth. And every other man and woman likewise. And every stained glass window, every mural, illustrated it. Everywhere a man turned a triumphant Church proclaimed the drama in which he was responsibly caught. The almost magical religious cycle of the Christian year celebrated it in festival after festival. Even the poorest and most destitute could be performers in that drama which spoke most to those the world had most abandoned.

How can we compare a Church which had that total function in and before the Dark and Middle Ages with a Church which functions, as most Churches in the West do today, without knowing why, in a muted and minimalized fashion? There can be no social drama of which the Church is the centre unless there is a social surrender to the drama. And today this is missing. There has to be a popular surge into the beauty and terror of the drama; into the heart of the sustaining myth. Without it the Gospel becomes a comment on an alien way of life and a toy for theologians, rather than life itself. This is what has happened to us.

If one asks what patterns a man's life in this total sense today, one cannot say the Church. It would be *individually* true of many men and women, but no longer socially true. It would even be difficult to say whether ideas or beliefs of any sort shape a modern man's life in the bold medieval way, unless perhaps belief in the nation. Apart from a number of hazy presuppositions about progress, and popular maxims about fairness and kindness, of which Richard Hoggart speaks in *Uses of Literacy*, what patterns a man's life today are the obligations of work and family. These fix him in routines, responsibilities, relationships and duties. It is typical of the secular world that beyond that nothing is of obligation except what may be demanded, even sacrificially, by the nation. The nation, perhaps, is the last refuge of the sacred in the modern world. Apart from the demands of the nation, severe and clear only in times of war, the world fragments his life in its own fragmentation. Perhaps today the mass media and the motor car have most influence. One cannot be sure. But these are means, not ends. They do not explain or justify his life, they merely provision it so that it may ramify still deeper into meaninglessness.

The ancient and the medieval pictures are so different that one is almost in another civilization. Of course, work and family then were the primary pattern-makers also, but both of these were caught up in the web of the Church which sanctified the great moments of life, blessing the harvest along with the birth, decreeing the holidays and great festivals, entering into the daily life of the people in guild meetings, mystery plays, charities and pilgrimages and the stories one told round the fire. Work and family were snatched up into a religious frame which both explained and justified, even glorified, the travail which was the life of man. As in quite primitive societies, the society was the *ecclesia*: the social pattern was a religious one.

I have no wish to idealize that medieval or any earlier religious life. Men then were as coarse and sinful, as brutal and lecherous as they are today: Chaucer tells all. I simply want to point to its totality. It was this which made the Church—and all over Europe of course, not just in England—a civilization maker. It is no longer such. This is the dramatic change. It may preach as powerfully as ever its old beliefs and scourge society with its criticism if it wants to, but it does not of itself change the direction of society. Forces it is the least equipped to understand do that. It has moved from the centre of society to the periphery and this is the transformation which compels us to look again at that historical continuity. What precisely is its value if it has led the Church into an ecclesiastical enclave from which it cannot escape into the larger society it once dominated? But again, what one says here of the Church of England only illuminates to a greater or lesser degree the situation of the major Churches and denominations of the West.

TWO

Moments of Crisis

THE thousand years were years of struggle, all the same, first for conversion and then for survival, then for unity, then for much needed organization which, like Augustine, came from Rome. In the seventh century there was a clash of two missions, the one coming north from Canterbury and the other moving east and south from Ireland. It amounted to confrontation between cultures and led to the Synod of Whitby (664) where what were virtually two Churches met to resolve their differences over the date of Easter. But if Easter was the occasion, the real issue was whether the English Church was to continue in a lonely monastic isolation or to be brought back into the mainstream of European religious life through obedience to Rome.

It was from Rome a few years after the Synod of Whitby that the Church of England received its forms of government. The Church, like the land, which was swept by plague emptying equally towns and churches, was near collapse. The Synod of Whitby had muted differences but provided no leadership. There had been no Archbishop of Canterbury for five years after 664. The Church was without law, forms of government, organization. Pope Vitalian sent what was virtually a second mission under Theodore of Tarsus whom he consecrated Archbishop of Canterbury. Theodore got together his own Synod in Hertford in 772 which gave the Church its Canon law, its national synods, manageable dioceses and its first school in Canterbury. He regulated the Church calendar, the marriage laws, the relationships between religious houses and their bishops. Here was the first systematic institutionalizing of the Church of England not a little of which survives down to the present day. From that point on, it is no longer an improvising missionary enterprise, somewhat eccentric in the eyes of Rome, but a national Church in the Roman discipline.

Greater trials were to come. The Danish invasions laid waste the countryside. Monasteries and churches were burnt, bishops and their priests fought and fell in battle. The new settlers were pagans, the Church was again a frontier Church holding the thin line of civilization against its destroyers. It was the role of Alfred, the greatest Christian monarch since Charlemagne, it has been said, to turn the defensive action into a basis for a Christian victory. From his Wessex Kingdom the Danelaw was slowly reconquered by his successors and the Danish settlers christianized. It was by Alfred's efforts that the religious and intellectual level of both Church and people was raised to standards closer to those of Europe, even in some things put ahead.

Yet the frontier role of Britain and its Church was to be illustrated again and again. Canute made England the centre of a vast and vague Scandinavian empire. It could not last. England was too strong and rich to be governed from far away. But it was still exposed. And it was the invasion of the North of England by Harold Hardrada of Norway, which forced Harold of England to fight at Stamford Bridge and lost England to William of Normandy. Escaping from Scandinavia, England was captured by Europe.

In the event, the Norman Conquest consolidated the Church of England and fixed it more firmly in the Roman orbit. But it planted both Church and people in a legalistic feudalism from which escape was made difficult by the system of national accounting called the Domesday Book, a technical exercise far ahead of its times. The feudal system was such that it was impossible for a village church to function outside the seigneurial jurisdiction. It formed part of the lord's domain. He probably founded it and provided it, and it was difficult to fit subservience to the lord into the system of Church government 'which assumed as a root principle that every clergyman in the exercise of his ministry must act in dependence on and under the authority of the bishop'.[1]

Who was the lord, anyway? He could be the King, a prince, a baron, a bishop, an abbot, a monastic house, a sheriff, a lesser lord, a dean of a cathedral. One has not to think of a Church trapped and made subservient by feudalism but of the Church as itself a great feudal power, lord or vassal as circumstances dictated. Not without reason modern critics have likened the Church of Rome, as it has come down to us, to a tight feudal institution still with duties and obedience owed upwards and responsibilities downwards. Certainly it was in the feudal centuries that it was forged as a disciplinary thing.

Inevitably the conflict of loyalties at the parish level—is the parson the lord's man or the bishop's man or somehow both?—repeats itself at the national level. Is the archbishop the king's vassal or the pope's? It is not exactly the Henrician question in medieval times—is the Church national or international?—for nationalism hardly existed. But it is the question, since everyone had to owe obedience to someone, and all owed obedience to the Church, to whom does the Church owe obedience, and how much? It was not sufficient, in feudal times, to answer 'God'.

---

[1] G. W. O. Addleshaw, *The Development of the Parochial System from Charlemagne (768–814) to Urban II (1088–1099)*, St Anthony's Hall Publications, No. 6, 1954, p. 6.

The Church did not forego the feudal obedience owed to it, but it resisted vassalage to the king. Wherever it was powerful it behaved as a kingdom in its own right, in opposition if necessary to the temporal rulers, as when its courts encroached on the sphere of lay courts and it claimed jurisdiction over all clerks, even those of minor orders, and protected criminous clerks from temporal punishment. The tension was never solved in medieval times. It could not be while the pope was both temporal monarch and spiritual overlord of Christendom. He was in this the man of two loyalties himself. The bitterness the tension produced cost Thomas Becket, Archbishop of Canterbury, his life. It was particularly explosive when Church life was obviously corrupt and the Church unable to reform itself, but must have been least bearable, it has been said, when the temporal powers found little occasion to reproach the Church. Speaking of the downfall of Rome which left the Church in a new position of independence, Herbert Butterfield remarks, 'The result was those conflicts between the spiritual and secular arms which prevented on either side the establishment of a cramping totalitarianism. . . . From those controversies concerning the spiritual and temporal power emerged that wealth of speculation concerning human society which made political theory so largely a Western European development. . . . More significant than this, however, was the establishment of the autonomy of the spiritual principle—the most important area of human life and activity was freed from subservience to the secular power, and the state was not presumed to dictate to a man the moral end for which he was to live and the highest law that he should serve.'[2] No man taking to heart the adjuration of the Church that he belonged ultimately to God, to whom finally he had to give account, could ever believe that he belonged totally to the state. That is the ignoble heresy which has appeared only in our times.

The case of Thomas Becket, subject of brilliant plays, films and biographies,[3] is well known and very illustrative. As one of the team of brilliant young men trained by Theobald, Archbishop of Canterbury, he attracted the attention of Henry II, became his close friend and his magnificent Chancellor. Henry nominated him for the Archbishopric of

---

[2] Herbert Butterfield, *Christianity in European History*, Collins, London 1952, pp. 28 ff. In *Civilisation, A Personal View* (BBC and John Murray, London, 1969, p. 20) Sir Kenneth Clark wrote, 'Maybe the tension between the spiritual and worldly powers throughout the Middle Ages was precisely what kept European civilisation alive. If either had achieved absolute power, society might have grown as static as the civilisation of Egypt or Byzantium.'

[3] T. S. Eliot's *Murder in the Cathedral*, of course, Anouilh's *Becket*. In *Thomas Becket*, London, 1971. David Knowles rescues the complex and devious Archbishop from the literary hagiographers and restores him to history. Cf. also M. D. Knowles, 'Archbishop Thomas Becket: A Character Study', *Proceedings of the British Academy*, vol. XXXV 1949.

Canterbury on the death of old Theobald with the clear intention of extending royal control over the Church. His friend was to be the instrument. It proved a fatal misjudgment. Becket served the Church with as single-minded a loyalty as he had previously served the King. His way of life became humble and ascetic. His reputation grew as the obstinate defender of the Church's prerogatives till the King declared that 'England is not a bush which can hold two such robins as the Archbishop and myself'.

The King answered Becket's consistent defence of the Church with two Councils. The Second, the Council of Clarendon in 1164, set up the famous 'Constitutions' which forbade appeals to Rome, unless approved by the King, denied the clergy freedom to leave the country and made 'criminous clerks', convicted in church courts, subject to secular punishment. In view of the corruption of the clerical courts and the readiness of the clergy to block secular action by appeals to Rome, the 'Constitutions' could hardly be regarded as altogether excessive in their demands, though they were incompatible with the Gregorian view of a self-disciplined Church. Becket furiously opposed them, gave in under pressure, almost immediately regretted his weakness and sought an open breach with the King. Becket went into exile and returned after six years to triumph and danger. His assassination, in his own cathedral, by the knightly instruments of the King and those bishops who also opposed him brought more than martyrdom, ironically it brought success to Becket's cause. In the face of the horror of the whole of Christendom, all royal proposals to discipline the Church were dropped like red hot coals. The extent of the disaster to secular policies is revealed by the fact that the Act of Benefit of Clergy, which meant that an accused man in orders could claim exemption from trial in lay courts, deeply resented in the twelfth century, remained on the statute books until the nineteenth.

The struggle between Church and the royal power was almost as violent in the thirteenth century under King John. Again the Archbishop of Canterbury was at the heart of the storm. He was Stephen Langton, the nominee of Innocent III to solve again a clash between the King's and the Church's claims over the archiepiscopal succession. The royal rage at his appointment was such that Langton was denied entry to England and lived in exile for six years. England was placed under a papal interdict and the King eventually excommunicated. The churches were closed, no masses were said, only baptism and burial were permitted, and the devout of the country were plunged into mourning over what must have seemed the death of God. It is almost unbelievable that this went on unbroken for four years and was only ended and the King brought to heel by the threat of deposition and invasion. The King made an abject surrender. He gave up his throne and his kingdom to Innocent III and received them back as the Pope's vassal on payment of heavy reparations. It is a clearer example even than the martyrdom of Becket of the depth of the Church's conflict with the state and of the reality of papal power.

The first real gains for secular authority in the struggle between the temporalities and spiritualities came in the fourteenth century, towards the end of which the papacy itself was weak and in exile at Avignon. Its French 'captivity' was resented in England—France was the traditional enemy—and so were the pretensions and excesses of the Church at home. Not even the Church was happy about the heavy taxation siphoned off to the papacy: it far exceeded the royal taxation. England had become a papal colony, a subject nation. The general determination to decrease the papal power in England, a process begun before the Great Schism, gave rise to four fourteenth century statutes, two of Provisors, which declared invalid all papal appointments to English benefices and the two statutes of *Praemunire. Praemunire* forbade the taking to a foreign court of any suits which could be tried in the king's court—and what could be tried there was a matter for the king to decide. The penalty for defiance was outlawry which meant too that the condemned's estates were forfeit. *Praemunire* was still on the statute books and formed part of the royal power over the Church of England until 1967. The dean and chapter of a cathedral who refused the election of the crown's nominee to the bishopric could be punished by outlawry, imprisonment and confiscation of possessions. As they never contested the royal writ in modern times the matter was never put to trial. In the Middle Ages *Praemunire* formed the first legal barrier to further papal penetration in the kingdom and the first means of diminishing papal exactions. It marked the beginnings of English nationhood.

Attacks on the papacy and on the Church's corruption were popular with the London merchants and their apprentices, who saw England being plundered by a lot of miserly ecclesiastical brokers 'in the sinful city of Avignon'. When the city of London celebrated the accession of young Richard of Bordeaux to the throne one pageant in the procession was a burlesque of the papacy—a mock pope surrounded by a court of cardinals, some wearing black masks like devils. What the merchants of London thought one day, the burgesses of other cities were likely to think the next. And it was from this rising, increasingly wealthy class, flourishing on international trade, but needing a strong, alert national government behind it to protect it and to help negotiate its trade privileges, that nationalism was born. The new class was not as a class less moral than others—indeed in some things it was already more strict and bourgeois, literate and pious than poor or peasant, cleric or lord— but it had its eye on wealth and possessions. For these it came into existence and for these it would fight.

The growing national consciousness was immensely strengthened by the labours of John Wycliffe, a harsh, critical, unafraid Oxford doctor, who denounced the corruptions of the Church and challenged its most basic assumptions, doctrinal as well as institutional. When he attacked the avarice of bishops, priests and friars he carried all men of good will with him. When he decried the mysteries of the Mass and the quasi-divine powers of the priest at the altar ('That Christ is not in the Sacrament essentially and really in his own corporeal presence') then he became a heretic, but one who strangely anticipated the very bases of the Protestant schism of the Reformation nearly two centuries later. His *De Officio Regis* even anticipates the theocratic theory of national kingship evolved to fill the vacuum created by the overthrow of papal power. Henry VIII might have written it for himself. Wycliffe's other great contribution to rising nationalism was his (or his followers') English Bible, though he would not have spoken of it in these terms but in terms of the necessity for everyone, no matter what language he spoke, to have direct acquaintance with the scriptures, which alone were the source of faith. His contemporary, William Langland, was forging the English language too. His visionary *Piers Plowman* was as ferocious as Wycliffe in his denunciation of the evils of contemporary Christianity, but he added another element to the amalgam, a dream of a loving Christian brotherhood dwelling in peace and beauty; 'on a May morning on Malvern hills' that marvel befell him.

Church and state were shaken by two other events in the fourteenth century. The first was the plague, the Black Death of 1348, which reduced the population by perhaps one-third. Manorial villages were wiped out. Parts of the country were laid waste. The best of the clergy —those who visited the sick and buried the dead—died of plague themselves. The pusillanimous clergy and the idle friars who fled, survived. Not only the numbers but the quality of the clergy therefore declined disastrously. Immorality and unbelief flourished everywhere as in the wake of some long and disastrous war. The second great blow to the feudal system was the Peasants' Revolt of 1381, in which priests took part. The wealthy prelacy was itself attacked and an archbishop was murdered. If Wycliffites did not actually take part they were judged guilty by the company they kept. They were in large part the creators of the ethos in which it was possible for a revolt against the very structures of feudal society to take place. The feudal system was never the same again and the Church though apparently secure enough in the fifteenth century was hard put to re-establish its moral authority. Perhaps it never did, completely, in England and other northern lands, for the intellectual basis of its authority had been seriously eroded. The high-water mark of the medieval world had been the masterly synthesis between Christ and Aristotle accomplished by Thomas Aquinas. Nothing else approached its rigour or commanded the same respect. Down to our day Thomist scholasticism has been the official philosophy of the Roman Church: in a modified way it continues to be.

The highly rational Thomist reconciliation between reason and faith was challenged most powerfully of all by William of Occam in the fourteenth century, and his scepticism slowly spread. On the side of theology Occam rejected the Aristotelian principle that we can come at the notion of God as First Cause or Prime Mover just because all observable motion appears to involve a first mover itself unmoving. He argued that self-induced motion occurred in the mind, for instance. He doubted too, whether infinite recession was unreasonable. The image we make of God in our minds is formed not by direct experience of him, he said, but of a union of many physical, moral and personal notions we find in the natural order or in mankind. Such concepts do not infallibly establish the existence of God, merely the possibility. In the same analytical spirit he treats of the unity of God. How do we know of his infinity and eternity? They cannot be demonstrated. Reason is not affronted if we suppose that there are many worlds and many Gods. One is reminded of the question asked by the intelligent child when told of the possibility of life on other planets, 'And did Christ die on each of them?'

In *Quodlibeta Septem* Occam made a strict analysis of the difference between knowing God in fact and in faith. The seeker after truth, he says, cannot come to any absolute knowledge of God through his knowledge of natural things, for the reason that if God were plainly exposed in natural things, not inferred through them, no one would be able to deny the existence of God, for it would be evident to every believer 'that God is by the fact that he sees that whiteness is'. But it is obvious that it would be a contradiction in terms to say that the unbeliever knows by the evidence of things that God is: if he did he would not be an unbeliever. Therefore it is manifest that we know God in faith and not out of natural evidences. By many routes the antithesis Occam posed between faith and reason penetrated Christian philosophy. We can therefore more easily understand the subjective, the existentialist stand of Luther on faith and the whole doctrine of justification by faith with its New Testament simplicities. Symptomatic too was Luther's demand that Aristotle should be banned from the universities.[4] It was as revolutionary and as foolish as demanding that Shakespeare be struck from the syllabus of English Literature.

And that of course reminds us of the importance of Renaissance humanism, and of Italy in particular, in a process which it took Europe about three centuries to work through, if we date the Renaissance from Petrarch. The new way of looking at man and the world, at art and science, at literature and classical texts—a direct, unclouded way of enormous significance to the new study of the scriptures in Erasmus and Colet and de Lyra—may indeed be said to have begun the creation of the

---

[4] Cf. A. G. Dickens, *The English Reformation*, Batsford, London 1964 pp. 63 ff.

world we are living in (and now destroying). In one way, Luther, child of that cultural avalanche, was also its opponent, living rather by the terminal debates of medieval scholasticism than by the new humanism.

As far as one can tell the Church in England in the fifteenth and early sixteenth century was curiously inert and unimaginative. It had lost the fire of Becket: it had not acquired the grandeur of vision of More and Erasmus: it did not understand, perhaps, what was happening to the world or if it did, felt that all it had to do was to sit tight and hold on to its powers till the storm blew over. The monks were not quite the villains the Protestant propaganda painted them, but neither were they the angels of light of the pre-Raphaelite imagination. Except perhaps for the Carthusians, who were devout and disciplined, they were no better than the average citizen. But as landlords, tithe-collectors, dealers, traders, employers with an eye on the main chance they must have seemed much worse, exposed as they were to the searchlights of the age. The sense that if all was not well with and for the Church the blame rested with the clergy and their evil lives was the theme of Dean Colet's sermon to the provincial council of 1510. 'If one did not know the date,' A. G. Dickens remarks, 'one would attribute his lurid phrases to the period of the Reformation Parliament twenty years later.'[5]

As he also makes clear in *The English Reformation*[6] the murder of Richard Hunne, a merchant tailor and freeman of the city of London, was the product of a sick Church concerned to protect its legal rights and privileges at whatever cost to its Christian credibility. It aroused secular rage and contempt. In March 1511 Hunne's little son died and the rector of the parish demanded the bearing sheet by way of mortuary fees. Hunne refused and the rector, a year later, instituted proceedings against him at the ecclesiastical court at Lambeth. The case went against Hunne. In 1513 Hunne lodged a charge of slander against the rector's assistant priest—a charge never settled—and later instituted *Praemunire* proceedings against his rector. The Bishop of London, Fitzjames, retaliated to this audacity by arresting him on a charge of heresy and imprisoning him in a cell in Old St Paul's. There, on 2 December 1514, he was found strangled. A jury brought in a verdict of wilful murder against the Bishop's chancellor, a Dr Horsey, and two of his henchmen, one of whom subsequently confessed. Compounding the ecclesiastical wickedness, the Bishop of London prevented the guilty men from standing trial and at a court he himself presided over condemned the murdered Hunne as a contumacious heretic and handed over his body to be burned by the secular authorities!

When one thinks of the centuries of conflict between Church and state over the Church's exemption from the secular law, between clergy and

---

[5] *The English Reformation*, p. 90.
[6] Ibid pp. 90–3.

laity over tithes and church fees, over the plunder—often papal plunder—of pluralism and land ownership and puts all this in opposition to the rise of secular learning and the wave of brilliant enlightenment sweeping over Europe the wonder is not that the Reformation occurred but that it arrived so late. The matrimonial troubles of Henry VIII were only the occasion. Without them, events would still have compelled him to confront the Church and to come to terms with what was happening on the continent. As More's discussions with son-in-law Roper show, a great mass of intelligent young people was already swinging to Protestantism long before any formal break with Rome.

Still, the upshot of the Reformation was that Christendom was broken into little warring pieces.

THREE

Henry VIII

I.ONCE drew a comparison between the birth of the English Renaissance at the beginning of the sixteenth century and liberal humanism of England of the twentieth century.[1] I spoke of the resemblance between the men of the new learning, Erasmus, More, Colet, Grocyn, Linacre, Fisher, at the beginning of the sixteenth century and Bernard Shaw, H. G. Wells, Bertrand Russell, G. D. H. Cole, R. H. Tawney and a score of others at the opening of this. The men of both centuries were excited by recent international triumphs—for the sixteenth the invention of printing, introduced to England in 1471, the discovery of America in 1492, the opening of the Cape route to India in 1497, the resurrection of Greek studies, and the glorious expansion of the human spirit which was the gift of the Italian Renaissance, to which the papacy itself had contributed not a little. Behind the early twentieth century prophets were the triumphs of transport and industrial science, the new planetary vistas opened up by Darwinian theory, universal elementary education, a new social compassion. The intellectuals of both centuries were ready to produce policies for universal peace, new systems of education, or blue-prints for a new society at the drop of a hat. The disappointments of More's age could no more be foreseen than those which lay in ambush for Comte's.[2] Centuries which began with tremendous hopes plunged into disasters generated by the hopes themselves. The price to be paid for Luther or Machiavelli was no more understood than the price to be paid for Marx and Lenin.

The generous spirited young Henry began his reign as a glittering Renaissance prince, patron of Erasmus, friend of Thomas More, studious in religion and devoted to Rome. No reign had more auspicious beginnings or more wretched an end. As every schoolboy knows, Henry's troubles began with his failure to beget a living son and heir and

---

[1] My *Sir Thomas More*, Faber, London 1953; Library of English Renaissance Literature, NY 1970.

[2] Ibid, pp. 16–17.

in so sensitive and narrow-minded a man there is no reason to doubt that, child of a superstitious age, he saw himself the accursed of God for his marriage to his dead brother's wife and could quote the Bible to prove it. Lack of a son promised to be a disaster for so short-lived a dynasty. But even if there had been an immediate son and heir the dynamic of the sixteenth century would still have carried England farther and farther from Rome towards that religious independence promised but never quite achieved by *Praemunire*. Or else Henry himself would have become the maker and manipulator of popes, beginning with Wolsey, which would have delighted his vanity! In the event the sad succession of divorces and royal executions converted the growing national independence into regal defiance of Rome, and the destruction of much that Catholicism had given to England. Though recent studies[3] have shown that there was more clergy opposition to Henry than was at one time supposed, nevertheless it is surprising how supine the clergy seem to have been on the whole, especially in Convocation. And how ready were the gentry, and even more the merchants, fashioned by the same kind of European learning and experience as Thomas Cromwell, to connive at simple plunder. It was perhaps More alone who saw what destruction was being done to European civilization, to the Christian consensus. More accused the Christians themselves of being even more ruinous to Christianity than the warlike Turks who were besieging Vienna in 1529. The Christian city held, though Austria suffered these ferocious infidel invasions until 1545. Meanwhile Christendom sundered itself.

In the *Dialogue of Comfort*, written by More in the Tower (and a treasonable manifesto if ever there was one) thinly disguised as a translation out of (Hungarian) Latin into French and out of French into English, Henry becomes the great Turk whose treachery and infidelity threaten Christendom. 'I have known him, and his father afore him too, break more promises than five as great as this that he should here make with you,' More's mouthpiece Anthony tells his nephew Vincent who speaks of the prince's promise that much earthly preferment will come of a small act of allegiance, and, 'For of this I am very sure, if we had the fifteenth part of the love to Christ that He both had and hath unto us, all the pain of this Turk's persecution could not keep us from Him, but that there would be at this day as many martyrs here in Hungary [England] as have been afore in other countries of old.'

The legal story of the breach begins with the fall of Wolsey, itself the product of his failure to secure the Pope's assent to the King's divorce so that the King might openly espouse Anne Boleyn, to whom he was already secretly married, and the expected heir be legitimated. In 1531 Henry

---

[3] Cf. for instance G. R. Elton, *Policy and Police in the Time of Thomas Cromwell*, Cambridge University Press 1972.

invoked the *Praemunire* statute to fine the Convocations of York and Canterbury for accepting the legatine authority of Wolsey. In the following year the clergy made their submission to Henry, promising never to draft new canons or ordinances or to do anything else unless licensed by the king to meet, and to secure his assent to what they promulgated. This 'Submission of the Clergy' is the accepted date for the beginning of the English Reformation.

The next step in the subordination of the Church to the king was the Restraint of Appeals Act in 1533. *Praemunire* had forbidden appeals to Rome unless by the king's consent. The new Act forbade them unconditionally—the demise of Roman authority was written into the constitution. A year later the Dispensations Act cut off supplies to Rome. It ruled that no person or persons shall from henceforth pay any pensions, censes, portions, procurations or any other impositions to the use of the Bishop or the See of Rome. *Inter alia*, it empowered the Archbishop of Canterbury to issue, with the king's approval, all those licences, faculties and dispensations formerly issued by Rome.

In 1531 Convocations had been compelled to recognize Henry as the supreme Head of the Church of England 'as far as the Law of Christ allows'. The Supremacy Act of 1534 now registered this undoubted usurpation in statute law. The Act dropped the clause about 'the Law of Christ' which had soothed tender consciences and asserted 'for corroboration and confirmation ... that the King our Sovereign Lord, his heirs and successors, Kings of this realm, shall be taken accepted, and reputed the only supreme head in earth of the Church of England, called *Anglicana Ecclesia* ...'.

The Pope replied with a Bill of Excommunication. He could do no other. It served no practical purpose unless to encourage England's enemies as well as Henry's. But it widened the ideological gap, of course, and spurred on the plunder of the monastic houses, set in train by the reports of Thomas Cromwell's Commissioners. The Act of Parliament authorizing the expropriation began with a direct smear on the monastic life; the preamble justified the Act because 'manifest sin, vicious, carnal and abominable living is daily used and committed among the little and small abbeys, priories, and other religious houses'. It was this Act more than any other which showed the social face of the Reformation. There were no longer to be any privileged religious groups. The wealth of the monasteries was forfeit to the King, to replenish his coffers and to buy political support. How far would the King go? His power was much to be feared. Expropriation was a recognized political weapon against opponents and potential rivals. There was the fear of endless expropriation, of a social revolution in which only the King and tough managers such as Thomas Cromwell would be the winners—which brought about the rebellion called The Pilgrimage of Grace, born in the far from Protestant north. A failure, but a warning all the same. It did not work out that the King was much enriched by monastic plunder, but rather that power in the land began to pass to the ubiquitous class of gentry—much enlarged in numbers, prospering exceedingly and full of a confidence that was ultimately to bring down kings. Nevertheless England was much changed.

'So, in the course of three years, was expunged from the face of England one of the greatest and most ancient of her institutions. It was monks who had evangelized England, whether from Rome or from Iona. It was monks who had kept scholarship alive in the Dark Ages, who had established the earliest schools, who had provided hospitality for the traveller and the pilgrim, who had fed the poor and nursed the sick. Now by the rapacity of a King and the subservience of Parliament the whole thing was brought to an end, the monastic buildings sunk into decay and ruin, a useful quarry for farmers who wanted good stone to build their barns and fences.'[4]

The diminished Church of England, as it has come down to us, is the product of four reigns, Henry VIII, Edward VI, Mary, and Elizabeth I. But for Henry, at the end of his days, the Church was in all essentials the Catholic Church he had worshipped in as a boy, or so he seemed to assert—with one important difference, the severing of allegiance to Rome. However, that was for Henry a political necessity, with no obligatory effect on doctrine or liturgy over which he appears conservative and orthodox. In *The Six Articles* of 1539—called 'the bloody whip with six strings' by the reforming party of the Church which had taken the great divorce as a signal for initiating liturgical changes—Henry asserted some of the most controversial Catholic doctrines as dogmas to be believed on pain of burning. They were—*transubstantiation* ('after the consecration there remaineth no substance of bread and wine, nor any other substance, but the substance of Christ, God and man'); *communion in one kind only is ordained*; *priests may not marry* ('by the law of God'); *laity who have taken vows of chastity must observe them* ('by the law of God'); *private masses to be continued* ('in this the King's English Church'); *auricular confession is expedient and necessary*, and must be retained and continued.

This Act closed the door on doctrinal reform and on Lutheran and Calvinist pressures for the rest of Henry's lifetime. But to make sure that it was understood he published *A Necessary Doctrine and Erudition for any Christian Man*—'the King's book'—in 1543, which expounded his rigid doctrines. He took his role as supreme Head most seriously—he was as good a theologian as most of his bishops—and sick, bloated, petty,

---

[4] J. R. H. Moorman, *A History of the Church in England*, A. & C. Black, London 1954 p. 175.

suspicious, lonely old tyrant that he was, did not hesitate to lecture parliament on the immorality of the country in his declining years.

'Charity and Concord is not amongst you, but Discord and Dissensions beareth rule in every place.... Behold then, what love and charity is amongst you, when one calleth another heretic and anabaptist, and he calleth him again papist, hypocrite and Pharisee? Be these tokens of Charity amongst you? Are these signs of fraternal love amongst you? ... I hear daily that you of the clergy preach one against another, teach one contrary to the other, inveigh one against another without charity or discretion; some be too stiff in their old *Mumpsimus*, others be too busy and curious in their new *Sumpsimus*.... I am very sorry to know and to hear how unreverently that most precious jewel the Work of God is disputed, rhymed, sung, and jangled in every Ale-house and Tavern.... And yet I am even as much sorry that the readers of the same follow it in doing so faintly and so coldly: for of this I am sure, that charity was never so faint amongst you, and virtuous and godly living was never less used, nor God himself among Christians was never less reverenced, honoured or served.'[5]

---

[5] There are several versions of this famous speech. This quotation comes from Edward Hall's *Chronicles*, 1548 edition, 'Henry VIII, the XXXVII year', pp. 365–6. But cf. *The Letters and Papers of Henry VIII*, vol. 20 ii, *1031*, p. 513, 'The King's Speech before Parliament, 24 Dec. 1545', HMSO 1907.

FOUR

The Search for Uniformity and Unity

HENRY left a prickly legacy to his successors—a plundered and servile Church presided over by an excommunicated monarch, the hostility of the papacy and all Catholic kingdoms (most of Europe, in fact), and the growth on the left of the formidable Protestant opposition of European origin—Calvinists, Lutherans, Anabaptists, what you will. Because of this polarization, and the rallying of privileged social classes behind the king, relations with the papacy could no longer be settled monarch to monarch. For the reformers, the old Church under a new head was not enough: there had to be a clean sweep of everything papistical, idolatrous, and superstitious. While the link with Rome remained, the Church brought strength from the outside to the maintenance of an inner social and political stability; it had a power and a will of its own to pit against other social groups. With the link gone, the Church became a political prize for which parties battled inside the nation. Whoever determined the shape of the Church determined in large degree the supremacy of other forces in the country, including of course its nationalism, and the role of its gentry and its growing merchant class.

It took three more reigns to arrive at the *Act of Uniformity* and more than a century after Henry's death to develop a liturgy finally suitable for a Church both catholic and reformed, yet received with hostility. Perhaps 1,760 dissenting clergy were dismissed.

Under the sad little boy king, Edward VI, by his father's mysterious edict educated by Protestant divines and *prepared* for a Protestant regency during his minority, the Church of England took a violent swerve in a Lutheran direction. By royal injunction a few months after Edward's accession idolatrous paintings and images had to be removed from churches, candles on the high altar officially reduced in number, bells silenced during Mass. Erasmus was ordered to be studied in parish churches that the congregations might begin to understand their faith in a new spirit. In a word, the glitter and parade of the surviving Roman liturgy was scaled down. A more sombre note had to be struck. Two of Henry VIII's doctrinal Acts of Parliament were repealed. All the Roman rigour of the Ten Articles and the Six Articles went down the drain, with merriment, and England began sacrificing its art treasures to an icono-clastic temper. The extent of popular support for the royal reform shows indeed how deeply the 'German doctrine' had penetrated the popular understanding. For the people the Mass had now indeed become a 'hocus-pocus', a dead magic.

The shape of things to come was revealed by the issue in 1549 of an English Prayer Book, the work of Cranmer, to replace the Roman service books. It was not well received everywhere, particularly in areas remote from the metropolis where Luther's thunder was reduced to a mutter and they were still faithful to Henry's understanding of reformation. In Cornwall there was an insurrection. The enigmatic Cranmer had done his work well, and the prayer book was a homogeneous spiritual whole in prose of such enduring splendour as to leave a permanent impress on religious and literary history. It was followed by a revised book in 1552 which revealed how much Cranmer had now fallen under the influence of Calvin and the rest of the Geneva reformers. The old King, dead only five years at Cranmer's second try, ought to have turned in his grave, especially as the Church was then again plundered by official decree and the poor deprived of many sources of charity and other simple forms of help and comfort the Church had provided. Convocation—still Henrician in character—was helpless and afraid, bishops humiliated or imprisoned and forced to give up their lands. The bishops Gardiner and Bonner, who had supported Henry VIII over the Supremacy, went to prison rather than accept the Protestantism of Edward VI. The rascally regency council, with whom power rested, succeeded in enriching its members (Protector Somerset principally) and after that the crown, the gentry, the merchants. Somerset House, built from Somerset's new found wealth and in large measure out of the stones of destroyed ecclesiastical buildings, became, though beautiful, the sign of a Protestant arrogance as unpleasant in its way as Wolsey's.

The sickly boy king died—what would he have made of his country if he had survived to maturity?—and Mary, daughter of the Catherine of Aragon Henry had spurned and humiliated, came to the throne (1553). She was the dedicated opponent of her father's religious policy and, married to Philip of Spain, stood in the minds of her fellow countrymen for the Spanish rather than the English supremacy. The influential Cranmer was dropped, to be succeeded by Reginald Pole. Bishops Gardiner and Bonner, Henry's rearguard, released, became the principal agents of the Queen's terror. Cranmer was burnt at the stake as a heretic and in his dying redeemed anything that had been base in his life. He had held the throne of Canterbury for twenty years—a most enigmatic man who had managed to marry subservience to his royal master and 'onlie begetter' with a deep spirituality. The Supremacy was dropped, the Protestant legislation of Edward's reign was repealed. Convocation reaccepted transubstantiation and Cardinal Pole, as papal legate, absolved the nation through parliament from its heresy and reunited it with Rome. The wealthy were, if not converted, consoled by the promise that they would not have to surrender their monastic lands.

Too many years had passed since Henry declared the Supremacy for the *volte face* to be achieved so easily. What began for many as a simple act of justice and restitution ended as a bloody purge. The heresy laws were resurrected. Worshippers were required to denounce Cranmer's prayer book. Every reign, including Henry's of course, had been marked by terror and persecution of religious opponents. Mary's was the worst. Five bishops were burned to death as heretics, including Latimer and Ridley. In a reign of less than five years three hundred people were burned to death because of their nonconformity to the new ultra-catholic regime. Not all those burnt were the clergy, by any means. Only twenty-one clergymen and eight gentlemen succumbed. For the first time in such persecutions, the obscure, the humble, the poor—what today we might call the working-class—suffered. Eighty-four tradesmen and one hundred husbandmen, servants and labourers were done to death, along with fifty-five women and four children. The figures for executions take no account of the fines, confiscations and imprisonments. The stench of faggots was stronger than the smell of incense. Roman Catholicism killed its own cause by the savagery to which it had recourse. After Mary, it was not to be freed from hostility and impediments until the nineteenth century.

What Elizabeth, who came to the throne in 1558, so clearly saw was how destructive religious differences were of the national unity and order. She had Sir Thomas More's sense that the nation could be put in peril by them. Her whole labour in a long reign, and in a day when Christianity was universal, was to arrive at a national solution of what was religiously acceptable. In this task she had to fend off the drive of the Anglican puritans towards Presbyterianism and of the 'Romish Catholics' towards Rome. But she did so in the firm sense that the Church of England belonged to the mainstream of Christendom and did not constitute a violent break from it. As J. R. H. Moorman reminds us[1] in the Bidding Prayer despatched with Elizabeth's injunctions in 1559, the faithful are asked to pray 'for Christ's Holy Catholic Church, that is for the whole congregation of Christian people dispersed throughout the whole world, and especially for the Church of England and Ireland'.

The intention of catholicity was there, even if not the Roman kind, the sense that there ought to be a universally acceptable form of worship for Christian people. There was in the person of Elizabeth a characteristically English instinct against extremes. The trouble, however, was to find the *via media* and to establish it.

---

[1] *A History of the Church in England*, p. 211.

Cardinal Pole died soon after Mary, but Elizabeth faced all the same a strongly catholicized episcopacy and parochial clergy. Those who had resisted Mary at all openly were dead, banished or deprived: only the romanized were left in office. Any return to the situation under Henry had to be accomplished in the teeth of the dead Mary's clergy. A new Act of Supremacy (1559) broke the link with Rome again and restored the sovereign powers that Henry VIII had claimed. But the verbal form was softer. The Queen ceased to be the 'head'. 'The queen's highness' the act said, 'is the only supreme governor of this realm, and of all other her highnesses's dominions and countries, as well in all spiritual or ecclesiastical things or causes, as temporal, and that no foreign prince, person, prelate, state or potentate, has, or ought to have, any jurisdiction, power, superiority, pre-eminence, or authority ecclesiastical or spiritual within this realm.' That was the hub of the oath every 'ecclesiastical person' and 'every other person having your highnesses's fee or wages' and every civil officer was required on 'a corporal oath upon the evangelist' to swear.

If Mary *had* succeeded in restoring the 'catholicity' of the Church of England, creating a clergy once again genuinely submissive to Rome and reluctant for their souls' sake to forswear themselves, Elizabeth's task would have been far harder. In any case she must have been ill at ease in face of the purged Church she had inherited from Mary and reluctant to face a new, even more massive purge. As it was, circumstances seem to have overtaken her and pushed her along the Protestant road faster than she intended to go. Though it was only twenty years since the monasteries had been suppressed England had transformed herself and was moving fast towards that form of secularization described so delightfully by A. L. Rowse in his *The Elizabethan Renaissance*[2] out of which grew that cultural wave, those works of genius never since surpassed: a brief golden age before the civil war. As to the causes of this secularization, which are hard to determine, the two most important must have been the removal of the Church from the position of central cultural authority (among other roles) in the land, and the changed stance, the transformed outlook of the gentry, who ruled England at the grass roots.

One potent factor was economic. A. G. Dickens finds it 'impossible to doubt that the laicizing of landed capital' was a most important factor for change.[3] Indeed he sees this as a more potent historical factor than Weber's Protestant ethic. And this laicization was directly the consequence of the monastic dissolution, which moved the Church from the

---

[2] And in particular, I suppose, in Volume Three: *The Elizabethan Renaissance: The Life of the Society*, Macmillan, London 1971.

[3] *The English Reformation*, p. 335.

economic centre of society just as other forces moved it from the cultural centre. Certainly, and as Dickens points out, there was a remarkable increase in the number of landed families throughout England from the mid-sixteenth century.[4] The increase was due, not only to greater prosperity, but to the direct promotion of yeomen into the ranks of the gentry, particularly those yeomen who had raised their status by the acquisition of monastic lands.

'If towns were at the intersections of the web of society, there is no doubt what constituted the filaments—they were the gentry, with all their affiliations and cross-connections over the borders of their native counties. If magnates ruled at the centre, in the Privy Council with its offshoots in Wales and the North, it was the gentry who ruled in the country as a whole,' A. L. Rowse wrote.[5] He traces the 'mounting pressure' of the gentry for seats in parliament which brought them all too often representation of the towns themselves, in place of their proper burgesses. Busy burgesses found it too expensive: the gentry had the money, the leisure, the political initiatives. In 1584, he points out, of the 460 members of parliament, 240 were country gentlemen and only 53 were townsmen. The townsmen, he shows, were at a further disadvantage. The merchant empires of the City of London did not endure. It was apparently rare for businesses to last more than a hundred years. Not only were commerce and merchanting mercurial—as against the enduring land—but living in insanitary towns, visited every decade by plague, was dangerous. Merchants bought themselves into the land when they prospered, if they were not already rooted there. The merchant body was renewed and refreshed in return from the younger sons of the gentry. Indeed every aspect of the national life could be seen to draw its strength from the gentry.

One notices the munificent gifts of the Elizabethan merchants to every conceivable charity: often those gifts were expressly to the needs of the home base in the countryside. They were no longer as once making legacies to the Church, setting up Masses for dead souls, or subsidizing expensive ecclesiastical building. (Marvellous country homes, rather than churches, were being built.) The ruling gentry, in alliance with merchants, had become so secularized by Elizabeth's day that they had begun to turn in some disgust from obsessive religion to a multitude of more fascinating and rewarding pursuits—to science and mechanics, natural history, the secular drama and romantic poetry, medicine, history, philosophy, alchemy, exploration. After all, only three quarters of the way through the century Drake was circumnavigating the globe. Francis Bacon's new scientific world was waiting in the wings.

---

[4] Ibid. p. 333.

[5] *The Elizabethan Renaissance: The Life of the Society*, p. 71.

Of the historic importance of the rise of the gentry A. L. Rowse writes that 'until the earthquake of the first world war of 1914–18, society remained recognizable as continuous, at least in rural England, from Elizabethan days. It exemplified an organic structure, which recognized a principle: it was based on hierarchical order, in which social class expressed social functions. People knew their place in it, where they stood and how they were expected to behave—always with a margin of exceptions, the inassimilable, the misfit, the criminal, in a word, the exceptional (a Marlowe, for instance).'[6]

It was the gentry who were at Elizabeth's accession a force to be reckoned with in the search for a religious settlement. Their allegiances were divided, of course: at the lower social end, and among the yeoman, puritan: in the North and among some great families, Catholic: yet for most part Protestant both as a reaction to Mary's reign and out of a patriotic sense that the break had to be complete or England remained perpetually under the Spanish threat. A Church which was not subordinate to the crown was a perpetual fifth column: a crown which was not itself Protestant menaced the national interest, as Mary's reign had shown. A decent Protestant monarchy served by a Church deprived of power, ambition and independence alone satisfied those newly born patriotic impulses which Shakespeare was soon so stirringly to exploit.

It would be wrong to attribute the Protestant attitude of the mass of the gentry only to motives of patriotism and self-interest. There was a genuine swing away from a priest-ridden hocus-pocus religion, exploiting the poor and ignorant, and obscuring, even dishonouring its biblical origins and a longing for a faith which was above board and gentlemanly and kept in its place. And in a Christian community not yet split into a multitude of sects but all contained within the one *Ecclesia Anglicana* Elizabeth's problem was to find a settlement so satisfactory to all factions that it would drive none into rebellion or recusancy.

Mary had caused many brilliant divines and laymen to flee into exile. But her reign had been short and they had no chance to become alienated from their native land. The Lutherans had fought shy of them on political grounds and it was in Calvinist towns and cities that they found a spiritual home and there that they had to decide whether to settle for a purified Anglicanism or the congregational puritanism of Geneva. It was not the most Geneva-oriented group which became influential in Elizabeth's settlement. John Knox, among others of them, was not permitted to enter England. The initiatives fell to such formidable figures as Dr Richard Cox, who was to become Bishop of Ely, John Scory who was to be Bishop of Hereford, John Jewel, to be Bishop of Salisbury, and many others who were Prayer-Book Protestants or Puritans and whose

---

[6] Ibid. p. 90.

influence seems to have been decisive in Elizabeth's first Parliament and in the choice of Cranmer's prayer book of 1552 against the more conservative variant of 1549. Their pressure preserved Cranmer's Articles of Religion. As the Thirty-nine Articles of Religion they became the doctrinal basis of the Elizabethan settlement and in theory have governed the Church ever since. They are not simply Protestant but even Puritan, Calvinist, in tone. Elizabeth said that she gloried in her father and it may have been her will to restore the Church (and the crown's relationship to it) to the situation both enjoyed under him. It was not to be. She was no theologian and on some things had to take a back seat—governor of the Church, like a president who leaves the detail to others, rather than Supreme Head. What was established by the revolution of 1559 was a Protestant Church in which the Puritan doctrinal position was clearly stated and carefully protected within an episcopal rather than a presbyterian discipline under the crown. It was not Henry's, or Edward's, or Mary's Church but something over against all of them. Much of its history under the Stuarts was a struggle to retain its new nature against hostile or recusant kings or sectarian or presbyterianizing reformers. In the end it bowed them all off the stage.

FIVE
The Civil War

'THE authority of the Holy Scripture . . .' the Westminster Confession of
1643 said, 'dependeth not on the testimony of any man or church; but
wholly upon God (who is truth itself) the author thereof. . .' The Second
(Baptist) Confession of 1677, spelt out the scriptural role and even more
severely, 'The Holy Scripture is the only sufficient, certain and infallible
rule of all saving knowledge, faith and obedience.' And for that reason, it
went on to say, nothing is at any time to be added to this total revelation,
either by supposed new revelations or by the traditions of men. If taken
seriously and fully this would have frozen fast all theology and removed
the need even for a Church at all which was nothing if not the
institutionalizing of 'the traditions of men'. 'The infallible rule', the 1643
Confession said, dotting all the i's and crossing all the t's, 'for the
interpretation of Scripture is the Scripture itself.' How hard can you slam a
door?

It would have been impossible to say all this before the invention of
printing, when books were few, and mostly in Latin and to be found
principally in the houses of the rich, in monasteries and some churches.
There was little point in being literate when there was nothing to read.
The scriptures would have been wholly unknown if they had not everywhere been read in churches and expounded in sermons and echoed in
prayers and credos taught even to very little children along with the
stories of the saints. That there were scriptures the final authority of
which it was possible to assert in the seventeenth century was due in
fact to 'the traditions of men'.

By the time the Presbyterian Confession was drawn up, printing had
had a run, of a couple of centuries. It was the mass medium of the
day, destroyer of a purely oral culture, and it transformed its users. The
man who could sit by his own fire and con his Bible, or bring his family
together and read it to them at prayers, or study it with friends, was not
only going to be affected by it at the deepest spiritual level, but was
made in a measure independent of Church and priest and critically armed
against both.

In a sense a third religious entity had been created for those who cared

27

to exploit it— the Book. The Church was no longer the ministry and the laity in tension and partnership, but the ministry, the laity and *the Book*. And those for whom the Book had absolute primacy over traditional worship were the radical nonconformity, baptists, presbyterians and so forth. For them Church reform by itself was not enough, there had to be a less superficial, more self-conscious, more heart-searching faith.

It is possible to argue that a new Christian religion was being created, the religion of the Bible. Owen Chadwick has beautifully summarized the rift.

'Reformed churchmen felt the breach from Rome to be an irreparable rending of a garment, the cutting out of a moth-eaten patch of the cloth and the renewal or cleansing of the remainder. They transformed the appearance and atmosphere of their churches, they found a strange or repellent or unintelligible atmosphere when they entered a Catholic Church, they had little sense of continuity with the Christian·past of the Middle Ages. When they looked into history for their Christian predecessors, they found them, not in the main stream of the tradition, but in the little persecuted groups of medieval Christendom—Hussites and Wycliffites and Waldensians. . . . [They] saw in the Pope of Rome the Scarlet Woman, or the Beast, Antichrist sitting upon the throne destined for another.'[1]

Elsewhere in the same book Owen Chadwick writes, 'The England of the middle seventeenth century was to test what happened when the "mechanik", the brazier and the feltmaker and the coachman, went into the Bible to fetch their divinity for themselves.'[2] But it was more than that. The Bible was the religion of that new class which was excluded from that hierarchical Chain of Being which Shakespeare celebrated —God, King, Nobles, Gentlemen, Yeomen. Religious independence was the fiercest form of expression of their social arrival, though not the less sincere for that. The rude mechanickals were not so typical of that class as the haberdasher, the tanner, the coachmaker, the wool merchant, the jeweller, the yeoman, the banker—masters all, but not ennobled, not members of a great estate, commoners rather who worked at their own trades even though they might employ many others. Some of them were self-taught. Others passed through the post-Reformation Grammar Schools. They mastered reading in order to master the Bible. They lived frugally, dressed sombrely in the black which became a Puritan uniform. They were thrifty, disciplined, austere and brought up their families to be as God-fearing as themselves. They were their own men, proud to work and to owe nothing to anyone. It was a bunch of this independent sort which set off to America in the Mayflower to establish religious

[1] *The Reformation*, Pelican Original, London 1964 p. 369.
[2] Ibid. p. 204.

colonies where men might live as they willed. Inevitably they were alienated from high Church bishops like Laud and from kings supported by them who claimed divine right to rule, and from all pomp and circumstance, clutter and extravagance of worship or of life. Religion was for them a conventicle of like-minded godly folk—a Bible school and plain religious workshop. These were the people who made and fought the Civil War in an ideological fury. But they were never the whole people. A less vocal majority stood somewhere in the middle praying to be delivered as much from the papistical terror and foreign influences which Mary had represented as from the grim fanaticism of the puritans. 'Between ... two wings lay a middle party' said J. R. H. Moorman (of the Elizabethan age), 'who wished neither servility to Rome nor subservience to Geneva but a Church of England truly catholic in all essentials and yet cleansed and reformed from ... abuses.'[3] Yet no one at the beginning of the Stuart era, or when the struggle between king and parliament, bishop and puritan was at its height, could have imagined that it would be this third party, the middle of the road group, which would emerge victorious by the end of the century, retaining the monarchy, a catholic but reformed Church on the one side but on the other a supreme parliament and a modest degree of religious toleration. It would have seemed the least, the most absurd possibility.

The Westminster Confession said, among other things, of the civil magistrate, that 'it is his duty to take order that unity and peace be preserved in the Church, that the truth of God be kept pure and entire, that all blasphemies and heresies be suppressed, all corruptions and abuses in worship and discipline prevented and reformed, and all ordinances of God duly settled, administered and observed'. A right royal charge indeed in a turbulent age! But the absurd powers they were prepared to award him were simply to call synods, to be present in them, and 'to provide that whatsoever is transacted' is 'according to the mind of God'—provided of course that God had been instructed not to regard Roman Catholics as of 'the true religion' but rather as the source and support of the Antichrist.

It is impossible even to sketch the long civil conflict of the seventeenth century which began with the accession of James I in 1603 and ended only with the accession of William of Orange and Mary in 1689. Virtually a whole century was lost in cruel religious and political strife. The first confrontation of James I's reign was a religious one—the Millenary Petition. It was handed to him on his way to London with the claim that it represented the views of a thousand clergy. It demanded 'no popish opinion to be any more taught; no ministers charged to teach their people to bow at the name of Jesus; that the canonical Scriptures

---

[3] *A History of the Church in England*, p. 200.

only be read in the Church'. (Erasmus out!) And, of course, 'that there may be a uniformity of doctrine prescribed'. But it is startling to note that the petition also asked that 'King Edward's statute for the lawfulness of Ministers' marriages be revived'. The king met Church divines of both parties at a conference at Hampton Court where to the antiprelatical party he made the famous declaration, 'No bishop, no king!' He made some concessions, but decided on the whole against the Puritans. James had his own preferences and so had Charles I and the Arminian or High Church Bishop Laud was the instrument of them. The Puritans had serious reason for religious and political offence. The religious was the political too. To what political uses a subservient Church could be put was shown very clearly when Charles, in 1640, dissolved Parliament and prolonged Convocation in order that it might pass canons defending the divine right—an act which the Long Parliament subsequently declared illegal.

The retort to all this was the Puritan fury which brought about the execution of Archbishop Laud—the first revelation of Puritan savagery —and the founding of the Solemn League and Covenant of 1643, which declared 'That we shall ... without respect of persons, endeavour the extirpation of popery, prelacy (that is, Church government by archbishops, bishops, their chancellors and commissaries, deans, deans and chapters, and all other ecclesiastical offices ...), superstition, heresy, schism, profaneness ... that the Lord may be one'.

So the episcopacy went by parliamentary decree, a 'Directory' replaced the Prayer Book, parliament became bitterly Calvinist, full of a persecuting zeal, and the Church was made over in a Presbyterian fashion which solved nothing. Ordinary people lacked the stomach to make it work or to change themselves by Act of Parliament. It took a despairing Cromwell, during the Protectorate, to make the effort to moderate the bigotry a little in his Instrument of Government, 1653, where he proposed that people should be protected in, not restrained from the profession of their faith and exercise of their religion and should not be compelled by penalties to do what they did not want to do.

That same Instrument of Government which promised a kind of status quo in the religious arrangements—'the present maintenance shall not be taken away or impeached'—was still quite ruthless about the spoiling of the Church. All the acts and ordinances of parliament previously made 'for the sale or other dispositions of the lands, rents, hereditaments of the late king, queen, and prince, of archbishops and bishops, etc., deans and chapters' were to remain *good and firm* it said.

A Church so mauled was bound to be in darkness and confusion. What Henry VIII had begun the Cromwellian era completed. Churches were desecrated, ornaments smashed or stolen, statues defaced or thrown out, stained glass windows destroyed. The churches were never to be as rich and beautiful again. It may not be as easy today as once it was to blame Oliver Cromwell. He himself was not a revengeful man, but the Civil War was after all a religious war and the parliamentary armies behaved towards the churches of their own country as the Lutheran armies had behaved at the sack of Rome in 1527. They were the seventeenth century iconoclasts. And thus 'the Lord was made one'. It must have been a relief to many that dancing, playing games, singing songs, acting plays and celebrating Church festivals were forbidden. There was so little left to be merry about.

The seventeenth century, Christopher Hill wrote,[4] is 'the decisive century in English history, the epoch in which the Middle Ages ended'. The century was decisive for Europe too, through the growth of new capitalist relations within states and in inter-state relationships, arising from the opening up of the world in the voyages of discovery of the previous centuries and the immense stimulus to trade which followed. Population grew and land was better farmed. There was inflation. All this took place within societies still feudal and broke them open. There occurred what Christopher Hill calls 'a consequent regrouping of social classes'. However, only in England, in the English revolution, was the breakthrough so decisive that the foundations were laid for the world's first industrial and imperial power. 'Within the seventeenth century the decisive decades are those between 1640 and 1660. In these decades the decisive figure is Oliver Cromwell.'[5] Elsewhere he says that the breakdown of Calvinism in the mid-century is 'one of the great turning points in intellectual history'.[6] So that was 'decisive' too.

It is quite true that the English revolution saw the rise of new classes of men who found in the doctrines of the Levellers an ideology to support their social demands. The New Model Army was full of men of lower ranks in society who were devoutly religious in the new puritan stamp. Cromwell defended the promotion of the best of them into officers at a time when it was still a scandal for soldiers to be commanded by other than gentlemen. The strongest support for the parliamentary side in the war came from the wool and clothing areas of the North and East Anglia, from London (a law to itself), and from the ports—in other words from the most industrialized, most wealthy areas of the country. Moreover, the political themes of the American and French revolutions —themes essentially middle-class—first had their airing. What right has a king to rule? Whence comes his authority? What rights have the people as a whole *against* the king if need be? Who had power to come between a man and his God and dictate the way he should worship? Freedom

---

[4] *God's Englishman: Oliver Cromwell and the English Revolution*, Weidenfeld and Nicolson, London 1970 p. 12, to which I am specially indebted in this section.

[5] Ibid p. 14.

[6] Ibid p. 215.

of conscience was a demand for political freedom—for who had the right to control political ideas? Oliver Cromwell said many things which put him on the side of the new wave. He could not abide, he once said, so anti-Christian and divisive a thing as the distinction between clergy and laity: again, 'I had rather have a plain russet-coated captain, that knows what he fights for and lives what he knows, than what you call a gentleman, and is nothing else'. And as to liberty, in his denunciation of the religious monopolism of the Scottish Kirk and in defence of independent lay preaching, he cried out, 'It will be found an unjust and unwise jealousy to deny a man the liberty he hath by nature upon a supposition he may abuse it'. 'The liberty he hath by nature' almost bows the American Declaration of Independence on to the stage of history.

Oliver Cromwell was himself a gentleman-commoner whose family had risen through the spoiling of monastic lands and had become well-connected. This promotion and his subsequent power illustrate as nothing else does the rise of the gentry in the land and the half-eclipse of the nobility. He was not one of the new classes, though he deeply respected them and depended on them and was the first ruler of the land to defend the meritocratic principle. Nevertheless, he was proud of being a gentleman and asserted that in the traditional social arrangement of a nobleman, a gentleman, a yeoman he saw 'a good interest of the nation and a great one'. He hated the levelling principle. One could not be a gentleman and not hate it, for levelling praised the man who worked at trade or commerce or industry and questioned the right to live on the labour of others.

The point is, of course, that Cromwell was no ideological revolutionary. He was a good, busy parliamentarian who became a superb general able to manipulate the ideological army he created with an iron will and to turn it into an instrument of government when parliament failed through indecisiveness. For if he was not an ideological revolutionary he was certainly a millenarian.[7] He was a man full to the brim with the sense of God. No speech but invokes God's name: he takes no action except that in which he believes God's hand guides him. And God loved England: in his Declaration of 23 May 1654, he claimed ecstatically that the place of England in the world was as if the Lord had said, 'England thou art my first-born, my delight among the nations, under the whole heavens the Lord hath not dealt so with any of the people round about us'. It was not sufficient to rout the king, whose death Cromwell engineered, turning him into a religious martyr for whom prayers were said in the Church of England until 1857; the millenarian dream had to be pursued. In practice this meant a broad, tolerant state Church with no man persecuted over questions of conscience and congre-

---

[7] Cf. *Godly Rule*, W. Lamont, Macmillan, London 1969.

gations calling their own ministers from among themselves. The Presbyterian lion was to lie down with the Independent lamb. The real unity was to be inward and spiritual, like the vision of Piers Plowman at Malvern, and, as Cromwell wrote after the siege of Bristol, 'as for being united in forms, commonly called uniformity, every Christian will for peace sake study and do as far as conscience will permit: and from brethren, in things of the mind, we look for no compulsion but that of light and reason'. 'Would that we all were saints.'

Of course, this was a Protestant millenarianism. The unity of saints excluded papists and the high Church. It was hostile, not so much to the idea of a national Church, a broad common way of worship, as to the whole apparatus of privilege and power by which the Church maintained itself, an apparatus tightly bound up with the ideology and the realities of kingship. With a divine monarch went along the divinity of the Church: ordinary men were not to question its rights and rules. Bodies, like the High Commission, which could impose religious disciplines and doctrines upon parsons, coming between parson and flock, parson and gentleman-patron, were as hated as the Star Chamber. Religious courts which could try laymen were feared and detested. Tithes were anathema, the battle around them was the supreme fiscal controversy of the century and one on which Cromwell, who promised to destroy them, changed his opinion. Enmity to the Church establishment focused on the hierarchy and this never changed. The bishops held immense estates and wielded great political and economic power, and parliament and Cromwell sought their destruction. The Elizabethan Settlement was seen as only half successful—it had failed to complete the reformation of the Church by abolishing the episcopacy. Only in this way could the back of Laudian royalism be broken.

The parliaments which opposed Charles I just as bitterly opposed the hierarchical Church therefore. They were strong for a Presbyterian Settlement of the kind that John Knox planned for Scotland. The Presbyterians were like the Laudians at least in this—that they wanted a uniformity of worship for Kirk or Church throughout the land and disciplinary means, and the powers of the state, to enforce it. The merchants, the traders and bankers, the shipowners, many of the new industrialists were strongly for the doctrines and practices of Geneva.

Cromwell, the parliament man who secured parliament's victory, was faced by parliaments which favoured a religious settlement he strongly opposed. The Calvinist cause might just have succeeded at Elizabeth's accession. In the mid-seventeenth century in England it was too late. As far back as 1580 Robert Browne had begun the establishment of independent, self-governing congregations operating abroad or secretly and in great danger in England in opposition to the established Church. From this impetus of the Brownists stemmed the Baptists, the Congregationalists, the Quakers and other free sects which naturally preached religious tolerance and freedom of conscience as a proper solution of the religious issue. The independent assemblies stood to the left of the Presbyterians, who were the conservatives of Cromwell's rule. They recruited easily men of lower social station, and were strongly attracted to Levellist principles. The New Model Army, I suppose the first revolutionary army of Western history, was full of such men. Cromwell, with this Army as his political instrument, prevented a Presbyterian Settlement. It was for this reason that parliament, though it succeeded in so much, and was the true victor of all the struggles of the seventeenth century, never created a Presbyterian England. In 'the decisive decades' freedom of conscience was the passion of the Lord Protector, to say nothing of his army. He was delighted with the Instrument of Government, the parliamentary source of his authority, because it gave him power to prevent parliament from 'imposing what religions they will on the consciences of men'. 'What greater hypocrisy than for those who were oppressed by Bishops to become the greatest oppressors themselves so soon as this yoke was removed?' [8]

We know that Cromwell, politically a pragmatist, veered right round the clock in many of his policies, that he rested on the army to stop the Presbyterians and on the Presbyterians to break the Levellers. The army in the end ceased to be a crusading Puritan force and was professionalized. The steam went out of it, as out of Oliver Cromwell himself. The millenarian idealism evaporated. Something went out of Calvinism too, which is perhaps what Christopher Hill meant by speaking of its seventeenth century crisis. It was the problem of the election—'By the decree of God, for the manifestation of His glory, some men and angels are predestined unto everlasting life, and others foreordained to everlasting death' [9]—and of the *politics* of election. It is certain that Oliver Cromwell felt himself called and justified by God. The New Model Army was full of men who believed likewise. Despite the Presbyterian hope of an accommodation with the king, for the army the battle was between the elect of God and the forces of darkness. It was not easy to hold on to this certainty once the king had been defeated and executed, and conflicts developed within the army, and between it and parliament. The elect fighting the elect? Was this part of God's providence too? Who were now the Saints? The disillusion was deep. Then, as we saw, Cromwell most certainly proclaimed the divine election of England in a combination of patriotic and religious euphoria, confident he saw everywhere God's hand in events. But an elect *nation* seems to spread predestination very thinly around and to threaten at the same time every individual right or freedom with subordination to the interest of the higher divine instru-

---

[8] Cf. *God's Englishman*, p. 184 et seq.
[9] *The Westminster Confession of Faith*, 1643.

ment. Indeed the divinizing of the nation was the next step in history, and is still with us.

The disillusion of Cromwell himself with the Puritan experiment was greater, if that is possible, than that of the nation as his rule came to an end. He held on to power for fear lest catastrophe should follow or so he seemed to say. 'God knows, I would have been glad to have lived under my woodside, and to have kept a flock of sheep, rather than to have undertaken this government.' By the time of the Restoration in 1660 the Puritan revolution was defeated and Puritans were never again to resort to arms for their religious or secular causes. The Restoration was a Laudian triumph. Laudians had worked and plotted assiduously for the day and the initiatives were all with them. But the Puritans did not simply disappear. Perhaps sixty per cent of the clergy were Puritan, and as J. R. Green told us long ago what came after the military failure proved more constructive than armies. He was thinking of the spiritual consequences of Milton's *Paradise Lost* and Bunyan's *Pilgrim's Progress* and of the growth of Puritan mysticism once the resolve to establish the Kingdom of God by force and violence had been broken.

'As soon as the wild orgy of the Restoration was over, men began to see that nothing that was really worthy in the work of Puritanism had been undone. The revels of Whitehall, the scepticism and debauchery of courtiers, the corruption of statesmen, left the mass of Englishmen what Puritanism had made them, serious, earnest, sober in life and conduct, firm in their love of Protestantism and freedom. In the Revolution of 1688 Puritanism did the work of civil liberty which it had failed to do in 1642. It wrought out through Wesley and the revival of the eighteenth century the work of religious reform which its earlier efforts had thrown back for a hundred years. . . . The whole history of English progress since the Restoration, on its moral and spiritual sides, has been the history of Puritanism.'[10]

---

[10] J. R. Green, *A Short History of the English People*, 1874, Everyman Edn., London 1934 p. 566.

SIX

The Restoration

THE Restoration produced the Clarendon code for the creation of uniformity, aimed somewhat harshly against 'the growing and dangerous practices of seditions and sectaries and other disloyal persons, who, under pretence of tender consciences, have or may at their meetings contrive insurrections'. The Conventicle Acts (1664 and 1670) closed the chapels, the Corporation Act (1661) forced public officers to swear to the allegiance and the Supremacy, and on oath to forswear the Solemn League and Covenant, and the Five-Mile Act (1665) exiled dispossessed Puritan incumbents from the livings they had once enjoyed and from the major towns. The Test Act of 1673, to smell out 'papish recusants', forced all prominent men to swear against transubstantiation. But legislation, even with so much swearing, was never enough to settle the religious issue and when it was disobeyed it settled the crown instead. James II's Declaration of Indulgence, giving Romans and Nonconformists the right to worship in their own way, but meant to give the 'Papish recusants' comfort and support, was a great folly in a nation which had all too recently almost established a Calvinist republic! Seven bishops petitioned against its being read in churches and were acquitted on a charge of seditious libel. Thereafter it was James who fled, childishly casting his great seal in the Thames as he made his escape to those foreign parts into which so many royal and prelatical refugees had dropped in the past.

By the opening of the eighteenth century the Church of England was in decline. Its spiritual life was dead. Daily services had ceased in most churches, holy days were no longer celebrated. Holy communion was out of fashion, the poor neglected, the buildings themselves decaying. It was, *faute de mieux*, an erastian Church, subservient to the state and its idle clergy were held in derision. Many of them were poor, forgotten men. The Church at the centre was no longer capable of controlling the clergy as in the past and the local church passed to the oversight of the gentry as the episcopal power diminished. The gentry were no lovers of episcopal interference in what they felt were their responsibilities.

The strange enigma was that though the Church itself was sadly demoralized, somehow after a century of buffeting an independent Anglicanism was secure in the minds and hearts of the people: or at least, of the silent majority. For this, though it is not easy to account for, we have to thank several events which redeemed an evil century. The first was King James's Bible, the Authorised Version, which established itself in the affections of all men, not simply Anglicans, and by its beauty and virility of language did more for the English tongue than any other single work. The second was the Book of Common Prayer of 1662, the final result of a century of prayer-book making in which the ancient catholic liturgy had been reshaped in the English tongue for the English ethos. Though the cause originally of dissension, Cranmer's Prayer Book seems to have caught on at last. Other rival forms, anyway, had dropped out of sight. The Prayer Book of 1662 in Cranmer's penitential mood was almost timeless. A superb liturgical achievement, it combined a Calvinist temper with Roman forms. For more than three hundred years these two works have been the principal religious instruments of the Church of England, its great source of strength and stability in all historical and doctrinal changes. If changes are now coming and the Authorised Version must give way to new translations for private and public reading it is because not even the Authorised Version can compel language to stay still and because scholarship can no longer condone its inaccuracies. With Cranmer's book too, the language barrier grows. Its rotundities and sonorities are strange and prolix to the modern ear: its abject mood unfelicitous. Nevertheless, like the Authorised Version, it stamps and limits all its would-be successors, and compels them to kneel to it.

The third event was the growth of a purely Anglican spirituality, something not to be predicted from say the scourging spirituality of Sir Thomas More a century and a half earlier.[1] It expressed itself in the Anglican philosophy of Hooker at the end of the sixteenth century, the first effort to give Anglicanism a solid, intellectual basis. His *Ecclesiastical Polity* was influential again with the Restoration. It shone in the exquisite mystical *Centuries of Meditations* of Thomas Traherne, in the poems to love and to God and the hammer-blow sermons of John Donne, in the serene George Herbert, in the metaphysical poems of Henry Vaughan, who lived for the 'white, celestial thought' of eternity, in the sermons and writings of Bishop Jeremy Taylor, who ruggedly defended Anglicanism in *A Letter to A Gentleman Seduced to the Church of Rome*, asking what could be wanting in the Church of England for salvation since we had 'the Word of God, the Faith of the Apostles, the Creeds of the Primitive church, the Articles of the Four first General

---

[1] Cf. *A Dialogue of Comfort*, 1534, written while More was in the Tower, and *Four Last Things*, 1522.

Councils, a holy liturgy, excellent prayers, perfect Sacraments, faith and repentance, the Ten Commandments, and the sermons of Christ, and all the precepts of a holy life'. But his letter expresses more than a loyalty to his Church: it is a warm, even tender assertion of the possibility of a deep spiritual life within the Anglican fold. 'We pray for all men. We love all Christians, even our most erring brethren. We confess our sins to God and to our brethren whom we have offended, and to God's ministers in cases of scandal or of a troubled conscience. We communicate often . . . And what could here be wanting to salvation?'

Nicholas Ferrar's community at Little Gidding was a practical demonstration of what this innocent and felicitous Christianity, poised between two fanaticisms, could be. In 1626 he gathered his own kin, with their enormous brood of children, in a manor house in remote Huntingdonshire. They restored the little church, which is still standing, occasionally used, and half museum. To find it, T. S. Eliot wrote in his famous Fourth Quartet,

> If you came by day not knowing what you came for,
> It would be the same, when you leave the rough road
> And turn behind the pig-sty to the dull façade
> And the tombstone. And what you thought you came for
> Is only a shell, a husk of meaning.

In manor and chapel Nicholas Ferrar's group created a new familiar life of Christian devotion and discipline, rising at four to say their first prayers and keeping a continuous Christian watch of prayer through every twenty-four hours. It was remarkable, so to make the family and the daily round the basis of a monastic discipline. Nicholas Ferrar died in 1637 when the community was just over ten years old. It continued another ten years, until, in 1646, the Puritans sacked what they called 'the arminian nunnery', burnt its treasures and dispersed the community. And that was the end of what Traherne would have called the life of Christian felicity there—

> . . . of people, not wholly commendable,
> Of no immediate kin or kindness,
> But some of peculiar genius
> All touched by a common genius,
> United in the strife which divided them . . .

What was it which united Anglicans in 'the strife which divided them'? In his editorial comments in *Documents of the Christian Church*[2] Henry Bettenson speaks of Anglicanism in the seventeenth century as more a loyalty than a doctrinal position. This was true then and is still true

---

[2] Oxford, 1943.

today and is why Anglicanism can embrace so much. But it is also true
that the Caroline divines held a strong doctrinal position *against* both
contending extremes; and that was to take their stand with the early
Church and to identify with it against both 'Papall and Puritan Innovations'. Against the Puritans because their censorious religion of the Book
sought to sever the Church from the sacramental fellowship which was
the Church of the Fathers: and against the Romans for such palpably
false innovations as the seven sacraments, the offering up of 'our Saviour
in the Mass as a real, proper, and propitiatory sacrifice ... and that
whosoever believes not is eternally damned'[3]; against the doctrine of
transubstantiation, doctrines of purgatory, of saintly power, of relics,
images which are prayed to, indulgences, none of which seemed to the
Caroline divines to be scriptural or to belong to the Church of the Fathers
or Martyrs.

The seventeenth century Anglican Church walked a tightrope,
accepting the real presence of Christ in the eucharist, but rejecting the
grosser transubstantiation; accepting the Lutheran doctrine of grace, but
rejecting as perilous 'the sentence of God's predestination'. But the
stripped down or reformed catholicism the English divines claimed was to
historic Rome an insolent heretical presumption; while to the angry
Puritans it was incomprehensible, the mere disguise for an ultimate
surrender to the scarlet woman, the whore of Babylon. The point of the
stand of the Caroline divines is more clearly seen today when both Rome
and non-conformity subject themselves to a scrutiny which in the
seventeenth century came only from outside.

It is extraordinary that in so violent a century so God-confiding, God-
seeking a religious mood should have been born. It witnessed to the
possibility of a serene and saintly Christianity which persecuted none and
was free of self-laceration. This surely must be the meaning of Traherne's
search for a Christian felicity and of George Herbert's plea, unheeded
in his day, to 'take the gentle path'. He was of course writing a poem
to God. But not only God could read.

> Throw away thy rod,
> Throw away thy wrath;
> O my God,
> Take the gentle path.

---

[3] Bishop John Cosin in 'A Letter to the Countess of Peterborough', *Works* IV, 332–6.

SEVEN

The Age of Reason and Revolution

'Differences of opinion', wrote Jonathan Swift in a *Voyage to the Houny-hnhnms*, 'hath cost many millions of lives; for instance, whether flesh be bread, or bread be flesh; whether the juice of a certain berry be blood or wine; whether it be better to kiss a post, or throw it into the fire; what is the best colour for a coat, whether black, white, red, or grey; and whether it should be long or short, narrow or wide, dirty or clean; and with many more. Neither are any wars so furious and bloody, or of so long continuance, as those occasioned by difference in opinion, *especially if it be in things indifferent.*'[1]

We may take this as the contemptuous and derisory verdict on the heritage of Christendom which Swift shared with Voltaire, Gibbon and many other critical minds of the eighteenth century. Religion had little rationally to commend it if it led to the disasters of the seventeenth century. But centuries are arbitrary divisions. The ideas and character of the eighteenth century were being created in the seventeenth century and if any one deserves the title of maker of the eighteenth century it is

---

[1] *Gulliver's Travels*, etc., Oxford 1935 p. 292 (italics mine). Swift could be a great deal coarser in his derision. In a *Tale of a Tub* (1704) he plays around merrily with the concept *anima mundi*, which he translates 'the spirit, or breath, or wind of the world'. And within a paragraph he has got 'wind' round to 'certain mysteries not to be named, giving occasion for those happy epithets of *turgidus* or *inflatus*, applied either to the *emittent* or *recipient* organs'. From that point it becomes pure music hall. He establishes that man brings with him into the world a grain of the universal wind which he must develop and not hoard but freely communicate to mankind. And so, understandably, some ancient sages, 'affirm the gift of BELCHING to be the noblest act of a rational creature'. Predictably, we are entertained to a spectacle out of Aristophanes: 'At ... times were to be seen several hundreds [of priests] linked together in a circular chain, with every man a pair of bellows applied to his neighbours breach, by which they blew each other to the shape and size of a tun....' We need not enter into what happens to the wind. It all leads up to the ironic syllogism, 'Words are but wind; and learning is nothing but words; ergo, learning is nothing but wind.' *But the point is that Swift was, as Pope said, 'a dignified clergyman'*—of the Church of England, who had, 'composed more libels than sermons'. He was thirty-two when the seventeenth century ended. His mere existence is a more ironic comment on a fanatical century even than his own satire.

John Locke, the philosopher, who was born in 1632. When, on that wintry day at the end of January 1649, Charles I stepped to his execution on a scaffold erected outside the Banqueting Hall in Whitehall, John Locke, a thoughtful youth of sixteen from nearby Westminster School may have been among the crowd which watched a king's head fall and the first European breach made in the civilized consensus about the sacredness of the monarch. Certainly as a scholar living within a stone's throw of the place of execution he could not have escaped the horror of that day. Forty years later we find the same John Locke returning to England from political exile in the ship which brought Princess Mary to the throne of England. He came as political godfather to the Glorious Revolution and principal formulator of the ideas behind the Bill of Rights. Significantly the title of his first published work is *Essay on Toleration*.

His most influential political work, *Two Treatises on Civil Government*, not published till 1690 because of his exile, but influential long before publication, consists of two groups of ideas, the conjunction of which marks an intellectual watershed, for the first is a reply to Sir Robert Filmer's *Patriarcha* which was a justification of the divine right by an argument from history intended to prove 'the ancient and prime right of lineal succession to paternal government'. Locke summarizes Filmer's largely biblical argument thus: 'That all government is absolute monarchy; and the ground he builds on is this: that no man is born free.' In the second treatise Locke breaks away from the appeal to the (biblical) past and argues from natural principles like a scientist engaged in a deductive exercise that in nature man is a free sovereign being, gifted with reason by his maker so that he may understand his life and order it properly, for the safety and good of himself, his family and his property. He surrenders his free sovereignty to society voluntarily in return for a pledge to protect his person, his property, his rights. In the light of this social contract doctrine society ceases to be a mysterious human *a priori* by which every man is captured but becomes a rational construction openly consented to, and designed for rational ends. In his *Essay Concerning Human Understanding* Locke does for the human individual what he had done for society—he rationalizes the object of his study. Man, like society, becomes a rational construct. He does not come into the world, like Platonic man, bearing an awesome past of experience and understanding in an immortal soul, which has only to be awakened in order to *know*, or like Christian man arrive God-instructed, possessed *a priori* of a moral character. On the contrary, he arrives a *nothing*, a *tabula rasa*, and is built into a natural creature by the instruction of his senses. Locke dismissed depth and mystery from man and society as in a way too René Descartes did by his recourse to extreme scepticism.

The teachings of Locke mark the end in British thought of the ideas of the schoolmen. Precisely this appeal to reason against a quasi-divine tradition lay behind the constitutional settlement of the Glorious Revolution—monarchy, yes, for this was a rational, unifying force in a nation, but monarchy subject to law, and law the product of parliament, and parliament the reflection of the will of the people and subject to their dismissal. Thus was the social contract writ large in British law. A highly gifted Anglican Bishop, George Berkeley, made a superb contribution to the development of Locke's empiricism but all foundered in the total scepticism of David Hume—the viper's sting which set Kant dancing. But the empiricism Locke established as the dominant school of British philosophy is still with us and productive as ever of negative, analytical and sceptical attitudes to religion.

Among other writings John Locke produced *The Reasonableness of Christianity* (1695) of which the title tells all. It was more or less the opening shot in the Deist controversy. Deism saddles God with the primal act of creation but little else, save as a Presence, perhaps a sustaining Presence, behind the universe. But from the moment of its creation the universe is subject to the laws of its creation: a second revelation and the miraculous and the supernatural elements which go with it are unacceptable, against reason. Briefly, this is Deism, under which the Gospel significance has to be reassessed. And so we find Matthew Tindal, Fellow of All Soul's Oxford, writing *Christianity as Old as Creation, or the Gospel a Republication of the Religion of Nature* (1730) which so exquisitely summarizes the contents that no further comment is necessary.

John Toland earlier, in *Christianity not Mysterious* (1696), paraphrased Locke when he wrote that 'what is evidently repugnant to clear and distinct ideas, or to our common Notions, is contrary to Reason'. He affirmed that he intended to prove that the doctrines of the Gospel, if they are the Word of God, cannot be against reason. God has no right to require the assent of his creatures to what they cannot comprehend. 'If by *knowledge* be meant understanding what is believed, then I stand by it that Faith is Knowledge.'

Deism, even in a torpid and latitudinarian Church did not go unchallenged. Indeed, the retorts became more influential than the works which had provoked them. Joseph Butler's *Analogy of Religion, Natural and Revealed, to the Constitution and Course of Nature* (1736) established itself as a Christian classic and William Law's *A Serious Call to a Devout and Holy Life* (1728) is still a living source of Christian spirituality. Indeed it was Law's book, more than any other, which fed the evangelical revival of the latter half of the century and the Methodist schism.

But at the end of the seventeenth century and the beginning of the eighteenth the Church was still enmeshed in the controversies of the civil war and the Restoration. The Laudian high church views had deep roots. Six bishops—including William Sancroft, Archbishop of Canterbury and the saintly Thomas Ken, Bishop of Bath and Wells—and four hundred clergy refused the oath of allegiance to William and Mary. To them a king was king by divine will and against a king no one had the right to rebel and James II to whom their love and loyalty had been given absolutely, as part of their faith, was still alive! And here was parliament offering the crown to someone who had no title to it, and as if they had the right to dispose of it to the highest (political) bidder in a Dutch auction! So the non-jurors, as they were called, were suspended and deprived of their offices and livings. They went into schism and formed a separate communion. They went on exercising a shadowy authority, even negotiating with the Orthodox Church. They were another wound in a Church stricken enough. All one can say about this magnificent stand on principle, is that, typically English, it came too late and in a lost cause. There had been too many compromises, shifts, improvizations, sacrifices, persecutions since Henry VIII had beheaded the Church of England. They were, as those who would stand on principle, a century and a half late. And standing on the wrong principle.

Yet they were not imprisoned or beheaded. The nation had moved on that much. The promise of Locke's essay had been partly fulfilled in the Toleration Act (1689) which, though it excluded Roman Catholics and Unitarians, at least permitted all other nonconformists to worship as they willed, in their own chapels, so long as they did not lock themselves in. Still, the tolerance of others manifested in the Act failed to soften the conflict of parties within the Church of England. The Convocations were bitterly divided. Their upper houses were Whigs—erastian and latitudinarian, except for the bishops who had become non-jurors: the houses of the lower clergy, still deeply influenced by Laud, were Tories and high churchmen. Indeed, so bitter were the conflicts of the clergy that Convocations were suspended and the church governed by royal injunction. It became, subject to conformity to the growing mass of Church law, a federation of dioceses rather than a single Church. Lacking a debating chamber or legislative assembly it was seriously crippled in the face of Methodism.

Methodism was nothing if not centralized. There was no central body of the Church of England capable of negotiating with it. It was not until 1852 that Canterbury Convocation met again and not until 1861 that York Convocation was summoned and not until 1970 that Church Assembly and the Convocations of York and Canterbury were united in one General Synod. And one of the first acts of that Synod has been to debate how free or unfree the Church is in its established status.[2]

---

[2] *Church and State. Report*, CIO 1970. See below p. 115 et seq.

EIGHT

An Economic Revolution

AT THE beginning of the eighteenth century English agriculture was still organized much as it had been in the Middle Ages, when villeins enjoyed their tenure of land in return for labour services to the lord of the manor, and the collective duties of a manor were controlled by a manorial court. Into this system Church and parson were fitted usually by the patronage of the manorial lord and so were themselves integrally feudal.

The manorial system had slowly decayed over the centuries as a money economy forced out labour payments. Nevertheless, eighteenth century England outside the cities was a land of peasants. The common fields were still the chief feature of each village, along with the glebe and the manorial park. The peasants, as owners or tenants, cultivated their strips in the common fields and pastured their beasts on the common waste. It was an agriculture of a low productivity, which shut out change. It was impossible to introduce new crops, or a higher breed of cattle into a village economy which was bound to move at the pace of the slowest mind.

Just as the technical and scientific investigations of the Royal Society (1660) were leading to a growth of interest in new industrial processes, so the voyages of exploration all over the world were exciting botanists and agriculturalists.[1] The great houses of England, already the heart of its culture, became centres of botanical learning and experiment. Through their enterprise a botanical revolution preceded the agricultural revolution. The combined pressures of new learning, the economic needs of the growing population, the self-interest of the landowners forced that revolution upon an unwilling, an uncomprehending peasantry by redistributing the common land in a way which excluded the small producer. The common field, by and large, was abolished, the peasantry disinherited. In 1760 one-third of the land was still being farmed in open fields, but by 1830 the open field system was extinct. Between 1710 and

---

[1] Cf. W. H. G. Armytage, *The Rise of the Technocrats*, Routledge, London 1965.

1760 nearly 350,000 acres, and between 1760 and 1843 nearly 7,000,000 acres of land were enclosed. Some of this land was common and waste land, but a large proportion was land previously under common field cultivation.

The consequences of this agricultural revolution were new and improved crops—hops, mangel wurzels, swede turnips, a substantial rise in the weight and health of cattle, and the introduction of many successful new field techniques. It was accomplished at the cost of social disaster—a new, destitute country poor, and a drift of the landless and uprooted into the towns: in fact by the creation of a landless proletariat, to use Marxist language.

The same technical advances which set in motion the agricultural revolution promoted the industrial revolution too. New machinery, first driven by water power and then by steam power, launched it. The revolution was already under way before 1750 with Kay's flying shuttle servicing the weaving industry. As early as 1735 Abram Darby transformed the smelting industry. In half a century iron production went up by eight times and as Adam Smith pointed out in 1776, for every independent workman there were now twenty working for a master. It was a foreign agricultural product, cotton, which enormously expanded the already powerful textile industry and created the cotton mills of Lancashire to match the woollen mills of Yorkshire.

The Midland and Northern towns, particularly of Lancashire, Staffordshire, Yorkshire and Warwickshire, expanded rapidly. In the seventy years from 1750 to 1820 the population of England and Wales rose from 6 million to 12 million. By 1861 it had reached 20 million. Only an extraordinary increase in productive capacity could have made that possible. A new and different society was being created, with a new alignment of classes, but it was at first hidden in the new towns of the North and the Midlands: the South, where government, learning, culture, pre-industrial wealth were concentrated, went unscathed. Until the railways connected up the land the North was more remote from the Southerner than Ulster is from the Londoner today. The population of London rose, in the half century from 1750, by about a quarter and that of Bristol, the main commercial centre of the South, grown rich on the profits of the slave trade, by one-third, while the population of Norwich, once the wealthiest wool city of England, hardly moved at all. Liverpool increased its population threefold and Manchester fourfold in the same period. That tells the story.

Was the Church aware of this vast social and economic transformation? On the whole it would seem not, at least until well into the nineteenth century. There was, of course, a piecemeal awareness. Many priests must have known of, and connived in, the sale of poor law children to the new factories. Many were magistrates, all were members of the parish vestry, the organ of local government. The clergy could hardly ignore the invasion of their parishes by factories and industrial housing. We do not hear of them putting all heaven in a rage. They were torn between pride in local progress and the wealth it would bring, alarm lest the invasion of the poor in search of work meant a higher poor law rate and a genuine but unworthy fear of the already alienated masses. Town poverty bore a different face from rural poverty. In a way that was more rare in the country, the poor in the town were being brutalized by their living conditions, particularly the overcrowding in disease-ridden housing Engels[2] was so vividly to describe, which they took to gin and sin to escape—abandoning the Church.

There was hardly even a national consciousness of what was happening until a series of government reports revealed conditions of virtual slavery in mills and factories. Church consciousness came in the 1840s with the Christian Socialists. Even then, lacking Convocations, the Church lacked also an *organ* of conscience. The Nonconformists more easily made the running.

The Church picked up much of its new consciousness about the new poor, not from Christianity itself, but from the utilitarian philosophy which began increasingly to prevail in the nineteenth century. Bentham's doctrines made every man the personal judge of his own happiness or self-interest. Christian apologists made use of his phrases and concepts: individual economic salvation suited evangelical principles. Tragically for Britain and the rest of the world, utilitarianism promoted *laissez-faire* at the moment when industry and commerce were most in need of governmental control and stern moral oversight to prevent the merciless exploitation so characteristic of the century. At the same time it placed the poor under the censorious judgement of all the secure and well-cushioned of the land. If you were poor and unemployed it followed that you were lazy, feckless or full of moral turpitude, unwilling to pursue your proper self-interest and so deserving of punishment. Hence the harsh Poor Law of 1834, which took from the parish the right to look after its own poor and handed it over to sour district Boards of Guardians determined to keep the poor rate down. It was they who established the punitive workhouses which Oliver Twist experienced.

The growth of a vast social gulf between the educated and able and well-off in society and *the rest* was inevitable when the working-masses were held to be of a different order of humanity—moral aliens, not simply alienated. (In the pew rents debate the cry against the poor was 'Unclean, unclean'.) The Church of England has never overcome this social heritage from the nineteenth century, this identification with masters and landed gentry *against* the poor. I would say that this, more than anything, was the great watershed in the history of the Church:

---

[2] *The Condition of the Working Class in England in 1844.*

a great class, both patronized and despised, then decided that 'the Church is not for us'.

To this theme I shall return.

NINE

Reason's Unreason

THE surprises of history are unending.

The age of reason ended in the most terrible and destructive unreason. It may be illustrated philosophically first. The teachings of David Hume were a total dead end. If accepted there could be no movement of thought beyond them. Events could be associated by contiguity and succession but never by cause or effect. One event may follow another in time or be associated with another in space but it is only a species of human folly which insists on relating them causally. 'Objects have no discoverable connexion together; nor is it from any other principle but custom operating upon the imagination, that we can draw any inference from the appearance of one to the existence of another.'[1] And so, 'reasoning is nothing but a species of sensation'—that is, reasoning is irrational. Morals too. But if Hume by and large bit only philosophers —except maybe the old lady who had heard bad accounts of him and would not drag him out of the ditch into which he had fallen till he recited the Lord's prayer—Jean-Jacques Rousseau affected all literate men in France and the masses too.

Hume, an authority on the role of feeling in human affairs (after all everything for him was a species of feeling), said of Rousseau, 'He has only felt, during the whole course of his life. He is like a man who was stript not only of his clothes, but of his skin, and turned out in that situation to combat with the rude but boisterous elements.'[2] This judgment was the consequence of an affecting interview in which the exiled Rousseau fell on Hume's neck and wept.

Rousseau, one of the progenitors of the romantic movement, exalted the world of nature and feeling and the natural man, the man of Eden, before civilization corrupted him. He turned Locke's artificial sovereign man into the noble uncorrupted being every man potentially was and made him a political symbol of revolutionary power. Over that fictional

---

[1] *Treatise of Human Nature*, Bk. I, Pt. III, Sec. VIII.
[2] *Life and Correspondence of David Hume*, ed. J. H. Burton, Edinburgh 1846, vol. II, p. 339.

man the French revolution was fought. True the revolution was sparked off by legitimate grievances but it would never have generated its terrible dynamic without this romantic vision of what man could be and ought to be in a new and egalitarian society held together by natural justice and untainted by the artifices of civilization.

Though the goddess of reason (in the shape of a dissolute young actress) was enthroned on the altar of Notre Dame, the course of reason was not saved. The revolution developed from regicide to general terror against the aristocracy and then began to devour its own sons. What followed it was, first, military dictatorship, then 'revolutionary' monarchy and the first really nationalist wars fought with indoctrinated mass armies—events which foreshadowed the wars and dictatorships of the twentieth century. The Church in France was particularly the object of attack, its wealth confiscated, its monastic houses dispersed and religious orders suppressed, its clergy tamed or executed. Early liberal support from England for the revolution—seen, like the American War of Independence, as a struggle for liberty and the rights of men—soon faded. Edmund Burke's *Reflexions on the Revolution in France* (1791) came more and more to speak for British opinion. Reaction in England was lamentably strengthened; radical views, sympathy for the protests of the poor, were regarded as dangerous revolutionary symptoms. Just about every influential and intelligent mind was hostile to the French 'solution'. Reform in Church and state—long overdue—was put back forty years: the poor were an enemy to be suppressed. When one contemplates the victory of reaction, side by side with the shallow utilitarian ideology which fed it, one can only feel sorrow for lost opportunities. What England needed most just then, despite the Napoleonic wars, was a period of gentle reform and social guidance. All it got was a stubborn gentry, greedy manufacturers, child slavery and a tormented king.

Yet, in the face of alien ideologies which seemed to abandon the new masses to the most wretched and defiling poverty, and over against an ineffective and corrupt Church of England absolutely identified with an establishment hostile to the poor, two movements gave comfort and courage to those whom God seemed to have abandoned—Methodism and Evangelicalism.

TEN

Methodism

IT HAS often been said that Methodism saved Britain from revolution. Conceivably so. But it was in its own way a social revolution. It was an unimaginable social phenomenon set in motion by a man whose labours were more considerable than those of Paul in the first century. John Wesley covered about a quarter of a million miles on horseback on preaching journeys which began in his thirty-fifth year and continued until his death fifty-two years later. Someone has reckoned that he preached 40,000 sermons. But how he preached! Four or five times a day, beginning at five in the morning! How could anyone persuade three or four thousand overworked miners to listen to him early on a winter's morning preaching on grace or justification by faith? It is only conceivable in a revolutionary situation and the pace could only be maintained by a religious genius preaching 'as never sure to preach again, and as a dying man to dying men'. Even at eighty-five his life discipline included rising at four and preaching at five, with no sense that he had earned a respite.

One cannot form today any proper idea of the magic of his oratory, but it was often accompanied in the early phases by the ecstatic phenomena of mass conversion and miraculous healing such as those which accompany the massive rallies of The Assemblies of God in South America and Indo-China today. Listeners were held in rapture: individuals changed colour, cried out, fell insensible, were overwhelmed with simultaneous conviction of guilt and salvation, roared out their hallelujahs and their hymns in the certainty of the presence of the Lord. Britain had never witnessed before such a wave of religious fervour as brought twenty thousand poor to listen together in one place to one Church of England priest. But it was socially significant too. For the period of Wesley's greatest influence was the second half of the eighteenth century when the agrarian revolution was creating the landless poor who were being absorbed as 'hands' into the dark, satanic mills. Lost, they found identity again through Wesley as souls deserving of salvation and made their peace with, and got their strength directly from, God. When society failed them, its norms and forms gone, its securities withdrawn, they took hope and courage from the Kingdom which transcended all societies. Thus was born a Christian stoicism which distinguished the working-class of Britain in the nineteenth century and brought it un-crushed through the evils of that bad time. It was a christianized philosophy of self-help the poor worked out for themselves.[1] By their own pennies they founded friendly societies, co-operative societies, trade unions, sick clubs, chapels, and flocked to the support of temperance societies. When Robert Owen appeared on the scene as the secular evangelist of the self-help of the poor he was in his own eloquent way John Wesley standing on his head.

The appearance of the moralizing, millenarian Owen on the scene reminds us of that other role for which Methodism, along with dissent generally, has been cast, which was to usher in the working-class as a self-conscious class with a sense of destiny, and so to help to create a viable class society in the nineteenth century. Harold Perkins argues[2] that what was required to bring a class to birth was something more than a conflict over wages, rent, profit, which has always been with us. A class needs a clear, even flattering image of itself *vis-à-vis* other (denigrated) classes, and of 'the ideal society in which it might find its right place'. 'Reluctant to be born, the new class society needed a midwife to help it into existence. It found one in the unexpected form of sectarian religion.'[3] As Harold Perkins sees it the old religious structures formed a kind of social sandwich, with Anglicans (and sometimes Romans) at the top and bottom and the old Dissenters, presently joined by new Methodists, in the middle—coming of course from those independent minded social groups which had once formed the nucleus of the New Model Army. As industrialism enormously expanded the working population, the 'filling' expanded too and 'ate away the bottom layer'. To be working-class was to be 'chapel'. A religious stratification took place which corresponded with and emphasized the class stratification

---

[1] No one without direct connections with the working-class poor of the nineteenth century can properly understand this fanatical working-class independence which took pride in poverty but had a horror of destitution. It was singularly without resentment or envy. My grandmother in Leeds holy-stoned her step and the pavement down to the gutter every day; windows, curtains, door knockers were kept spotless, the house immaculate. She 'kept herself to herself' in her own words, even in widowhood, 'owed nothing to nobody', 'would sooner starve than ask anyone for help'. And as for strong drink 'She'd sooner die than let a drop pass her lips'. In my grandfather's best years perhaps a pound a week was coming in to the house: that was his pay as Leeds' first sanitary inspector. See in this connection Richard Hoggart's account of his childhood in Leeds in *Speaking to Each Other. Vol. 1. About Society*, Chatto and Windus, London 1970.

[2] *The Origins of Modern English Society*, Routledge & Kegan Paul, London 1969 p. 218 ff.

[3] Ibid, p. 196.

—Anglicans at the top, Nonconformists underneath.[4] It provided society with the means to understand its complex and changing patterns. Let it also be said that 'chapel' provided the working-class with a morally superior picture of itself and of the future society it would attain which has coloured working-class politics right down to this day.

Of course, after the charismatic leadership of John Wesley came the routinization of the charisma, as Max Weber would describe it. Methodism became a 'connexion', a great society, efficiently run by a national conference, depending more and more on local preachers, hiving off from the Church of England into its own buildings, controlling and vetting its members by compelling their attendance at weekly class meetings—a powerful source of the self-education of the best strata of the lower middle class and of the poor. It is a matter of history that the Church of England did not know what to do with the religious revival John Wesley handed to it on a plate. Lacking Convocations, it had no means of negotiating nationally with Methodism, which was the first modern democratic organization and a model for almost every national society since. And so, with a clear reluctance, the new Methodism, while its High Church leader was still alive, and under his direction, began the ordination of its own ministers and established itself as an independent denomination, presently to be riven by schisms some of which pointed in a revivalist, others in a democratic, direction. The Wesleyan Methodists had no real doctrinal quarrel with the Church of England. Its allies in the Church of England, the Evangelicals, had.

---

[4] As to the haziness in which 'class' was viewed, K. S. Inglis points to this in *Churches and the Working Class in Victorian England* (London 1963) by quoting from an 1858 pamphlet by a layman, 'Why are our churches closed?' The anonymous author speaks of 'the upper and middle classes (those whom we term churchgoers)'. Inglis feels that this casualness indicates the imprecision with which the notion of class was handled even as late as 1858, despite, one might add, the nascent Marxism and the birth of the Workingmen's International, Robert Owen and all.

ELEVEN

The Evangelical Revival

METHODISM, it has often been said, was for the most part Arminian in its theology: it rejected predestination. Warm, passionate, and confronting the hungry masses with the promise of salvation it could not, by emotion and instinct, go along with a doctrine which taught the salvation of a predestined élite. Such determinism would have destroyed its impetus. But it had its Calvinistic wing in the followers of the eloquent George Whitfield. Wesley took him up while he was still at Pembroke College, Oxford and sent him as a missionary to Georgia, USA, before even he had taken his priest's orders. He began, reluctantly, to break with the Methodists in 1741 but his influence with them continued till his death. Able to reach crowds of twenty thousand with his voice, and preaching more than forty times a week and infallibly reducing them to tears, he looms even now a prodigious figure.

Whitfield's followers were called 'the Countess of Huntingdon's connexion', he having become her chaplain in 1748. The formal break with Methodism came in 1781. There were to be other secessions, destroying the original unity, of which the Methodist New Connexion of 1797, the Primitive Methodists 1811, and the Bible Christians 1815, were the most important. The United Methodist Free Churches, 1857, reuniting three schismatic groups, marked the beginning of the reunion movement in Methodism. All the same Methodism early displayed the extreme Protestant impulse toward fragmentation into sects, a tendency in the end quite self-defeating.

The Church of England experienced its own profound Evangelical revival, which ran parallel with Methodism, but it was spared from further breakaway movements of the Methodist kind. The Evangelicals remained loyal to their Church. It was that much easier for them to do so because their theology was Calvinist and they could point to the Thirty-nine Articles and argue convincingly that the Church itself was Calvinist. Their revival was therefore aimed in their view at maintaining the purity of doctrine and practice of the Church of England, a position they still maintain.[1]

Indeed the most cursory examination of the Articles puts right on their side. The Articles are most explicitly Calvinist. The Anglo-Catholic party is still legally in the wrong as the Evangelicals consistently asserted all through the nineteenth century and still do, though with less enthusiasm. The real point, however, is how far the Church is still *governed* by the XXXIX Articles, the law notwithstanding, or ought to have been governed by them even in the eighteenth century. It is undeniable that the Evangelicals could claim at their birth to be in the true tradition of the Tudor and Caroline reformation. The high church appeal to the historic Church, to the long traditions of Christendom, had always an element of casuistry in it. The lesson, however, is that a Church so bound by old laws it was itself incapable of changing could only grow and develop by becoming a law-breaker. This is what has happened in the last two centuries and in a way is still happening. The basic doctrinal law of the Church goes by default and only a general assent to the XXXIX Articles is required of the ministry, an assent which is more truthfully a non-assent, though now this is being legalized.

One of the early leaders of the Evangelical revival was John Newton (1725–1807) who went to sea as a boy, became captain of a slaver, lived a far from blameless life and through a sudden conversion in 1748 launched himself into the Evangelical movement. He had difficulty in getting ordained, but succeeding, at the hands of the Bishop of Lincoln, received the living of Olney. There he attracted the melancholy William Cowper to his side and built up a village atmosphere imbued with that piety and spiritual devotion which had characterized Little Gidding a century earlier. Cowper himself—*The Stricken Deer* of Lord David

---

[1] Article IX of the Church of England Articles of Religion says, 'Original Sin standeth not in the following of *Adam*, (as the Pelagians do vainly talk;) but it is the fault and corruption of the Nature of every man, that naturally is ingendered of the offspring of Adam: whereby man is very far gone from original righteousness, and is of his own nature inclined to evil, so that the flesh lusteth always contrary to the spirit; and therefore in every person born into this world, it deserveth God's wrath and damnation.' Article X 'Of Free Will'—'The condition of man after the fall of Adam is such, that he cannot turn and prepare himself, by his own natural strength and good works, to faith, and calling upon God.' Article XI commends Justification by faith as 'a most wholesome doctrine'. Article XVII lays down the doctrine of election: 'Predestination to life is the everlasting purpose of God, whereby ... he hath constantly decreed by his counsel secret to us, to deliver from curse and damnation those whom he hath chosen in Christ out of mankind, and to bring them by Christ to everlasting salvation, as vessels made to honour ... Predestination, and an Election in Christ, is full of sweet, pleasant and unspeakable comfort to godly persons....' The Articles are Calvinistic too in tone in their condemnation of the errors of certain Church Councils and of Romanish and ritualistic practices.

Cecil—added a poetic dimension to Evangelicalism of which the hymn—

> O for a closer walk with God,
> A calm and heavenly frame,
> A light to shine upon the road
> That leads me to the Lamb!

is typical in its quietism. The redoubtable Newton made his own contribution to the hymnal: 'Glorious things of thee are spoken', still a regular congregational hymn, and the masterpiece—

> How sweet the name of Jesus sounds
> In a believer's ear.

One remarkable leader of the later evangelicals was Charles Simeon (1759–1836). Brought up in a high church tradition, he suffered a conversion experience as an undergraduate at King's College, Cambridge. Convinced that only an inner spiritual worthiness, an experience of salvation, justified him in receiving the sacraments, and that no mere conformity would substitute he joined the Evangelicals. He devoted himself with such ardour to what seemed almost a new faith that when he was appointed perpetual curate to Holy Trinity Church in 1782 there were demonstrations against him and he was mobbed in the streets. A man of both courage and learning, and a great preacher, he became a power not only in Cambridge but throughout the land. An unfortunate memorial to him is the Simeon Trust, which, founded in his lifetime, and by his inspiration, bought up advowsons in order to secure the appointment of evangelical incumbents to vacant livings—and so to freeze their churchmanship in perpetuity.

What sort of men were the Evangelicals? Werner Stark spoke of them as 'being Calvinists, however emotional in the beginning, who came in the end to produce a steely type of man, who would master, if not suppress, his emotions', as against the Methodists who would be 'loving, yielding, even soft'.[2] 'Outside their religious practice evangelicals are highly ritualized in their behaviour,' David Martin wrote with some irony.[3] He goes on to speak of the thrift, sobriety, hard work and earnestness of the latterday Puritan—the perfect English example of the Protestant of Weber's Protestant ethic, except perhaps that he drew back from the greed and gambling of high capitalism or the harsh tyranny of the industrial master. This strict private sense of morality and respectability which spread to and sobered the gentry changed the profile of a whole

---

[2] *The Sociology of Religion, Vol. III, The Universal Church*, Routledge, London 1967 p. 398.

[3] *A Sociology of English Religion*, SCM Press, London 1967 p. 62. The whole of his Chapter Three is illuminating in its analysis of religious attitudes.

century. Gentlemen took to black coats and stovepipe hats and left off their swords. The dissolute ways of the Georgians were no longer condoned and if pursued were hidden behind lace curtains. Cock-fighting and bear-baiting went. Sexual frankness went underground. Later, Temperance Leagues flourished.[4] The ideal of the nineteenth century was the modest, puritan professional gentleman with a house and garden in the suburbs, and the high esteem of his chapel or church. To this ideal the lower middle classes almost universally aspired: it was called *respectability* which did not in its heyday carry a derisory ring but meant precisely 'worthy of respect'. It gave birth to the solemn English Sunday: the Lord's Day Observance Society still expresses that Evangelical hostility to pure enjoyment.

The ideal of Evangelicalism was curiously classless. The whole conception of the historic Church I have examined in earlier chapters involves what David Martin calls 'a carefully graded cultural hierarchy, generally based on some concept of an accumulating richness of awareness and intellectual distinction'[5]—or of religious status. The pope (or for England, the archbishop) was by definition nearest to God, indeed his chosen earthly representative. Logically, it followed that all others were set at a further distance from God, in a descending scale until one reached the most poor and ignorant to whom God was only accessible at all by the mediation of the other, culturally privileged members of society. Evangelicalism changed that, even for those who were not evangelicals. This was the basis of Wesley's power too. The personal experience of conversion or salvation, the motion of God directly into the heart of man, the inner proof of election, these were independent of all hierarchical chains and cultural privileges. 'Assurance is democratically available', David Martin writes. So, equally, was eternal damnation. 'The rich man in his castle and the poor man at his gate were equals in sin and in the experience of redemption: a point which many rich men in castles found distinctly unpleasing.'[6] It was probably no social accident that the Evangelical revival coincided with the growth of democratic aspirations in British society.

Evangelicalism cannot be understood unless it is seen as crossing denominational boundaries. Loyal though the Anglican Evangelicals were to the Church of England as by parliament established, their hostility to the high church party was even greater than their hostility to Rome, for it was nearer home: invoking the law against them, they became the bitter persecutors of the Anglo-Catholics all through the

---

[4] Cf. B. Harrison, *Drink and the Victorians: the Temperance Question in England, 1815–1872*, London 1971.

[5] *A Sociology of English Religion*, p. 59.

[6] Ibid, p. 59. 'I suppose that undenominational evangelicalism is in many ways the Englishman's folk religion, isn't it?' Mr. R. M. Turner in a note to me.

nineteenth century. Their *true* spiritual brothers were the evangelicals
—Calvinists and biblical fundamentalists—of *other* denominations and
the founding of the Evangelical Alliance in 1846, which drew 900 clergy
and laity from all over the world, was an international, ecumenical
assertion of their common doctrinal position. One might even say that
it was this bridging theology which united the moral consciences of the
otherwise fragmented Nonconformity with the Low Church, and that
what dominated the nineteenth century was not so much the Nonconformist as the Evangelical conscience. This was certainly the back-
bone of the temperance movement and the two great movements which
acted with astonishing power on the politics of the age, Wilberforce's
drive against slavery, coming from the brilliant Clapham Sect, and
Lord Shaftesbury's long campaign against evil conditions in factories
and mines which succeeded in the end against the cruel, utilitarian
ideology of industrial merchant capitalism. It is remarkable that they
were both the products of evangelicalism. Neither the Anglo-Catholic
Movement nor the Christian Socialists can claim comparable social
successes. The Christian Social Union succeeded in inspiring a formidable
minority but perhaps not until William Temple began to preach a new
Christian social involvement in the twenties and thirties of this century
does a real *Anglican* social conscience again emerge.

It is worth noting what the Evangelical Alliance actually declared. The
project was militantly intended 'to associate and concentrate the strength
of an enlightened Protestantism against the encroachments of Popery
and Puseyism, and to promote the interests of a scriptural Christianity'
and was therefore in its birth a hostile reaction to the Tractarians.

Its doctrine cut deeper. It affirmed

'Evangelical views in regard to the divine inspiration, authority and
sufficiency of the Holy Scriptures; the right and duty of private
judgment in the interpretation of the Holy Scriptures; the unity of the
Godhead and the Trinity of Persons therein; the utter depravity of
human nature in consequence of the Fall; the incarnation of the Son of
God, His work for atonement for the sinners of mankind, and His
mediatorial intercession and reign; the justification of the sinner by
faith alone; the work of the Holy Spirit in the conversion and
sanctification of the sinner; the immortality of the soul, the resurrection
of the body, the judgment of the world by our Lord Jesus Christ,
with the eternal blessedness of the righteous and the eternal punishment
of the wicked; the divine institution of the Christian ministry, and the
obligations and perpetuity of the ordinances of Baptism and the Lord's
Supper.'[7]

Except for the points about the ministry and the sacraments, it is a

---

[7] Cf. A. J. Arnold, *History of the Evangelical Alliance*, London 1897.

Christianity which has little need for a Church, for it would be best expressed through a private life or family group. An ordained ministry and a confessional or credal Church could come between a Christian and 'the right and duty of private judgment'. In the sense that the Alliance moved across Church frontiers, it transcended them and this is what the Evangelicals willed and brought about through their austere life style. One can see why the Church of England was so specially acceptable. It was not, finally, under the control of an ecclesiastical hierarchy, but of parliament, that is of laymen who could be trusted to resist foreign papacy equally with home-brewed prelacy. Evangelicals were correct in their judgment of parliament right down to the 1928 Commons which threw out the Catholic-inspired new Prayer Book. Then again, the parochial system gave extraordinary freedom to the individual incumbent to live and preach his churchmanship position. According to John King[8] it was only at the Keele Conference, 1967, that evangelicals began to bend thoughtfully to the notion of the historic Church to which they owed some obedience and to move away from the concept of the Church of England as a mere federation of self-governing parishes with parliament holding the ring.

However, to return to the nineteenth century, if the impact of evangelicalism was astonishing on the politics, humanitarianism and missionary zeal of the century it was as effective, often, on provincial life. E. R. Wickham presents us, in *Church and People in an Industrial City*[9] with a vivid picture of the impact of a solid, cross-Church evangelical ministry in Sheffield.

'Sheffield was no Jane Austen world, no Barsetshire; in Sheffield there were no fox-hunting clergymen, no ministers "standing on the same holy ground as the pheasant and the partridge", in spite of the proximity of the moors! Nor were there absentee pluralist vicars or starving curates. From early in the century Evangelicalism was firmly entrenched in Sheffield Christianity. The appointment of Thomas Sutton, a strong evangelical churchman, to the living of Sheffield in 1805, which he occupied until his death in 1851, was responsible for a long sequence of evangelical clergy in the parish, and in 1841 the advowson was purchased by a few individuals to ensure the appointment of a successor with similar views, with the result that the clergy were much in line with the essential theological outlook of the Nonconformists ... all the churches were solidly evangelical, throughout all the phases that Evangelicalism itself passed right up to the twentieth century.... All those many causes that Evangelicalism initiated or espoused were strong public causes in Sheffield, widely supported by

[8] *The Evangelicals*, Hodder, London 1969.
[9] Lutterworth, London 1957.

Christians of all denominations except where strong political undertones divided the Establishment and Nonconformity. Apart from these issues, they both vied with one another and supported one another in the same good works, in Sunday Schools and day schools, Foreign Missions and Abolition Societies, and in local auxiliaries of all the national religious societies, besides such town projects as the "Bettering Society", Libraries, the Mechanics' Institute, Saving Banks, the Infirmary, the Literary and Philosophical Society, and so on.... And if not as Christian philanthropists, the same laymen led the town as Commissioners of Police, Overseers of the Poor, officers of the Cutlers' Company, and Directors of the Gas Company!'[10]

E. R. Wickham does not see the nineteenth century situation as the Church 'doing things' *for* the people of Sheffield, as from some position of authority and isolation, but as the Christian people of Sheffield promoting with almost a ferocious activity a whole range of social services. The figures he quotes for 1840 show almost all the education in Sheffield in the hands of the Churches. Nearly 13,000 children were in Christian Sunday Schools and another 6,000 in Christian Day Schools. Five thousand children were in private schools but all these would have been at least nominally Christian, and a number run by ministers. The population of the parish was around 112,000. It meant that very few children, perhaps only the very poorest in the slums, missed *some* education. This fervour of social zeal—so characteristic of so many cities of the north led by Evangelicals—hardly confirms the dictum of Dr Thomas Arnold that Evangelicalism handed over the temporal affairs of men either to national laws or the devil. Indeed, the theology of Calvin always led towards theocracy rather than to quietism or social indifference.

All the same the 'image' of the Evangelicals (to use the fading cant of our time) has not been a good one in this century. If one looks back to the birth of the Oxford Movement and *Tracts for the Times* one might say that all clergy were then fundamentalist, accepting the inerrancy of the scriptures. In this century the stand on biblical infallibility has been characteristic of the self-conscious conservative Evangelicals (though not of course so implacably of the more liberal sort) and this placed upon them the necessity to oppose modern scholarship, the higher criticism and to a large degree modern science—that is, to struggle against some of the most significant cultural movements of the very centuries in which they were most active. Meanwhile, much of the Church had moved on to the tacit acceptance of the view that it was impossible totally to hold Christianity to the thought and culture systems of the first or any other century without impoverishing itself.

---

[10] Op. cit. pp. 82–3.

In general, the life-styles of the Evangelicals, derived from puritanism, seemliness of dress, frugality, the rejection of the world and of sensuous experience, tended to make them the enemy of the arts, and of all other distractions from godly living. The voluptuousness of painting, of the erotic poem, the scandal of the novel tempting to idleness and self-indulgence, the sexy frivolity of the theatre above all appeared to the devout as, along with strong drink and smoking, the works of the devil. (In our own day the licence of the cinema and the mass media, the rise of pornography to both profession and highly profitable industry, must have confirmed the view.) The detestation of Roman Catholicism was strengthened by the sensuous appeal of the glittering, incense-clouded churches of Rome. One was nearer to God in the spirit on plain pine benches. But as to what *characters* this prayerful self-discipline produced one is reminded by Anne Arnott's studies of her evangelical doctor father in *The Brethren*[11] and *Journey into Understanding*.[12] A man of this century, he was in the true devotional and spiritual strain of William Cowper. His spiritual home was with the Plymouth Brethren.

However, Evangelicals have to be seen against the nineteenth century background of their ritualist and Tractarian opponents, who seemed to them to have one horrifying intention only—to drag the Church of England back into submission to Rome.

---

[11] London 1969.   [12] London 1971.

TWELVE

The Oxford Movement

THE Test and Corporation Acts, barring recusants and Nonconformists from public offices, were repealed in 1828 and the Catholic Emancipation Act was passed in the following year. Public opinion had advanced to the point where the creation of second class citizens by legislation was no longer tolerable. In 1832 the Whigs came to power with a direct mandate to reform a corrupt parliamentary system—and by implication a corrupt Church too. The Whigs were representative of the middle and lower middle classes who were strong in dissent and radical in opinion and resentful of Church of England privileges.

In the twenties and thirties there were many widely publicized attacks on the injustices and abuses of the Church. One of the first was *The Black Book, or Corruption Unmasked* (1820–23) and another *The Extraordinary Black Book* of 1831. There was much other scurrilous pamphleteering. In a Trollope Church world there was rich material for popular exposures of a *Private Eye* character. The reform period witnessed to the growth of newspapers and magazines run by bright young men from the middle classes who played the iconoclastic role in society which the television interviewers performed in Britain in the fifties and sixties. It took a long time for the Church to discover that they even existed, let alone should be answered. A writer in *Fraser's Magazine* wrote, 'When we see the clergy represented, both in the Lords and in the Commons, as proud and indolent, and enemies to freedom and education—when their property is designated a burden upon the state, and themselves held up to public odium as drones that fatten on the industry of the people— can we wonder if the people, aware of their own distresses, and eager by every practicable means to alleviate them, should believe what their rulers assert, and, as a necessary consequence, abhor the Church?'[1]

---

[1] *Fraser's*, August 1832, pp. 88 ff. Quoted in Olive J. Brose, *Church and Parliament, The Re-Shaping of the Church of England 1828–60*, Stanford Univ. Press and OUP 1959 pp. 22–3. I am indebted to Olive Brose in this chapter.

There was reason to abhor it. In the early 1800s pluralism and absenteeism were rife. The revenues of the Church were simply being plundered by lazy but greedy men. 332 men drew the revenues of 1,496 parishes. Another 500 those of 1,524. A Prebendary of Durham, who happened to be Wellington's brother, was rector of three parishes. The superior clergy often held four or five livings. And the value of many of their higher offices in any case put them among the richest in the land. Making safe a valuable living till a little son or nephew came of age was a habitual practice. In 1813, out of some 10,800 benefices, 6,300 were without resident incumbents; they were served by curates on forty to sixty pounds a year.

There is a curious parallel (even to the scandals) between the attacks of the Benthamites, or Philosophical Radicals, on the Church in the nineteenth century and the Henrician attack on the Roman allegiance in the sixteenth. The common point was property. What right had the pope to all those fees, tithes, Peter's pence, procurations and so on which poured out of the country? Who would enjoy their reversion when they ceased? If monasteries did not deserve to survive, who could properly usurp their properties? We know what answers came. In the nineteenth century, with the Church morally condemned by radicals, dissenters, members of parliament, the manufacturers, the poor, the intellectuals, she was necessarily, even justly, threatened with disestablishment. Indeed, when the state recognized, *de facto*, all religious sects and opinions it had become politically expedient that the state should appear religiously neutral and dissociate itself from one particular Church, however exalted, however inextricably woven into the nation's history. But immediately the question rose—what would happen to the property of a disestablished Church? Sir Robert Peel laid it down that the mark of an established Church was an inalienable right to its property. But *disestablished*? The cupidity of the middle classes was excited—at least in the degree that they were dissenters. Jeremy Bentham, in *Mother Church Relieved by Bleeding*, argued that the life of the Church was 'her gold—taking away her gold you take away her life'. And if the 'gold' of the Church could be regarded as public property, that is, state property, and if on grounds of utility it was no longer expedient that there should be a national Church, then the process of disestablishment could strip her of the 'gold' she so plainly misused: justice would be seen to be done and the happiness of all except the priesthood greatly augmented.[2]

It was an intellectual conjuring trick which promised enormous political dividends. The tide was running against established Christianity. There were many straws in the wind. For example University College,

---

[2] Cf. Olive Brose, *Church and Parliament*, Chap. 11, 'Church and State in Turmoil, 1832–3.'

London, was founded in 1828 as an answer to the Anglican-saturated older universities. It banned theology from the curriculum and imposed no religious tests. The endless scurrilous abuse of the clergy, particularly bishops, often resulted in violence against them. There were religious riots. The Bishop's Palace in Bristol was destroyed by a mob. Thomas Arnold saw the danger and complained that 'The Church as it now stands, no human power can save; my fear is, if we do not mind, we shall come to the American fashion, and have no provision made for the teaching of Christianity at all.' Unless the Church reformed itself speedily—and even under attack it was reluctant, perhaps even impotent to do so— it would be destroyed. His answer to the attacks was to propose to get rid of 'that phantom uniformity which has been our curse ever since the Reformation' and to establish a National Church which included all the dissenters who wanted to come in. (This proposal is curiously revived today in the argument that the 'established' Christian presence should be the British Council of Churches rather than the Church of England.)

It was also a *social* rather than a purely ecclesiastical Church he demanded. We have already seen that he thought the Evangelicals abandoned man's temporal life to the devil. The high church, he argued, had retreated into a ritualistic sectarianism. 'What is the good of a National Church if it be not to Christianize the nation, and introduce the principles of Christianity into men's social and civil relations, and expose the wickedness of that spirit which maintains the game laws, and in agriculture and trade seems to think that there is no such sin as covetousness?'[3]

A Church under attack does not cease to function. The Church of England still continued to draw its tithes and church rates and to say its prayers. The rates were designed to raise money to maintain the Church fabric and were particularly galling to dissenters who did not use the Church and saw no reason to pay for it and who gave, often generously, to chapel building funds. The only way for dissenters to get the tax reduced, before the repeal in 1868, was to get themselves elected parish overseers. Bishop Frank West describes[4] a quarrel in Walkeringham Vestry. The Vicar, Mr. George Gorham, had rushed through the election of a sympathetic group of overseers before the dissenters arrived and was proceeding gleefully to the next business on the agenda when—

'There was a sound of heavy footsteps in the lobby outside. He stiffened as he stood, his eyes fixed on the door. Every head in the room turned. Then the door was flung open and a dozen or more men came

---

[3] A. P. Stanley, *Life of Dr. Arnold*, 1858, vol. 1 p. 227. See also Thomas Arnold, *Thirteen Letters addressed to the Editor of the Sheffield Courant*, 1832, and discussed in E. R. Wickham, *Church and People in an Industrial City*, Lutterworth, London 1957 pp. 86 et seq.
[4] *Sparrows of the Spirit*, SPCK 1961, pp. 91-2.

tramping in . . . the dissenting faction in force, with Morris [a powerful Methodist opponent of the Church] at its head. His hands trembling slightly, the vicar announced with as casual an air as he could muster, that the first business was concluded and the late comers were invited to sit down.'

The late comers did not sit down. The meeting must begin all over again. A shouting row began.

'Thomas Bown, urged on by Morris, came up to the table and grabbed the vestry book. Mr. Gorham snatched it back from him, and the two men stood glowering at each other, the book clutched between them. Thomas Bown took a step forward and grasped the vicar roughly by the lapels of his coat . . .'

In the end the meeting was adjourned as riotous.

If that was the temper of the quieter sixties, what must it have been in the ugly thirties? Jeremy Bentham once pertinently said—apply it all to Ireland! For there was the Church of Ireland, newly united with the Church of England, enjoying tithes and church rates raised from parishioners almost entirely Roman Catholics.[5] At least the church taxes in England were raised from parishioners the majority of whom (in most, but not all, parishes) were Anglicans! The tax collectors in Ireland met pitchforks, dung and dogs. One draws a veil over the hatred the church taxes evoked in the Irish—never an easily taxable or easily governable people anyway. A bill was introduced into Parliament in February 1833, to reduce the number of Irish sees from 22 to 12 and so to save money, reduce taxes and produce a more governable Church.

It produced a sudden storm of Anglican protest both in England and Ireland. It was felt by many to be another sinister development of the Catholic Emancipation Movement. Many clergy of a Church they were themselves unable to reform could not endure that others might reform it for them! The protest was totally illogical. The bill was eminently sensible and just, and only parliament, the ultimate legislative assembly to which the Church by its own will owed obedience, had power to act. The Church had been erastian without option since Henry VIII's day and a department of state since the silencing of Convocations in 1717. Now, in an era dominated by Church-indifferent Evangelicals, and in the presence of Church corruption no one bothered to reform, and amid a chorus of anticlerical taunts from the radical pamphleteers the rights and high dignities of the Church were raised over against the menace of the usurping secular state, as though the Church were guiltless.

It was an astounding performance. Even a lost cause. Appropriately it began in the heart of the establishment with an Assize Sermon preached

---

[5] Cf. Kevin B. Nowlan, 'Disestablishment: 1800–1869', in *Irish Anglicanism, 1869–1969*, ed. Michael Hurley, S.J., Figgis, Dublin 1969.

in Oxford by John Keble on 14 July 1833. It was a highly political sermon and its title was, significantly, 'National Apostasy'. From it John Newman dated the beginning of the Oxford Movement.

In the preface to the printed edition Keble wrote:

'Calamity ... has actually overtaken this portion of the Church of God. The Legislature of England and Ireland ... has virtually usurped the commission of those whom our Saviour entrusted with at least one voice[6] in making ecclesiastical laws on matters wholly or partly spiritual. The same legislature has also ratified, to its full extent, this principle,—that the Apostolical Church in this realm is henceforth only to stand, in the eye of the State, as *one sect among many*, depending, for any pre-eminence she may still appear to retain, merely upon the accident of her having a strong party in the country.

'It is a moment, surely, full of deep solicitude for all those members of the Church who still believe her authority divine.... How may they continue their commission with the Church established (hitherto the pride and comfort of their lives) without any taint of those Erastian principles on which she is now assumed to be governed? What answer can we make henceforth to the partisans of the bishop of Rome, when they taunt us with being a mere Parliament Church? And how, consistently with our present relations to the State, can even the doctrinal purity and integrity of the MOST SACRED ORDER be preserved?'

How indeed? A high doctrine of the Church was born, after three centuries of submission. The basic issues of Church–state relations had at last been raised in the heart of the Church itself. Things were never to be the same again. Of course, the Oxford Movement was a movement of Church intellectuals arguing with Church intellectuals. Nothing speaks more incisively to the remoteness of the Church from the upheavals of society than that the most important ecclesiastical event of the nineteenth century began with a sermon in Oxford preached before assize judges and was passionately concerned with a high doctrine of the Church and all that legally followed from it, in indifference to the role of the Church in society.[7] The contrast with, say, Wesley's campaign or that of the Salvation Army later in the century is painful, the Christian Socialist movement notwithstanding.

---

[6] All the sad, compromising history of the Church of England is to be found in the unscriptural thought that the Church had *only* '*one*' voice' in its laws ecclesiastical and spiritual.

[7] 'Late in life Cardinal Newman told Charles Marson that "he had never considered social questions in relation to faith and had always looked upon the poor as objects for compassion and benevolence".' G. Kitson Clark, *Churchmen and the Condition of England, 1832–1885*, London 1973, p. 38. G. Kitson Clark is quoting from Charles Marson, *God's Cooperative Society*, 1914 p. 71.

All the same it was a necessary movement if the Church itself was not to grow ever more corrupt and supine. It was one kind of answer to Bentham's Philosophical Radicals. It helped to bring to an end the latitudinarian tendencies of the clergy, who were roused ultimately to the importance of Church order and the role of the sacraments in the life of the faithful, and began to see again the beauty of their inherited liturgy. It raised again, after generations of little Englandism, the status of the Church of England as a world Church in Christendom and sought to wean it from its entrenched localized protestantism. The Oxford view was that the Church of England had a spiritual primacy in the world in an unbroken connection with the primitive Church through apostolic succession. It exaggerated, but it had a point. It could claim therefore a kind of parity with the mainstream Churches—Roman and Orthodox.

The Oxford Movement grew out of the *Tracts for the Times* it published as an exercise in dialogue about the Church. The last tract was No. XC which challenged the XXXIX Articles. It was a disingenuous effort by John Newman to re-assess the articles to make them compatible with high church doctrine. The style of the *Tract* can be shown by contrasting some important passages. Article XXVIII asserts among other things: 'Transubstantiation (or the change of the substance of Bread and Wine) in the Supper of the Lord, cannot be proved by Holy Writ [earlier said to contain all things necessary to salvation]; but is repugnant to the plain words of Scripture, overthroweth the nature of a Sacrament, and hath given occasion to many superstitions. The Body of Christ is given, taken, and eaten in the Supper, only after an heavenly and spiritual manner.'

Newman quotes examples of 'grossly corporeal' Roman doctrines of transubstantiation and concludes, hardly honestly, that it is only against *these* that the Article is directed. He writes:

'We see then that by transubstantiation an article does not confine itself to any abstract theory, nor aim at any definitions of the word substance, nor in rejecting it, rejects a word, nor in denying a *mutatio panis et vini* is denying *every kind* of change, but opposes itself to a certain plain and unambiguous statement, not of this or that council, but one generally received or taught both in the schools and in the multitude, that material elements are changed into an earthly, fleshly, and organized body, extended in size, distinct in its parts, which is there where the outward appearances of bread and wine are, and only does not meet the senses . . .'

Of course the Article rejects that view, but also any less corporeal doctrine which asserts a change of substance. The Article is clear in its point that the sacraments are the vehicle of the spiritual body, received in faith, and not the Saviour's flesh and blood. When it comes to the Mass, Newman appears to find that Article XXXI, which says that 'the sacrifices of Masses, in which it was commonly said, that the Priest did offer Christ for the quick and the dead, to have remission of pain or guilt, were blasphemous fables, and dangerous deceits', somehow excluded the sacrifice of the Mass from its condemnation, because it used the plural Masses! He believes the Article therefore permits a Mass as a commemorative offering for the quick and the dead for the remission of sins.

In his conclusion to the Tract Newman urged that it was

'a *duty* which we owe both to the Catholic Church and to our own, to take our reformed confessions in the most Catholic sense they will admit; we have no duties towards their framers. ... The Protestant Confession was drawn up with the purpose of including Catholics, and Catholics now will not be excluded. What was an economy in the reformers is a protection to us. What would have been a perplexity to us then, is a perplexity to Protestants now. We could not then have found fault with their words: they cannot now repudiate our meaning.'

Of course words and meanings could not be stretched so far. The Protestants turned out to be more angry than perplexed. They had expected that this was that it would all lead to.

Orthodox churchmen protested vigorously against the 'Jesuitry' of the Tractarians, questions were asked in parliament, the Bishop of Oxford put in his oar and the Tracts ceased publication. But the issue which then faced Newman was this—was the Church of England the true Church or was it all make-believe? He gave his answer by resigning his living in 1843 and two years later entering the Roman Church. Many followed him. The Movement was unable to survive the loss of its greatest leader, one who already enjoyed an international prestige, but ritualism, Puseyism persisted.

What followed was the growth of a high church party which, though less inclined to challenge the Thirty-nine Articles directly, pursued vigorously the romanization of the liturgy, stretching every rubric as far as it would go. They introduced (or should one say, remembering the continuity of the Church, *re-introduced*?) vestments, altar candles, incense, reserved sacraments, auricular confession, the doctrine of the sacrifice of the Mass and of transubstantiation. Precisely all this involved them in legal conflict with the Church of England and over this they were ready to accept martyrdom. In 1860 the English Church Union was founded to strengthen and support the ritualists. A few years later the Church Association was created to prosecute them. Once again the Church of England was polarized between high and low church parties. It was principally an internecine war of the clergy themselves. In the absence of Convocations, not revived until 1852 (Canterbury) and 1861 (York), and of proper means by which the voice of the laity could be heard one does not know what the silent majority of the Church really felt. As someone has said they went to Church to learn to be good and doctrinal subtleties shot over their heads. The persecution of one clergyman by another made no strong appeal to their sense of goodness, though the cry 'No Popery' could still arouse them.

The watershed for the Church in the ritualistic controversy was the hooliganism at St George's-in-the-East, an old parish church near the Ratcliffe Highway, with a population of 30,000, 'dunes of empty pews and fifty or sixty faithful worshippers. It was the land of docks and sailors, of dining-saloons and filthy bars, of public houses offering squads of harlots. The 733 houses within four streets of the church included 154 brothels' Owen Chadwick wrote.[8] He also said that the established church was never quite the same after the promoted strife of St George's where the Anglo-Catholic Rector, Bryan King, assisted by loyal curates, Charles Lowder and Alexander Mackonochie, was at war with a hostile parish over candles, vestments and confession. It has to be said that there was nothing wrong with such church ornaments as candles and a cross on the altar. The Act of Uniformity permitted such ornaments of the church 'and of the Ministers thereof' as were in vogue in the second year of the reign of Edward VI. Nothing in the Prayer Book would seem to rule out vestments, or private confession, though the rubric at the beginning of the service of Holy Communion does charge the priest to stand at the north side of the Holy Table. The Act of Uniformity does give some latitude for changes brought about by time and custom. It seemed to be the case that the Church had 'protestantized' itself in the anti-popery reaction in defiance of its own legal basis. The mind of the Protestant Laity, Owen Chadwick remarks, could not be satisfied with the comprehensiveness of its own Church. It stood amazed at ritualism. 'As Lord Shaftesbury was reported to have said, "If the rubrics allow it— well then, away with the rubrics!"'[9]

Owen Chadwick explains that for almost a year after June 1859, 'Sunday afternoons at St George's were the zoo and horror and coconut-shy of London.' The parish had elected an aggressive Evangelical as the lecturer and the church became a battleground of two parties. 'The best days witnessed pew doors banging or feet scraping or hissing or coughing or syncopated responses. The worst days witnessed gleeful rows of boys shooting with peas from the gallery, fireworks, flaming speeches from tub-orators during service, bleating as of goats, spitting on choir boys, a pair of hounds howling gin-silly round the nave, cushions hurled at the altar, orange peel and butter, kicking and hustling of clergy.'[10] A pew was used as a privy. There was even a bodyguard to protect the clergy. The riots were only stopped when Bryan King went on

---

[8] *The Victorian Church*, Adam and Charles Black, London 1966, Pt. 1, p. 497. This section owes much to Professor Chadwick.

[9] Ibid. pt II p. 320.

[10] Ibid. pt II p. 501.

a prolonged holiday, from which he never returned to the old battle ground. Understandably these incredible events formed the background for the struggles of the next few decades. It was Protestantism which was tarnished in reputation by its bully-boys and the Anglo-Catholics who took on the martyr role.

The Church Courts had a busy century. In 1833 supreme jurisdiction in ecclesiastical matters was taken over by the Judicial Committee of the Privy Council in whose hands it remained until 1963. Some of its decisions were sane and liberal. It supported the Rev. G. C. Gorham against the Bishop of Exeter when he refused to institute Gorham to a benefice because Gorham did not accept unconditional regeneration in baptism. It supported two modernist contributors to *Essays and Reviews* (1860) against their suspension and condemnation for heresy by the Court of Arches. When Bishop Colenso of Natal published an attack on the historicity of the Old Testament and was deposed by Bishop Gray of Cape Town in 1863, the Judicial Committee declared that Bishop Gray had no power to act.

In 1866 ritualists received many episcopal censures: an ecclesiastical exhibition staged to impress the York Church Congress that year ruffled protestant feathers. There was an unequivocal condemnation of ritualism by the bishops in Convocation early in 1867, the Lower House concurring, but soon after controversy was stirred up again when Dr Hamilton, Bishop of Salisbury, asserted in a sermon the supernatural gifts of the priests and the divine presence in the sacrament. That year saw the first trial by the Court of Arches of the Rev. A. H. Mackonochie who had transferred to St Alban's, Holborn, for ritualistic practices specified as the use of incense, mixing water with the wine, and elevation of the elements. The trial became a *cause célèbre*, and went to many appeals. Mackonochie managed to evade all the sentences of suspension passed upon him. Finally, *fifteen years later*, in 1882 he lost his appeal to the House of Lords, received a three years' sentence of suspension and resigned his living at the request of the Archbishop of Canterbury. He resigned a second living the next year after being sentenced to deprivation. The saga was not over. He died a few years later from exposure, having lost his way in the snow on Scottish hills on a December day.

Such was the general *brouhaha* that a memorial against romanist teaching and practice, signed by 60,000 people no less, was presented by the Church Association to the Archbishops, who replied that they were aware of the dangers and of their duties: they struck a modern note by saying that, 'We live in an age when all opinions and beliefs are keenly criticized, and when there is less inclination than there ever was before to respect authority in matters of opinion. In every state, in every religious community, almost in every family, the effect of this unsettled condition may be traced.' The establishment response to the disorder was the

Public Worship Regulation Act of 1874 to suppress those acts in worship the Royal Ritualist Commission had earlier condemned. The Act came into operation in 1875, and by it a new judge was appointed to serve the Provincial Courts of Canterbury and York. He was Lord Penzance.

The first case before him involved the trial of the Vicar of Folkestone for illegal practices. In the second the Rev. Arthur Tooth of the parish of Hatcham, in South London, was admonished for his ritual acts. He denied the authority of the court to deliver on such matters and continued his ritualistic services in defiance of the court until January 1876, when he was pronounced contumacious by the judge in the Court of Arches and imprisoned for a month in Horsemonger Lane jail. When he came out he broke into his church, which had been locked against him and celebrated the eucharist in the proscribed form. Proceedings against him were quashed on appeal because of a legal technicality.

The most famous of trials was that of Bishop Edward King of Lincoln by Archbishop Benson and other bishops on seven ritualistic charges. All the charges were dismissed except two—breaking the bread and taking the cup in a manner invisible to the people and making the sign of the cross at the absolution and benediction: on these he was convicted as making unjustifiable additions to the ceremonies of the Church, and ordered to discontinue them. It was a kind of acquittal and led to the secession of a small body of clergy to form a new evangelical sect.

Neither the ecclesiastical war nor the growth of illegalities ceased as a result of the Bishop of Lincoln's quasi-acquittal. Some celebrated parish churches had moved so far that they were Roman in everything except the ordination of the priest and the source of his benefice. They even said their services in Latin.

The struggle went on well into this century. When the high church Canon Gore was appointed Bishop of Worcester a 'Petition of Right' was launched to prevent it and it led to a high court case dismissing the right of Church authorities to question the appointment. When a celebration of the eucharist was announced at St Paul's Cathedral in commemoration of those who died in the Boer War it was attacked as a revival of the Roman use of prayers for the dead.[11] The service was abandoned. Deputations to the Archbishops, from both sides of the controversy, continued throughout the first decade. The opponents carried the war into the camp of the ritualists who had long claimed that the justification of their liturgies and doctrines was to be found in the teachings and practice of the primitive Church. What they *did*, however, often seemed no more than a reproduction of extravagant contemporary Roman forms. Early in 1905 the Archbishop of Canterbury was forced to receive a deputation arguing that nothing ought to be accepted as

---

[11] A matter which still agitates General Synod during the debates on the new liturgy.

Catholic which had not received general assent before the seventh century. The demand of the deputation was endorsed quite soon after by an almost unanimous decision of the Lower House of the Convocation of Canterbury.

But is this *all* that the Church was about? Whether to make the sign of the cross in communion, to add a little water to the wine, to elevate and to reserve the sacraments, to hear private confession and to wear vestments? If the heady disputes and legal tangles of the nineteenth and twentieth century are a true witness, the Anglicans began more and more to resemble the Lilliputians in their tragic dilemma as to whether to start eating one's egg at the big or the little end. There were serious doctrinal differences between the high and the low church—over the real presence for example—but they were often lost in the war about candles.

And of course this was not all that the Church was about. The North seemed hardly disturbed by the ritualistic debate, and what the Church was about there is perhaps better seen in what E. R. Wickham tells us of the Church in Sheffield in *Church and People in an Industrial City*.[12] The rural churches seemed barely affected; they continued their bare, comely way under the eye still of the gentry, as Kilvert's diaries tell us: if change there was it was towards the increasing dominance of the clergy as social and political developments reduced the dominance of the gentry and diminished the role of the laity in church affairs. Speaking of the last century, Owen Chadwick wrote, 'We enter the most clerical age of English life, clerical in the sense that the parson had more individual power in his parish church than ever before or after. The symbolic limits of this "clerical" age may be dated to begin with the abolition of Church rates in 1868, and to end with the parochial church councils measure of 1921.'[13] But as Owen Chadwick goes on to point out, the age of clerical power began much earlier and ended long after 1921—if, indeed, in rural parishes it has yet ended.

No small part of this expansion of clerical power and authority must be attributed to the Evangelical and Oxford Movements we have just examined, rather than to the law. Both movements demanded a religious intensity which could only be maintained by a religious professional or exceptional laymen, in the absence of a fervour sweeping the country. It was beyond the average Englishman's conception of what religion should be. There was no such movement of fervour after Wesley's until the Salvation Army in the latter part of the nineteenth century (and the Army had limited appeal). The professionalization of a certain clerical religious intensity was part of the role of the theological colleges, most of them products of the nineteenth century. How significant it is that they, too,

---

[12] Op. cit. pp. 77 ff.

[13] *The Victorian Church*, pt. II p. 322.

divided along Church party lines and produced their own specia'
bigotries. The maintenance of party lines in church congregations anɷ
church offices became the prime task of the college trained élite! How
could lay congregations have gone along with that complicated clericaliz-
ation of the Church, even had means been open to them? They surrendered
the Church to the clergy and allowed themselves to be led. The buying of
advowsons by Church parties to freeze the party allegiances of individual
parishes shows in what contempt, really, the laity was held.

There are other social reasons certainly for the advance of ritualism.
One was the break-up of many old parishes into conventional districts.
The Parish of Old Battersea Church, with William Blake's name on the
marriage register, was so divided, the rector holding the advowsons.
Every conventional district struggled to become a full-blown parish with
its own church, vicarage and endowments. It was part of the praise-
worthy attempt of the Victorian Church to reach the masses in the
swollen cities of the industrial revolution. But it was also an invitation to
sectarianism. The new district church usually imposed pew rents and so
'selected' its congregation. It tended to have at its heart a group
enthusiastic to promote the liturgical practice of a particular Church
party, even to extremes, and to exclude by its ethos those worshippers
not of the same persuasion. Most of the prosecutions for what were
called illegal practices fell on the priests of what had begun as
conventional district churches. The point is that they provided the
opening needed for brighter, more colourful services, more cheerful
decoration. Nobody needed to be offended, because as Owen Chadwick
remarked, 'nobody needed to go, nobody could be disturbed by sudden
changes of old custom'.[14] Still, it was a move away from the broadness of
the old parish churches and we have seen something of the stir it created.

There was perhaps another social reason—the reaction of the middle
class in particular against the drabness of the Victorian age. The revolt
of Ruskin and Morris, and the Pre-Raphaelites against dull philistinism,
against the dark satanic mills and their surrounds, moved many Victorian
minds to long for splendour again. The Oxford Movement was saturated
with a nostalgia for medievalism. What splendour the age had was royal
or military—and the royal share was muted after Victoria was widowed.
There seems to have been a movement to find some glory again in the
churches. Choirs were increasingly robed: by 1901 a quarter of all
churches saw their priests in vestments and over a half had candles on the
altar. Incense had got a foothold. Only a few clergy clung still to the
northward position.[15] A revolution of sorts had been accomplished.

---

[14] Ibid. p. 316.
[15] Figures collected by Owen Chadwick, op. cit. p. 319, from *The Tourists' Church Guide*,
1902.

THIRTEEN

The 'Warring Atoms'

WE HAVE already seen something of the social order of the eighteenth and nineteenth centuries over against which the Church of England functioned as the third estate of the realm. But we have not seen all: not as yet the worst. A panic-stricken government passed, in the wake of the French revolution, the Combination Laws of 1799 and 1800 even though 'combinations' to raise wages were already illegal under both common law and the Conspiracy Acts, for the reason that under the mercantile system the state or the municipalities were presumed to control industry and wages. Although by the end of the eighteenth century governmental efforts to control wages or industry had been abandoned in the interests of *laissez-faire*, the Conspiracy Acts remained on the statute books. The Combination Acts made the repressive powers more precise and persecutory. Strikes became illegal and even four or five workmen jointly applying for a rise in pay risked persecution. Just to attend a meeting to discuss raising wages or shortening hours carried the penalty of three months' imprisonment.

Out of such oppressive laws the Tolpuddle Martyrs were born. But there were many other less celebrated working men who suffered grievously for an elementary freedom: inevitably a system which left the fixing of wages and conditions in the hands of rapacious employers was bound to breed revolutionaries. It is surprising that there were so few.

For almost the first half of the century labouring conditions grew worse. Real wages fell because money wages were outstripped by rising prices. There was an actual fall of wages between 1790 and 1820 though during that period rent was doubled and interest nearly so. Taxation fell very heavily on workmen. Even in 1834 half the labourers' wages went in taxes.[1] The Combination Acts of 1799 and 1800 were not repealed till 1825. Child labour was a social horror. Adult unemployment and under-employment were rife, particularly in those areas where the craftsmen

---

[1] *The Industrial Revolution of the Eighteenth Century in England*, Arnold Toynbee, London 1913, pp. 106 ff.

were made redundant by the new mills and factories. Living conditions in the new areas were miserable and degrading and epidemics were widespread. There were virtually no public health regulations. The independent craftsmen, weavers, nail-makers, spinners and such were driven into poverty and extinction, because the machines replaced them. The forties became the hungry forties. A witness said of Colne in Lancashire in 1842,

'I visited 88 dwellings selected at hazard. They were destitute of furniture save old boxes for tables and stools, or even large stones for chairs; the beds composed of straw and shavings. The food was oatmeal and water for breakfast, flour and water with a little skimmed milk for dinner, oatmeal and water again for a second supply ... all the places I visited were scrupulously clean. The children were in rags but not in filth. In no single instance was I asked for charity.'

The same witness found only 100 of Accrington's 9,000 inhabitants fully employed: some had food only on alternate days. No wonder he saw the Burnley weavers 'haggard with famine, their eyes rolling with that fierce and uneasy expression common to maniacs',[2] as they demanded employment: or that he found them Chartists to a man. Conditions in the old slums were worse than in the new barrack streets. The philanthropists of the century sought out abandoned children sleeping and dying, out in the alleys and yards. Indoor conditions were desolating.

In Wyld Court, Drury Lane, when Victoria began to reign:

'The first bed contained the defendant, his wife, a boy of sixteen and a girl of fourteen, with another boy of ten and an infant. In the second bed there were a woman, a girl and a child; in the third bed, a man, his wife, a girl of sixteen, and two boys (twelve and seven): with a fourth bed, a woman and two boys; and in the fifth a man. There were no partitions of any kind to separate the sexes. The total number of persons in the room was twenty, but seven only were [legally] allowed'.[3]

In 1856–7 in the St Clement Danes district of the Strand, *deaths equalled births*, according to the Sanitary Inspector's Second Annual Report. In the rest of the Strand district, including Drury Lane, the excess of births over deaths, per 10,000 living, was much less than half the figure for London as a whole (43:115).[4]

One can understand Robert Owen's passionate advocacy of decent working conditions, non-employment of children, fair wages, and his

[2] C. R. Fay, *Life and Labour in the Nineteenth Century*, p. 178.

[3] Quoted in *The Worm in the Bud: the World of Victorian Sexuality* by Ronald Pearsall, London 1969 p. 114. The author says, 'These accounts are contained in the notes to the mid-Victorian publication of Don Leon, supposedly by Lord Byron.'

[4] Conway Evans, M.D., John Churchill, London, 1858, p. 47.

experiments with communist colonies in Britain and in the United States. The great trade union revival of the thirties was his inspiration and it nearly succeeded in creating a British syndicalism. One understands too the influence of Chartism which between 1832 and 1848 continually raised the spectre of revolution through rallies and riots and physical force agitation. It was the time of the confluence of great new forces in the world, above all of the birth of an international working-class consciousness about to be given expression in Marx and Engel's *Communist Manifesto*, from which we can perhaps date the modern world.

The expected revolution, stillborn in England, succeeded in France (which had acquired the habit) when Paris threw out Louis Philippe and installed a government of liberals, socialists and idealists. John Malcolm Forbes Ludlow, a colonel's son, a barrister and an earnest Christian, who had spent most of his life in France, rushed to France to rescue his sisters from the revolution. He was a young man of distinction, deeply learned in political economy and well acquainted with the socialist and co-operative theories of Charles Fourier and Louis Blanc which dominated the new French government. He wrote home to Frederick Denison Maurice about it all. Maurice was then Professor of Theology at King's College, London, a post from which he was to be dismissed in 1853 for the allegedly heretical tendencies in his teaching. Maurice's doctrines, in *The Kingdom of Christ* particularly, were powerfully in opposition to the *laissez-faire* ideas of the times. He believed in a life illuminated by knowledge of, and fellowship with God and therefore lived in fellowship with men, and he meant *economic* fellowship not hat-doffing at the lych gate. This Christian social fellowship was the bond between man and man and class and class and it was the Church's mission to preach and practise it and to save society from the selfishness which the prevailing philosophy had grafted on to the nation, destroying it politically and the working classes physically.

Maurice was a shy man. But he had many friends who were not— Charles Kingsley, parson and social novelist, Clough the poet, Grove the musician, Furnivall the philologist and Thomas Hughes, athlete, member of parliament, judge and author of *Tom Brown's Schooldays*, and Vansittart Neale. They were an élite in their way and of too independent a temper to be held back by episcopal disapproval. Ludlow, Maurice and Kingsley were brought together over the possibility of violence at the 10 April 1848 rally of Chartists on Kennington Common. The Chartists there planned to bring the maximum pressure to bear on parliament. The demonstration which might have sparked off the necessary revolution was a fiasco. The Chartist cause which had attracted millions shrivelled to a procession of hansom cabs bearing a monster and part-fraudulent petition to the House of Commons. But the Christian Socialists sprang from the crisis and launched themselves on a remarkable campaign of propaganda and practical help to the poor. Their first broadside, *Politics for the People*, appeared within a month of the Chartist meeting. It was a paper promoted 'to consider the questions which are occupying our countrymen at the present moment, such as the extension of the franchise; the relations of the capitalist and the labourer; what a government can or cannot do to find work or pay for the poor'.

This was the first time that a Church of England group had emerged which identified itself with working-class *aims* and was not merely patronizing or pietistic. *Politics for the People* ran for three issues only, but its circulation reached two thousand and it penetrated the industrial towns; its message that the Bible was the revolutionist's handbook quickly reached the working classes. Maurice presently declared the practical aims of the group when he said that 'competition is put forward as the law of the universe. That is a lie. The time has come for us to declare that is a lie by word and by deed. I see no way but associating for work instead of for strikes.' 'Christian Socialism is the assertion of God's order.'

The group launched itself into a struggle to found workingmen's associations or self-governing workshops to produce goods co-operatively of which the first was the Castle Street Working Tailors' Association,[5] formed in 1850. There followed a series of powerful tracts on Christian Socialism 'which will', in Maurice's words, 'commit us at once to the conflict we must engage in sooner or later with the unsocial Christians, and the unchristian socialists'. Later in the same year the group established their periodical, *The Christian Socialist, A Journal of Associations*. Two years later they launched the thoroughly practical society for promoting Working Men's Associations which got printers, smiths, hatters and pianoforte makers organized in self-governing workshops. They were also successful in promoting legislation (The Industrial and Provident Societies Acts, 1852 and 1862) which protected these fragile new institutions and others like them.

In the field of consumers' co-operation a healthy, secular start had been made by the Rochdale Pioneers in 1844. Robert Owen's inspiration was behind it. This small society had many imitators and the modern consumers' movement is based on it. The Christian Socialists were active in bringing the two movements—the self-governing workshops and the consumer societies—together in the Co-operative Union. Perhaps their last and greatest achievement was the foundation of the Working Men's College in London with the expelled Maurice as its principal. It numbered among its teachers such influential (and anti-industrial) teachers as Ruskin, Rossetti, Tyndale, Ford Madox Brown and J. R. Seeley.

---

[5] It was a nineteenth century pleasantry that one could tell a Christian Socialist by the cut of his jib.

The working life of the group was hardly more than ten years. It spent a lot of money but the Working Men's Associations failed one by one. Someone wisely said that the beaten Chartist workmen of 1848 had no ears for well-meaning parsons and gentlemen who were going to teach them how to run their lives. They looked for the catch! All the same, the Christian Socialists stimulated and helped to protect many forms of that working-class self-help of which I have already spoken. It would be untrue to say that they changed the image of the Church of England, which remained stonily conservative, more prepared to tolerate a Benthamite under the bed than a Blanquist in the parlour. But it provided the Church with an alibi and appealed to those generous spirits in the Oxford Movement who held that the pursuit of gain was the root of all evil and not the moral source of improvement, virtue and happiness the utilitarians argued it to be. The purely economic man was a disaster, his role incompatible with the high calling of the human soul. The Oxford Movement and the Young England Movement looked back, like William Morris, to an idealized medieval Christendom of saintly craftsmen.

At least the Christian Socialists looked forward and made, as they had hoped, a christianized socialism possible and promoted indirectly not only the entrance of Christian priests into the Labour movement (William Temple was a member of the Labour Party for a time) but some magnificent priestly work in Britain's slums and industrial towns by what Stephen Mayor calls 'Slum Ritualists'.[6] It was unfortunately to prove a localized and personal Christian socialist enterprise rather than the product of a broad national movement. Its influence was considerable just the same and on its roll of honour are the names of laymen and priests—and Nonconformists—who have helped to shape modern society, William Temple, Stewart Headlam, Scott Holland, John Scott Lidgett, Dick Sheppard, Geoffrey Studdert-Kennedy, John Groser, Wainwright of the docks, Basil Jellicoe of Somers Town, Tubby Clayton, George Lansbury, Stafford Cripps, Lord George Brown, Lord Soper, William Dick of Trinity Church, Poplar and scores of others.

There was an extremely colourful cross-fertilization between the Anglo-Catholics and Christian socialists of various hues of which Conrad Noel's bright band of followers from highly rural Thaxted, with their medieval banners, are a gay example. They were to be found marching alongside trade union and political contingents in many May Day parades after World War One.

The mantle of Christian Socialism proper fell on the Guild of St Matthew founded by Stewart Headlam, an Anglo-Catholic who carried

---

[6] Stephen Mayor, *The Churches and the Labour Movement*, Independent Press, London 1967, is an important guide.

his ritualism into curacies at Drury Lane and Bethnal Green and chose to live in workers' tenements. The Guild, formed on St Peter's day 1877, illustrates the conjunction of Anglo-Catholicism with Christian Socialism. Its aims which read as though they were dashed off the cuff were—

'(1) To get rid, by every means possible, of the existing prejudices, especially on the part of the Secularists, against the Church, her Sacraments and doctrines, and to endeavour to justify God to the People.

(2) To promote frequent and reverent worship in the Holy Communion and a better observance of the teaching of the Church of England, as set forth in the Book of Common Prayer

(3) To promote the study of social and political questions in the light of the Incarnation.'

The Christian Social Union, founded by Scott Holland in 1889, followed. There was much rivalry between the two bodies. There is, however, a long succession of Christian bodies which sought to promote either socialism or social understanding, or both. One may mention the Church Union School of Sociology, founded by the Christendom Group, the *Lux Mundi* group, of which Bishop Gore was the kingpin, the Christian Socialist Society and the Church Socialist League, the first Christian society to be affiliated to the Labour Party. Even Guild Socialism, with which the names of G. D. H. Cole and that redoubtable High Church Anglican layman, Maurice Reckitt, must ever be associated, had its Christian Socialist dimension.[7] Two of Maurice Reckitt's books, *Maurice to Temple, A Century of Social Movement in the Church of England*,[8] and his autobiography, *As it Happened*,[9] document the social movements admirably. These movements fed all that tremendous work which William Temple undertook through COPEC,[10] and other organizations between the two wars to promote social justice.

Coming down to the present day we may notice such radical movements as the Fellowship of Reconciliation, the Anglican Pacifist Fellowship, and Christian Action. Christian Action, an ecumenical body, under the inspiration of Canon L. John Collins of St Paul's, kept the Christian social conscience alive and active during the dead days of the nineteen fifties and sixties. It spawned the Campaign for Nuclear Disarmament and took charge of the British end of the struggle against apartheid in South Africa with a Defence Fund which topped a million pounds.

---

[7] Cf. Maurice Reckitt and C. E. Bechhofer, *The Meaning of National Guilds*, London 1918.
[8] London 1947.
[9] London 1941.
[10] Christian Organizations' Political and Economic Conference.

It is significant sociologically[11] that working-class movements on the continent grew up, especially in France, on an inflammatory anti-clericalism. The Church was as great an enemy as the capitalists—and a more easily identifiable and caricaturable one. Socialism and Christianity were, on the continent, mutually exclusive terms. Hence the persistence of persecution of, and organized terror against, Christians beyond the iron curtain. If we in Britain have been saved from this polarization some small credit must go to Frederick Denison Maurice, J. M. Ludlow, Charles Kingsley and others of that generous original fellowship.

Maurice's Christian Socialism attracted reformers, such as Edward and Augustus Vansittart Neale, who were not Christians and cared for the work but not the title of the band. They wanted to permit socialists who were not Christians to join the society. Maurice produced a celebrated formula to make this possible. It ran—

'(1) That human society is a body consisting of many members, not a collection of warring atoms.

(2) That true workmen must be fellow-workmen, not rivals.

(3) That a principle of justice, not selfishness, must regulate exchanges.'

The formula was adopted in March 1853. In 1859 Charles Darwin published *The Origin of Species*. From then on the 'warring atoms' were on top again.

---

[11] Cf. David Martin, *The Sociology of English Religion*, London 1967.

FOURTEEN

The Ongoing Revolutionary Rumpus

THE world of intellect had moved in the age of Copernicus and Galileo to the discovery that the earth was not the centre of the universe, with the heavenly spheres moving sublimely round it, but a planet, a minor body, moving round its sun, one of a universe of suns. Newton showed how it all worked. Of course this was a mildly shocking notion, robbing the earth of its uniqueness, but the sun still rose in the east and set in the west and the stars were far away, however bright, and the relevance of the discovery to the daily life of man was not very obvious.

Men were awed by, but not as frightened of the silence of the great galaxies as Pascal was. Rather they were impressed. For all those vast distant bodies moved with such an impeccable timing that their positions could be predicted far into the otherwise unknown future. The universe swung with the grace and precision of a Swiss timepiece and appeared to be in itself, and without man, the flawless handiwork of a perfect creator. From Ray's *The Wisdom of God in the Works of Creation* in 1691 to Paley's *Evidences of Christianity* just over a century later this reverent admiration for the works of God in the universe was the inspiration of Deism. If beyond that it was possible theistically to believe that the creator of so vast a cosmic machine had created and continued to care for man, as the crown of his works, then the Newtonian universe could be a source of the flattery of man and supportive of Christian optimism and rationality. There was no reason to suppose that man was not a superior being, with the quasi-divine destiny to which his reason testified. Nothing in that silent universe contradicted this and the need for a consciousness to contemplate the majesty perhaps demanded a creature such as man.

The new evolutionary studies of the nineteenth century changed all that. They introduced a sombre, tragic and even savage element into human history and destiny which humanity, as if it has a special interest in proving it true, has been ferociously acting out ever since.

Of course the idea of evolution was alive and active in the world before Darwin, and Darwin himself was busy on it from the day of his return from his voyage to the Galapagos Islands in H.M.S. Beagle in

1836. His survival theory was inspired by reading the work of an Anglican parson, Malthus, *On Population*. Lamarck had already taught an evolutionary theory which amounted to the belief that evolution was an act of will—that the struggle of animals to outreach themselves produced new characteristics which were then passed on. Herbert Spencer, who was to become the first great philosopher of evolution, was speculating about evolutionary theory in the same period, moving from Benthamism to an evolutionary deism. Evolution was everywhere in the air. So too was discussion about the age of the earth. The discoveries the geologists were making about the rock strata, the improbability that the sedimentary rocks could have been laid down in the 4004 years Bishop Usher had allowed for the age of the earth on biblical evidence, the mystery of fossil creatures deep in rock and no longer known on the earth all pointed to the inadequacy of the timetable Christian humanity had accepted as the frame of its history.

Darwin's *Origin of Species* made evolutionary theory both cogent and exciting, by exposing what had happened and revealing the mechanisms by which it must have taken place. Man was not excluded. He was firmly fixed in his place in the animal order. *The Descent of Man* dotted the i's and crossed the t's of *The Origin of Species* and rebuked man for his moral inferiority to animals. It was a revolution of more than Copernican gravity. The shock to the Christian system arose from two consequences. The first was the assertion of the inauthenticity of the Bible. The Bible was for millions in Europe and the Americas the revealed Word of God. Almost literally they believed—they were all fundamentalists—that this was what God himself wrote, just as he had engraved the tablets of stone for Moses. How could it be inaccurate? If it was inaccurate, then Christianity was untrustworthy and the sacred edifice was threatened with collapse. The second consequence was the assertion that the rise of man had been secured by cruel and merciless means. How could man, a being of reason and morals, stand on such godless foundations? Would he continue his (apparently guaranteed) evolution by such means? What then of Christ and his teaching of mercy and forgiveness? Were the claims made for his divinity equally false? Even so bald a statement of consequences reveals what the emotional recoil must have been. Christians were being asked (they thought) to give up their faith and to surrender their doctrine of man not for an arguably higher concept, such as the eighteenth century concept of a rational autonomous being no longer needing the Almighty, but for a baser concept of man as the fortuitous product of a struggle 'red in tooth and claw' in which the Christian claims of mercy, pity, love were an irrelevance if not a hindrance.[1] Disraeli's remark in 1864

---

[1] It is still a living issue as I sought to show in *Alternatives to Christian Belief*, Doubleday, New York 1967. Cf. too, my *The English Philosophers*, Faber, London 1953, Ch. XI 'Philosophers of Evolution'.

to the Oxford Diocesan Society summed up the religious dilemma: 'The question is this—Is man an ape or an angel? My Lord, I am on the side of the angels.' J. R. H. Moorman succinctly summed up the contemporary anguish[2] 'How could a God of Love design so hideous a universe in which everything preyed on its neighbour and only the strongest could survive?'

In *Principles of Biology* in the same year as Disraeli's immortal remark, Spencer faced Christians quite brutally with the moral dilemma:

'Those who espouse the hypothesis of special creation, entangle themselves in other theological difficulties... Without dwelling on the question why... during untold millions of years there existed on the Earth no beings endowed with capacities for wide thought and high feeling, we may content ourselves with asking why, at present, the Earth is so largely peopled by creatures which inflict on each other and on themselves, so much suffering? Omitting the human race, whose defects and miseries current theology professes to account for, and limiting ourselves to the lower creation, what must we think of the countless pain-inflicting appliances and instincts with which animals are endowed?...Whoever contends that each kind of animal was specially designed, must assert either that there was a deliberate intention on the part of the Creator to produce these results, or that there was an inability to prevent them.'[3]

T. H. Huxley capped it by declaring 'The very plants are at war'.

The consternation produced in Christians can be imagined by re-reading the accounts of the legendary debate between Bishop Wilberforce and T. H. Huxley in the Museum Library at Oxford in June 1860. At Oxford the very dons were at war. Wilberforce declared in the *Quarterly Review* that the principle of natural selection was incompatible with the word of God, contradicting the revealed relations of creation to its creator. This was the thesis he debated with a cleverer man than he on an occasion noted, alas, for its hysteria rather than any advance in understanding and from which ladies were carried out fainting and clergy almost died of apoplexy. No one just then, and for a long time afterwards, was quite sane about evolution, as I have remarked elsewhere.[4]

But the attack on accepted Christian foundations came from inside the Church as well as outside. In 1860 *Essays and Reviews* was published at the height of the Darwinian debate. Its mood was sympathetic to the new scientific learning. Among its contributors were clergy of such standing as Frederick Temple, subsequently Archbishop of Canterbury,

[2] *A History of the Church in England*, p. 177.
[3] Op. cit. London 1864 pp. 340–1.
[4] *The English Philosophers*, London 1953 p. 222.

Rowland Williams, Baden Powell, Bristow Wilson, Benjamen Jowett, C. W. Goodwin. The views expressed in the symposium so innocently titled threw light on the attitude of the dons and the more enlightened divines to the evolutionary controversy, and they bear more weight from having certainly been arrived at before the publication of *Origin of Species*. Temple, who was then headmaster of Rugby, in his essay, 'The Education of the World', advanced a developmental, even a Hegelian thesis—the slow increasing revelation of the Spirit in human history. The Church was the paradigm. 'If the Christian Church be taken as the representative of mankind it is easy to see that the general law observable in the development of the individual may also be found in the development of the Church.'[5] He made an eloquent appeal for intellectual liberty within the Church. We have no right, in the understanding of religious truth, to stop short in the exercise of our intellectual powers. 'If geology proves to us that we must not interpret the first chapters of Genesis literally; if historical investigation shall show us that inspiration, however it may protect the doctrine, yet was not empowered to protect the narrative of the inspired writers from occasional inaccuracy; if careful criticism shall prove that there have been occasional interpolations and forgeries in that Book, as in many others; the results should still be welcome.'[6] This was the maturity of mankind. Benjamin Jowett said openly that the new speculations concerning 'the chain of animal life' might lead to 'new conclusions respecting the origin of man'. He asked people 'to read scripture like any other book' and welcomed what came to be called the higher criticism. Criticism was a great help to religious communion. 'It does away with the supposed opposition of reason and faith. It throws us back on the conviction that religion is a personal thing, in which certainty is to be slowly won and not assumed as the result of evidence or testimony.'[7]

Bristow Wilson argued that religion was not theology 'and it is a stifling of the true Christian life ... to require of many men a unanimity in speculative doctrine, which is unattainable, and a uniformity of historical belief, which can never exist'. C. W. Goodwin, who showed the folly and dishonesty of trying to reconcile Genesis with contemporary geological science, protested that 'it would have been well if theologians had made up their minds to accept frankly the principle that those things for the discovery of which man has faculties specially provided are not fit objects of a divine revelation'. Baden Powell, an erstwhile Oxford professor of geometry, thought that revelation was most credible when

---

[5] Op. cit. 12th edn 1869, p. 49. This edition marks the passages which were the subject of legal action.

[6] Ibid, p. 56.

[7] Ibid, p. 525.

it did least violation to the laws of nature. 'If miracles were in the estimation of a former age among the chief *supports* of Christianity, they are at present among the main difficulties and hindrances to its acceptance.'[8] And so on.

The book caused a stupendous row. The bishops met to express their disapproval. Convocations asked for punitive action. Eleven thousand clergy and 137,000 laity signed a petition against the book. Bishops instituted legal proceedings and Rowland Williams and Bristow Wilson were suspended for a year by the Ecclesiastical Courts. Privy Council cleared the work of the accusation of heresy, but Convocation solemnly condemned the book in 1864. However, within a generation or so, the views modestly expressed in *Essays and Reviews* were to become the commonplaces of educated churchmen. Frederick Temple's role in the matter did not prevent his appointment to the See of Exeter in 1869 or his translation to the throne of Canterbury in 1896. It took a long time for the dust to settle. The Modernist movement both among Anglicans and Romans had a rough passage.

Looking back we can agree that the opponents of evolutionary theory, though often most foolish in the manner of their opposition, were right in many of their moral fears. No one was content to leave evolutionary theory in the biological arena to which it properly belonged. Everyone determinedly socialized it, even Darwin, who should have known better. Spencer, in *The Man versus the State*, was the first to adopt (fortunately in words only) a ruthless evolutionary 'morality' by opposing any acts of charity to keep the unemployed alive. 'The command', he wrote, '"If any would not work neither should he eat", is simply a Christian enunciation of that universal law of Nature under which life has reached its present height—a law that a creature not energetic to maintain itself must die.'

The doctrine of 'death to the weak' which Spencer propounded was not only a decided turnabout from that conception of a beneficent nature extolled by Rousseau, hymned by Wordsworth, and preached by the first philosophers of evolution, but it was the negation of all hitherto accepted European morality. In alliance with Benthamite ideas, it strengthened the enmity of the rich, powerful and successful towards the poor and helpless; in alliance with revolutionary idealism, it confirmed revolutionaries in the belief that only terror and violence succeeded; in combination with nationalism it created the ethos in which any military ruthlessness was justified in the interests of national or racial expansion. If one believes (as I do) that ideas make history then the consequences of Darwin for world history have been disastrous. This is not to speak of evolution as 'untrue' but rather as still imperfectly

---

[8] Ibid, p. 168.

understood[9] and dangerous when the concept is lifted into the sphere of human history where no one knows how to apply it, if applied it can be. There have been many efforts to humanize and even Christianize evolutionary doctrine. They began perhaps with T. H. Huxley's Romanes Lecture of 1893 where he flatly condemned the notion that evolutionary processes could determine human ethics, arguing indeed that they arose in defiance of the cosmic process. One must mention among the liberalizers Henri Bergson, Lloyd Morgan and A. N. Whitehead, all of whom sought a transcendent dynamic behind the evolutionary process. William Temple, in *Nature, Man and God*, married Whitehead's process philosophy to his own special Christian idealism. Whitehead has proved the source of the new Christian process theology which Norman Pittenger describes and defends in *God in Process*.[10] This is very much an American philosophical debate[11] and its penetration into European theology has been slight compared to that of Bultmann and Tillich, exploring 'Being' in the wake of Heidegger.

By now, the whole thinking world knows Teilhard de Chardin, idol of a cult. For him, in *The Phenomenon of Man*[12] and elsewhere, evolution becomes a mystical act, the glorious unfolding flower of God moving to a spiritual apocalypse at the Omega point. Teilhard, the latest gift of the Jesuits to the world, hands back evolution to the poetry of Wordsworth.

There has been much hand-clapping at his prestidigitation.

One wonders whether that is enough.

---

[9] I.e. is it a purely fortuitous process and therefore might have gone anyway but happened *this* way, or is it motivated (teleological) and if so by what or by whom? What does a *one-way* notion of evolution do to the concept of time?

[10] London 1967.

[11] Cf. *Philosophers speak of God*, Chicago 1953 and Schubert M. Ogden, *The Reality of God*, New York 1967. David Edwards provides a useful critique of the debate between the 'Being' school and the 'Process' school in *Religion and Change*, Hodder, London 1969. Chap. 8. I discuss the whole 'Nature v. History' controversy in *Nature into History*, Faber, London 1957, and critically examine A. N. Whitehead's *Process and Reality* in *Persons and Perception*, Faber, London 1961, Chap. 3, 'The Protest against Bifurcation'.

[12] London 1959.

FIFTEEN

Parish and People

THE nineteenth century Church which debated ritualism was, almost unawares, a changed Church. The latitudinarianism of so much of the eighteenth century had gone: it had become a troubled Church. Legally, it had lost its exclusive position in the establishment. Politically, it presently ceased to be part of local government. Parochially, it had become, almost unaware, a new thing, even in the countryside.

'How full the year was for the Elizabethans, filled and tricked out by custom! One has the same sense of surprise as one has in reading Hardy's novels at how occupied simple people's lives were with the diurnal routine of labour, markets and fairs, feast days and holy days, sport and gatherings, fasts and rejoicings; observations of this and that, days when one mustn't do one thing and must do another; wassailing, maying, dancing, Shrovetide games, Whitsun ales and plays, Christmas disguisings; customary obligations and beliefs, ghosts, fairies, witches, spirits, souls of the departed; the events of the family life, birth, marriage, death.'[1] And all, as A. L. Rowse points out, geared to the seasons and the Church. The folk life and the Church life were intimately intertwined. In that common life the parson, farming his glebe, going to market, collecting his tithe was a yeoman-farmer like his parishioners. And in many of the duties and responsibilities of the parish and in the maintenance of the church, and in public order, the yeoman could be the equal of the parson. Certainly he could not be ignored. When one remembers too that the church building was used for an infinite number of secular purposes including church ale feasts, and the churchyard for archery, sports, and games, particularly on a Sunday afternoon, it is easy to see the Church as a focal institution bound up with every aspect of the life of the land.

The Victorian Church was a different institution. It was less of a folk institution and more of a moralizing institution. But it was not the faint-hearted *modern* Church. To assume that is to do a great injustice

---

[1] A. L. Rowse, *The Elizabethan Renaissance, Vol. III, The Life of the Society*, 1971 p. 200.

to Victorian Christianity, which was certainly not of a peripheral character. Christianity was *necessary* to Victorian society in a way we can hardly conceive of today. People, ordinary people, common people went to church or chapel or meeting house in immense numbers on Sunday, which was still the *religious* day of which Addison wrote in *The Spectator* in the early eighteenth century, arguing that people would become savages and barbarians but for the Sunday which cleared away most of the whole week and refreshed notions of religion. 'I am always very pleased with a country Sunday and think if keeping the Sunday holy were only a human institution, it would be the best method that could have been thought of for the polishing and civilising of mankind.'[2]

On Easter Sunday in 1970, 1,600,000 Anglicans received communion out of a population of 46 million people. If one assumes that communicants will be aged fifteen or over that gives less than 50 per 1,000 population. On an average Sunday perhaps 3·3 per cent of the population is at an Anglican church.[3] I do not suppose total religious attendances do more than double that. The Victorians would have been horrified and thought the world at an end. When Horace Mann made the Religious Census of 1851, the church and chapel attendance was, on census Sunday, no less than 10,896,066 people out of a total population for England/Wales of just under 18,000,000! After making all allowances for those who attended twice, or those who could not go every week, and for babies, the figure remains prodigious. It exceeded the total number of 'sittings' or seats in church or chapel, and even the number of people Horace Mann estimated as always *able* to attend. The Church of England share of total attendance was 52 per cent, and this approached a quarter of the population.[4] Indeed the great concern of Horace Mann was with the people who did not attend places of worship. (Five million were able to attend but did not.) Was it lack of free seats? There were nearly five million free seats but almost five and a half million rented pews. Was it lack of places of worship? Twenty-thousand had been built since 1801 and he complained that there were still too few and that 2,000 new churches and chapels were needed in the large towns. Accepting the norm of Sunday worship, Horace Mann found the missing five million a problem. In his search for answers he could not help but see that the poorest people and the labouring classes were the worst attenders. He gave several reasons for failure to attract this (growing) sector of the population—social distinctions, indifference of churches to social problems, misconception of the motives of ministers, poverty and

---

[2] *The Spectator*, Monday 9 July 1711. Cf. N. Sykes, *Church and State in England in the Eighteenth Century*, Cambridge 1934 p. 231.

[3] *The Church of England Year Book*, 1973, Table 1, pp. 174–5.

[4] *Census of Great Britain, 1851*, 'Religious Worship in England and Wales', Routledge, London 1854.

overcrowded dwellings. They all amount to one—alienation of the new industrial masses. Yet though this altered the stance of churches and chapels it would be a mistake not to see Christian observance in the last century as an established way of life and the influence of preachers as tremendous.

In what way did the stance alter? This is so hard to say. One can feel for the ethos of the century which, for all its confidence and success in industry and empire, was an anxious and an earnest one. One suspects that the Church—*vide* Horace Mann—felt itself slipping as the focus of the common life, not only through the rivalry of Nonconformism, but from the growth of secular emphases too, hence a certain scolding in its appeals. As the century progressed the churches became centres within society for the promotion of Christian doctrines and practices, it seems, rather than the inevitable expression of society itself. The Salvation Army called their early local headquarters barracks or citadels— meaning centres from which the Christian soldiers sallied forth to do battle for the right. Now Anglican churches were never as militant as that: but they were increasingly the local nuclei of groups and societies designed to influence society, or to train the young, to support missions or to strengthen the Church, or one or another of its parties: presently the military parallel found its way into titles—brigades, armies, crusades—of all sorts of denominations. And in hymns. 'Onward, Christian Soldiers' belongs to this era. Powerful though the Church still was, it was now one group in society—one pressure group—forced to direct its work *at* society—a society not always prepared to listen. All denominations shared this situation—indeed denominationalism itself by its very competitiveness forced this situation upon Christians. They were in conflict with one another for support: society was their fishing ground. The embattled stance the Salvation Army took up, as though at war with society itself, symbolized the new role of the churches faced with a society increasingly secular.

The Church of England did a remarkable service to society in the provision of education through Sunday schools and day schools: its identification with education from the universities and public schools downwards was so close that it accepted without question its role as provider and what it had accomplished created the basis for the national system which came with the 1870 Act. And despite all that has been said about ritualism, which captured so much publicity and concerned the unity and credibility of the church, education could be said to be the Church's primary nineteenth century social concern absorbing much of its energy. Every parish church set out to create its own parish school (if it had not got one) in addition to the work it was doing in Sunday School, and both were as concerned originally with the three Rs as with religion. But education too became a battleground for the denominations, and over religion itself. The Act said that in the new public elementary schools, 'no religious catechism or religious formulary which is distinctive of any particular denomination shall be taught in the school'. And as for any existing school qualifying for a grant, 'such grant shall not be made in respect of any instruction in religious subjects'. Perhaps nothing quite so well illustrates the secularization of the age and the curious isolation of the Church that in this field where it was overwhelmingly the primary provider its will could not prevail over the teaching of the established religion. And so it found itself in opposition to the new Act it itself had made inevitable.

In the essay on the Reverend George Gorham, Vicar of Walkeringham, 1855–73,[5] Frank West speaks of him as in pretty continual conflict with the Nonconformists for most of his ministry and sometimes with the village too. The Wesleyans celebrated the Act by founding their own school. 'Mr. Gorham's immediate response to the Education Act was to divide the [Church] School into "a *secular* branch" (which must conform to the new Education Act) and "a *religious* branch" (which will not recognize its provision in any way)! One of the dissenters sent a copy of the Vicar's rather absurd rules to the Board of Education and it was hardly surprising that "that bureau should show some disposition to challenge them!" In fact, it sent down an inspector two years later at an unpropitious moment...and a very adverse report was recorded. The following year the vicar was informed that the Education Department would in future ignore his school "as an instrument of education".'[6]

In 1870, of the 8,919 schools receiving grant aid, 6,974 were Church schools. It appears that a great number of them had refused aid in order to keep their religious independence. Certainly the system of voluntary schools grew after the 1870 Act and the Church of England which had nearly 11,000 schools in 1878 had close to 12,000 by 1885. Thereafter the numbers began to decline. Inevitably the new educational system was a new source of secularization—partly because of the conflict between Anglican and Nonconformist interests—and education itself became polarized between 'religious instruction' and 'the rest', or *versus* the rest.

In other spheres, as the Sheffield story tells us, both the Church and the Nonconformists were leaders in the social and cultural life. All the same the popular lectures and lantern lectures, local drama and sport, evening classes, brass bands, penny readings, clothing and shoe clubs, savings banks, parish excursions became more and more secularized and the church increasingly functioned in secular society through its satellite organizations. A straw in the wind of the slide away from the Church's universalism is provided by the irate Mr Gorham who put up a notice on the occasion of a school feast which went:

'The vicar invites parents of children in the schools and all members of

[5] *Sparrows of the Spirit*, SPCK, London 1961 p. 91.
[6] Ibid, pp. 103–4. Frank West is quoting from the Rev. G. Gorham's diaries.

his congregation with their friends AND NO OTHERS. Working men will be welcome, if properly dressed and willing to help in keeping order. NO BOYS ADMITTED EXCEPT SCHOLARS.'[7]

The Mothers' Union was typical of the satellites. It owed its birth to experiments made by Mary Sumner in the seventies at the very moment that Church Sunday Schools began their slow decline. It is rather striking that the Mothers' Union began to grow as the schools began to fail the Church, for it operated directly on the home, insisting on a Christian piety and discipline in the family no matter what might be happening in the outside world, and with remarkable effect. It has been the proto-type for many similar lay enterprises.

The Church expressed its growing uneasiness at its new situation in many ways. It attacked governments for moving into a neutral or potentially hostile position in relation to the Church as betraying the spirit of the Elizabethan Settlement and it broke into self criticism over its relation to the working man and to the laity. It became conscious of how middle class it had become—but just this sharp class conscious-ness, as against rank or status consciousness, was itself the mark of a great change. There had always been the poor but they had to wait for Bentham to be considered as a group in society anathema for their poverty. But no one thought of them till the nineteenth century as a *class* in the modern sense. And it was soon realized that the poor or the working man—terms almost interchangeable by the mid-century—had no place in the church, a notion inconceivable in Elizabethan or even in the eighteenth century days.

In *Religious Worship in England and Wales* (1854) Horace Mann said that

'Workingmen, it is contended, cannot enter on religious structures without having pressed upon their notice some memento of inferiority. The existence of [rented] pews and the *position* of free seats are, it is said, alone sufficient to deter them from our churches; and religion has thus come to be regarded as purely middle-class propriety or luxury.'

Much of the steam behind the campaign to abolish pew rents came from the belief that the system excluded the poor and the working people. That was certainly true, but it did not follow that its abolition would bring them in. Church going, even chapel going, had become alien to the way of life of a vast sector of the working population. To enter a church, unless for baptism or marriage, was an unusual step. As a poor (and perhaps solitary) person, one was immediately exposed to a criticism not always silent from the prosperous ethos so clearly manifested in the dress, manners and deportment of superior persons.

---

[7] Ibid, p. 99.

Perhaps one was in debt, not always sober, particularly on the night before Sunday, raggedly clothed, unable to afford even a threepenny bit for the plate, and ashamed to be naked in one's poverty before the well-to-do. The nineteenth century saw the heyday of the eclectic church of the fashionable preacher to which the rich were driven in carriage and pair. And as for *them*—among them there was a fear akin to the racial fears of today. The poor were a mysterious, hostile group, full of envy. They were sexually dangerous. Probably they stank, spat and had fleas. They might be helped, but it was better not to have them sitting beside you. These fears were one reason why the campaign to get rid of pew rents, begun in 1850 at St Barnabas, Pimlico, notorious presently for its ritualism, took half a century to complete. But it was still common when I was a boy attending church before the First World War to discover a printed notice in the church porch which said that rents for pews had been abandoned in this church and all seats were free. But still the poor did not come to church. Charles Booth saw the class gap that had grown when he remarked about working-class converts that the movement that really comes about, 'is not so much *of* as *out of* the class to which they have belonged'. Weber's Protestant ethic still promoted people! It can be said even now that churches and chapels are ladders in upward social movement. A nineteenth century saw had it, 'Carriage and pair never pass church door for more than a generation'.

As to the laity who were not poor, they were not being used in a clericalized Church. A committee of the Canterbury Convocation on the spiritual needs of the masses declared in 1885: 'the time has arrived for turning to account that large body of intelligent lay people, whether men or women, who have at heart the cause of Christ and His Church'. 'Let the laity do their part', said a layman at the Church Congress of 1886, 'and the Church's influence may be amazingly extended in a very short space of time. There is no other method I know for bringing a large amount of influence to bear upon the lapsed masses.'[8] So began discussions even of the priesthood of the laity and an influential movement to bring lay people back into the organs of Church government. As a consequence Houses of Laymen were added to the Convocations of Canterbury and York in the eighties and parochial church councils were presently being approved and set up.

Nevertheless the 1902 Report, *The Position of the Laity in the Church*, saw in the nineteenth century legal and social developments we have scanned only a sad fall. It protested that it was not only that private patronage began to decline with the decline of the squirearchy, and episcopal, collegiate and party forms of patronage began to increase in

---

[8] K. S. Inglis, *Churches and the Working Classes in Victorian England*, Routledge & Kegan Paul, 1963, p. 47.

strength and importance, but that legislation itself removed the Church farther and farther from the laity. It made a recapitulation: in 1836 the civil registration of births superseded the old church registers. In the same year the law recognized marriage by civil contract. The Church Building Acts of the century made it possible to charge pew rents: 'The ability to rent a seat became a qualification for taking part in public worship, in the place of the spiritual birthright of every baptised person.' Church rates were abolished in 1868. The Local Government Act of 1894 withdrew all but ecclesiastical duties from the churchwardens of the parish. The old universities ceased to be 'the exclusive heritage of Churchmen'. The state took over education. Parliament itself was no longer the supreme body of the laity of the Church of England. And so on, and so on. What was in fact a weakening of the social and political power of the Church and a loosening of its bonds with the state, the Report saw as especially the reduction of the authority of the laity through whom so many of those powers were exercised.

The introduction by Dr Norman Sykes to the 1952 edition took note of all these points and began briskly with a quotation:

' "What is the province of the laity? To hunt, to shoot, to entertain. These matters they understand, but to meddle with ecclesiastical matters, they have no right at all." Such were the sentiments expressed by Monsignor George Talbot to Archbishop Manning in a letter of 25 April 1857, à propos of signs which he discerned of the English Roman Catholic laity's beginning "to show the cloven hoof", by putting into practice "the doctrine taught by Dr. Newman in his article in *The Rambler*", entitled *On Consulting the Laity in Matters of Faith*. From Dr. Thomas Arnold, when asked, "what is the laity?" the reply came at once, "The Church—minus the clergy".'[9]

Despite Newman's lead and Dr Arnold's resolute stand, it was not the conception of the primacy of the laity which gained ground in the nineteenth century, at least not until the end. The Oxford Movement naturalized the Roman view of the priesthood in the Anglican Church. The clergyman was no longer the promoted layman, the younger son of a gentleman made safe for life by the purchase of a living and as good a Christian as the next man, but a sacred member of a sacred order, the earthly vehicle of the divine charisma, set apart for life, and as such possessing unquestioned authority over the laity. The promulgation of Papal Infallibility witnessed to the apogee of a similar process of sacralization within the Roman Church. The movement which slowly gave more status to the Anglican laity in the last quarter of the century only secured for the laity a third share in the government of the Church

---

[9] Op. cit. p. iii. We should notice that Monsignor Talbot's laity are the leisured gentry. Others, humbler, or even working, do not exist.

in the first quarter of this. The Roman Church has not yet moved thus far, though the voice of its laity is heard far more effectively today than at any time past and a new theology of the laity has been developing fast.[10] But this is to anticipate.

---

[10] Cf. Hendrik Kraemer, *A Theology of the Laity*, Lutterworth 1958; F. R. Barry, *Asking the Right Questions*, 1960; Yves M. Congar, *Lay People in the Church*, London 1957; Kathleen Bliss, *We the People*, London 1963; Gibbs and Morton, *God's Frozen People*, Fontana, London 1964, etc.

SIXTEEN

The Birth of the Modern Church

ONE might date the modern Church of England not from the Convocations revived halfway through the nineteenth century, important though this was, but from the Houses of Laity created by them in 1885. It was the first step in recognizing that the Church of England was not just its ordained ministry and a lay parliament. Many consequences were to flow from it. Earlier the voluntary Church Congress, first meeting at Cambridge in 1861, had begun to popularize the idea of lay participation and of democratic processes in Church government and to dispel the vulgar criticism of the Church as nothing but a club of wealthy and reactionary bishops and absentee parsons. Indeed the Congress in the year of the Second Exhibition marked the high seriousness of the middle and late Victorian Church. It was a Church of a vastly greater learning and social energy than it had been a century before, though still in chains to a feudal structure and an erastian law. It had become part of the moral earnestness of Victorian England and this muted the disestablishment campaign against it. Then, by the growth of an empire Britain had assembled 'in a fit of absent-mindedness', it had become a world Church and the first Lambeth Conference (1867) marked this.

Perhaps the most significant Anglican publication of the late nineteenth century was the symposium *Lux Mundi* (1889) with its thoughtful socialist bias, which began to move the Church away (at last) from the dominating utilitarian philosophy of the century. In the same year as its publication Sion College promoted a conference of 'Churchmen in Council' at Westminster Guildhall 'to promote the relief of the Church by obtaining for it, from the state, the power of settling its differences in doctrine and ritual in a liberal spirit, by the agency of convocation'. But the retort to this kind of thing was the founding of the Protestant Churchmen's Alliance with a Lord as president.

Perhaps one could date the birth of the modern Church from the drive by Bishop Blomfield to get two hundred new churches built between 1828 and 1856 to serve the expanding population of London diocese, or even leave it as late as the Canterbury Convocation of July 1905, when the Lower House presented to the Archbishop in the Upper

House a resolution asking for the appointment of a joint committee to consider the creation of a province of London, served by suffragans with territorial responsibilities. This has a decidedly modern ring. The agitation had already begun, a decade before 1914, for an *aggiornamento* to adapt the Church of England to the mass society which had overtaken it.

One would like to single out, as the closing drama of the nineteenth century and mark of the Church's piety before its history, the gigantic pageant, 'The Conversion of England', celebrating the landing of St Augustine in Kent 1300 years before. It took place in Canterbury in 1897. The Roman Catholics had earlier staged their rival show. One might also single out as the bitterest medicine of the century the papal bull of 1896, which condemned Anglican orders as 'absolutely null and utterly void'—a decision disastrous to all those high Anglican hopes of an early reunion with Rome. But even that was less important than the ongoing conflict between the Church parties. Petitions, deputations, conferences, books, pamphlets were endless and went on until the outbreak of war in 1914. The din of the ritualist battle drowned everything else. Some priests were burning candles and incense and reserving the Sacrament and others were prosecuting them for it. Fortunately no priests were yet disposed to burn other priests. So, ironically, the new century, the twentieth inglorious century after Christ, was heralded in, on 19 January 1900, by the demure presentation to the Archbishop of Canterbury, from the hands of the Duke of Newcastle, the Lord E. Churchill, and Mr R. W. Burnie, of a petition against the ban of the Archbishops on processional lights and incense, signed by 14,000 people. The Archbishop affirmed that he based his ban entirely upon the Book of Common Prayer. No doubt he was right. Entirely.

This obsessiveness is painful to look back upon: the narrow mindedness hurts. Yet there were issues of world consequence facing the Church in that first decade of the new century and decisions made about them which the ritualist debate obscured. The Lambeth Conferences of 1897 and 1908 marked the emergence of a third world Church on to the stage, with its autonomous provinces and native entrants to the priesthood. In 1908, the year of the fifth Lambeth Conference, a vast Pan-Anglican Congress, attended every day by about 17,000 people, marked the greatest effort ever made to educate Anglicans and others about the nature of their Church, its problems and teachings and world-wide spread. Perhaps, despite its party strife, in that year the Church came to a high water mark never reached since.

In 1910 the World Interdenominational Missionary Conference in Edinburgh—which will forever be associated with the work of John R. Mott and J. H. Oldham[1]—opened up a new frontier. There was born

---

[1] Cf. Kathleen Bliss, *We the People*, SCM, London 1963; chapter 3 has a special tribute to Mott and Oldham.

the Ecumenical Movement which in the end was to bring the world Protestant Churches together in the World Council of Churches and so to change the Protestant presence to the world and to end that embattled isolation which afflicted Churches and had for so long governed their attitudes to one another. Edinburgh, 1910, was significant for its lay initiatives and perhaps for the fact that it sought to impress on the home Churches the realities of the field mission experience. A host of denominational birds came home to roost.

The traumatic event of the century, and not alone for the Churches, was the First World War with its total destruction of the mass armies of a continent, one after another. There was an awful chasm between the idealism and valour of the young men of country after country going to fight in 1914 and 1915 and what the war eventually proved to be in impersonal slaughter. There was the postwar loss of the moral and political primacy of Europe, the beginning of a new era of class and national and racial violence, to which we are still party. Something in Christianity and in European civilization was gone for ever. Christendom stood fragmented before the catastrophe, its impotent little pieces adhering to the warring local nationalisms.

I spoke elsewhere[2] of the social shock that 'The Great War' administered to the Church of England. It discovered the industrial masses as a living powerful social element in the Tommies who went so gallantly, so uncomplainingly, to their deaths for a country which had never done very much for them or valued them highly. It discovered through its chaplains working-men as heroes rather than as ignoramuses, social delinquents or Benthamite failures. It found that England was being saved, not by the ploughboys of old time, or by the social scum of Kipling's poetry, but by millworkers, miners, clerks, steelworkers, shop boys, tram drivers. Chaplains in the Forces came to know these men as good, dogged, faithful representatives of 'the apparently inexhaustible reservoir of manpower of our great cities'. The Church discovered with a shock its almost total estrangement from them, and their suspicion of a Church completely identifiable with the ruling classes. It was a humbling experience. The day of patronage by a priesthood of superior persons was over.

I spoke in the same place of the shock to the Church in its moral security. The whole ethos of the upper and professional classes, and of much of the middle class was that

'country life was the right kind of life which anyone of any consequence as a matter of course wanted to live and that the industrial areas were monstrosities, aberrations, and cities in general only toler-

---

[2] In *The Death and Resurrection of the Church*, Hodder and Stoughton, London 1968, Chap. 1.

able at certain seasons or for certain tasks for certain people—*trades* people. Even the suburban villa growth of the period emphasized the belief that though you lived in a town you ought to make it as much like the country as possible. The country squire has been described as the permanent English ideal of manhood. The Georgian poets with their passion for country walks and week-end cottages celebrated a static rural peace [and] spoke nostalgically for a national mood that England was still nothing more than a charming rural island, outside the boring town.'[3]

The parson shared and fostered this view. The country was the place where most parsons were securely bedded down. And this was where they were quite certain they ought to be. The war did not completely destroy these illusions—they are not dead yet—but it jolted many, including the best minds, out of a long complacency. William Temple's National Mission of Repentance and Hope and the Life and Liberty movement which followed it were born out of spiritual dismay. The Enabling Act of 1919 which set up the Church Assembly was the result of a campaign which meant more than—give the Church a national governing body! There was a great longing to have the workers and the lower middle class represented on it, to have a national forum from which to address the people, and to bring to an end what many saw as an upper class monopoly of the leadership of the Church. It was reflected too in a postwar campaign to recruit ex-servicemen into the ministry. A crash ordination course was run at Knutsford, Cheshire, engendering the same kind of intellectual and spiritual excitement as that produced by Brasted Place College after World War II.

The campaign failed in its total objectives. Church Assembly became a legislature grinding out measures rather than a national forum. Only the rich, the elderly, some vicars' wives, and superannuated laity could afford to belong to it in the twenties and thirties. There was little provision to compensate working-people for loss of working time. Three full weeks of service was a lot to ask of people in their active years and when the usual holiday firms granted was only a fortnight.

Church Assembly was defeated in its first major legislation affecting its relations with the state, the new Prayer Book, rejected by Parliament in 1927 and again in 1928. The Evangelicals in particular lobbied for parliamentary opposition to it, hating its Anglo-Catholic tenor. But Dr Walter Matthews saw the Commons' defeat as hailing from the same kind of combination as has in this decade frustrated Anglican–Methodist union.

---

[3] Ibid. pp. 12–13.

In his autobiography which spans the best part of a century he writes:
'What study I was able to give to the text of the proposed revised
book of Common Prayer led me to agree with Archbishop Brillioth
the Lutheran Primate of Sweden, that the 1928 Book liturgy of the
eucharist was the finest liturgy in Christendom. . . . Two things however
troubled me deeply. The first was the movement which defeated the
new Book. The loud-voiced protests, which undoubtedly had their
effect on the Commons vote, came from the two extreme parties in
the Church. There was an unholy alliance between the extreme
Protestants and the extreme Anglo-Catholics[4]—the former because
they feared the Mass and the latter because they feared they might
be prevented from saying the Latin Mass in their churches. When
the 1928 Book became legal, the chaos in episcopal regulation would,
it was hoped, be halted and excuses for "supplementing" and
"supplanting" the Holy Communion by the Roman liturgy would be
abolished. Allied with this was my feeling of dismay at the optimism
of the bishops.'[5]

Of course, Parliament was perfectly entitled to do what it did, and
the first class row hit all the headlines and encouraged the satirists:

> Sir William Joynson-Hicks is mad,
> The bishops aren't behaving well,
> They've turned the Prayer Book inside out,
> They're selling people short on Hell.

But the rebuff to the Church's new found sense of autonomy was
severe. In the light of the defeat the unity of the Church appeared
fragile indeed. A minority had resorted to the extra-ecclesiastical
authority to defeat the will of the Church's own supreme chamber and
were prepared to see it crushed rather than submit to the legitimate
decision of a majority. There is nothing so deadly as the hatreds of
really godly men. It was an ominous indication that the struggles of a
century were not over and that the Church was finely balanced still
between low Evangelicals and High Churchmen. Perhaps only the
resources of the Ecclesiastical Commissioners kept them under the same
umbrella.

In 1922 the Church appointed a Commission on Doctrine. The
reasons were not far to seek.

' "It is clear that one of the dominant purposes of the Archbishop in
setting up the Commission was a practical one," Dr Matthews said
in *Memories and Meanings*. "The conflicting currents in the Church of

---

[4] This alliance first occurred in 1860 over *Essays and Reviews*, in 1928 over the new
Prayer Book, in 1972 again to defeat the will of the Church over reunion with the Methodists.
[5] *Memories and Meanings*, Hodder, London 1969, p. 149.

England had become violent. The extremes on either side aimed at purging their opposites from the Church and both agreed that the majority who were attached to the middle way and hoped that they were both Catholic and Reformed were feeble compromisers. The expressed aim of the Commission was to formulate the limits within which disagreements were tolerable." [6]

If the Commission, of which Dr Matthews was a member, owed its birth to a sense of doctrinal urgency it soon forgot to hasten. Appointed in 1922, it reported in 1938 and the Report was then lost in the other urgencies of the Second World War. Many of the original team of twenty-five theologians and philosophers had in any case died by the date of publication. The hope of Dr Matthews and many others (one speculates) that the Report would replace or lead to the modification of the Thirty-nine Articles was dead from the beginning. Such an effort would have led to a split as traumatic as that which attended the new Prayer Book. Dr Matthews felt that the bishops were timid. In the circumstances, it is not surprising.

The tone of the Report is scholarly and urbane. It explains discursively a great many things and tends to be all-embracing when it comes reluctantly to anything like a definition of a doctrinal point. On the sacrifice of the Mass it says: 'The character of the sacrifice varies with the varying relationship in which those who offer it may stand towards God and towards one another. Thus sacrifice may be regarded simply as a gift, or as a pledge and means of fellowship, or as the formal sealing of a covenant, or, where the sense of sin is present, it may have a propitiatory or expiatory character.' This, and like statements, did not really advance the solution of doctrinal difficulties.

Original sin, the Thirty-nine Articles affirmed, is of such a nature that 'in every person born into this world, it deserveth God's wrath and damnation. And this infection doth remain, yea in them that are regenerated. . . . The condition of man after the fall of Adam is such, that he cannot turn and prepare himself, by his own natural strength and good works, to faith, and calling upon God. . . .'

It is a strong, even passionate, statement of man's total depravity which includes lust and concupiscence in 'the nature of Sin'. One does not have to believe it before one acknowledges its power. The Commission repudiated total depravity, but accepted a human bias towards evil, and was forced to confess that in interpreting this bias, and relating it to the purpose of God, it was not agreed. It put forward views which it regarded as 'not illegitimate' in the Church of England.

'(1) Since man is by his very nature social, we are involved in some

---

[6] Op. cit. p. 144.

form of social solidarity, so that, evil having beyond question found
an entrance into human life, all are brought under its influence.

(a) Some hold that this influence of social environment upon each
individual is a sufficient explanation of facts.

(b) Some hold that, in addition to social inheritance, there is a
racial inheritance of evil, a biological transmission of moral
taint.

(c) Some, whether accepting (b) or not, hold that more than (a) is
involved, and that there is a transcendental solidarity of the
human race in evil which creates or determines a proneness to
sin in each individual.

(d) Some hold that the very essence of man as a finite spirit is a
sufficient explanation of the facts.

(2) In regard to the question of God's responsibility for sin.

(a) Some hold that God, having made man free, has no further
responsibility for sin, which falls outside His original purpose for
man.

(b) Others hold that from the beginning sin falls within that purpose, though among these, again, there would be a difference
as regards the directness with which the responsibility for it is
to be attributed to God.'[7]

One is awestruck that so earth-shaking a concept as 'God's responsibility for sin' could at the end of sixteen years of deliberation be
dismissed in language so flaccid and inept. One can only surmise that
the Report's tepidity arises from, or rather is a part of, the total intellectual inadequacy of the interwar years, in theology as elsewhere. Men
lived the progressive dream still, as if there had been no Great War and
there would never be another war. Liberal-minded England and America
had no idea what they faced in Stalin's Russia and Hitler's Germany.
The Commission indeed found it difficult in that meliorating climate to
believe in sin or evil at all, except as something a pre-arranged evolution
would presently eliminate. Sin is certainly not an easy meal to digest if
one is a modernist or liberal theologian. How does one possibly *sin*
against Teilhard de Chardin's grand design or Whitehead's process? It
seems an impertinence to mention it. The Commission had nothing as
trenchant to say about sin as William Golding's aphorism—'man distils
evil as a bee distils honey'.

The perfunctoriness of the report belongs to a theology not yet in
crisis. It had not yet felt the blows of Kierkegaard, that one had to
have faith with twenty thousand fathoms beneath one, nor had it heard
Barth quoting Luther that man has a passion against deity, he cannot
abide deity. Brunner seemed unheard and the existentialism of Sartre was

[7] *Doctrine in the Church of England*, SPCK, London 1938, pp. 62–3.

yet in the womb of time. Perhaps I put too much on one report—but yet, sixteen years to produce a theology totally without grief! Where did they go to?

Just as astonishing as the Report was the outcry that erupted. Both Church parties took the warpath against it. Some eight thousand clergy signed a petition condemning it. The bishops mildly welcomed it 'as a survey of the currents of thought and belief within the Church' and desired that the Report should be widely and tolerantly studied. But, they warned, it was not a *declaration* of the doctrine of the Church which was as always the faith set forth in 'the Creeds, in the Prayer Book and in the Articles of Religion'. A Lower House resolution in Convocation, which carried the day, attached the Church firmly to the Nicene Creed and attacked any attempt to liberalize theology 'by private interpretation [of] the historic meaning of those clauses which state the events of the earthly life of our Lord Jesus Christ'. An amendment to this resolution, by Dean Matthews of St Paul's, to get the Thirty-nine Articles revised in the light of the Doctrine Commission's findings was defeated by a large majority. And after that the Report died. In 1938 and 1939 men had other things to think about. The Archbishops have appointed another Commission on Doctrine, which is now sitting. It is to be hoped that it will not continue to sit as a way of life.

The Church is left with the Lambeth Quadrilateral as the only acceptable modern statement of doctrine. It is the product of the Lambeth Conference of 1888, on the initiative of the General Convention of the American Episcopal Church. It was revised a little and reconfirmed in 1897. According to this statement, the four essentials upon which the world Anglican Church must stand (as it were, four square) are—the Old and New Testaments, the Nicene Creed, the two Gospel Sacraments, Baptism and the Eucharist, and the Historic Episcopacy locally adapted. It makes no mention of the Thirty-nine Articles.

Halting this summary in the early decades of this century one ends something between 1400 and 1800 years of the history of the Church of England. Clearly it has proved a tough institution, not easily changed, except by the hardly discernible processes of history, or the fiats of governments, successfully resistant to all attempts to break it. Despite its corruptions its enemies proved unable to destroy it.

England is a country with a remarkable institutional continuity: one thinks of parliament and the crown as well as the Church. The continuity of the Church down to this century, despite all the oppressions, the crises, the execution blocks and the Smithfield fires, witnesses at least to its social significance. Only in this century has it ceased to look so 'embedded' in the structures and infra-structures of society and as if, at some time, it might be shaken loose. Its historicity, like its holiness, has had perpetually to be rediscovered. The renewal of its historical awareness was what the Oxford Movement achieved in the last century: it brought to Victorian Anglicanism the surprised consciousness that it might be closer to the primitive church than the two great world fortresses, the Roman and the Orthodox. Even the Evangelicals were deeply affected by this new understanding, which we see now was only half true. The Lambeth Conferences began to spell out the international independence and authority its overseas growth promised, adding the humbler note that perhaps the Church of England might eventually disappear for the greater glory of the greater Church of God.

All the same one has to recognize a turn around. The significance of the Church of England during the Reformation was that, catholic or protestant, it was the Church of *England*, and be hanged to only the *Roman* supremacy. The significance of the Church of England in the eighteenth and nineteenth centuries is that it was too protestant, too insulated from the continent to feel *rapport* with the historic Church. It helped to spread missionary enterprises all over the world, to the dark and heathen continents as well as to new colonies, but it hardly conceived of Rome as Christian at all, rather as some dangerous extravagant, superstitious 'other world'. The Catholic understanding of an Anglican universality in a Christian universalism, the gift of the Oxford Movement, has born fruit only in this century. The Evangelicals themselves, for all their social courage, would never have brought to an end the sense of the English Church as the private 'thing' of middle-class morality, as Doolittle would have put it.

Continuity notwithstanding, the price paid for the Reformation has been tremendous. The exchange of king for pope was a poor bargain, the poorer for the royal terror which accompanied it. Since that day the polarization of the Church has been almost schizoid—the swings of giant Church parties tugging it first to Geneva and then towards Rome and paralyzing its native spiritual initiatives. One gathers from its post-Reformation history that it never collectively knew what it was. How could it, either, when its Convocations were so long silenced and it enjoyed the role of a department of state governed by royal injunctions? Since the Henrician supremacy it has been a subordinate and dependent institution, too much attached to the state's apron strings. And we all know what happens to children who are not allowed to grow up. They cease trying. Their spirits wither.

In relation to society the Church at the end of the nineteenth century was in a totally different situation from that of the first millenium. As I have said in the introduction, the Church of the early centuries was teacher, prophet, master. It bore within its bosom the spark which lit the fires of civilization in these islands. Learning, literacy, culture, the arts, were its monopoly. One may speak of its monasteries as teaching, not only the word of God, but industrial arts and crafts, strict accounting, business economics and even planning. The Church was all-pervasive and its Christianity the final dynamic of society, the very drama of being.

At the end of the nineteenth century it was society which had become the teacher, the Church the pupil. Secular society had grown away from the Church, come of age. Its intellectual presuppositions were not, outside the sphere of morals, Christian ones. Its science was autonomous and displayed all the confidence in its own future and in that of the societies under its guidance which a new religion develops. It thought of itself, as once Christianity had thought of itself, as the sole source of demonstrable truth. Some of the best minds of that century spoke of the Church as nothing more than a rubbish swept down from the past which blocked the road to progress. The new role of the Church in the new century was to resist being thrust out of society by secular forces beyond anyone's control, to insist upon its presence as in itself a judgement upon the direction civilization was taking. But it was, too, the wayward child of its time, too often turning a blind eye to the traffic signals and counting the candles on the altar with its good one.

PART TWO

The Church Today

'The church is a pilgrim walking through time and history, going from stage to stage along a way as yet incomplete.'
          Cardinal Suenens in *The Future of the Church*

'By the Church therefore in this question we understand no other than only the visible Church. For preservation of Christianity there is not any thing more needful, than that such as are of the visible Church have mutual fellowship and society one with another. In which consideration, as the main body of the sea being one, yet within divers precincts hath divers names; so the Catholic Church is in like sort divided into a number of distinct Societies, every one of which is termed a Church within itself. In this sense the Church is always a visible society of men.'
          Richard Hooker in *Ecclesiastical Polity*

'The mistake of ecclesiasticism through the ages has been to believe in the Church as a kind of thing-in-itself. The apostles never regarded the Church as a thing-in-itself. Their faith was in God, who had raised Jesus from the dead, and they knew the power of his Resurrection to be at work in them and in their fellow-believers despite the unworthiness of them all.'
          Michael Ramsey in *The Future of the Church*

ONE

What the Church is Legally

CHURCH law is in part canon law and the canon law of the Church of England is the nearest thing to a written constitution and clergy disciplinary code that it possesses. The makers of canon law have been the Convocations of Canterbury and York, clergy legislative bodies from which the laity were generally excluded, and the canons passed by them 'are binding *proprio vigore* on the clergy'.[1] In 1970, however, Convocations were amalgamated and, with a House of Laity, constitute the General Synod to which power to make or amend canon law now passes. The present revised canons promulged by Convocations in 1966 and 1969 come down from the Code of 1603 and include many canons unchanged in form and wording. Canon A5 'Of the doctrine of the Church of England' spells out the basis of the Church's life: 'The doctrine of the Church of England is grounded in the holy Scriptures, and in such teachings of the ancient Fathers and Councils of the Church as are agreeable to the said Scriptures. In particular such doctrine is to be found in the Thirty-nine Articles of Religion, The Book of Common Prayer and the Ordinal.'[2] Clergy discipline is founded on the Declaration of Assent (Canon C15) in which a clergyman was required before ordination and at every subsequent change of post to swear that he solemnly assents to the Thirty-nine Articles of Religion, the Book of Common Prayer and the Ordinal—the specific doctrinal and liturgical legacies of the English Reformation of the sixteenth and seventeenth centuries.* Canon Law comes down to the Church from pre-Reformation days, but the post-Reformation canons proclaim in no uncertain voice the Church's loyalty to its Tudor and Caroline origins. Indeed the very first canon speaks of the Church of England as established according to the laws of this realm under the Queen's majesty.

---

* But see below, footnote to p. 133, for the new form of assent passed by General Synod, July 1973.

[1] *The Canons of the Church of England: Canons Ecclesiastical promulged by the Convocations of Canterbury and York in 1964 and 1969*, Introduction by the Archbishops of Canterbury and York, SPCK, 1969, p. xi.

[2] Ibid. p. 3.

Before the Reformation English canon law was grounded upon the canon law of the European Church as a whole, and subject to the authority of popes and Councils, but that link was deliberately broken by statute law, in particular by *The Submission of the Clergy Act*, 1533, which 'severely curtailed the Church's power to legislate by canon:

(a) by limiting it to the English Convocations if and when summoned by Royal writ (Section 1)

(b) by requiring the Royal Assent and licence for all canons (Section 1),

(c) by prohibiting the making of canons contrary or repugnant to "the customs laws or statutes of this realm" (Section 3).'[3]

The powers of the Act show how easily the Church down the centuries was silenced and made submissive. Indeed from 1603 until this century the order and discipline of the Church were determined by statute law, that is by parliament, or by royal injunction. For over a hundred years, Convocations were never called.

It would require a separate study to analyse and codify the mass of ecclesiastical legislation passed by parliament between the Submission of the Clergy Act of 1533 and the Enabling Act of 1919 which established Church Assembly as the ecclesiastical legislative chamber. But how important Church legislation was and how seriously parliament took its task has surely been made clear by the historical chapters which preceded this. What is quite certain is that, despite its own legislative powers, the Church today stands legally in the position determined for it by the successive Acts of Uniformity of 1548, 1558 and 1662. For our purposes 1662 is definitive. It required the clergy to use the Book of Common Prayer in what we may speak of as its finally approved form (still in daily use), and especially for the morning and evening prayers of the book to be said in all churches on Sundays. The 1662 Act put in statute form the central disciplinary doctrines of the Canons of 1603. Two hundred and sixty-two years later, the Clerical Subscription Act, 1865, drafted amidst the ritualist controversies, dotted the i's and crossed the t's of the earlier legislation and enshrined the Declaration of Assent already described in Section 1 of the Act. There could not be the slightest doubt as to what the Church of England was in terms of statute law. It was the body entrusted to maintain the forms of public worship contained in the Book of Common Prayer, to sustain the doctrines of the Thirty-nine Articles, to recruit and ordain ministers obedient to these requirements according to the forms prescribed in the Ordinal.

Is it still that? The Code of Canons of 1603 has been replaced by the Revised Code of Canons of 1964 and 1969 which has of course received the necessary royal assent. The Law Reform (Repeals) Act 1969 has got rid of the Clergy Subscription Act. But the Act of Uniformity 1662 will be repealed almost wholly if the 1972 Worship and Doctrine

---

[3] *Church and State, Report of the Archbishop's Commission, 1970*, Appendix A 'The Law of the Church of England', CIO, p. 88.

measure is accepted by Parliament. It has been softened already in its liturgical rigour in one respect—The Prayer Book (Alternative and Other Services) Measure of 1965 (a Church Assembly measure, of course) authorizing alternative forms of service to those prescribed in the Prayer Book for an experimental period which will end in 1980. There are stringent safeguards to make sure the experimental services do not depart from 'the doctrine of the Church of England'. A measure needs the approval of parliament. If received it has the force of an Act of Parliament. It is this close relationship between Church Assembly—but since 1970, General Synod—and parliament which causes one to regard the Church's supreme legislative body as an extra-parliamentary ecclesiastical legislative chamber. As a sub-body its powers are limited, as it discovered when the Revised Prayer Book of 1928 was twice rejected by parliament.

What did the Enabling Act achieve? It is an odd Act. It did not draft a constitution for Church Assembly. Convocations did that. Virtually, it recognized the right of the Church to govern itself in all matters where parliamentary sanction was not required and, where it was, it laid down how that sanction was to be obtained. Measures passed by Church Assembly had to be submitted by the Legislative Committee of the Assembly to the Parliamentary Ecclesiastical Committee of both Houses of Parliament. Ultimately, a Measure is laid before both Houses, accompanied by a Report of the Ecclesiastical Committee, and on the passing of a resolution of approval goes to the Queen for assent. What applied to Church Assembly applies to General Synod. No Measure passed by it has any validity without parliamentary approval. It may pass resolutions: they only have moral force. Parliament has not surrendered its ultimate control over the Church, but simply transferred to it the detailed legislative work for which it was no longer fitted and had no time. Of course it has been of enormous benefit to the Church that since 1919 it has been *de facto* the creator of its own legislation. Nevertheless the special role of the state is set out in a clause of the Enabling Act which charges the ecclesiastical committee to look on any Church Assembly Measure in the light of 'the constitutional rights of all His Majesty's subjects'. The Commission's report, *Church and State* (1970), comments significantly about this: 'This phrase has been much discussed, and it is thought to mean the rights of the people of England, and not merely those who take an active part in church affairs or are regular churchgoers, to worship when they wish in their parish churches and to receive the sacraments and ministrations of the clergy. These rights have been upheld in cases in the courts, and they are also guaranteed by the parochial system extending over the whole country and by the obligations involved in the care of souls.'[4]

---

[4] Op. cit. p. 95.

The law does not allow the Church to behave as a voluntary society. What it can do and cannot do, whom it can admit or turn away, are strictly circumscribed by law. Its right to make its own law subject to parliamentary sanction precisely expresses its established but dependent position. That dependence still leaves the appointment of its principal leaders in the hands of the crown. In the case of archbishops and bishops the appointments are still determined by the Appointment of Bishops Act of 1533 which gives all power to the crown, which today is subject of course to the advice of the prime minister. The crown issues a *congé d'élire* to the dean and chapter requiring them to elect the person nominated by the Queen within twelve days. A not dissimilar procedure governs the appointment of deans of cathedrals. Under the Suffragan Bishops Act 1534 a diocesan bishop submits two names to the Queen who by tradition appoints the first. The Queen holds rights of patronage of many important livings—by the lowest estimate of my own Report, some 726 livings, or 6 per cent of the total, are in crown hands.

Reciprocally, the law requires the sovereign to be in communion with the Church of England, to swear to maintain the laws of God, the Protestant reformed religion established by law, to preserve the settlement of the Church of England and its doctrine, worship, discipline and government, and to protect bishops and clergy in their legal rights and privileges. By the Accession Declaration Act, 1910, the sovereign must declare himself a faithful Protestant who will uphold the Protestant succession. An atheist, a Roman Catholic, a Methodist could not in present law ascend to the throne. The coronation itself takes place within the context of a holy eucharist in Westminster Abbey and it is the Archbishop of Canterbury, attended by the Moderator of the General Assembly of the Church of Scotland, the Archbishop of York, the Bishops of London and Winchester, who anoints the sovereign with holy oil and places the crown upon her or his head.

The establishment role of the Church gives her a bench of twenty-four bishops and two archbishops in the House of Lords but debars her ministers from sitting in the Commons—a deliberate decision to prevent crown nominees from creeping into the Commons and creating there a servile clique. And also because, in Convocation, the Church was presumed to have her own legislative chamber having parity with the Commons. The establishment's protection extends to the Church courts. The ecclesiastical courts, stolen from the pope, were established as crown courts with the same standing as civil courts. The Ecclesiastical Jurisdiction Act of 1963—the last in a long line—freed lay persons from their jurisdiction and set up the current procedure. Under these, court proceedings may be taken against bishops and clergy for disciplinary reasons (unbecoming conduct, neglect, doctrine, ritual) or faculty reasons (ceremonial, church order, buildings, dress). At the episcopal level trial is by commissions of bishops appointed by Convocations, with the Dean of Arches presiding, with right of appeal to a review commission appointed by the Crown (three communicant Lords of Appeal and two bishops from the Lords).

For what used to be called the 'inferior' clergy, matters concerning doctrine, ritual and ceremonial go to a new body, the Court of Ecclesiastical Causes Reserved, which the crown appoints, and appeal is to a Commission of Review assisted by episcopal and theological advisers. In cases of clergy conduct, trial is by consistory courts (that is diocesan courts), with appeal only to provincial courts. Faculty proceedings are similarly handled except that in those which do not involve doctrine, ritual or ceremonial appeal may still go as far as the Privy Council. The 1963 Act cleared away a legal jungle worthy of the pen of Dickens in which every diocese had eight or nine courts or tribunals with legal power and every province had at least six. Even though the court system has been rationalized, one notes that church and civil powers both combine to create means by which people (clergy mostly) can be tried for ecclesiastical offences in ecclesiastical courts. It is the price of establishment by statute law. If statute law appears to be broken there must be means to try offenders for the 'crime' or 'offence'. If there are verdicts of guilty there must be 'sentences'. These vary from admonitions to total deprivation of office, status, livelihood—the process of 'defrocking', that is. It is sad that clergy discipline has to be maintained by judicial processes. Churches which are voluntary associations are spared this medievalism. It is not surprising that Church courts are little resorted to and their intimidatory pressure therefore the less felt.

The tight hand of the law shows itself in all the authorized procedures for parochial reorganization and reform. The Pastoral Measure, 1968, a consolidatory measure which embodies a number of proposals from the Paul Report, gives quite considerable powers to the statutory pastoral committee of every diocese. As well as the general supervision of the pastoral arrangements of the diocese it can produce and carry through schemes for the re-organization of designated areas of the diocese and the disposal of redundant churches. A pastoral scheme can involve the creation, whether by union or otherwise of new benefices or parishes and the dissolution of old ones, the redrawing of boundaries and the creation of extra-parochial places. It can establish group and team ministries and in the case of team ministries determine the tenure of the clerical group. Patronage and freehold rights can be withdrawn where the scheme makes this necessary and incumbents compensated for the loss of freehold. Churches made redundant by any scheme are handed over to the consideration of the Advisory Board for Redundant Churches which has to seek a suitable use for the church before advising its demolition, and in any case has to report its activities to the archbishops and indirectly to the Church Commissioners and General Synod. Every diocese has, too, its statutory Redundant Church Uses Committee which reports directly to the Church Commissioners and from which the Commissioners may demand a direct account of the proposals for the disposal of any particular church.

The Church Commissioners have as important a role where the fate of pastoral schemes is concerned. A scheme moves in this way and by statutory authority: the pastoral committee prepares it; it then consults interested parties—incumbents, patrons, parochial church councils, archdeacons and rural deans, local planning authorities—granting interviews where necessary; the scheme, amended or unamended, then goes to the bishop; if he approves it, it goes to the Church Commissioners; they may make amendments and in any case if a redundant church has to be altered or pulled down they must consult the Advisory Board: if all is finally approved the Commissioners now prepare a legal document—a draft pastoral scheme or pastoral order to give effect to the proposals.

Now everything starts again. The scheme or order is submitted to all interested parties inviting written representations within twenty-eight days. If it involves redundant churches the Advisory Board has to be notified and notices inserted in the appropriate newspapers. If the Church Commissioners are of the opinion, representations or no representations, that the scheme should go through they submit it to 'Her Majesty in Council'. The Privy Council publishes the appropriate order. If not a scheme but a pastoral order is concerned the legal document goes to the bishop who applies his seal to it to make it effective. Not all is over yet. 'Any person who has duly made written representations with respect to the scheme may appeal to Her Majesty in Council against the scheme or any provisions thereof by lodging notice of appeal with the Clerk of Privy Council before the expiration of a period of twenty-eight days beginning with the day immediately after the date of the first publication of the notice of the submission of the scheme....'

The Privy Council may order an appeal to be heard by the Judicial Committee of the Privy Council. Her Majesty in Council may allow the appeal and then dismiss the scheme, or dismiss the appeal and confirm the scheme, or do neither and ask for another scheme. If the scheme is returned to the Commissioners they can withdraw the scheme, re-submit it to the Privy Council just as it is, or amend it after the Bishop and Pastoral Committee have seen it again. It takes endless time even if all the Dickensian circumlocutory processes are successfully surmounted and an order has appeared in the London Gazette. But it may have been wrecked on the way, perhaps by one determined individual, who may not have to bear any share of the legal costs. A pastoral committee is naturally reluctant to start a second round for a scheme lost or spoilt on the first round. Consultation, appeals, representations there must be, of course, or we have church management by the backroom boys. But whether they need to be so labyrinthine and tortuous or to land up in the lap of the supreme legal body in the land is open to doubt.

The Privy Council everyone knows. The Church Commissioners on the other hand constitute a collective *éminence grise* behind the Church of England. The Commissioners came into existence in 1948 through the amalgamation of Queen Anne's Bounty and the Ecclesiastical Commissioners. The Commissioners hold, invest and administer the ancient endowments of the Church and distribute the income to the ordained servants of the Church. Every incumbent's salary cheque comes from them and their financial skill determines by and large the level of stipends. Over this they have a good record. Their second function is to act as an administrative body. To some extent how they act is described above in the rigmarole involved over Pastoral Measure schemes. Sufficient to say that no parish is created or dissolved, no church built or demolished, no boundary changed without the approval of the Commissioners.

They draw their authority from parliament where questions could be asked about them but seldom are. They are not responsible to Synod. They must rank as part of a department of state. They submit their annual report to the Home Secretary. They are governed by two Church Commissioners' Measures, 1947 (amended 1964), and 1970. No mere resolution of Synod would be operative against them. They have, nevertheless, an enormous board—all the bishops and archbishops, something like fifteen other clergy, ten laity appointed by Synod and four by Her Majesty, nominees of the archbishop, judge representatives of London, York, and the Universities of Oxford and Cambridge. But effective management is in the hands of the three Church Estate Commissioners, one of whom has to be a member of parliament.

I have not exhausted the legal complications of the Church of England. They are in fact inexhaustible. It is doubtful if any institution in the land is so bound round with legal complications: they determine just about everything from the words of its (authorized) prayers to the ornaments and memorials on the walls of its churches, from the rights of patrons to the coronation oath of the Queen. Perhaps it is best to say that the Church is (institutionally) primarily a legal body watched over by lawyers. If not the whole truth it is not an untruth. Certainly its over-legalization goes along with and stands guard over its over-institutionalization. But there is no one church law on the statute book, creating and defining it (the Act of Uniformity, 1662 comes nearest) but scores and scores of laws, which increase year by year as first Church Assembly expressed, and now General Synod expresses its legislative will. Always, always subject to parliament which may not interfere but has the power to. Indeed, General Synod, at its birth, faced with the *Church and State Report* is having to decide whether it must ask for complete power to determine its own liturgy and for greater power over the appointment of bishops. The legislative dependence of the Church of England is illustrated by the *Church and State Report* itself. It contains as an appendix the draft of a Measure designed to give the Church control over its doctrine and liturgy. A schedule shows that sixteen Acts or Measures ranging over four centuries would have to be repealed in whole or in part to achieve just that.

The Church of England (Worship and Doctrine) Measure, introduced in November 1972 and discussed in the next chapter raises the number of Acts or Measures affected to seventeen. The three Acts of Uniformity, 1548, 1558, 1662 would be almost wholly repealed: this is the measure of the quiet liturgical transformation of the Church of England. The Measure also shifts the emphasis from legislating by Measure to legislating by Canon—a procedure legally simpler which avoids parliamentary complications. Canons go directly to the Sovereign for assent. The new form of clergy assent (footnote, p. 133) also marks the shift of the Church towards greater doctrinal and liturgical freedom.

TWO

The Nature of the Establishment

AT THE November 1972 sessions of the General Synod a Measure[1] was introduced with a clear mandate from 42 dioceses—to give Synod control of the forms of worship of the Church of England and of the lay and clergy forms of assent to the Church's doctrines. In other words, to release parliament of the obligation to legislate on the prayers and declarations of assent of the established Church. The first part of the first clause says:

'It shall be lawful for the General Synod to make provision by canon with respect to worship in the Church of England including provision for empowering the General Synod to approve, amend, continue or discontinue forms of service, but such provision shall ensure that the forms of service contained in the Book of Common Prayer continue to be available for use in any parish or any guild church where it is decided to use them or any of them.'

This constitutes one step towards church autonomy and it springs from the Report of the Archbishops' Commission, *Church and State* (1970), already quoted, the tenth report this century to deal with the establishment and its many unsolved problems. 'We regret we cannot be unanimous', the Commissioners said on the opening page, but 'all of us would welcome some change in the present relationship between Church and state'. Three did not sign the Report, but presented minority reports, and so the Report goes on, 'all but three of us feel that these changes need not, and indeed should not, lead to formal disestablishment'. But those, the majority of the Commissioners who opposed disestablishment, could nevertheless not agree as to the 'special relation' of the Church with the state when it came to the appointment of bishops. All were able to assert that the Church should command its liturgy—and this is a very serious assertion in the light of the legislation at which we have looked in which parliament binds the Church to it through the Book of Common Prayer—but they were not able to agree

---

[1] *Church of England (Worship and Doctrine) (No. 1) Measure.*

that the Church should appoint its own bishops. One group put forward 'Proposal A' the other 'Proposal B'. We are saddled with this clumsiness in attempting to discuss them.

Proposal A (pp. 96 ff.) presents what we may speak of as an insider's point of view of Church–state relationships in the context of the prime minister's crucial role in the appointment of bishops. Of course we recognize that the Church is not quite the sleeping partner it may seem to be in these appointments. Through the work of the Howick Commission (it reported in 1964) a Vacancy-in-See committee is set up in a diocese and convened when a vacancy occurs and its views are made known to the prime minister and to the archbishops. Undoubtedly, then, representations are made, though their exact form is not known. But the final decision on the appointment is in the hands of the prime minister in his advice to the crown. Constitutionally, the advice must be taken. Today, and for long past, it is the prime minister who is the Supremacy. But the nature of the Supremacy is not much changed by that. It is still what was intended in Henry's Submission of the Clergy Act. The Church shall not be allowed to appoint its own hierarchy: to the state alone that power shall belong. The Act was deliberately an instrument to compel the Church to submit to the will of the state, albeit a Christian, even an Anglican state.

In Proposal A the brutal political conflict for the control of the Church is seen in another light, in the light of the state as itself a spiritual entity. It is amplified in a *Note of Dissent* by Sir Timothy Hoare. Government, the Proposal A argument runs, is more than an exercise of power: it is concerned with the whole life of the people, economic, social, cultural and spiritual; with the care of the sick and old, with education, leisure, social justice and compassion. Why not therefore with religion? It is an argument that seems to lean towards the award of totalitarian responsibilities to the state. Proposal A certainly equates the compassionate role of the state with a state religious commitment. 'We believe that this dimension should be recognized and emphasized, and that a divorce between the interests of the Church and the interests of the state would damage both.' It is not far short of the assertion that the state is a religious force, or has a religious dynamic, and that nothing should be done to obscure that or to put difficulties in the way of it, by, say, forcing the state into a secular role. Bellah[2] says much the same about the United States where he speaks of the civil religion of American society—briefly, a belief that American society must be justified by God, is held under God's judgment, is in a covenant relationship with God like Israel marching to the promised land. 'God's own people'

---

[2] Robert N. Bellah, 'Civil Religion in America', *Daedalus*, Cambridge Mass., Winter 1967.

is more then than a vainglorious phrase; it is the definition of a religious position. English society, of which the proper spokesman is the British government, defines its religious position through the Church Establishment.

For such or similar reasons the Proposal A commissioners decided that the appointment of bishops is not a Church affair only, but genuinely a national concern. 'Far more people than Anglicans in a bishop's diocese have a concern in the kind of man he is.'

In any case, the argument goes, the electoral systems of the Church are extremely faulty and not productive of truly democratic results. One can point to a vast 'silent majority' outside its representative system. Those who get elected to church bodies represent one (clericalized) group in society because a series of filters operates to restrict the participation of ordinary people in Church government. In General Synod one occupational group is grossly over-represented—the clergy. Parliament is a much better representative of the national (Christian) will because it can speak for the inarticulate mass of the Christian laity in a way the Church cannot.

Sir Timothy Hoare spells it out in figures: 'At no time since 1930 have the electoral rolls included more than 41 per cent of the confirmed or 16 per cent of the baptized members of the Church. Recent members on the rolls (1968) are about a third below these peaks that is to say, 27 per cent of the confirmed or 9·5 per cent of the baptized. Only a dramatic increase in the number of those signing the rolls can give the Synod an electorate comparable with the wider membership of the Church.'[3]

Support for this view is obtained from the sociological evidence appended to the Report itself—that between 60 and 70 per cent of the population—twenty to thirty million!—is prepared to declare itself Church of England and without distinction of sex, age or class, yet is inadequately or not at all represented in Church government at any level. Hence, 'the crown and the prime minister, acting together, represent the Christian people of England in a way in which the organization of the Church does not'. Again, 'Some of your Commission go farther, and say that the prime minister acts as representative and trustee for the nation, in the discharge of its duties to God and his Church.' This useful empirical evidence is left behind by others who declare a Laudian doctrine of the union of Church and nation, under the crown, and feel, if they do not actually assert, that something close to divinity attends the monarch. But even so, the Proposal A group of the Commission would like more consultation with the Church over prime ministerial appointments to the episcopacy than happens at present. The Proposal B group

[3] *Church and State*, p. 85.

urges a system of election by a small electoral board representative of the Church as a whole and of the individual diocese concerned. The group would also stay with Establishment, which it too values, if not quite as mystically. The Proposal A group sees that the breaking of the crown link over the appointment of bishops is a measure of disestablishment which could ultimately mean 'the severing of the organs of the state from all public connexions with Christianity' and 'a measure of disendowment'. Both of these would entail, they say, damage 'to the effective work of the churches in this country'. Which is what Bentham and his Philosophical Radicals hoped for a century and a half ago, but did not achieve.

I regard the Proposal A as standing very pat upon the insider's point of view that the Church is an immense and venerable institution which has always worked in a certain kind of way as part of the state apparatus and as a participant in, and contributor to, a certain national Christian ethos and that to tamper unnecessarily with its structures and relations is to invite disaster. The insider sense of all this is that any privileges the Church of England may possess over other churches are part of the 'special relation' and therefore deserved. That they may be offensive to other communions and make the Church appear a 'parliament Church' and a bar to ecumenical developments is brushed aside. That the world has moved on since Gladstone and presents a more frightening profile, that the Church—the churches—are in crisis and must regain their souls if they are to be effective again is muted, though not by all members of the Commission. Indeed the Report is quite wise and humble over a number of these issues.

A considerable debate on Crown Appointments took place in General Synod in February 1973 on a resolution by the Dean of Worcester to instruct 'the Standing Committee to bring forward proposals to secure for the Church a more effective share in the making of these [episcopal] and other senior ecclesiastical appointments'. In the debate, Synod was critical of backstairs methods and showed anxiety over the failure to promote good men but to prefer the safe. A radical amendment, from the Earl of March, which substantially argued that 'in any new system of appointments the final choice should . . . rest with the Church' was carried overwhelmingly and moved Synod into the Proposal B camp.

A member of Synod said after the debate, 'Synod is more radical than the establishment' and 'the establishment is being chipped away bit by bit'. And disestablishment was the subject of a remarkable 'Memorandum of Dissent' from Valerie Pitt in the *Church and State Report*. She wrote:

'Although the Commission genuinely intends to devolve responsibility from the state to the Church it preserves intact the legal apparatus of Establishment, and so leaves the state with a real, though no doubt formally exercised power, in the Church's affairs.' With incisive irony she writes, 'Establishment discussion about the Establishment tends to dwell on the "givenness of English life" as though the Elizabethan settlement were a platonic entity, an idea laid up in the mind of God.' But, she says, though the legal relations of Church and state may be tangled and irrational, they are not obscure. All those matters of doctrine and worship, appointment of bishops and so forth debated by the Commission (and over which the statutes are quite clear) are the fruit of the sixteenth century determination to safeguard the Royal Supremacy. The Establishment 'is a legal edifice resting on twin Tudor pillars: the King's power and right to direct and oversee the Church's life; the subject's obligation to attend and maintain the Church "by law established"'. She senses the establishment temper which made Elizabeth I write to an obstructive bishop: 'Proud Prelate, you know what you were before I made you what you are now. If you do not immediately comply with my request, I will unfrock you, by God. Elizabeth.'

What Valerie Pitt makes clear is that the Establishment works at two opposed levels, the personal and the constitutional. At the constitutional level, in the appointment of bishops, the prime minister advises the crown, and the crown has to act on that advice. This is not to say that the crown may not have exercised counter-advice at some point: this is the sovereign's prerogative: but the constitutional proprieties are always carried out and we all know where we are. The Supremacy at the personal level, however, and as an echo of personal Tudor power is a different thing. Here there is no parliamentary intervention, but a monarchical decision, even if it is a decision taken in consultation with the Church itself. Valerie Pitt instances the appointment of suffragan bishops by the crown. The diocesan bishop concerned submits two names. By convention the prime minister endorses the first name. Here parliamentary intervention is a mere formality, no more than a process of taking note in a direct relationship between crown and bishop. Perhaps this is slender evidence: a more formidable example concerns the Revised Canon Law, already discussed. This went straight to the Queen for royal assent in 1969 because this was the procedure laid down in Statute Law and operated on the last occasion the canons were revised in 1603.

Why this procedure operated in the seventeenth century is no mystery. It derived from the ideal of Church and state relations which was at the basis of Reformation theory in Henry VIII's time. The king stood then on different twin pillars from those mentioned by Valerie Pitt. On the one side parliament, uniting and speaking for all civil authorities and secular affairs, and on the other Convocations in charge of the spiritualities, each theoretically equal legislative bodies, each with direct access to the sovereign whose assent was required for all their legislative acts. But history took over and parliament grew while Convocations diminished and the more the sovereign chose to act, or was compelled by circumstances to act, through parliament, the more he became not king, but first king-in-parliament and then constitutional monarch subject to parliament, and thus parliament usurped that supremacy over the Church which was at first entirely the personal royal prerogative. This is the theme of a brilliant little book by Professor Peter Hinchliff called *The One-Sided Reciprocity.*[4] The reason why the Revised Canons went direct to the Queen in 1969 was because, since nothing had happened to the canons since 1603, parliament had overlooked this possible breach in its constitutional position as the only source of access to the crown in matters of law. And over the submission of the revised canons there was, Valerie Pitt points out, the personal intervention of the sovereign herself. 'Two Canons, that on the marriage of the unbaptized and that on the seal of the confessional were discreetly withdrawn from the code presented for the Royal Assent because it was intimated that they were unlikely to get it.'

The special point of Valerie Pitt's argument is this: the more radical of the Church and State Commission's proposals (Proposal B on crown appointments) that 'the part of the prime minister should cease, and that the Electoral Board should elect the bishop, and present his name directly to the sovereign' leads the Church back to the point where the sovereign once again would exercise the personal supremacy last exercised by the Stuart dynasty. Parliament, by surrendering control over the liturgy and by ceasing to exercise through the prime minister its right to appoint to the episcopacy, will then have withdrawn from the 'special relation'. Supremacy will be exercised directly by the sovereign herself on those occasions that the Church's representations require it. It may be exercised purely formally, just as it is now in so many parliamentary matters. But it could be exercised personally, idiosyncratically, and this surely is Valerie Pitt's point. Or else parliamentary control could be asserted indirectly—if the prime minister chose to tender advice to the sovereign on ecclesiastical affairs—over acceptance of a new Prayer Book, or the appointment of Y or Z to the episcopacy, for example. He could not be restrained by any outside power, nor could his advice be rejected. No one could stop him. It would be his constitutional right or duty.[5] Statute could not restrain Parliament in the exercise

---

[4] SPCK, London 1966. According to Dr Hinchliff, the Tudor settlement was 'a deliberate and self-conscious attempt to create a relationship, enshrined in legislation, which was advertised as being in theory an equal partnership. In creating this partnership the state took the initiative. . . . And once the state had acted in this fashion, the projected partnership ceased to exist . . . after 1559 parliament could, but Convocation could not, undo or alter the settlement' (p. 215).

[5] 'But suppose the board proposed by the Commission should elect some future Dean Swift or Bishop Bell: it has and can have no power to compel a reluctant sovereign to accept its choice, nor could it offer to use the prime minister as an intermediary. Indeed, the prime

of any power it chooses to exercise, because Parliament makes statutes and could always overthrow any restraint it objected to. Restraint of parliament could only be achieved by a change in the constitution and would require a written constitution which defined the powers of parliament and established a supreme court, on the American pattern, to declare illegal any acts of parliament which overstepped its powers. No one imagines that there will be a political devolution in Britain in that direction. All that would be left to restrain parliament in the event of the restoration of personal monarchical supremacy would be precedent. There would be a precedent that the prime minister did not interfere. But precedent depends for its recognition on a certain gentlemanly code in British politics. It is important, but it may not last for ever.

Of course, all the difficulties which could present themselves over the appointment of bishops and on which the Commission has not agreed to ask for absolute autonomy, could arise over the liturgy, on which it has. Thoughtful and honest though the Report is, Valerie Pitt's Note of Dissent demolishes it by its clear-sightedness. Any modification of the Establishment one can contemplate, or which the Report proposes, still leaves the Church in the state of submission to the secular powers demanded by the Act of 1533, and therefore shorn of the autonomy necessary to an institution which by its nature and origin must swear to 'the absolute claim of Christ to the allegiance of his Church'.

Valerie Pitt therefore proposes the dismantling of the legal apparatus of the Royal Supremacy so as to give the Church of England the status of all other British churches, with the exception of the Church of Scotland.[6] To achieve this the following acts would have to be repealed:

---

minister might himself be an obstacle; for whether the Church's nomination is made direct to the sovereign or by convention, through the prime minister, it is clear that no sovereign could appoint a bishop who, though chosen by the Church, was unacceptable to the government of the day at least, not while the Church remains established' op. cit. p. 71.

[6] The *Church and State Report* summarizes the quasi-established situation of the Church of Scotland in Appendix E, p. 121. It says: 'The constitution of the Church of Scotland has been ratified and confirmed, rather than conferred, by the state, and all Statutes, Acts, Canons, etc., inconsistent with the constitution and powers conferred and recognized by the Act of 1592 have been repealed by it. Adhering to the substance of the faith of the Reformed Churches, and to the presbyterian form of church government, the Church has a right to:
(1) frame its subordinate standards;
(2) constitute its own courts;
(3) legislate and judge in all matters of doctrine, worship and discipline, membership and office;
(4) appoint its agents and their spheres of service;
(5) alter its own constitution within prescribed limits and in accordance with prescribed procedure.
The authority and power of the Courts of the Realm is fully recognized in matters of property and civil right.
The patronage system was reformed by the Church Patronage Act of 1874 which... declared all rights of appointment to be vested in the congregations of vacant churches and parishes, subject to Regulations of General Assembly...'

The Submission of the Clergy Act 1533, which deals with the Royal Assent to Canons: *The Appointment of Bishops Act 1533, The Suffragan Bishops Act 1534, The Suffragan Nominations Act 1888, The Act of Supremacy 1558, The Clerical Subscriptions Act 1865*, and *The Acts of Uniformity*.

Valerie Pitt accepts the logic of her radical proposals. She thinks it is for the nation to decide whether the Church, as a community within the community, should have episcopal seats in the House of Lords. The Church has no more right to them than other communities. She would like the ceremony of episcopal homage (the kissing of hands) to go and sees no point in the oath of allegiance to the crown taken by beneficed Anglican clergymen but not required of ordinary citizens. 'Christian ministers are lieges of Christ, the servants of peace, not the military vassals of a feudal sovereign.' For the rest she stands with the proposals of the Commission for the Church's control of its worship and doctrine and for the election of bishops by an electoral board (made by the Proposal B group) 'with the proviso that the bishop elect should be presented to his diocesan synod so that they may formally receive him as their father in God'. She makes a characteristic demand, too, for an inquiry into the work and powers of the Church Commissioners to find ways to make 'the corporation' directly answerable to the Church of England. What kind of oddity the Church Commissioners is, even within the framework of such a legal oddity as the Church of England by Law Established, I have already explained. It is a part of the mystification, if not the mystery, of the Church.

THREE

How the Church is Governed

IN AN earlier chapter I pointed to the shocked reaction of the Church towards autonomy when, in the thirties of the last century, the state moved towards impartiality in religious matters. Church leaders saw in the repeal of the Test Acts a threat to the establishment status, even a betrayal of it. If the state was no longer to be trusted to maintain the 'special relation' then the Church had to revive its traditional forms of government.

The *Church and State Report* gives a list of events, Acts and Measures, which signpost the steady and consistent progress of the Church towards control of its own affairs. It is important to reproduce it for it charts the progress of more than a century.

'1852 The Convocation of Canterbury resumed debate.

1861 The Convocation of York resumed debate.

1866 First diocesan conference.

1885 House of Laity attached to the Canterbury Convocation.

1892 House of Laity attached to York Convocation.

1870–1903 Development of parochial church councils.

1904 First meetings of Representative Church Council, combining both Convocations and House of Laity.

1919 Representative Church council is turned into National Assembly of Church of England (Church Assembly) and given the right to pass Measures which with the assent of Parliament have statutory force. Parochial church councils made compulsory.

1947 Process of revising the Canons (begun), substantially completed 1967.

1963 Ecclesiastical Jurisdiction Measure removes the highest court of appeal and substitutes a court of appeal in cases of doctrine and ritual devised by the Church Assembly.

1965 Alternative and Other Services Measure permits Convocations and House of Laity to sanction (for an experimental period ...) new forms of service.

123

1969 Synodical Government Measure reconstructs representative system in parishes, rural deaneries, and dioceses, and associates House of Laity with Convocations in all the work of the Church, including doctrine and liturgy.'[1]

Perhaps one should first make clear the difference between the Church Assembly system of central government and the new synodical form. Assembly government was essentially bi-cameral or even tri-cameral. Not, however, bi-cameral in the traditional parliamentary manner of Commons and Lords, with the Lower House having the power and the Upper serving as a revising and delaying body, but bi-cameral in the sense of two sorts of legislative bodies, Assembly and Convocations, directed at different legislative ends and responsible to different electorates; one might almost say, belonging to different worlds. 'One system, exclusively clerical in membership, is concerned with the *doctrines, beliefs and practices* of the Church. The diocesan synod[2] is the local assembly, and above it is the synod of the province, consisting of the Upper and Lower Houses of the Convocations of Canterbury and York respectively. The Convocations of the two provinces can combine to form a national synod of the Church of England.' So Guy Mayfield succinctly explained it.[3]

Dr Walter Matthews, in his *Memories and Meanings*,[4] speaks with affectionate ridicule of the antiquated procedures of Convocation in his days as prolocutor (speaker) of the Lower House. The archbishop controlled the order of business and the Upper House, over which he presided, sent matters for debate down to the Lower House, which then had to drop everything to attend to the episcopal message. When the Upper House wished to communicate with the Lower House, they did so verbally.

'The prolocutor would be summoned to attend His Grace and their Lordships where they were assembled. . . . The effect of this was to hold up progress in the Lower House because, though they could go on debating, no motion could be put to the vote until our return from the Bishops' House. . . . When the ostiary (doorkeeper) ushered us into the meeting of the Upper House, we found the Archbishop and bishops all in canonical dress, sitting at a long table with the Archbishop at the head. He and the bishops remained seated all the time and we remained standing. His Grace the President delivered his instructions and communicated the results of the debates in the Upper House. As I was standing, dressed in cassock, doctor's gown

---

[1] Op. cit. p. 14.
[2] A purely *clergy* synod in this case of course, which describes the situation before the introduction of synodical government.
[3] *The Church of England: its members and its business*, OUP, Oxford 1958, p. 121.
[4] Hodder, London 1969, particularly Chapter 15, 'Convocation'.

and bands, I could not make any notes and had to trust in the memories of my companions.... I am ready to admit that on these occasions I was nearer to Presbyterianism than usual and to their principle of "the parity of ministers".'[5]

In this grave and archaic way the doctrines and disciplines of the Church were maintained or not, as the case might be, by Convocations. The Church Assembly, on the other hand, functioned like parliament under a Speaker who was one of the archbishops. Its tasks were primarily legislative, legal, financial and administrative (as a legislative body subordinate to parliament). As its lay basis it had the statutory parochial church councils, the ruri-decanal and diocesan conferences. Lay members of the parochial church councils were elected from those on the electoral roll of the parish. One begins therefore with an almost exclusively lay electorate which appointed representatives to ruri-decanal and diocesan conferences. The lay members of the diocesan conference elected members to the House of Laity of Church Assembly. In 1955, according to Guy Mayfield, this total lay electorate was 17,832 distributed over 43 dioceses. Only about 57·6 per cent voted. This method of election was one of the filters which prevented the election of other than members of select, comfortably-off groups to the House of Laity. It is generally agreed that lay members of the Assembly were drawn from the retired, the wealthy, the wives of clergy, officials, and others who could afford the expense and the time. The proposal of the Selborne Committee on *Church and State* (1916) that 'A certain number of wage-earners' representatives—not less than 5 per cent of the lay members of the Conference—should be selected by the Committee of each Diocesan Conference, and be eligible equally with other members of the Diocesan Conference for election to the House of Laymen,'[6] was stillborn. Perhaps it was as well that the Church of England was unable to exhibit its tame working men at Church Assembly as Conservative conferences once had the habit of parading Tory trade unionists. The idea was well-meaning but patronizing and its five per cent 'quota' pathetic.

The clerical houses of Church Assembly, however, consisted exactly of the Upper and Lower House of Convocation of Canterbury and York. Convocations therefore, just as they were, were married to a new House of Laity to create Church Assembly. And, of course, it was Convocations which drew up the constitution. But as Professor Eberhard Wedell has pointed out[7] even Convocations after the 1919 reforms failed to be very representative of the inferior clergy. Canterbury Lower House had 89 *ex officio* to 71 elected. Two unrepresentative Convocations

---

[5] Op. cit. pp. 302–3.

[6] Op. cit. p. 44.

[7] *The Reform of Church Government*, Prism Pamphlet 20, 1965.

combined with one unrepresentative House of Laity to form one representative Church Assembly! An unwieldy one too, for it had 746 members, more than the House of Commons and one in which, in any case, 15,000 clergy had roughly the same representation as 2,500,000 lay people. There was a built in balance of power. Houses could elect to vote separately on any issue. A negative vote of *one* House could extinguish a Measure or anything else proposed.

The Church Assembly suffered other defects. The Church of England functions by parishes, not by deanery or diocesan synods, and not only in the legal sense, for it is only at parish level that members meet frequently and come together at least weekly in worship and fellowship. But parishes were not themselves directly represented on Church Assembly either by clergy or laity. If they received reports even, it would often be at second or third hand. About 700 clergy or lay members distributed around 12,000 or so parishes meant in round figures one Assembly representative to every seventeen parishes. The parishes without representation would year in year out hear little of Church Assembly except from what appeared in the press or on the occasions when the parson wanted to damn it from the pulpit. What would be the occasions for which it might be damned? Guy Mayfield in *The Church of England* (p. 128) let one cat out of the bag. 'In its early days the Church Assembly tended to legislate with the enthusiasm of a child playing with a new toy. Underlying many of its early measures was a desire to weaken the freehold status of the clergy in order to make it easier for the bishops to deal with the few cases of lazy or unseemly clergymen. This untutored phase has now passed but it lasted long enough for the Church Assembly to fail to win popular support among the parochial clergy.'

The implication is clear. Church Assembly was acceptable so long as it did not actually try to govern. One understands Guy Mayfield's caustic remark 'The Church of England Assembly may not have alienated the parochial clergy, for that implies that it once held their sympathies'.

Of course, there is an issue of great importance wrapped up in the distrust of, or hostility to, Church Assembly by the parish clergy, and that is their attitude to central authority of an impersonal kind. The list of events quoted from the *Church and State Report 1970* shows the Church moving with the inevitability of a slow historical landslide towards self-government. But, however democratic the processes of government, there have to be administrators to execute decisions and departments to service the legislature. There has to be a degree of centralization and efficient organization, by someone somewhere. To the hostile, this is simply bureaucracy, in its pejorative sense. Side by side, therefore, with the movement towards autonomy there has been equally inevitably an unwillingness to foot the political bill because this meant an increase in centralization and the emergence of new, dark powers —committees, commissions and faceless secretaries in back rooms only to be seen, if ever, by appointment. This opposition arose not only from a detestation of bureaucracy but from another consideration altogether—the clergy did not feel themselves 'governed' by Church Assembly but by their bishops. And in some degree the freehold and Convocations were a protection against *Them*! We are back indeed to the primacy of the parish and to the fact that the clergy mistrusted all institutions except parochial ones. But there is also a conflict of ideology. To those who administered the complex organization of the Church, centralization appeared inevitable and they did not think of efficient administration as hated bureaucracy. To those little concerned—rural divines, cathedral clergy, university professors, high churchmen—'their emphasis was not on the articulation of the church system with society, but on the articulation of the system with the supernatural which acted through the system'.[8] And such an emphasis made central 'interference' appear a presumption, if not something positively destructive. Then too a central administration, and its governing assembly had to be in *London*, the source, to a Church predominantly rural, of everything that was alien and inimical to the established countryside order! Church Assembly was extra-ecclesiastical, but unlike parliament not *the* government, tolerated as such because this was the accepted price of Establishment, but an anonymous body, held to be unnecessary, interfering, even persecuting.[9] On the other hand, though there is quite a formidable opposition to bishops among the clergy, the relation of a clergyman to his bishop is very direct. He is known to him. He sees him before he is ordained by him, may go on retreat with him, is inducted and licensed by him, has access to him, the 'Boss'. He may dislike this, but understands it in a Church which is episcopal through and through. This direct paternalistic relationship never existed between clergymen and Church Assembly. It could not, in the nature of things.

Which leads us to the point that episcopacy is yet another form of government of the Church of England, indeed the most ancient form, and in a great measure independent of assemblies and synods. Into this, and to the opposition to central bureaucracy, we shall look again. At the moment we must ask—what difference does the new synodical form of government make?

It has to be emphasized that three bodies, the (reformed) Convocations and the House of Laity now become one Synod. The second is that a

---

[8] Kenneth A. Thompson, *Bureaucracy and Church Reform: the Organizational Response of the Church of England to Social Change, 1800–1965*, Clarendon Press, Oxford, 1970, p. 35. Thompson brilliantly exposes the problem.

[9] Though it is early days to be sure about this, General Synod seems less exposed to this resentment.

synod, by historical tradition, is concerned with the doctrine and practices of the Church, previously the reserved powers of (clerical) Convocations. The government of the Church, is therefore, since 1970 in the hands of one chamber with power over the whole range of the Church's life. Not without protest though. The Lower House of the Convocation of York said, in reference to the Synod, 'We cannot think it right that there would be taken from the ordained officers of the Church the power of final veto. We desire to see the final authority of the Church in doctrinal matters vested in the Convocations of Canterbury and York as at present constituted'. And indeed the Convocations continue a shadowy existence with a power of veto! Thus, the Measure declares:

'A provision touching doctrinal formulae or the services or ceremonies of the Church of England or the administration of the sacraments or sacred rites thereof shall, before it is finally approved by the General Synod, be referred to the House of Bishops, and shall be submitted for such final approval in terms proposed by the House of Bishops and not otherwise.

'A provision touching any of the matters aforesaid shall, if the Convocations or either of them or the House of Laity so require, be referred, in the terms proposed by the Bishops for final approval by the General Synod, to the two Convocations sitting separately for their provinces and to the House of Laity; and no provision so referred shall be submitted for final approval by the General Synod unless it has been approved, in the terms so proposed, by each House of the two Convocations sitting as aforesaid and by the House of Laity.'[10]

If this escape clause is used to defeat the will of Synod, Synod will become a broken-backed body, of course. Yet, clergy jealousy of synodical powers notwithstanding, *the will is there* to create the one national body to handle all the problems of policy and doctrine for the Church of England and to act as final authority in the event of disestablishment.

Then too, the body is smaller—543 members compared to an inflated Church Assembly of 746—and its houses do not sit in separate blocks. Its chairman or moderator does not have to be one of the archbishops, who are left free therefore to lead the chamber rather than to discipline it as a species of 'Speaker'. Its third meeting was outside London—at York University in the Summer of 1971. It might develop the ethos and the will to give a new kind of leadership. Time will show.[11] The issues before it are formidable. They include Church and state relations,

---

[10] *Synodical Measure, 1969*, Sch. 2, Sec. 7 (1), (2), p. 12.

[11] See Margaret Duggan, 'Synod Grows Up', *Church Times*, 18 February 1972, in which the work of the February 1972 Synod is looked at refreshingly and critically by a member who is also an able journalist.

deployment, liturgical revision, the whole financial future, as immediate issues. And who knows what spectres wait in the wings?

A further difference between Assembly rule and Synod rule arises out of the new local structures the Synodical Measure sets up. The old diffuse, large and cumbrous diocesan conferences have gone. They were often simply platforms for episcopal policy, rubber-stamping decisions made elsewhere, too uncomfortable and brief for proper debate, their time often taken up by invited speakers. They were, in a sense, exhibition pieces.

The new diocesan synods—between 150 and 250 members—are small enough to be debating chambers. They may discuss any matters relating to the Church. They are not limited simply to the concerns of the diocese. The General Synod refers matters to them for opinion or decision. Upon them falls the responsibility for the application of many General Synodical decisions to the diocese. The electorate for the lay members of the diocesan synod consists of the lay members of the deanery synods (formerly ruri-decanal conferences). Precisely as General Synod refers business to the Diocesan Synod, so that body in its turn refers business to the Deanery Synods, on which each parish in the deanery is represented. The clerical and lay members of the diocesan synods are elected by the clerical and lay members respectively of the deanery synods. There is thus intended a synodical devolution right down to the Parochial Church Council which is a statutory body, elected by the members whose names are on the Church Electoral Roll attending the annual, statutory Parish Meeting. There is therefore, 'if it works, a channel of communication, even a chain of command. Ever menacing, however, is the time lag the structure dictates, which could defuse the most burning issues—the movement of reports and resolutions up and down the chain is endlessly time-consuming. General Synod meets only three or four times a year. Diocesan Synods usually twice or three times a year, and Deanery Synods quarterly at least. This could be costly in terms of administration and democratic effectiveness. And where, on the lay side, all is voluntary and comes out of the time of busy people, the difficulties in the way of the creation of an articulate and informed lay opinion, able to influence legislation, are immense. Those who have the time for a surfeit of voluntary church activities are not those most representative of the population, or even of that laity which confesses a commitment to the Anglican Church.

Though a legislative body modelled in its own legalities on the House of Commons, the General Synod does not function like it. There is no official 'government' and 'opposition'. There is just no parallel at all to a legislative programme proceeding from a policy-making cabinet whose proceedings are secret. Even though there is an acute party division in the Church at large, which deeply influences Synod, it is not reflected in the way Synod runs itself. It is true that Synod has a Standing

Committee which is charged, among other things, with co-ordinating all work done in the Synod's name; with keeping under review the overall needs of the Church and with making proposals to the Synod for such action as seems appropriate; with advising on policy and priorities. But it is impeded from exercising a cabinet form of government by the manner of its appointment. It has an elected and an ex-officio group. The ex-officio group consists of the two archbishops, the prolocutors of Convocations, the chairman and vice-chairman of the House of Laity and the chairmen of the five principal boards of General Synod and a Church Estates Commissioner. The chairmen of the boards are usually bishops. Eighteen more members—two bishops, eight members of the house of clergy and eight from the house of laity are elected. The laity are thus heavily out-numbered and the solid core of the Committee is constituted by departmental heads who by the nature of things are always present. The weight of what we might call in another context, 'the permanent civil service' is very strong. Of course, in every election, each Church party tries to get the maximum number of its own 'reliables' elected and this operates to produce a stalemate in the Committee. A body so appointed, so balanced between the 'machine' and the Synod, and again balanced between parties, might be appropriate as a revising and delaying chamber but is unsuitable as a policy-making body except where a consensus already exists and it can propose a time-table of priorities. It is more like an agenda committee than a cabinet.

How then does Synod work in default of leadership and/or a policy-making body? In all its ongoing work—at Church House—it operates through boards, councils, committees, all pretty autonomous, some of them with a history which goes back before Church Assembly, some with independent financial resources. All of them report to Synod and receive budget allocations. For new work, for movement forward, Synod depends on the setting up of commissions, which is accomplished by resolution of Synod. Invariably, the reports of commissions are scholarly and thorough and (if they are not paralysed in their conclusions by trying to reach a balance between High and Low Church views) it is from them that Measures usually result, though nothing prevents the individual member from acting on his own. He may not, however, move a Measure himself, but seek through a motion to persuade Synod 'to instruct the Standing Committee or any other committee or body responsible to the Synod to introduce a Measure to give effect to the proposals specified in his motion'.[12]

Any new canon is subject to much the same procedures. Only an effective resolution of Synod can compel the Canon Law Standing

---

[12] *General Synod Standing Orders, 1970,* CIO, p. 28.

Commission to introduce a draft of a proposed new canon, apart that is from its own initiatives. It then goes through the stages appropriate to a Measure. When one recalls that Synod must submit certain business to diocesan synods, to the House of Bishops, to the ghostly Convocations for separate decision, that it must handle important financial business, and that it must do this in about twelve days in any given year one readily understands that its agenda is crowded and the individual members feel oppressed by its ponderousness, and ask, time and again, in different ways whether the work of Synod need be so heavy-footed.

It is easier to see the weaknesses of the new synodical structures than to devise better forms. Perhaps these weaknesses derive from the effort through Synod to marry 'popular' with 'professional' government. The House of Laity is a 'popular' chamber, or at least intended to be so though in fact paid church officials and clergy wives get elected to it.[13] But Convocations, the House of Clergy, the House of Bishops, these are bodies of professionals whose influence over Synod and the Church at large is paramount. It is hard to find a parallel to this form of government anywhere else except where a body is entirely devoted to professional interests. The British Medical Council or a trade union, spring to mind. One understands the point Sir Timothy Hoare made about the unrepresentative nature of Church government in the *Church and State Report*. But then a church is a peculiar institution anyway in which the status of its ministers can never be only that of the paid, professional servants of a supreme body. They are who they are and where they are because they have been given authority over the Church. That authority has been awarded them in the Church of England by its bishops who do not have to ask anyone for permission to do so. No role exists for the laity here as yet. And it is to the bishops the clergy look as the final authority over them.

I think it is true to say that it is in the direction of 'popular' government, rather than government by a professional élite that the Church has been moving since Convocations were (temporarily) given Houses of Laity in the middle nineteenth century. But popular government depends on the will of the populace to interest itself in government at a serious level and with fidelity and constancy through the years: not notable virtues in our times. The risks involved in popular government are those the Church seems commanded to make as the State retreats from its Reformation role. But in that case what does it do with its bishops? The episcopacy also constitute a government of the Church which of its nature is not 'popular' government.

---

[13] Cf. what was said about the clericalized laity p. 91 et seq. and p. 117.

FOUR

The Episcopacy

THE Church of England following the historic tradition is, of course, divided into dioceses. There are 43 dioceses in the provinces of Canterbury and York and because each archbishop has a diocese, 41 bishops and 2 archbishops. Every diocese is divided into rural deaneries and every deanery into parishes. This would seem to be an acceptable description of the territorial organization, or local government of the Church of England. But is is quite inadequate. To begin with, rural deaneries are not 'divided into' parishes: parishes are grouped into deaneries: the parish is primary. Then, strictly, the Church of England is not 'divided into' dioceses—one does not begin with a national Church which now establishes dioceses but with a certain territorial grouping of dioceses which constitutes the Church and adopts synodical forms to discipline and protect itself. In other words, we do not begin with a national association with decentralizes itself through branches but with an historic institution in which two forms have always had primacy, the parish and the diocese and in which therefore two men have always played a key role, the parish priest and the bishop.

We have already seen that though the bishop and parish priest differ enormously in status, they play the same role. The bishop is a priest, the first priest in his diocese and the parish priest exercises his ministry for the bishop and only with the bishop's authority. However, only the bishop has full priestly powers.[1]

The parish priest has the local care of souls. In his parish church he must provide, by statute, open morning prayer and evensong on Sunday while he himself openly or privately must say matins and evensong daily. He will celebrate Holy Communion at least once each Sunday and preach at least twice and provide such weekday and festival services as he thinks fit. He will promote and perhaps run a Sunday School. He will

---

[1] Guy Mayfield puts it rather unfortunately: 'The Bishop of the diocese is the normal minister of the Church, because only he can supply the entirety of the Church's ministrations while priests and deacons with their lesser powers may be regarded as subnormal ministers'. *The Church of England*, p. 30.

baptize, marry and bury those who request or require it and prepare candidates for confirmation. He must keep an electoral roll, see that the parish meeting and parochial church council are summoned, and chair them, keep watch on the church accounts, and on the church fabric and interior and ornaments and keep the graveyard tidy. He is expected to visit the sick and bring them consolation and communion. He will probably visit his parishioners. Beyond that his work will ramify almost as he pleases, for he is a free agent. He may lock himself in his study or cultivate his glebe or his garden or enter as fully as any man into teaching or local political or social work, youth work, or work with the satellite organizations of the church.

Nevertheless he is a man under authority. Assent was required to the Thirty-nine Articles, the Book of Common Prayer, the Ordinal, to testify to his obedience to the law concerning the Church of England. He must take an oath to the crown.[2] At his institution he receives his cure from the bishop. He is handed the instrument of institution with its episcopal seal with the words, 'Receive this care of souls which is both thine and mine'. The induction which follows immediately is more down to earth. It is the archdeacon, very much the business man or manager of a diocesan area, who hands the new incumbent the key of the church and says to him, 'I do induct thee into the real, actual and corporal possession of the Rectory (Vicarage) and Parish of Blank, with all the rights, members, and appurtenances there unto belonging'. The incumbent may have a 'mine and thine' care, but the appurtenances, the benefice are his alone and not the bishop's. Unless he commits a crime or defaults from his duties he cannot be deprived of them. He is no longer in fact as absolutely the bishop's man as episcopal theory would have us assume. His entrenched, legally safeguarded position, reflects the primacy of the parish in the ecclesiastical structure. It is not an accident, for there the incumbent is officially 'The Church'.

---

[2] In the liturgical reforms, and reforms 'with respect to the obligations and forms of assent or subscription to the doctrine of the Church of England and the interpretations of that doctrine' (as the preamble to *Church of England (Worship and Doctrine) (No. 2) Measure* puts it), before the General Synod in the seventies, the loyal oath remains unchanged. But a new Declaration of Assent has been drafted. The old one, Canon C15 of the revised Canons of 1969, bluntly demanded 'assent to the Thirty-nine Articles of Religion, and to the Book of Common Prayer and of the Ordering of Bishops, Priests and Deacons'. The new assent after a preface which declares the Church's unity in faith with the other Christians in all parts of the world, mentions 'her historic formularies—the Thirty-nine Articles of Religion, the Book of Common Prayer', etc., almost in passing as part of her witness and demands only of the minister—his affirmation of loyalty 'to this inheritance of faith'—'I, A.B., do so affirm, and accordingly declare my belief in the faith which is revealed in the Holy Scriptures and set forth in the catholic creeds and to which the historic formularies of the Church of England bear witness; and in public prayer and administration of the sacrament, I will use only the forms of service which are authorised or allowed by Canon.' This is the Assent (G.S.116a) accepted by July 1973 General Synod, but subject to final revision. So, the sun of the Thirty-nine Articles sets! What a change is there.

Bishop

Nevertheless, the completeness of the priesthood is to be found only in the bishop. He has the power to do all that the parish priest does and much more that the parish priest may not do. He is responsible for order and jurisdiction. In diocesan synod he is a separate 'House' or 'authority' the consent of which is necessary to conference decisions, but he may withdraw from diocesan synod any matters which belong to his personal episcopacy.[3]

The diocesan bishop does not bear the same relation to his archbishop as a parish priest does to his ordinary. He is not the archbishop's man, but the crown's appointment. An archbishop is *'primus inter pares'*. He has a few legal powers not possessed by the diocesan. The Archbishop of Canterbury, 'Primate of All England', has the right to crown the Sovereign; by tradition rather than right, the Archbishop of York, 'Primate of England', crowns the Queen's consort. The duties of the Archbishop of Canterbury outside his diocesan role in Canterbury, are presidential, advisory, counselling. Pre-eminently he is expected to be a scholar and spiritual leader. But the times demand good administrators too and the growth of the world Anglican Communion imposes a certain world status on him. Nothing, all the same, makes him an Anglican pope. The powers over the Church which Henry VIII and his successors stripped from the pope were usurped by the crown not the archbishops. It was very convenient to them that England, by historical accident, was divided between two Church provinces where it might have been one.

The Church had a history of democratic procedures in its primitive days. The followers of Jesus met at Pentecost to elect a successor to Judas. The Christians of Hippo made Augustine bishop by popular acclaim. Early Christian communities had a say in the appointment of their leaders and officers. The Letters Paul addressed to the churches of Asia Minor reveal the existence of quite stubborn, self-willed Christian fellowships not easily persuaded to surrender their idiosyncratic inter-pretations of Christianity and to accept a discipline from outside. The conflict between the primitive Pauline and the Petrine churches shows that the Church did not begin as a disciplined unity. In a rough and ready way majority opinion was locally decisive. The prolonged and angry early Councils tell how bitter was the battle to arrive at satisfactory doctrines consistent with the known facts of the life and teaching of

---

[3] One of the functions which the Synodical Measure entrusts to the Diocesan Synod is 'to advise the bishop on any matters on which he may consult the synod'. As to diocesan synodical procedure, all questions before it are decided by the votes of all the members sitting together, the assent of the three houses, clergy, laity and bishop 'being presumed, unless ten members present demand that a separate vote of each of the houses of clergy and laity be taken, or unless the bishop requires his distinct opinion to be rendered.' (Sch. 3, Sec. 28 (1) (f).) Thus each house has a veto, the bishop included, which could override the view of the other two houses.

Jesus. The monarchical form of the papacy does not come in until the Constantinian settlement, but from then on more and more apes the imperial style. The pope becomes '*pontifex maximus*' as were the emperors before him. In the Eastern Empire pope and emperor become one. The imperial style greatly suited the feudal ideology. The pope, the vicar of Christ on earth, drew his authority from God, enjoyed God's power; he owed obedience upwards to God not downwards to the priests or the commons who attended church. To them he was authority: from them he expected and received submission. In this doctrine of power flowing downwards there was no room for democratic practice. The bishop was 'pope' in relation to those in his diocese beneath him: the priest the 'pope' of his parish. There was no point in the chain of command downwards and of fealty upwards where processes of criticism or assent might operate, anymore than in a military system. (Of course, the feudal system *was* a military system.)

Unless the feudal ideology and with it the monarchical model of the Church are rejected *ideologically*—and not just grumbled about or made fun of as Erasmus did in his *Praise of Folly*—then a system so tight-jointed is bound to grow in strength by the discipline it feeds on. If the theory of the Church is that authority is at the top then all authority is likely to accumulate there. One logical result is papal infallibility. If the pope is not to be infallible on basic matters of doctrine then the processes of criticism and debate must begin. The joints have to be loosened. It is happening now in the Roman Church, with consequences which cannot yet be foreseen but which must end in its de-feudalization.

What happened in the explosion of the Reformation was of course the rejection of the feudal ideology by reformed Churches generally and the assertion of the rights of the congregation as, with its elders and presbyters, the true Church, on the primitive model. This re-assertion of the Church as a popular entity—as being in an existential sense the Church of God here and now in a worshipping congregation and its own authority—was perhaps only pressed to a logical conclusion in Congregationalism. Elsewhere it turned out, 'new Presbyter is but old Priest writ large'. Yet what was important was not so much the degree of institutional success as the rejection of the feudal inheritance in the reformed churches. The Geneva bankers, the Hanseatic ship owners, the merchants of the City of London who had by-passed feudalism in their lives were ready to reject it in their religion.

The English, typically, went their own way. The English Church describes itself as 'Catholic and Reformed'. A more accurate description might very well be 'Protestant and unreformed'. Henry VIII broke the fealty of Church and crown to Rome but usurped the authority over the Church which the pope had enjoyed. True, he disposed of the monasteries to his friends but this was not intended to break the disciplinary chain the feudal Church had established. Of course, that chain reached the populace, which had to be religiously disciplined. The battles over uniformity were just about that—how to get people to church to worship in the prescribed manner in seemly fashion, without riot and disorder. The parish priest was the king pin in the effort. And he was a man under the monarchical authority of the 'defender of the faith' to whom he swore allegiance. At the same time he was a member of an élite charged with the maintenance of an institution, the preservation and propagation of its doctrines, the instruction and discipline of its laity. There was, therefore, a clean division between the layman and the man in holy orders. The men in holy orders *were* the Church and in a sense then in which it was inconceivable (until the Reformation) that the laity could be the Church.

While reformed Churches generally moved over towards the greater authority of congregations and their ideological integration into the body of the Church, the Church of England remained unreformed. The hierarchical structure was unchanged. The suspension Convocations removed the only synodical form which could keep the bishops in check, and so strengthened the monarchical episcopacy and took away the representative voice of the inferior clergy. The consultative system was put in a deep freeze.

We may depict the Church of England therefore as a double system, as on the one hand a hieratic system, corporately owning vast wealth in buildings, land and endowments (most unequally distributed among the members) and its clergy, under a chain of command which begins with the crown, set aside from common people and marked as an élite by ordination, powers of ownership and control, ideology and even uniform: in a word 'the cloth'. On the other side the mass of the faithful laity: not 'the Church' finally, but as indispensable to it as voters are to a candidate for Parliament.

Without doubt, however, there is a crisis in the episcopacy which takes many forms not easy to describe. At one, of course, we have looked—whether the crown or the Church in independence should appoint bishops. It is not necessary to go over that again except to say that, autonomy apart, the *form* of appointment does make a difference to the quality of the episcopacy. Apologists for the crown appointment system defend it on the grounds that it enables outstanding men to be mitred where synods would have chosen only safe, middle-of-the-road men. They point to Gore, Barnes, Hensley Henson, Temple and similar outstanding men as appointments a diocesan conference would not have made. A Conservative prime minister, they say, could appoint a socialist Mervyn Stockwood where no one else would have done. It is debatable, however. The obvious man to succeed William Temple during the war was Bishop Bell of Chichester. Given the choice it is reasonable to suppose that the Church would have elected him. For political reasons, Winston Churchill would not have him. The political ban on the obvious man could come down again if ever Church and state clashed over social policies. In the postwar years the bench has been filled with good administrators, with safe elderly men, in fact. One can think of only a few outstanding appointments. One obvious difficulty is that the Church has no career structure. Only 43 priests could at any one moment be diocesan bishops: there are 18,000 clergy approximately. An incumbency is top of the ladder for most clergy. The elaborate sifting processes must favour the middle-of-the-road men when it comes to promotion. Nevertheless one recalls so many outstanding men who have been overlooked, and asks why? There may be good reasons, but the procedures are so secret one can never know.

The other crises I am thinking of would arise whatever the nature and capacity of the bench. I would name three—the relation of episcopal authority to synodical authority; the size of a bishop's pastoral charge; the nature of the episcope itself.

As to the first, the episcopacy as it has come down to us from pre- Reformation times, and surviving all Presbyterian plots against it, is monarchical. Its ethos survives in the triumphalist service of installation and enthronement of a new Bishop, who is shown forth with fanfare as a great lord taking possession of his see and threatening the Church's and the Sovereign's enemies. It is a feudal occasion. It does not work like that in practice: all is much humbler. But the sense of the bishop as the Lord with the last word in his diocese and as there with authority over, rather than from, his clergy and laity remains. The plans and projects of his diocesan boards and committees do not usually survive his opposition. With his support synodical projects flourish, but without it they may wither. He is by nature of his office an authoritarian figure.

This does not place him in permanent opposition to his clergy or laity or to General Synod and all its works. Rather the contrary. It would be true to say that his clergy and laity expect him to act with authority and are reluctant to push opposition to him too far. Among the clergy there is a traditional distrust of—or apprehension about—an individual bishop (lest he carry his authority too far) together with approval of the office and unwillingness to see it devolve upon a committee. It would be untrue to place the bishop in opposition to General Synod. The bishops form a House of Synod and could block anything they disapproved there. Matters the Synod itself cannot solve are sometimes referred to them. The bishops meet regularly in conference to concert policy and do not publish their minutes. It is open to them, as to other members, to use Synod to promote policies. Moreover, bishops usually chair the boards, councils and commissions of General Synod. They are, therefore, more intimately concerned with the day-to-day running of the national Church than any other body, and the most well informed, for they can see more easily than most the local consequences of policies stemming from the floor of Synod. And in some ways they constitute the group most concerned to see Synod work, particularly on the lines of establishing uniformity in order, doctrine and clergy discipline. Long experience has shown them that Church disorder multiplies their diocesan difficulties tenfold. It is not that the House of Bishops 'manipulate' Synod as a presidium manipulates a conference—that would be a caricature of the situation. It is the case though that they necessarily value it, and it is more important to them, the supreme professional body, than it is to the clergy or the laity. Whatever then may be said about the 'monarchical' episcopacy and 'popular' government through Synods there is, in the integration of the two, the emergence of an instrument of government which reconciles and advances the power of both. Only the clergy may remain uneasy in this situation, despite their right of veto as a house: what they appear to fear is an alliance of laity and bishops against them: Guy Mayfield voiced these fears in his criticisms of Church Assembly.[4] It goes along with that clergy unease about the laity and disquiet about episcopal powers at which I have looked.

2   The second episcopal problem is the debate about what the proper episcopal charge should be. The two provinces of England have dioceses which differ in population from 245,000 (Hereford, 1970) to 3,695,000 (London, 1970). Even by 1963 figures there were four dioceses and in 1970 five, with over two million population, and in 1970 twelve with populations between one and two million. Today only five dioceses have populations of under 500,000 each. Dioceses tend therefore to be huge. They differ extensively in area. Lincoln consists, at one end of the scale, of 2661 square miles, London of 282. There is no uniformity. The majority of the dioceses are the products of very ancient history: eighteen were founded before the thirteenth century: only ten have been founded in this century. The last great effort at diocesan expansion was in 1926–7. They are certainly not the fruit in general of some contemporary effort at equalization of tasks or of mission efforts to the great conurbations. Of course the number of active, full-time clergy per diocese varies as widely as area and population. London has 952, Oxford approaches 755, Bradford has no more than 170, Sodor and Man, 26. The number of parochial churches and chapels ranges from 861 (Oxford) to 184 (Porstmouth) to 48 (Sodor and Man).

In a survey I conducted among clergy attending courses at St George's House, Windsor,[5] 45 per cent of the clergy answering my questionnaire agreed *very strongly* that dioceses were too large and 33 per cent that there was too much administration, and when it came to ranking the

---

[4] See p. 126 supra.

[5] *Clergy Attitudes*, unpublished. The Survey was conducted among 386 clergy attending courses at St George's House, Windsor between October 1966 and July 1968. 295 filled in the questionnaire.

importance of the duties or work of a bishop the order they proffered turned out as follows:

1. Pastoral oversight of the clergy.
2. Pastoral oversight of the laity.
3. Outspoken leadership in moral and spiritual matters.
4. Exposition of doctrine.
5. Confirmation.
6. Ecclesiastical duties.
7. Scholarship.
8. Administration.
9. Representing the Church on major national and local occasions.
10. Outspoken participation in the political and economic affairs of society.

It is a curiously protective assessment. Perhaps it is not fair to call it inward-looking, but it exhibits a concern for maintaining the steadfastness of the Church as the primary pastoral job while mere administration and extra-ecclesiastical activities are given the lowest preference. Even scholarship takes seventh place. On this research and in the Paul Report research it was pressed on me very sharply in conference and interview with the clergy that the bishop's primary job ought to be pastoral oversight and of the clergy first, and that dioceses were too large to permit this, though in the Windsor research only seventeen per cent agreed *strongly* that bishops were too remote and fifty-nine per cent *disagreed* that he was out of touch. One might conclude that what the bishop does in the diocese for his clergy and laity is strongly approved but that there is not enough of it because administering a large diocese gets in the way!

A caveat could be entered against the clergy attitude because it suggests an ignoble emotional dependence on the bishop by men who find themselves terribly at sea in a secular world which apparently has less and less use for them. Certainly dependence on the bishop goes oddly with the clergy's defence of the freehold (only fourteen per cent of the Windsor clergy wanted to reform the freehold) which, in the majority clerical view, protects them from the encroachments of the bishop and the laity! The primacy of the parish in the Church life suggests anyway that the priest is expected to be his own man, the local leader, teacher, father, source of charisma. Perhaps the bishop should be dealing with his clergy as a general deals with his commanders, not as a comforter but leading them into a battle where he expects them to be men of might and resource! At least let me say that the clergy attitude to the episcopacy, and the clinging to the freehold, suggest a frightened ministry.

There remains the problem of the size of the dioceses. Should they all be subdivided to the point where a bishop will know all his clergy and his principal laity personally? Or should they remain large and related to their historic pasts and associated in some sense with a great civic area? Of course, it is the second type of diocese that we have in the Church of

England already. What is not known is at what point the subdivision of existing dioceses, if it takes place, should stop, at what point a given area and population becomes viable pastorally in the sense that the critics of large dioceses mean this. To subdivide the dioceses until all dioceses had approximately the population of Hereford, for instance, would involve the creation of 150 new dioceses or about 190 in all. Most of them would have to be carved out of the great conurbations and these might prove as socially and civically meaningless as the great urban parishes we already have and do not know how to service or to transform. An unknown number of such new urban dioceses, with a population of between 200,000 and 250,000 of the most alienated to serve, would undoubtedly become client-dioceses, dependent for their very existence on the benefactions of richer sees. Hereford, which we have taken as a model, is perhaps the most rural diocese. The bishop has care over 467 churches and chapels and 166 parochial clergy: but he has 1,670 square miles to cover and must spend a lot of time travelling. Perhaps *this* is still too large for the critics of large dioceses to accept? If we give the 166 clergy 12 or so prominent laymen and women each (and that is not quite five per church) we have a hypothetical figure of 2,000 privileged laity for whom pastoral oversight is asked. If one adds the laity of societies, schools, universities, the hospitals, the prisons, the forces one soon sees that though a bishop of a small diocese may know all his clergy, his outreach to the laity is going to be limited indeed. At the same time, in a small diocese, socially insignificant, the ordinary's outreach to his people through press, radio, television, might prove to be negligible. The point is that we do not know what the ideal size of a diocese is and we should be beginning at the wrong end by seeking to solve the Christian pastoral and mission problems by creating smaller ones on grounds of principle. It is with the parish that we have to begin and while ever we have parishes of between thirty and forty thousand population each run by one incumbent (and not a team) we have not even begun to reform the mission of the church in the great cities and industrial areas. The parish needs to be truly local and identifiable with a living community or a named neighbourhood. The diocese cannot do the neighbourhood job. In any case, standing between the dioceses and the parishes we have the rural deaneries—nearly 800 of them—strongly entrenched now in the system of synodical government. In the Paul Report I urged as eloquently as I could that they should be raised in importance and the rural dean given greater status and authority. I would now say that in the rural deanery the truly local episcope should rest and that it would be better to concentrate on developing this rather than to exhaust the legislative energies of the Church for a decade, and embitter it with local battles, over the reduction of the size of dioceses.

The large diocese plays a key role in establishing the civic and social presence of the Church. A proliferation of small dioceses might destroy that. The social and civic role of the Church might even in cases demand the enlargement of dioceses. It would be reasonable to enlarge the diocese of Portsmouth so that it might cover the great conurbation which now stretches from Porstmouth to Poole Harbour. It would be sensible to extend the diocese of Birmingham to cover Telford New Town, at present straddling across the diocesan boundaries of Hereford and Lichfield, and to give the diocese more of a rural hinterland. It is of great value if a diocese at least covers a *zone humaine*. London, in population the largest diocese, still does not cover the London conurbation: it shares it with, at least, Southwark, Rochester, Chelmsford, Oxford and the Croydon portion of Canterbury diocese. With London so huge there is perhaps not a case for one single diocese to cover it. But there is no case for its fragmentation among several. The nineteenth century proposal for a province of London has much to commend it: but for the Church to speak with one voice in the capital city the provincial would have to be endowed with more authority over his dioceses than the Archbishop of Canterbury or York over theirs. That is why the proposition spoke of suffragan sees under an archbishop truly a metropolitan.

The Archbishop of Canterbury appointed a Commission under Sir John Arbuthnot to study the diocesan boundaries of London and the South East. It reported in 1967.[6] Its terms of reference rather turned it away from the solution of organizational and pastoral problems by the multiplication of very small dioceses. It was instructed to take as a norm a diocesan area which would reach a population of 900,000 or a total of 200 incumbencies—an ideal a little larger than Coventry and a little smaller than Rochester dioceses. But the Commission was instructed to 'take in view an alternative of smaller dioceses including the need for co-operation between them, in the event of the adoption of a general policy of making them smaller'. It had therefore a choice of policies.

The principal interest of an expert report rests in the proposals for greater London, and the Oxford dioceses. It proposed that the diocese of Oxford should be divided into three dioceses—Oxford, Aylesbury and Reading—and that the bishop of each new diocese 'should have the help of one suffragan who should also be an archdeacon'. At the same time it opposed new cathedral establishments for Aylesbury and Reading, but wanted the centralization of certain common activities, financial, educational, for all the Oxford 'group'. For London it proposed five separate radial dioceses, London, Southwark, Barking, Croydon, Kensington. In broad terms London diocese would have been divided into three, Southwark into two, subject to certain other boundary adjustments. It was intended that the dioceses should be autonomous and of

---

[6] *Diocesan Boundaries*, being the Report of the Archbishop's Commission on the Organisation of the Church by Dioceses in London and the South-East of England, 1965/7, CIO 1967.

the same status as all other dioceses but that 'in the Greater London area some functional responsibilities might be made the specialized concern of an "auxiliary" bishop who could act over the whole region' (p. 112). 'Dioceses of the Greater London area must cooperate to the full. They will require individual diocesan conferences, or synods and boards of finance, but those matters which can be most efficiently dealt with jointly should come under a joint administration. A regional council under the chairmanship of the Bishop of London should be set up by statute [with] responsibility for the policy-making necessary to coordinate the Church's work over the whole of the Greater London area' (p. 114).

The Commission therefore, in Oxford and London, proposed what was indeed a new thing—the diocese federated with other dioceses at its birth, by statute. But it shrank, in London, from the idea of a new province, with dioceses federated under the provincial—which was the strict logic of its case. The Report has made no progress because of diocesan opposition. But London diocese has now created suffragan territorial areas in which the suffragan 'is' the bishop—an internal federation, as it were, served by an episcopal team ministry.

Oxford diocese is creating much the same. A Commission of the Diocesan Conference, reporting in 1970, proposed a collegiate structure to run the diocese. 'The Diocese should be administered as four areas, each the responsibility of a bishop. To make this possible the diocesan bishop should agree to delegate to three suffragan bishops as much of his jurisdiction as the law allows, and proclaim that in his own area the suffragan should be responsible in full. Each area bishop should be supported by his own Council and Synod ... [but] the general policy of the diocese including all matters of finance should continue to rest with the diocesan bishop, the Diocesan Bishop's Council and the Diocesan Synod.'[7] Apart from an area around Oxford and Cowley, designated for the Bishop of Oxford, three suffragans would preside over separate territories—the suffragan Bishops of Reading, Buckingham and Dorchester. The Report was accepted and in *Ad Clerum III*, December 1971, the Bishop of Oxford laid down the responsibilities of area bishops. The list is a long one and includes the pastoral care and discipline of the clergy, the appointment of rural deans and of curates, confirmations, institutions, suspensions of presentations and much else. Yet the advantages of centralization are not to be lost to this great and historic area, and it is a sign of the times that Oxford preferred this to partition into three separate dioceses. Interestingly the Report referred to, drew attention to a novel situation on Tees-side, where a new city straddles the diocesan boundary of York and Durham. There the Archbishop of York

---

[7] *The Division of the Diocese*, The Report of the Bishop of Oxford's Working Party, Oxford Diocesan Board of Finance, Jan. 1970, p. 45.

and the Bishop of Durham have granted the suffragan Bishop of Whitby full episcopal authority to act as their plenipotentiary.

Melbourne Diocese, in Australia, had much the same problems. One single diocese covered a city of over two million population and its hinterland. It had an Anglican population of 650,000 covered by 225 parishes. In 1964 the Synod set up a Commission to produce a 'Paul Report for the Diocese of Melbourne'. One of its charges was the problem of episcopal care. The final result of all the deliberations, in which I took part, has been not only the revision of the terms of clergy tenure but the establishment of a team episcopal ministry to serve the diocese under the ordinary (who is the archbishop).

The diocese is now divided into three 'Regions of Episcopal Care' each with its local bishop whose duties and authority are set out in a resolution of Synod.

'The regional Bishop will have the episcopal care and oversight of the parochial clergymen in his region, and, in addition, his normal functions in such region would include confirmations, inductions, the recommendation to the Archbishop of all faculties, the dedication of buildings. He will also normally, at the Archbishop's request, chair Boards of Nomination of the parishes in his region.'

'Each Regional Bishop remains a Coadjutor Bishop of the Diocese of Melbourne with right of access to all persons and places in the diocese on personal matters. He will continue to have spheres of responsibility, as directed by the Archbishop, which may take him to parts of the diocese not within his own area, and to persons not under his immediate Episcopal supervision. The formation of regions of episcopal care does not alter the relationship of the Archbishop to the clergy and people of the diocese, who retain their right of direct access to him, and his right of access to them is also retained.'[8]

What is spelt out so carefully there is a double function for each regional bishop. As a regional bishop he will be responsible for every episcopal function in his area; as a collegiate bishop, a member of a team, he is free to move about the whole diocese pursuing his special responsibility (industry, education, hospital chaplaincies, etc.) and in council with the rest of the team under the archbishop assist in developing the diocesan policy. The Church benefits by retaining 'a single presence' in a great and growing city. The report discussed in the Introduction, *Bishops and Dioceses*, which I had a hand in framing, says:

'If the entire environment of most people living in a metropolitan area—their homes, their place of work, their movement to and from

---

[8] Diocese of Melbourne, 'Regions of Episcopal Care', Inauguration Paper, 1971. Cf. also *Reports of the Archbishop's Committees on Diocesan Reorganization*, Diocese of Melbourne, 1969.

work and leisure—were within a single diocese and belonged to the single episcope of a college of bishops, there the college would be able to work out a strategy for the Church within that area, and its members would share together the responsibility for enabling the Church to carry out that strategy. The individual bishops would be responsible for particular geographical areas and for particular functions of society throughout the diocese, but the leadership, the authority, of the Church in the diocese would be given to the College of bishops as a whole. . . .'[9]

The report gave birth to an aphorism which sums up all that happened in Melbourne—'*the college of bishops is the bishop of the diocese*'. It felt that there were important recent precedents for the principle of collegiality (which it was prepared to trace back to Cyprian, Bishop of Carthage (248–258)), for instance the declaration on collegiality in the 1968 Lambeth Conference[10] and the Second Vatican Council's procedure in summoning a college of bishops. But the interdiocesan collegiality now well established by Rome demands, the Report insists, an equal collegiality *within* a diocese where more than one bishop serves it.

Though Rome stands by the monarchical form of episcopacy, it has its problem 'auxiliary' bishops and 'coadjutor' bishops. Can there be two kings, even though one might be the crown prince waiting for the monarch's demise? The Church of England has its suffragan and assistant bishops, who occupy the most ambiguous of positions in the hierarchy. Normally, the suffragan has no territorial responsibility and only such other responsibilities as the diocesan bishop cares to delegate to him and then never as a bishop acting in his own right but only as his superior's commissary. A Report, *The Nature and Function of the Episcopate*[11] spoke witheringly of his office. 'In the Church of England we have at present two classes of bishop, both in full-time employment as bishops of the Church. The members of one of these classes, suffragans and assistants, have no place by right in the conciliar government of the Church. Their exercise of episcopacy is deprived of its collegiate aspect. They have no share in corporate guardianship of the faith and discipline of the Church which the bishops of the province should exercise together.' These humiliated men are little more than episcopal curates, without even the certainty the deacon has of promotion. In the Paul Report, I urged that there should be two suffragans to every diocese and that each suffragan should have territorial responsibility and canvassed the idea, on the basis of experiments in Norwich Diocese, that every suffragan

---

[9] Op. cit. p. 27.

[10] 'The principle underlying collegiality is that the apostolic calling, responsibility, and authority are an inheritance given to the whole body or college of bishops.'

[11] Church Assembly, Misc. 14, June 1967.

should be an archdeacon. I no longer think this is adequate. Wherever there is a group of bishops in a diocese they should have equality of status, with the diocesan as *primus inter pares*. Belatedly the Church itself is moving to raise suffragan status. A proposal came from the House of Bishops to Synod in 1973[12] to include 'some suffragan bishops in the membership of the Upper House of the Convocations and thus in the House of Bishops of the General Synod'. Suffragans should elect six of their fellows to Canterbury Convocation and three to York.

The strong note on episcopal collegiality in *Bishops and Dioceses* raised again the problems discussed in the introduction. What is the Church? Where does final authority reside in the Church? The report which led to synodical government, *Government by Synod*,[13] made no bones about it:

'Theology justifies and history demonstrates that the ultimate authority and right of collective action lie with the whole body, the Church, and that the cooperation of clergy and laity in Church Government—and discipline—belongs to the ideal of the Church.'[14]

And the report on Church union in Australia[15] said that 'a truly episcopal church is one that takes seriously the *episcope* given by Christ at every level of the Church's life'.

The monarchical and hierarchical theory of the Church supposes the flowing down of the divine charisma through the agency of religiously superior persons, ordered in rank, until, diminished and diluted, we may suppose it reaches the laity. On the other hand, the theology which argues for the Church as the Body of Christ cannot possibly support this medieval notion. A body does not begin its life in its head, from which ponderously it suffuses life into its many parts. It is instantly, equally, vividly alive in all its parts and the head would soon suffer were that not so and it was deprived of nourishment. By analogy, and with Pauline authority behind it, the whole Church is the living body which dwells in the Christ. Within it there are many important differences of function, but none of rank. In the age we are living in, the concept of the corporateness of the Christian fellowship, of the community of the baptised, not only makes theological sense, but prepares the way for the humbler Christian presence the world seems to be waiting for. It justifies that collegiate episcopacy I have been arguing for which in this perspective becomes the proper form to express the corporate episcope of the whole Church.

---

[12] *Synodical Government (Amendment) Measure*, GS 142, Appendix 1, 'Bishops and General Synod'.

[13] CIO 1968.

[14] Op. cit. p. 14.

[15] *The Church: its Nature, Function and Ordering*, Report of a joint Commission of Congregationalists, Methodists and Presbyterians.

FIVE
The Parish

I HAVE spoken of the parish as the primary form or structure of the Church. This is the Church in the locality, on the ground, and this is where the church life begins in the weekly and often daily services of worship, in the oft-repeated eucharist which brings the faithful to the Lord's table, in the baptisms, marriages, confirmations and burials in the sacred ground which in so many places still surrounds the church. Though, since 1850, it has been true that more people in England have lived in towns than in the country, the popular (one might say tourist) image of the Church is still that of the village church, its spire rising above the trees, the villas and cottages bowered protectively around it. It is still the case that England has far more churches in rural than in town areas and far more clergy employed in the country than in bursting towns. It would be wrong to dismiss the beauty and significance of churches in a rural setting because times have changed. The builders, the architects, hankered for beauty and significance. The churches they erected were the dwelling place of God, rich in the symbolism of his presence. Rising in some central place in the village and in the dignity of their own grounds they expressed the centrality of the Church in the neighbourhood life and in a way proclaimed sovereignty. Even the dead were summoned to rest round its walls, or under its flagstones, still under its eyes. It was a dominating even a triumphalist presence. It is now a shrinking presence. But it was, unquestionably, a clerical presence.

By tradition it is the parson's church. The tradition is a lay tradition. Sir John Lawrence, editor of *Frontier*, once asked, 'What does the layman really want? He wants a building which looks like a church; a clergyman dressed in the way he approves; services of a kind he's been used to, and to be left alone.' Dr John Robinson, commenting on this, said[1] 'I think this is a pretty fair summary of what the average layman demands of the Church of England. And as Bishop Barry of Southwell put it in his book, *Asking the Right Questions*, the nominal Church of England man

---

[1] *Layman's Church*, Lutterworth Press, 1963, p. 10.

146

is still on the Latin side of the Reformation. He believes that religion is the business of the parson.'

Legally, it *is* his business. He is ordained 'to minister the doctrine and sacraments, and the discipline of Christ, as the Lord hath commanded, and as this Church and Realm hath received the same, according to the commandments of God; so that you may teach the people committed to your care and charge . . . banish and drive away all strange and erroneous doctrines . . . use both public and private monitions and exhortations, as well to the sick as to the whole. . . .' But before he swears obedience to the ministry in the ancient phrases of the Ordinal he has to testify that he thinks himself truly called to 'the Order and Ministry of Priesthood'. Put briefly he is *called* to the priesthood, he is *sent* to a care of souls. The 'care of souls' tells us for *what* he is *sent*. He is a man given spiritual authority over others. 'Whose sins thou dost forgive, they are forgiven; and whose sins thou dost retain, they are retained.' The service of Communion in the Book of Common Prayer offers him exhortations to read to the people (which today he never does), 'So it is your duty to receive Communion in remembrance of the sacrifice of his death, as he himself hath commanded; which if ye shall neglect to do, consider yourselves how great injury ye do unto God, and how sore punishment hangeth over your heads for the same; when ye wilfully abstain from the Lord's Table, and separate from your brethren. . . .' The Book of Common Prayer gives the priest also 'A Commination or Denouncing of God's Anger and Judgements against Sinners' to be used on the first day of Lent, which begins with ten resounding curses against offending men and is full of the sound and fury of a revenging God[2] and his inquisitorial Church.

The point that needed to be made at this length is that the parson came to his people in the past from the Church outside and beyond as an authoritarian father figure. He was not called by his flock. It was not for them but for others to discipline *him*. But it was his job to discipline them. This was immensely important when all were nominally Christians, and Church of England at that, and the majority did attend places of worship under duress of law. He, the parson, was the only man with the right regularly to summon, rebuke, lead in prayer, preach to, instruct, the whole community. Even badly, negligently exercised it was a tremendous, a unique power. Zealously done it was the maker and breaker of people and communities.

The existence of lay representatives and helpers—churchwardens,

---

[2] The 1928 Prayer Book offers a gentler alternative to this Calvinistic ferocity. 'God shall judge', it proposes in place of 'Cursed is he. . .'. Both services have fallen out of use, though not completely: nevertheless the Commination will remain part of the liturgy while ever *The Book of Common Prayer*, 1662, is retained.

sidesmen, verger, choir, organist, Sunday School teachers—did not reduce the parson's responsibility for, authority over, the local church life. Perhaps it increased it. The fact that no one could remove him except for a crime against civil or religious law, locked the door on his authority, barring all comers. And it was because of the nature of the parson's authority and its source that religion came to be conceived of as the parson's business and passivity was expected of the laity.

Nevertheless the laity have always played a role in the administration and local government of the Church of England. The landowners of the past, through patronage, appointed their own parsons to the churches they or their fathers had built. In the days of their power the gentry not only supported or defended their clergy but rebuked them too. The priest was expected to be, though he never wholly was, his lord's man. In the days of the great house, when the ministry was itself largely a class presence, the patron's power of presentation was a means of keeping it so and of helping the right man up. Then of course lay influence was strong in the parish when parish and vestry were units of local government, as we have seen.

The Church in this century granted the laity a statutory role in the government of the Church through the Parochial Church Councils Measure of 1921. 'It shall be the primary duty of the Councils in every parish to co-operate with the incumbent in the administration, conduct and development of church work both within the parish and outside.' What the PCCs became were bodies in love with the building but hardly committed to mission. They showed a distaste for all the disturbing aspects of the Christian faith and an affection for all its consoling, comforting and conservative aspects. They tended to become the administrative and financial committees of the parishes, money raisers, concerned with fêtes and jumble sales and with finding teachers for the Sunday Schools and leaders for the Cubs. They have seldom been great instructors, though often effective obstructers. Their very ethos has paralysed many a young priest eager for mission and reform. Parish congregation structures are not these days representative of the population structure as a whole. The dominant group in society is the married group between 25 and 45 or 50, the group in its productive prime. This is the group least represented in Church congregations. There, the strongest groups are the young and the elderly, and the most powerful group is usually the over 50s, from which most PCCs are drawn. Almost by definition PCCs are elected from that group in society most fearful of change and likely to be most attached to the Church because it represents to them the ideal of an unalterable past. The PCC base is the weakest part of the Church's electoral system.

We have to recognize though that the terms of the measure hardly invite the PCCs to take the reins into their own hands: they concede on the contrary the primacy of the incumbent. And many PCCs feel shy and ill-equipped to make a contribution to anything seriously Christian in the presence of a full-time religious professional.

Nevertheless, when the weaknesses of the PCCs are acknowledged, the meaning of their immense presence—14,500 PCCs with an electoral roll of nearly 2,600,000 churchgoers—has to be recognized. They form part of the movement of the Church towards autonomy: they are a socializing presence in society as well as the electoral basis of the synodical system.

They can change the nature of the parish if they are at all effective. Where they have taken over and run Christian Stewardship campaigns the results are often electric. Not only is Church giving transformed but attendances immediately rise. In general, as the figures of the Statistical Unit of the Central Board of Finance show, the attendances at churches which run stewardship campaigns are always significantly higher than those which do not. The usual Sunday attendances for the stewardship churches in a random sample of 1,567 parishes (but excluding cathedrals and eclectic churches) is 205, for non-stewardship parishes, 82.[3] The moral seems to be that when the laity find, as a body, some valuable role to fulfil, their relationship to the Church takes on a new life. They believe themselves wanted, trusted, and able to contribute. The parish church really becomes their church. It is a pity that the Church turns to the laity's expertise mostly over money. The need is to seek its co-operation over mission, over the Christian life of the community. When the PCC is effective in some creative way then the lonely, authoritarian, isolation of the incumbent, a life in which he has often taken refuge to escape the shallow religiosity of his flock, can be brought to an end. He may then become the servant, the executive of his Christian community rather than no more than a Sunday liturgical performer. Perhaps it is a minimal step towards the true laos, the people of God, but it is a step. Sadly, the will is often lacking to carry it beyond the mere boring formalities of a PCC meeting a few times a year.

All that has so far been said conceives of the traditional parish as the unalterable basis of the Church. In fact, in area after area, the parish is being transformed. This is not to say that there are no parishes successful both in their community life and missionary zeal. The Paul Report isolated a group of successful parishes, such as those which reported high attendance figures and gave other evidence of vigorous life. They constituted less than seven per cent of the whole, a figure I am inclined to regard now as an underestimate. At some of these parochial power-houses we shall look later. They tend to be of three types (1) the town church (2) the suburban church (3) the eclectic church. The eclectic church is usually a famous church, such as St Martin's-in-the-Fields,

---

[3] Cf. *Church of England Year Book, 1971–72*, Tables XXI, XXIa, XXIb, pp. 198–9.

or that other St Martin's, in the Bullring, Birmingham, which draw their congregations from far afield and could not possibly thrive on the basis of the local population. One at which I looked had a parish population of 593, an average Sunday attendance of 500, and 379 Easter communicants, results only possible by drawing worshippers from other parishes, to the detriment no doubt of their attendance figures. The thriving, lively centre gathers its congregation from a very wide area and it sometimes has an added pull if it is situated in the heart of a city. There is a lesson to be learnt here over the future of churches.

I produced a table of some successful parishes. I reproduce it here:

Some statistics of representative successful parishes[4]

Livings	Reported Pop.	Easter comm.	Av. Sun. attend.	ASA per 1,000	ASA per church	ASA per clergy
Suburban	23,000	930	600	26	600	300
Suburban	45,000	800	1,000	22	1,000	286
Suburban	30,000	750	900	30	300	300
Rural	1,600	180	135	84	34	90

Any parson in his senses would rejoice at these results. Yet in another sense they are failures. The average Sunday attendance per 1,000 population (Col. 5) falls below the national average as computed in my sample, except for the last entry. The national average was 31·1 per 1,000. And this bears out a consistent trend shown by my own statistics which is that as the density of population rises diocese by diocese so the average size of congregations tends to increase. There are more people to draw from. Yet the impact socially can still be less than in rural areas because attendance, as a percentage, falls. It has already been pointed out that fewer people attend church per thousand population in the towns than in the countryside. Indeed over a whole range of figures pastoral results are in inverse ratio to the density of population.[5] One incumbent reported to me that he constantly warned his congregation that their vigorous and thriving church life could mislead them—their impact on the parish was still fractional. It can occur that a church will from year to year improve its figures and come to feel that the battle is won, yet year by year reach a smaller and smaller percentage of the parish population. Of course, that does not disqualify the success of the church as a centre of a gathered congregation but it is a salutary reminder that this is not the most reliable measure of its outreach.

I have said that the parish is under great pressures. The unalterable is being altered. Hard economic and social facts are leading to the

---

[4] Leslie Paul, *The Deployment and Payment of the Clergy*, CIO 1964, p. 67.

[5] Ibid. Graph 5, 'Attendance at Church' p. 80.

suspension of livings, the merger of parishes into some form of corporate ministry, such as a team or group ministry. Dioceses are selling ancient churches or otherwise disposing of them. The shortage of clergy makes it difficult to fill the poorest and most remote livings in the country and the depopulated down-town urban livings. Lack of congregations jeopardizes even such services as may be provided and makes a *parish* life out of the question and an elected PCC an impossibility.

Where country parishes have long been under an interregnum through failure to find a new incumbent the church itself may exhibit decay —untended churchyards, crumbling fabrics, neglected interior, bird droppings and dead flies on the altar, damp. When the populations depart the faithful laity who cared for the church go too. In down-town areas where churches are shut they become the target of every kind of vandalism and vileness from the young of a population no longer much moved by any sense of the sacred. It is indeed clear from the debates of General Synod over the possibility of government aid for churches of historic value that part of the architectural heritage of the nation could be endangered because of the inability of the Church to raise the money for restoration and maintenance, or to provide the guardians.

Other social factors erode the parochial structure. One of course is high population mobility and the other high personal mobility both social and geographical. The first industrial revolution which shifted millions of families from a settled rural life in which church going was part of the pattern of community acceptance to industrial towns where it meant little or nothing, lost them to church life. The same is happening today. When a Welsh miner from a mining village with its chapel moves because of redundancy to Acton Town to work in a plastics factory, he loses chapel and all sense of community in one blow. But he may acquire a motor car and so achieve on Sunday the high personal mobility which is the special mark of the contemporary world. What is the community to which the ex-miner, who lives in Acton, works in Wembley, sends his children to school in Ealing, spends his summer Sundays at Brighton, his Saturday afternoons at Chelsea Football Ground, his holidays in Majorca, supposed to relate? In any real sense it does not exist, unless it is as a handful of neighbours or the chaps he meets in the Red Lion. He might not even know of church or chapel there to serve him, or that he had the privilege of membership of 'a parish'. It could even be true that he did not know the name of the Greater London Borough of which he was a citizen.

The parish in a great conurbation is often quite meaningless, particularly if in the last century it was carved out of a few streets in order to make a church available at every third street corner for the non-worshipping working-class. Do parishes make much more sense in the great housing estates, those great deserts of architectural and social mediocrity, which mar the landscape? It is hard to believe that giving

St Olave's the north side, St Mark's the South side, and St Stephen's the rural fringe makes much more sense than an agreement between canvassers, 'You take the first twenty streets and I'll take the next...' and so on.

Geoffrey K. Nelson and Rosemary Clews studied the religious consequences of geographical and social mobility in Dawley.[6] They found, *inter alia*, that in moving house six miles was a critical limit.

'People were much more likely to continue to attend the same church if the distance moved was under 6 miles than if it was greater than this amount. 60% of movers over short distances compared with 14% of those who moved further afield continued to attend the same church after the move. To some extent this result was expected. We did not imagine that people would travel very great distances to church. The fact that a proportion as high as 14% maintained their membership of the same church was of interest and confirmed the results of a Study of the membership of St Martin's-in-the-Bullring in 1967. It was discovered that 57% of the members of that church travelled over 3 miles to worship and 11% more than 6 miles.'

Then again, the co-authors state,

'If, however, the first move is greater than 6 miles 20% will leave church altogether. The first move is thus seen to be most important in detaching a person from church membership.'

'Broadly speaking', the authors say in their conclusion, 'geographical mobility reduces participation in corporate religious activity whereas *social* mobility [up or down in class or status] increases such participation.'

In a society more and more geographically mobile, the consequent erosion of membership, with all its cumulative effects is bound to be serious, for established religion flourishes best in stable societies.

The reaction of the Church to the problem of the erosion of the parochial structure was for a long time to unite parishes in the country and to increase their number in the towns. This was a simple way of adjusting parishes to population increases in towns and to decreases in the country. Bishops had the choice of uniting parishes by uniting benefices, which meant creating one parish, with one parochial church council and one vicar or rector, or causing several parishes to be held by one clergyman, who was therefore vicar of several parishes and chairman of several PCCs simultaneously. The first solution may easily make one or more churches redundant. It may, too, raise the question of the identity of the community the parson serves and the PCC

---

[6] *Mobility and Religious Commitment* by Geoffrey K. Nelson and Rosemary A. Clews, University of Birmingham Institute for the Study of Worship and Religious Architecture, 1971.

represents. The second keeps all the parochial machinery going but the parson himself becomes itinerant. In either case the old parochial concept, *church and parson here, for this parish and no one else*, loses meaning.

The Parochial Measure, 1967, under the influence of the proposals of the Paul Report, introduces new powers and blesses new methods for the grouping of parishes. Whole designated areas can be swept free of the old parishes with their freehold and antiquated patronage and reformed into team ministries responsible for a major parish. What clearly has to be intended by such schemes is the serving of some greater community than that given by a small, closed-off parish and to bring the new, major parish into some relation with civic boundaries if that is possible. The Church then has a chance to become *the Church of this area* and to be seen to be so. Its significance in the ministry to a new town can hardly be exaggerated where a community has to be brought into being and a parochial fragmentation of the town could only be socially divisive. A team ministry provides the structure whereby specialist ministries can grow and be provided with a territorial base. Church reformers, church radicals have placed much hope on these. Specialist ministries have grown-up largely in independence of the parochial system[7]—an army chaplain, a prison or hospital chaplain, a diocesan youth officer, an industrial missioner may happen to live in Parish X or Y and work in Parish A or B. But neither parish is essential *to his work*. He could be without a parish at all and still do his work. Sometimes he can do his work better if a parish priest is not looking over his shoulder. I recall a parish priest who forbade an industrial missioner to visit the factories in his parish on the grounds that they were his, the priest's responsibility, though he never visited them. In the enlarged area of a team ministry to a major parish the specialist priest would be a member of the team: it could not exclude him and do its job. In part, the team could be recruited to bring together such specialists.

One phenomenon of the sixties has been the growth of specialist ministries. It is estimated that nearly a quarter of the total ministry will soon be at work outside the traditional parish ministry. The parochial system provides for curates, incumbents, rural deans and so forth, up to the diocesan bishop. Parochial responsibilities lead to territorial responsibilities, but not usually to specialist posts. By and large, the specialist is outside the parochial system and no provision is made for him in synodical government. He is an alien and he could miss the promotion ladder.

---

[7] They are very adequately documented and discussed in *Specialist Ministries*, the Report of a Working Party of the Ministry Committee of the Advisory Council of the Church's Ministry, CIO 1971.

Only through incorporation in a team ministry could the specialist be brought back into a proper alliance with the parochial system and rejoin the main stream. A group ministry is not so appropriate a means for no clear place is provided for the specialist within it. But where a team ministry cannot for various reasons be contemplated as a corporate exercise, a group ministry may suffice. This is an agreement between incumbents to combine their ministry or mission without surrender of individual incumbencies or parish boundaries. Under the Pastoral Measure a group ministry constitutes a scheme which must be given legal status to prevent its break up by changes of incumbents or patrons. Again it is an instrument for more effective ministry to an area which can no longer be conceived of in terms of its separate parishes.

Of course, despite the Measure, the Church of England's ministry must for a long time remain parochial in the older traditional sense I have described, though the small, one church parish with under a thousand population will faster disappear. The significance of the new instruments of ministry is not that the church will cease to be local—that finally it must always be: that which is not local is not real, Chesterton said—but that it will be increasingly territorial rather than parochial in the great cities, the new towns and housing estates, and the more remote countryside.

The parochial system, by its very structure, has another mechanism which stands in the way of effective territorial (plus specialist) ministry. It is this: only one incumbent can be appointed to a benefice. He may be assisted by one or more curates, but their distribution is not necessarily related to the work-load of parish priests, rather indeed to the ability of parishes to pay for them.[8] Curates are young men under instruction and under authority and not experienced colleagues. In the nature of things they are 'juniors' anxious to move on. A priest with a parish, say, of 20,000 or even 30,000 souls is denied by the nature of his appointment the services of colleagues of equal status, however hard he is overworked and however desperate his situation, at least short of a scheme which would transform his and other parishes into a major parish.

The Morley Report[9] proposed reforms which would have dissociated ministry of incumbent status from the parochial anchor. Every man on ordination would go on to the strength of his diocese, if proposed, and would remain there, paid and housed, in or out of a post, until his retirement. He would reach 'incumbent status' after his post-ordination

---

[8] Other factors, including parochial training and post-ordination training, govern their distribution. But parishes must be able to pay the stipend laid down by the Diocese. See the *Deployment and Payment of the Clergy*,

[9] *Partners in Ministry*, CIO 1967.

training and stay there. Status would not be dependent on a particular benefice. Under such a basis of employment a team of the best men available could go into a parish in a desperate missionary situation—and immediately, without costly and lengthy pastoral schemes. The Morley Report was rejected by Church Assembly in 1970, a funereal act appropriate to the Assembly's demise. The safeties of freehold and patronage were preferred to the challenges of mission.

The result was not unexpected. No Church is just a Church in a mission sense, all else forgotten. It is also a social institution. Even the disciples of Jesus were sometimes more concerned with their status after victory than the immediate dangers ahead. Would they, they asked, receive preferment? A Church as a social institution represents a deep investment of wealth and power. It is natural for even the most well-meaning of men to interpret their mission in terms which leave their privileges intact or even enhance them. An established Church more easily falls victims to these temptations: the values of the establishment become its own yardstick.

The difficulties and problems of the parochial structure are shown up by the actual pattern of distribution of the clergy. The parochial system—the ecclesiastical parishes of the land by law established—forms a grid over the land. Not a grid of unyielding squares, but something like an irregular wire mesh which can be pulled and pushed a little this way or that but remains an inescapable superimposition upon the geographical and demographic map. This superstructure grew slowly through the centuries with the intention of providing church and parson for every living community. But once established, each church and parish became a self-regarding unit which defended itself against change. Change in adjustment of parish boundaries could be accepted so long as it was not too radical. After all, a parish remained. Abolition affected the *amour propre* of the parishioners, threatened the security of the parson and the rights of the patron. Vested interests, in fact, of freeholder, patron, parishioner (together with the investment in buildings) tended to freeze the parochial system. The wonder is that so much power has been taken by Assembly or Synod to adjust the pattern. But the principle of inviolate parish, freehold, and patronage has not *yet* been invaded, except marginally where the Pastoral Measure makes provision for elaborate schemes. And even these guarantee the right of compensation for loss of the property called the freehold.

Because of this slow-changing parochial system the clergy are very badly distributed. Most of the clergy are in the countryside while most of the population are in the towns. It is an aphorism which cannot too often be repeated. It is a promising way to secure the deconversion of England, if of course this has not been achieved already.

SIX
Class and Élite

I HAVE said a great deal about the Church as part of the establishment. One of the themes of Philip Elliott's *The Sociology of the Professions*[1] is the close relation between the earliest professions (medicine, law, the military, the Church) and the gentry. In the case of the Church of England that relationship is more obvious after the Reformation than before. In more recent history the novels of Jane Austen or the diaries of Woodforde and Kilvert tell all. The ministry became a special dimension of the life of the gentry—a statement made here without irony, for with the gentry rested so many, often arduous, social duties. They paid for some of their privileges with public responsibilities.

The close connection of the most privileged groups in English society with the Church, and their consistent support—a support so great that the Church would be impoverished without it—can be shown in many ways. One of the exercises carried out for the Paul Report argued that recruitment for the ordained ministry from the best public schools and the older universities was far above mere statistical expectation.

Research was conducted into 94 selection boards between 1954 and 1962[2] at which 1,525 candidates for ordination were fully or conditionally accepted out of 1,921 men interviewed. The conclusions were instructive. Over the period the recruitment from Oxford and Cambridge was approximately fifty per cent greater than the total from all other universities put together, though in the academic year 1960–1 Oxford and Cambridge housed only one-quarter of all male university students. (The actual figures for male students in England then were 63,328 of which Oxford and Cambridge accounted for 15,796: the accepted ordinands from Oxford and Cambridge in the period assessed were 278; from all other universities, 191.)

---

[1] Macmillan, London 1972.
[2] Attended by Mr. Geoffrey Heawood, General Secretary of CACTM. See *The Deployment and Payment of the Clergy*, p. 275 ff. 'The Fayers-Heawood Research'. The Rev. H. D. F. Fayers examined and tabulated the records of the boards attended by Geoffrey Heawood.

In the total applications from schools, the *public* schools, though accounting for only 7 per cent or so of the school population, contributed 557 candidates; the grammar schools contributed 993 or 52 per cent, though representing only 28 per cent of the school population; the LEA schools, 65 per cent of the school population, contributed only 19 per cent of the candidates, 355 in all. Rejections too, told their story: less than 15 per cent of public school candidates were rejected as against over 30 per cent of those from LEA schools.

Where the ordinands trained was also important. The Report tabled[3] a rising scale of public school recruitment to theological colleges, beginning with Brasted Place pre-Theological College with a score of 10 per cent and climbing to Ridley, Cambridge, with a score of 65 per cent. In a thesis on bishops,[4] quoted in the Report, David H. J. Morgan reviewing the episcopacy from 1860 to 1960 proved that a public school background, common in the ministry, is almost *de rigueur* for bishops. Ten leading public schools accounted for most of the bishops. They were Eton, Winchester, Marlborough, Shrewsbury, Rugby, Harrow, Westminster, Charterhouse, Haileybury, and King Edward's (Birmingham). All contributed four or more bishops in the century under review. Eton contributed 25. The pyramid narrows as one ascends. Oxford and Cambridge also played a dominant role and three colleges in particular, Trinity, Cambridge, and Christ Church and New College, Oxford, a predominant one. They contributed 25 per cent to the episcopacy. Four theological colleges, Cuddesdon, Ridley, Westcott, Wells, trained between them more than 25 per cent of the bishops. Their influence grew. Of the 58 bishops instituted in the duo-decade, 1940–59, 19 came from these four colleges. The number jumps to 31 in 1960.

To have been at a leading public school, at one of three select Oxbridge colleges, to have attended one of the four principal theological colleges (only one of which, Wells, is not at Oxbridge) enormously increases the chances of donning the purple. There are other factors. It proves statistically important to have a father in the Anglican ministry and to be well-connected by birth or by marriage to the peerage or the landed gentry. To put it no higher all these factors increase the probability (still) that one will be noticed, heighten the possibility that one will be selected. The Victorians would have said that one needed to be well-bred as well as well-educated to become a bishop. And sometimes one needed only that. The appearance from time to time of spiritual and intellectual giants in the episcopacy suggests not only that the system was capable of producing them—and this is beyond doubt in every field in

---

[3] In a contribution from Dr Anthony M. Coxon, p. 280.
[4] *The Social and Educational Backgrounds of English Diocesan Bishops, 1860–1960*, unpublished M.A. thesis of Nottingham University, 1965.

the nineteenth century—but that other possibly 'meritocratic' factors also influenced selection processes.

The importance of public school and Oxbridge background in the Church of England repeats itself in the House of Laity of the General Synod, according to an investigation by Kathleen Jones.[5]

'Nearly half the men (49%) had been to public schools, and 34% to grammar schools or direct grant schools. Of the small group remaining, the majority did not state their educational background. Only seven men (4%) recorded education in the less privileged sectors of the educational system—technical or secondary modern schools, or the equivalents before the Butler Act of 1944.' Of the women members, '14% were at girls' public schools and 35% at grammar or direct grant schools. Of the rest, the majority recorded privately educated ... Of the whole group, 59% were graduates. Again there was some disparity between the sexes, more men than women having a university background (62% men against 45% women). One man in three (35%) had been an undergraduate either at Oxford or at Cambridge ... Some of this group had reached Oxford or Cambridge from grammar schools, but 25% of all men had the traditional combination of public school-and-Oxbridge.'[6]

Class and élite factors in the ministry have been taken further by Anthony Coxon.[7] He saw men entering the ministry from two main streams, the younger traditional stream in which the public school element was particularly strong, and a group of older entrants with a far less privileged educational background and a skilled manual or clerical parental background far remote from any social élite. This group tends to offer itself to the ministry after testing service at parochial level and through long-held private aspirations.

Coxon's older group would seem to be less professional than the first. It is less likely to be a graduate group: it is most likely to be a married group. According to *Theological Colleges Tomorrow* the groups aged 40–59 and 30–39 constituted collectively about 43 per cent in 1966. When it is recalled that another 4 per cent of entrants were over 60 it can be realized that late entrants are coming up to the 50 per cent mark. By 1966 the young entrants had slipped to 53 per cent. The older group would be less 'professional', less likely interested in the career structure in the Church which would be more the concern and opportunity of the public school–Oxbridge sector of the younger group. At a time too when

---

[5] *Crucible*, July–August 1971, 'The House of Laity in The General Synod: a membership analysis', pp. 104 ff.

[6] Ibid. pp. 104–5.

[7] Cf. *A Sociological Study of the Social Recruitment, Selection and Professional Socialization of Anglican Ordinands*, unpublished doctoral thesis by Anthony Coxon, University of Leeds, 1965: Anthony Coxon, 'An élite in the making' *New Society*, 26 November 1964: 'Patterns of occupational recruitment: the Anglican Ministry', *Sociology*, January 1967.

every other profession and some non-professions too, have moved over to graduate entry the ministry at first moved away and then began to recover as more stringent terms of entry were demanded. The following graphs tell the story.

The graphs would seem entirely irreconcilable with all that has been said about the role of the universities and of the leading public schools. Not so. The dignitaries of the Church will continue to be recruited, as far as one can see into the future, fairly exclusively from the public school–Oxbridge element of the ministry. They will therefore be selected from a narrowing sector of the ministry and so they could become something of a superior caste! One could see many possibilities for friction and

Proportion of Graduates in Training

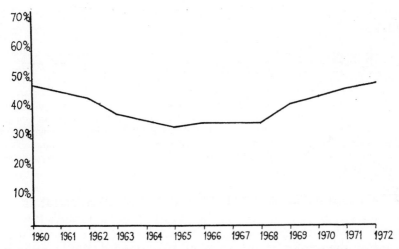

Fig. 1. *The proportion of* graduates *in training for the ministry of the Church of England is again rising after a dismal period in which it fell well below 40 per cent. Stricter terms of entry are producing results.*

misunderstanding if such a situation ossified. The bishop is already the target of the dissatisfactions of the inferior clergy: the House of Clergy in General Synod delights in cocking a snook at bishops.

Yet one point should not be missed. It is that the contribution of the grammar schools, secondary modern and comprehensive schools to selection boards is over 70 per cent. Ordinands from these schools form an absolute majority. If more than half the grammar and comprehensive school boys who come forward have not been to university but possess university entry qualifications—as they now must have—the mystery is explained: they are treating their theological colleges as universities.

Though there is a division of the ministry into two groups, the graduate

Age-groups of Deacons Ordained

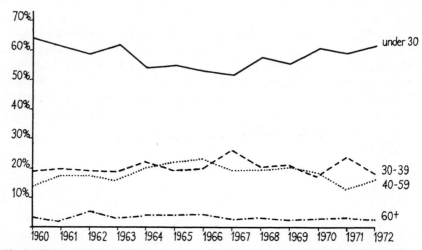

Fig. 2. *The proportion of younger men entering the ministry is again rising. Too great an inflow of older men raises the average age and reduces the average expectation of ministerial life. The two graphs are based on figures supplied by the Advisory Council for the Church's Ministry which brought up to date the graphs on page 23 of* Theological Colleges for Tomorrow (The Bunsen Report) 1968. *The figures also show a consistent rise in the number of married men in training. In many colleges they are now the majority group.*

and the non-graduate, lack of a degree makes no difference at all as far as I can see at the grass roots of the ministry where a man's talents do not have to be academic and the impact he makes does not usually depend on the school or university he has attended. But in promotion to dignities it is important. Those who promote are clearly looking for men of their own public school stamp. There is a consistent, strong bias, one expert noted, towards the public school candidate.

Is it surprising? Does it matter? It is, of course, not surprising. It would be very surprising if an established Church did not repeat in its ministerial structures the accepted social and class patterns of society at large. An established Church is by definition a 'conservative' Church, and beginning with the royal supremacy is bound to support society as it is rather than prove restless or experimental socially. It is unwilling to be radical about those parts of church structures which relate to the norms of society. In this it only reflects the conscious or unconscious standards of so many of society's institutions—the Foreign Office, the Services—which display the same biases. In one sense one could say that the behaviour of the Church is proper. If the public school–Oxbridge élite really is the nation's élite then it makes sense that the Church shares it and promotes it. This is one answer to the question—does it matter?

There is another answer. It is that dictated by the shifting social pattern, perhaps more fluid now than for many generations past. The gentry and the landed aristocracy still hold their ground: they still have incomparable status. Highly successful farming and the constantly renewed links with finance and industry sustain and refresh them. The wealthy middle class still buys itself into land. 'The County' has meaning. Yet even here the technological farmer, the farmer as business man, grows in importance as great houses decline and the paternal landlord–tenant relationship disappears. The countryside is being mechanized and losing its population and surrendering its dwellings to the urban, and the retired and to commercial firms.

A discernible shift has taken place in the nature of the public schools and the older universities too. The latter now have more undergraduates from outside the public school system than within. The student ethos— the ethos of the junior staff too—approximates more to Sussex or Birmingham or Essex than to the traditions of (establishment) hearties and (establishment) aesthetes with a few exquisites and eccentrics as décor. The youth cult uniform prevails. All the young men, as someone remarked, look like Joan Crawford. All the young women look like Bernadette Devlin. The attitudes to sexual promiscuity, abortion, family, drugs, Church are predictable. What applies there seems to apply *a fortiori* to the public schools. These quondam fortresses of the establishment, imposing a uniformity of conduct and life style acceptable to the establishment, have been taken over by the youth cult the values of which are painfully anti-establishment. It is not the point as to whether this is good or bad. The point is that the youth culture is hostile to establishment institutions. For them they are hypocritical, reactionary, oppressive or meaningless. Any religious explorations the culture makes are into experiences remote from conventional western religion. The youth culture field must prove a poor recruitment ground. How long therefore can the Church expect to rely on those traditional Oxbridge sources for the most important élite group in its ministerial structures? But these are the last academic institutions to be openly Anglican in their religious provision! The state schools, though committed to a syllabus of religious instruction, are neutral towards actual denominations. The new universities are positivist in attitude for the most part and remote from, and uninterested in, any form of institutionalized religion except as a field for specialized research. It is not likely therefore that any decline of recruitment from the public schools and universities will be compensated for by increases from other sources. If the establishment itself is changing, or must change, which is what this analysis also implies, then the Church, committed to a scene now vanishing, could find itself more isolated and more confused about its role. I think I have shown that the justification of the recruitment from the public schools and Oxford and Cambridge lay in the fact that this provided the Church with a share of the national élite. By this path some of the best minds, and best trained minds, entered the ministry. If that source does dry up, while the non-graduate entry increases, the Church of England will prove a duller, more denominational institution, less able to communicate with the leaders of the nation. The national élite, losing its share of the ministry, will itself be impoverished. It may be deplorably undemocratic to speak in élite terms at all. But élites are not elected: they flow from all sorts of subtle social and cultural processes, very often indefinable. It is important that a national Church, established or not, should reflect in its own structures the social and cultural structures of the nation. I am not sure that it can do much about it when it fails to. Or what happens to a national Church when the prevailing culture becomes anti-Christian.

One began with a monarchical, triumphal Church imposing its will on society by its economic, social and spiritual strength. One ends with the feeling of a Church slipping away from the élite centres of power, impelled by centrifugal social forces, and uneasy about its future, less powerful role, its archaisms clanking about it still like a suit of rusty medieval armour.

PART THREE

The Church in Trouble

'The old house has collapsed behind our backs and when we came to take our place in the homes of the young, they hadn't yet found out how to build their own, and we found ourselves in an indeterminate sphere, among the stones and the rafters, in the rain.'

Georges Bernanos (trans. R. C. Zaehner) in
Un Mauvais Rêve

'The more profitable vision that arises in the debate is of *a Church genuinely Christian.* Such a church would approximate, as closely as possible for sinful mortals to the single-mindedness implied in Dietrich Bonhoeffer's arresting phrase for the Church: "Christ existing as a community". In some sense it would be an "extension of the Incarnation", to use another bold phrase popular in some of the century's Anglican theology. It would recover for the life of Christians, as scholarship has recovered in theology, the New Testament's sense that the Lord who speaks to the churches is continuous with the Lord who spake in Galilee.... That is the presence would be personal. ...'

David Edwards in *Religion and Change*

'The danger is that God will once more be treated as an in-group totem.'

Alasdair MacIntyre in
Against the Self-Images of the Age

ONE

The Proper Use of Men and Resources

EARLY in the sixties the Commission on Faith of the World Council of Churches set up a Study Group on 'Spirit, Order and Organization'. I was privileged to take part in its work. It was intended to be a dialogue between sociologists and theologians. Its concluding report[1] makes illuminating and unhappy reading—illuminating because of the theological responses to sociological techniques and insights, and unhappy because the study group and the projects it planned came to an end for lack of funds. The bridge which it was building never reached beyond the first span. Those apparently inexhaustible American research funds ran dry, I imagine.

To some of the report's insights I will return but I find myself moved by one of its opening paragraphs: 'We witness today a profound crisis of human institutions. The values which served as ordering principles for human life in society in the past have lost much of their validity. More and more the Churches are drawn into this upheaval and efforts toward Christian unity appear in a new light. Far from being settled the old questions of continuity and change, of unity and diversity or plurality are forced upon us with new urgency.' The report enters upon—or provokes—critiques of Church 'order' in the light of this and similar insights. All those intimately concerned with the work of Churches will understand how deep a crisis is implied when the report asks whether Churches should not now understand order in terms of the functional rather than the normative and think of 'organization' rather than 'institution'. Much of the resistance of the clergy to my own report (*The Deployment and Payment of the Clergy*, 1964) arose because I was more concerned with function than tradition and with effective organization than historical institution. That being said, it must be emphasized that there are problems of deployment of the clergy *because* of critical changes in society and in the Churches. The years have underlined and made more acute the anomalies and absurdities I sought to expose ten years ago and their consequences for the Christian life and for ecclesiology. They were wider than just deployment, but deployment, in the

---

[1] Fall 1970 issue of *Study Encounter*, World Council of Churches, Geneva.

Church of England especially, reveals the clash between concern for effective function and the preservation of tradition and 'normalcy'.

As we have just seen the Church of England bases itself upon the ecclesiastical parish, the boundaries and status of which can only be altered by what are in truth acts of law. But legal entities become the more ossified with time the more difficult they are (legally) to change. Each parish in the past was bound up with properties fiercely preserved and defended—glebe, tithe, church, parsonage, endowment. Communities might decay or prosper, explode or vanish, but the parish, swathed in legal tape, was preserved intact through all the changes. Only the Pastoral Measure (1968) breaches in some degree the autonomy of these ecclesiastical bastions.

The rigidity of the deployment of the clergy by benefice or living can be vividly shown by the following figures:

1. 10·5 per cent of the population of the two provinces is grouped in livings of under 2,000 population. (There were 5,199 such livings, 3,545 of them under 1,000 population by 1963 figures.) *They are served by 38·2 per cent of the parochial clergy.*
2. 55·8 per cent of the population is grouped in livings of between 2,000 and 9,999 population and enjoys the services of 45·2 per cent of the parochial clergy.
3. *33·7 per cent of the population is grouped in livings of 10,000 and over and has to make do with 16·6 of the parochial clergy.*

This has nothing to do with original sin at diocesan or synodical level but with the simple fact that the clergy are distributed according to the availability of benefices or livings and not distributed according to any other plan or need unless they are placed in specialist, unbeneficed posts. Even after combining parishes to make a reasonable 'living' and to provide a man with almost a real job to do (there are 5,441 parishes covered by 3,545 livings of under 1,000 population) *the point remains that half the livings of the Church of England cover only ten per cent of the population. At the other end of the scale, the heavily populated end, less than ten per cent of the livings cover about a third of the population. This is the measure of the bankruptcy of the parochial system.*[2]

In fact one can take the analysis a stage further and then the implications are even more frightening. In 1969 there were 97 livings with 20,000 population and over 15 of them were over 30,000. The largest parish is still Kirkby St Chad in Liverpool with a population of over 50,000. I estimate that these 97 livings embrace a population greater than

[2] Figures have slightly changed since 1963. The 31 December 1969 figures for livings of under 1,000 show a rise to 3,624 which may be accounted for by depopulation of the countryside and certain inner city areas, and just these livings absorb nearly 3,000 parochial clergymen out of a total of only 14,250 (*Church of England Year Book, 1971–72.* Tables IV and V, pp. 175–6).

3,700,000. They are served, according to the *Church of England Year Book, 1971–72*[3], by 93 incumbents and 246 curates, a total of 339. At the other end of the scale something like 3,000 clergy look after about three million people. The discrepancy is simply appalling.

One concludes from this that the Church of England is still a rural-based Church only half-heartedly concerned with great cities. As the cities grow and the countryside depopulates the disparity between clergy deployment and mission need—and that is to say between traditional forms and effective function—must widen year by year. One projection of population growth for the two provinces[4] is that it will rise from 44 million in 1963 to 61 million in 2003. Projections such as these can falsify themselves, but they remain useful indicators of the serious problems ahead. A population density which was 333 persons per square mile in 1851 was 911 in 1968 and is expected to be 1,210 in 2003. In a half century, 1911 to 1961, the number of parishes with populations of 20,000 and over, doubled. Possibly over 80 per cent of the population of the country is already living in cities. What the ecologists are saying about the social and human consequences of this urban growth has yet to be assimilated by the Church.

Does it matter? It can be argued that at grass roots level these statistics mean little. Wherever there is a church and a parson one gets, one finds, a self-regarding congregation, large or small according to local circumstances, and this is the be-all and end-all of deployment. Redeployment might only kill a number of congregations unnecessarily without adding new ones. There is truth in this. Old congregational patterns based on ancient institutional forms—the forms of a gentry-dominated society—may not survive the abolition of the form and if they die may never be replaced. But left alone they can be tenacious of life while the form remains, it is said. But this argument in favour of the *status quo*, of a kind of 'rightness' in historical forms, was already dying in the last century in the wake of the industrial revolution. Somehow the traditional forms could not then reach the crowded urbanized masses, already partly secularized but fiercely moral. It took Salvation Army unorthodoxy to spark the imagination of those masses, to produce vivid loyalties or physical opposition—to make a mission impact. But the argument can hardly hold either in the light of the rapidity of social change, the mobility, affluence, secularization and disrespect for institutions so characteristic of our cities, or the rise of the new, lively, derisory masses and their hostile-to-history young.

There is another reason for rejecting the appeal to traditional forms. Though the Church of England parson is still (like the Queen) a corporation sole, this is a legal fiction disguising his dependence. Only a few

---

[3] Op. cit. Table VII, pp. 178–9.

[4] *Facts and Figures about the Church of England*, No. 3, CIO 1967, Tables 1 and 2, Diagram V.

parsons here and there have parochial endowments which enable them to live without outside supplements whether from the Church Commissioners or diocesan funds. When I wrote my report the endowments (benefice) element of stipends was already (in general) less than 50 per cent. So that if the traditional clergy status survives it is because of the sophisticated investment techniques of the Church Commissioners and the organizing zeal displayed with all contemporary bureaucratic efficiency at diocesan level. The point is, the clergy financially is a body dependent on ancient national funds administered by an autonomous civil service department, and upon the generosity of the laity. The battle against rationalization, or effective function, is on the financial side already lost and it is fortunate for the clergy standard of living that it is so.

The anomalies in the deployment of the Church of England clergy are not limited to the contrast between town and country. There is a similar disparity between ancient boroughs and townships and new or newer urban areas. The mostly rural Isle of Wight has some forty-six livings for its 106,000 population. At the time of my report it had one parochial clergyman to every 2,255 persons, but even built-up Ryde could boast a ratio of 1:2,654. Old towns and cathedral cities such as Exeter, Winchester, Canterbury, Cheltenham, Windsor and new ones such as Weston-super-Mare had similar ratios but in Norwich the ratio dropped even to 1:1,317 excluding cathedral clergy. I pointed in my report to the fact that, 'Bradford diocese, with a population of 600,000 (city 290,000) is served by 150 clergy. Two Chelmsford deaneries, Romford and Barking, with a population rising 700,000 have not more than 70 clergy at work.' Not only ancient forms but elements of luck seem to govern the distribution of clergy. On the whole the old has it better than the new.

As these last comments show, inequalities in deployment produce ratio differentials markedly to the disadvantage of great urban areas like London, Southwark, Manchester (1:4,500) and Birmingham, Liverpool, Sheffield (approx. 1:6,000) as against Hereford, Norwich, Exeter (approx. 1:1,500). But there are serious problems connected with the overall ratio of clergy to population. The average annual number of ordinations from 1955 to 1959 was 694: a bulge started in 1960 with 598 ordinations. Until the middle sixties the Church of England was signally fortunate. The number of men being ordained into the ministry was averaging 600 a year, the highest level for thirty years and this gave (1961) a ratio of one full-time clergyman to 2,838 of the populations of the two provinces. But a projection based on recruitment at that rate showed a worsening ratio and to maintain a ratio of, say, 1:2,500 a full-time ministry of nearly 24,000 men would have been required by the year 2001, an increase of nearly two-thirds! A vain hope! What one could not anticipate was that recruitment to the ministry would fall dramatically in the late sixties. As the Rev. David M. K. Durston (of the Grubb Institute of Behavioural Studies) has pointed out in a privately circulated paper, 'In the past six years ... there has been a sharp fall in the number of men being ordained from 636 in 1963 to 478 in 1968 and 420 last year (1969). The fact that there are now only 888 men in theological colleges going through a three-year period of training for the Church of England ministry indicates that within two or three years the number of ordinations will fall to around 300 a year.'

What faced the Church in the early sixties was the prospect of a slowly increasing ministry and a sharply rising population. But a sharply *decreasing* ministry together with a sharply *rising* population makes hay of all projected ratios. As Durston points out, just on the manning basis, 'The size of the shortfall will increase from around 100 a year in the mid-1970's to 200 to 250 a year by the end of the decade. This shortfall is of course accumulative, so that the total shortage is likely to reach 700 to 1,000 over the next ten years.'

However, there is an official estimate of the shortfall of a still more serious character than Durston's. It is that computed in Table X in *The Church of England Year Book, 1971–72* (pp. 182–3), the title of which tells all, 'Parochial Ordained Manpower of the Dioceses estimated for 31st December, 1972 contrasted with Actual Numbers serving Full-time in the Parochial Livings at 31st December, 1969'. The estimates there, ranged by dioceses, are proof already of Durston's thesis. The heaviest ministerial deficit is expected in Birmingham (35·9%), Chelmsford (29·7%), Lichfield (26·0%), all either heavily urban or facing heavy urbanization; the smallest is Hereford (1·6%). The figures for the provinces are York, 24·3 per cent and Canterbury, 16·7 per cent and the national shortfall will therefore be 18·9 per cent. *At the end of 1972 the Church of England will almost certainly have three thousand men fewer than it once estimated it ought to have to do its job properly on the basis of the present style of deployment.*[5]

Mr Durston discusses some of the consequences of the impending shortfall. It is not likely to spread itself evenly over the whole country but to result in competition between dioceses for clergy to fill their livings. There is already a drift south of men in their second curacies. Trained and recruited in the north, more and more find their way into softer livings (softer climatically, socially, economically) in the south. The north, no better at finding men for the ministry than the south, is far better at losing them. Durston points out that minimum stipends vary by as much as £200 a year between 'the largely suburban and hence relatively affluent dioceses and the poorer dioceses which include the centres of the country's conurbations'. Expenses of office, while often generously covered in suburban parishes, are seldom met in inner city

[5] Other ways of estimating are possible. 'Unless, therefore, the declining trend in ordinations is reversed, there are likely, as we indicated, to be 1,500 less (*sic*) parochial clergy by 1975 and up to 3,000 less (*sic*) by 1980.' This is an estimate based purely on wastage. *The Church's Needs and Resources*, Sixth Report, CIO, 1972, p. 19.

parishes. The clergy of these, already at an income disadvantage, may pay all or most of their expenses, perhaps to the tune of £200 a year, out of their own pockets.

To be poorer by possibly £400 a year will certainly drive men out of inner city livings to more prosperous ones. The effect of competition for increasingly scarce clergy will be to deprive the inner city areas of ministers. The rationing of men by 'price' will increase that maldeployment my figures have already shown. Prosperous suburban or quiet not-too-demanding country parishes (where the stipend is adequate, expenses low) will score all the time. The densely populated areas will suffer.

There is no easy, or immediate answer to all this. There is no remedy in drafting underemployed country clergy into the towns. Country clergy are on average ten years older than their town cousins. There are other social reasons against it too. What is needed is a national policy on staffing and deployment which gives men opportunity to move by their own initiatives and brings the freehold and patronage as at present understood to an end, which equalizes pay and expenses of office as between dioceses, with due allowances for differentials in the cost of living. Every diocese needs to make forward financial estimates to cover stipend increases to the clergy, which ought to run at about five per cent per annum if the clergy are not to suffer a steady decline in their standards of living. But pay structures are a jungle as the tables at the end of the Paul Report show. There are about 14,000 different ways of paying the clergy (I gave examples) and 43 different diocesan ways of equalizing that pay. The Church of England strangles in its own red tape.

Two major reports since the Second World War have recommended ways of rationalizing deployment and pay. They are *The Deployment and Payment of the Clergy*, 1964 (the Paul Report) and *Partners in Ministry*, 1967 (the Morley Report). I set out below their contrasting proposals for overcoming the obstacles to rational deployment of the clergy.

The Paul Report

Freehold: the transformation of the freehold into a leasehold (i.e. limited tenure of every incumbency to ten years, renewable for another five). Every incumbent should have the opportunity before the end of seven years to plan his future in consultation with his bishop. *Patronage*: in the traditional sense this should be ended and replaced by a staffing or appointments system and on a named day all patronage outside regional boards should be extinguished. *Staffing*: A clergy Staff Board should be set up at national level with corresponding regional boards, eight in number, at inter-diocesan level. They should seek, in consultation with the central board and diocesan committees, to plan deployment of the whole area and therefore to name men to the appropriate bishop for vacant posts. The bishop could accept or reject such nominations. Every newly-ordained man should be subject to direction for the first five years of his service; after that movement would be by consultation between the clergyman, his bishop and the regional board. *Pay*: benefice funds should be pooled to create a common stipendiary fund: regional machinery would be used to negotiate a common stipendiary level for the dioceses in each region, related to a national scale: Church Commissioners should make block grants to each diocese for the payment of living agents: the distinction between beneficed and unbeneficed men should be ended: all would become salaried men, on a graded scale with increases for special responsibility. Men should be able to retire at 65. *Parishes*: group and team ministries should be given a legal form and a new entity, *a major parish* should be created run by a college of clergy all of whom would enjoy 'incumbent status'. There would be neither leasehold nor freehold: tenure would be written into the appointment. Single incumbent parishes would then become *minor parishes*.

There were many other ancillary proposals, but the above were those which would have created a new system of deployment.

The Morley Report

Freehold: the freehold would be extinguished and replaced by a staffing system: tenure would be for a term of years, with the possibility of renewal by mutual consent or without a term of years but subject to review. A Diocesan Ministry Commission, wide in scope, would make all diocesan appointments; a national commission would seek to secure the deployment of clergy according to mission and pastoral need. *Patronage*: patronage would be extinguished—Diocesan Ministry Commissions would become the sole appointees. *Staffing*: Every man upon ordination would go upon the *strength* of the diocese. As long as he remained so he would be paid his appropriate stipend and housed. In this role he would continue, whether in a post or not, until he retired. If he moved into another field of work or outside the diocese he could still remain *on the books* of the diocese. An elaborate system of appeals and referees is proposed so that the objections of a man to being moved to or removed from a post are given the utmost consideration. The distinction between beneficed and unbeneficed men would go. *Pay*: the commission could not recommend basic or incremental scales for clergy because it could not see that funds permitted this, but it asked for a five-year scheme for reorganizing the diocesan stipends systems: it proposed the pooling of capital sums and glebe to create a central fund and that statutory fees received by incumbents should be passed on to the diocese. There would be guarantees to incumbents that their annual income would not fall as a result of the schemes proposed. *Parishes*: proposals for legal group and team ministries, by this time in the Pastoral Measure, were endorsed and reorganization recommended along the lines of the powers given in the Measure.

The Paul Report was subjected to a series of debates at Church Assembly and of explanatory memoranda by the Central Advisory Council for the Training of the Ministry which had commissioned it. The memoranda were, *A Study of the Paul Report on the Deployment and Payment of the Clergy*, February 1964; *The Paul Report: The Next Steps*, July 1964; *Issues Raised*, February 1965. The second paper led to the setting up of the Pastoral Recommendations Committee which was required to consider the proposals of the Paul Report which related to pastoral reorganization, and its recommendations led to the embodiment of many of them in the Pastoral Measure (1968). The debate on *Issues Raised* led to the setting-up of the Morley Commission. The Morley Report was finally defeated in the last session of Church Assembly in July 1970 and *yet a new committee* was set up to see how to do many of the things recommended in two reports without interfering with patronage and freehold.

Its first set of recommendations came before the July 1972 sessions of the General Synod.[6] It proposed, firstly, the establishment of a Central Stipends Authority (set up in November 1972) which would have the

Table to show per cent clergy and laity in favour of some recommendations of the Paul and Morley Reports
(Industrial Administration Research Unit, University of Aston*)

	Laity in favour (%)	Clergy in favour (%)
A common stipendiary fund for all the clergy	72·3	81·2
One single system of payment of all clergy with increments for length of service and special responsibilities	86·4	85·0
Upon ordination, the placing of a man on the diocesan strength and payment of him whether or not he has a job	58·3	70·4
An open central registry to bring available men in touch with available posts	97·2	93·2
Substitution of Parson's leasehold for Parson's freehold (i.e. a maximum of 15 years in any one parish)	59·9	59·3
The encouragement of group and team ministries	78·0	80·7
The establishment of lay street teams and other organized forms of lay activity in the parishes	80·5	95·7
Stepping up the co-ordinating work of rural deaneries and the status of rural deans	80·5	69·0

* Research in Birmingham Diocese conducted by Alan Bryman and C. R. Hinings. *Research Bulletin, 1973*, Institute for the Study of Worship and Religious Architecture.

[6] *First Report of the Terms of Ministry Committee*, CIO, June 1972.

Table to show per cent clergy in favour of some Paul Report recommendations
(St George's House, Windsor, Research)

	Clergy in favour (%)
A common stipendiary fund for all the clergy	49·6
One single system of payment of all clergy, with increments for length of service and special responsibilities	75·3
An open central registry to bring available men in touch with available posts	73·1
The right for clergy to retire at 65 on full pension if they want to	81·2
Occasional sabbatical leave for clergy (without reduction of stipend)	82·8
Substitution of parson's leasehold for parson's freehold (i.e. a maximum of 15 years in any one parish)	46·3
The encouragement and legalization of group and team ministries	63·3
The union of parishes in difficult areas into 'major' parishes run by colleges of clergy	61·6
The grouping of dioceses into regions principally to make the deployment of the clergy easier and more sensible	48·6
The conversion of such regions into archiepiscopal provinces	26·1
The establishment of lay street teams and other organized forms of lay activity in the parishes	76·3
Stepping up the co-ordinating work of rural deaneries and the status of rural deans	60·7
Direction of men for the first five years after ordination	60·7

power of oversight of the pay of all clergy from diocesan bishops downwards, and of the pay of lay workers too. One intention would be to secure common standards between dioceses and for this purpose the Authority would have power to submit payment schemes to the General Synod. But, of course, the stipendiary system is plagued by the inequalities of parochial benefices—for each parochial benefice is a kind of private trust fund secured to the incumbent—and the crunch of the Ministry Committee's proposals came in the recommendations of a 'Measure to secure the pooling of benefice endowment income, including glebe income, and the transfer of glebe into diocesan ownership'.[7] The upshot would be that endowment income and glebe 'would cease to be secured to benefices'. It was accepted by Synod.

In Section 2, the Report proposes that the House of Bishops shall set up a working group 'to formulate guidelines for the fairer distribution

[7] Ibid, p. 8.

of the available clerical manpower'[8] and that a new post, a (clerical) adviser on appointments, should be created. Section 3 proposed special care for men returning from appointments overseas. All these proposals can be traced back to the Paul and Morley Reports. Section 4 sought to by-pass the controversial earlier Reports which aimed at the abolition of the patronage system by proposing modest reform: all the same it went far towards satisfying the case for regional boards of appointment made in the Paul (but not the Morley) Report.

'We ourselves see considerable attractions in a suggestion that there should be a regional board for each group of dioceses, which would be formed by merging the existing diocesan boards of patronage on a regional basis so that one board would in future serve a group of dioceses. Diocesan boards of patronage have suffered in the past because their role has been narrowly circumscribed within a single diocese. The proposal is that the new regional board should take over the responsibilities of the diocesan boards it would supersede. It could also take over any patronage which existing patrons wish to relinquish.'[9]

At the parochial level the Committee asked for a Parish Appointments Committee, called whenever there was a vacancy, in which patron, diocese and parish would be represented in 'even balance'. It would seek to secure agreement on the nomination of a new incumbent by consensus, 'not a decision by majority vote'. It asked too for a Measure to be introduced 'covering the dissolution of pastoral relationships in cases of disability or ill-health of an incumbent, and in cases of pastoral deterioration'. The latter case meant—getting rid of a parson who was patently doing harm to his parish.

The Synod had debated on the same day the Sixth Report on *The Church's Needs and Resources* which drew attention to the predictable steady fall of the parochial clergy manpower from 11,000 in 1975 to 10,000 by 1980 and beyond at a sharper rate and called for a restructuring of the whole ministry. Synod approved the establishment of a central stipends authority and the pooling of benefice income and other proposals, including the compulsory retirement of a clergyman from his freehold at 70, but on patronage system it sent instructions to the Committee to reconsider radically its proposals for the reform of patronage in the light of the manpower situation described in *The Church's Needs and Resources* and overall problems of clergy deployment. *The Second Report of the Terms of Ministry Committee* (GS 154) was presented to Synod in July 1973, with proposals for establishing diocesan staffing panels and Parish Appointment Committees. The Report was

---

[8] This Committee first met in January 1973.

[9] Ibid. p. 17. My proposal was that the board should take over *all* patronage in its region.

defeated by a substantial majority for failing to deal courageously with patronage, and the life of the Committee brought to an end.

Of course what is happening to the Church of England is only a special case of what is happening to Churches and denominations in the West generally. The expansive days are over. Few Churches will be able to afford, in the long run, lavish buildings on spacious plots used for only a few hours a week. Few, too, will be able to recruit and maintain well-paid, well-educated full-time professional ministers and preserve them as a privileged élite or to distribute them around the country in the off-hand, gentlemanly way the Church of England does (as though they were two-a-penny). All those resources will be increasingly precious, rare, expensive. Churches must become Churches of a ministry shared with a conscientious laity if they are not to become ecclesiastical systems divorced from the laity (or even without laity) or put up the shutters altogether.

Which brings me to the paper I discussed at the beginning of this chapter. It spoke of the necessity to think of church 'order' in functional rather than normative terms—to ask whether the 'order' is doing what you want it to do rather than 'being' what traditionally it always was. This way of thinking leads one to prefer the notion of 'organization' to 'institution'. The advantages of this preference were summed up by the sociologist Mady A. Thung as follows.

'Organization allows for the distinction between conscious planning and unconscious processes in institutionalization. Seen as a process of goal-orientated action, organization brings in the element of "orientation to a common purpose". It takes account of the "informal and unorganized processes" which accompany formal order. It avoids therefore identifying church life with church order. It leads to a functional understanding of formal order as being subservient to purpose. It brings to awareness the frustrating potential of all formal order.'[10]

Much of this sociological thinking was deeply theological (or, to use the strange language of sociologists, had 'a strong theological potential'). What then of the Holy Spirit to whom, in some views, everything can be comfortably left? But, said someone early in our study, the Holy Spirit *is* God at his most empirical. The work of God through the Church is not always best served by subservience to the traditional. It is of course the traditional church structures in the Church of England and elsewhere which stand in the way of the proper deployment of human and material resources. These have everything to do with historical forms and the stubbornness of tradition, but very little, I am inclined to think, with Christianity.

---

[10] The Report of the WCC Study Group, 'Spirit, Order and Organization', *Study Encounter*, Fall 1970.

TWO

Cities and Decay

IN THE early sixties the Rev. Nicolas Stacey was appointed vicar of St Mary's, the parish church of Woolwich, a grey, eighteenth century church with great square balconies, standing on a little eminence over-looking the main road and the industrialized river Thames. He found the church with an average Sunday attendance of fifty and left it eight years later, his mission a self-confessed failure, with its Sunday attendance doubled. He had probably raised the attendance by almost one-half per cent of the parish population. In the meantime, he had transformed the church, enclosing the galleries to create a social centre with a coffee bar and lunch counter, opened a discotheque in the crypt and housed the offices of the local Council of Social Service, incidentally one of the oldest in the country. He had created an ecumenical team ministry, founded a successful housing association, engaged a professional sociolo-gist, become the rural dean, watched over the religious problems of the birth of the new town of Thamesmead, proved that the Church cared—and then abandoned it all as failure. He quite saw that what he had accomplished in a social service sense was impressive and that some people were deeply moved to see this coming out of a Christian context. But in terms of the Christian longing to bring people to the redemptive Gospel, to the fellowship of the eucharist, to the community of the faithful, he was still without impress on ninety, perhaps even ninety-eight per cent of the population.

Perhaps far more than two per cent *cared* that the Church was caring. If so attendance at church, active church life did not seem to them convincing ways of acknowledging this. Many things were against him. He was set down in the great secular suburban desert of south-east London, a commuter land with a population of about 1,000,000, as great indeed as that of some member nations of the United Nations, but culturally a wasteland, one vast subtopia.[1] Was eight years enough to tackle his portion of it? Woolwich itself had a long tradition of

---

[1] For instance, Trinidad and Tobago have just over 1,000,000 population, Panama 1,400,000.

radicalism and agnosticism stemming from its Arsenal and river front workers, its socialist pioneers and its *avant-garde* co-operative society. Nicolas Stacey was confronting, relatively alone, a social and historical tide symbolized by its adjacent Powis Street pointing at the Arsenal where the secular power lay.[2]

It is significant that his local suffragan was then Dr John Robinson, Bishop of Woolwich, whose *Honest to God* was published during Stacey's incumbency. Basically Robinson was asking what are we *saying*? *What really do we believe*? and his episcopal ministry was part, equally with Stacey's, of the religious crisis, a crisis related not only to what people believe of themselves and of God, but to the shape society is taking, the shape of shapelessness. It is not surprising that Southwark diocese has felt the impact of all this, for it is one vast housing area from the first streets by the riverside to the hills of Kent and with no one true centre south of the river. It has a population of over 2,000,000. It has grown up as a dormitory for the service of London's commerce, business and government, and highlights the problems and the nature of the great conurbations, all of which have inner suburbs like those covered by Southwark diocese.

An energetic Parochial Reorganization Committee set up by the diocese looked at the parishes to consider what its long-term strategy should be and published a report[3] on 'the principles and pattern towards which it should be working'. It gave the following account of religious attendance in the Diocese:

	Population	Parochial Units	Average Pop.	Easter Comms	Average per Unit
Inner London	1,501,010	188	8,000	29,436	156
Outer London	653,960	80	8,200	24,214	303
Surrey	165,250	37	4,450	8,479	229
Total diocese	2,320,220	305	7,600	61,129	204

The report comments on these figures that over half the Easter communicants in the diocese come from the outer areas which have only one-third of the total population. 'Moreover, parishes in those areas (suburban and rural) attract nearly twice as many communicants on

[2] The Arsenal has now gone, except as a symbol and the name of a football team. Nicolas Stacey has written an account of his ten year ministry in *Who Cares?* (Anthony Blond, 1971.) It belongs to an important group of clerical protests: *The Impatience of a Parson*, Dick Sheppard; *Parson in Revolt*, Joseph McCulloch; *Odd Man out*, Eric James; *What's Wrong with the Church of England* by Nick Earle. Nicolas Stacey abandoned the ministry to become Deputy Director of Oxfam, then Director of Social Services for the London Borough of Ealing.

[3] *Tomorrow's Parish*, introduction by Bishop of Southwark, ICF Press, 1969.

average as those in Inner London. If the Inner London figures were broken down so as to exclude middle-class areas where religious practice is relatively high, the contrast would be even more striking.'

The Report mentions investigations into the state of affairs in the Battersea Deanery, a convenient area to investigate since its boundaries at the time ran with the then Borough borders.[4] These investigations make plain the grimness of the situation of a not untypical inner city area. A 1965 survey showed that less than one per cent of the population of the deanery was in an Anglican Church on an average Sunday. There were 16 Anglican and 14 Roman and Nonconformist places of worship in the deanery. My own look at the situation[5] could not convince me that more than two per cent of the population were in Christian places of worship on an average Sunday. The extent of the disaster is perhaps better shown by the fact that the Anglican churches provided seating capacity for 7,700 people, but less than a thousand made use of them. In 1965 the percentage of use was 12·5.[6] By the 1970 figures from the deanery it looks as though only 1 in 144 persons is now in an Anglican Church on Sunday.

A certain depopulation of the old Battersea Borough through slum clearance and massive rehousing, and statistical difficulties caused by its union with Wandsworth to make a new London Borough, debar precise conclusions about everything, but it does seem true that all pastoral results except marriages in church fall from year to year—Christmas communions by nearly 14% and baptisms by nearly 15% in one year (1967–8)—faster than for the diocese as a whole, while the fall for the diocese in basic pastoral results has been faster than the results for other dioceses, though comparable to the changes taking place in great metropolitan dioceses such as Birmingham, London, Manchester and so on. What I mean can be shown from figures from my own report. The average Sunday attendance I gave for the Diocese of Hereford was 88 per 1,000 population—just about nine per cent—whereas Southwark had only an attendance of 23 per 1,000 population, or not quite two and a half per cent. *The Battersea deanery figure at roughly the same time was less than 1 per cent.* The situation is not greatly improved if one turns to Easter communicants. There a table best expresses the contrast. Another table shows the percentage decline for some of the most significant pastoral results.

---

[4] There are two Reports: (1) *Battersea Deanery Survey, 1966*; (2) *Battersea Deanery Organization Committee*, 1971, both published by Battersea Rural Deanery.

[5] I lived in the deanery for sixteen years and have a special knowledge of and affection for it.

[6] A fire and a church reorganization have sent the usage of available seating up to 14·3% though actual attendances have continued to decline.

	Population	Easter Comm.	per 1,000 Pop.
Battersea Deanery (1964)	110,076	1,659[7]	15
Hereford Diocese (1962)	228,670	26,654	135
Southwark Diocese (1962)	2,359,080	77,870	24

Battersea Deanery

	Period in years	% change
Attendance at main Sunday service	6	−23·06
Easter Communions	5	−22·72
Christmas Communions	5	−30·78
Baptisms	5	−54·04
Weddings	7	−37·14

Making all allowances for population mobility, the influx of immigrants and changing social patterns, the impression such percentages give is of a dying Anglicanism in Battersea. Perhaps one could extrapolate a line and show that the Church will hypothetically be extinct there by the year X. A Baptist Commission has done this for the Baptists showing its hypothetical reduction to 100,000 in the year 2001 and a falling curve leading to extinction at some point beyond.[8] Of course Battersea is no more the whole country than the seven tailors of Tooley Street were England. But it would be an ostrich ritual to deny these figures a wider significance. What strikes one is the fall in baptisms and weddings in Battersea. Not only do these represent the Church's future but they are part of the sphere of traditional religion, of rites of passage, where the Church of England has always been strong.

The Deanery Reorganization Committee, taking a hard look at the statistics of decline, recommends that all the Battersea parishes with the exception of the ancient parish church of St Mary's, by the riverside, where Blake's signature is in the marriage register, should be turned into Pastoral Units. A Pastoral Unit, as defined by the diocese, is a centre rather than a church, 'with accommodation for one or more clergy or lay workers, and space suitable for varying numbers of people to meet for worship and other activities'. They propose this, they say, 'Because we believe a local Christian presence to be important and because it seems that the closure of a church building leads to an accelerated decline in Church membership.' However, economics are important. The

---

[7] By 1970 the figure had dropped to 1282, about 12 per thousand, or half the diocesan rate.

[8] *Ministry Tomorrow*, Report of the Commission on the Ministry, Baptist Union, London, undated, p. 19.

Total Membership of Baptist and Associated Churches in UK (1861-1961) projected to 2001

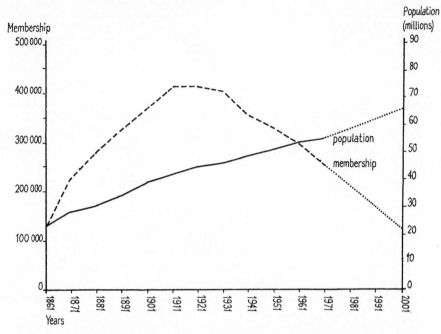

Fig. 3. *The point of the double curve of this graph is to show an absolute decline in Baptist membership side by side with absolute rise in population, both curves projected to the year 2000. So absolute a decline in membership is improbable—the curve is almost certain to flatten out. The graph is adapted, with permission, from Fig. 1 of* Ministry Tomorrow. *The Report of the Commission on the Ministry, authorised by the Council of the Baptist Union in November 1967, p. 19.*

Deanery is always in the red. Approximately half the money required to finance the Church in Battersea comes from outside. Yet the Church is rich in property, owning over eight acres of valuable urban land, the disposal of part of which would finance the redeployment of the Church at strategic points as the committee proposes.

The Deanery proposals are not unique. Indeed they stem from a wider conception of a new pattern of ministry for the whole of Southwark Diocese[9] involving the setting up of new parishes or major parishes with a population of 30,000 to 60,000 and devolving down to pastoral units of the sort Battersea Deanery argues for. Southwark Diocese owes the concept to the genius of the Rev. Leslie Harman, one time Director of Religious Sociology for the Diocese. Into this I shall look again in more detail presently. For the moment let us return to Battersea Deanery and its consciousness of the human element.

---

[9] *Tomorrow's Parish*, Introd. by the Bishop of Southwark.

'The implementation of these suggestions will, we appreciate, be a cause of pain and grief to many faithful Church Members. We believe this has to be frankly and honestly acknowledged. Many members of our congregations have struggled with great sacrifice and loyalty to preserve buildings which we are now suggesting should be pulled down or converted. Such a course must seem to them like an admission of defeat. Talk of rationalization may not impress them. We, all of us, the Committee included, have experienced emotional attachment to buildings. All we can suggest by way of consolation is that our policy is probably less painful, in the long run, than the alternative which we foresee; the further deterioration of our churches for lack of adequate resources to provide for their support'—and the reduction of the Church's mission to a desperate effort simply to keep the buildings going. In some places it has reached this point.

What is happening, or is about to happen, to Battersea churches is not something isolated or unexpected. It was estimated by the Bridges' Commission[10] in 1960 that nearly eight hundred churches were expected to become redundant in the sixties and seventies and that of these 'nearly 450 might be considered for preservation'.[11] Dr Gilbert Cope, of the Institute for the Study of Worship and Architecture spoke of the possibility of some six thousand redundancies. The Advisory Board for Redundant Churches thought this 'far too pessimistic' but argued on the other hand that the Bridges figure was a serious underestimate.[12] In the long run many churches will have to go, even medieval village churches of outstanding beauty, and the traditional landscape of England, already violated by motorways and high rise towers, will suffer further impoverishment. There is a limit to the preservation of what people no longer have a use for.

The closing of a church can be a traumatic experience for many more than those who actually attend church. The Battersea Deanery recognized the attachment of local people to 'their church' and to its symbolism on the skyline. The Rev. D. M. K. Durston wrote, on the preservation of ancient churches, 'The significance of this aspect of a parson's work ... can easily be misunderstood. Many people in this country perceive church buildings as symbols of the Christian faith, and the sight and presence

---

[10] The Archbishops' Commission on Redundant Churches, Chairman, Lord Bridges, 1960.

[11] *Redundant Churches Fund, Second Annual Report, 1970*, Faith Press, London, p. 4. The 1971 Report says: 'Thirty-three months of the operation of the [Pastoral] Measure should have been long enough for the pastoral committees to get in their stride, but by the end of 1971 the fund had been notified of only 136 declarations of redundancy....' There were 105 declarations of redundancy in 1972.

[12] *Annual Report*, 1971, p. 17.

of these buildings arouse powerful emotions in them. While these emotions may be of a very primitive kind and often inarticulate, they frequently have a profound influence on people's behaviour. They reflect people's need for a religion of some kind, a need which in this country they expect the Christian Church to fulfil. When they hear of clergy recommending that churches should be closed and demolished, or allowed to fall into disrepair, they feel that the clergy have now lost confidence in the Christian faith.'[13] One wonders what they think when they hear of clergy protesting, or even demonstrating, against the repair of York Minster or St Paul's Cathedral on the grounds that the Church has got its priorities wrong?

To the symbolic presence of the Church and its role in an unformulated national religion I will return. The point has been made that Battersea's dilemma, for that matter Southwark's dilemma, is only the national dilemma of the Church in urban areas. What it is suffering now other urban areas will be suffering in a decade or so, if they are not doing so already. There can be no remedy without unstitching a great deal that is precious—a backward fall into an anguish of nostalgia will not avail. It is perhaps the more important to say this because a mention of the Southwark Diocese evokes a derisory impatience in many sections of the Church. It is the 'Left Bank', the home of theological heterodoxy and general crankiness, of which its problems are argued to be the product. Few pause to see it the other way round—that its problems, whether of theology or parish life, may be the product of that grinding urban secularization to which so many have already drawn attention, and that what some described as mere gimmickry represents attempts to escape from a religious death to a living relationship with a community.

I have always argued that the core of the Paul Report was its findings about urbanization. England is an urbanized land, perhaps the most urbanized in the world.[14] Its urban populations derive very largely from those migratory masses who became alienated from religious practice when they moved from village society to the ghettoes of the industrial revolution where it was a psychological mockery as well as a social impossibility to worship. Those who have moved up in this urban society to lower middle class or middle class status have moved in fact from groups disposed to dismiss the Church as not their Church, 'nothing to do with me'. The hold of the Church on these groups and their living

---

[13] *The Times*, 5 July 1971.

[14] England had a population density of 911 to the square mile in 1968. Only the Netherlands with 949 exceeded that in Europe. Many small or island states such as Singapore (8,836) vastly exceed that. The density of the USA is 57 and of the USSR in Europe is 65 (RSFSR). Great Britain has the highest density in the world of vehicles per road mile—more than twice that of the U.S.A.—and expects to have 20 million cars on her roads by 1980.

Average Sunday Attendance in the Church of England (1962 & 1970)

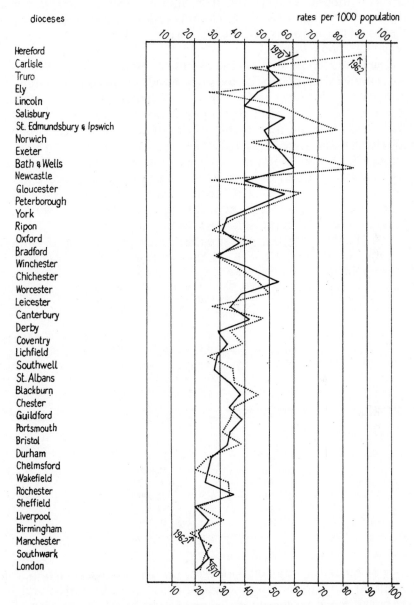

Fig. 4. *The Paul Report collected Sunday Attendances at church and correlated them with population. Subsequent collections made by the Statistical Unit of the Central Board of Finance makes it possible to compare 1962 with 1970 figures. Both curves show that the figures for attendance per 1.000 population decrease as urban density rises. The position on the whole is stable, except that the very rural dioceses seem to have lost their high peaks. The countryside—it is a guess—may be slowly becoming 'urbanized. in its religious outlook and practice, a sad look-out.*

areas has always been tenuous. As it slips, so the claim it has on the cities threatens to vanish altogether. But since its urban masses constitute the overwhelming majority of the population its loss of the cities means the loss of the nation as a whole. Some rural and suburban successes avail very little against that.

The Paul Report showed the extent of the urban slide. When Easter communicant figures and average Sunday attendance figures were graphed for dioceses placed in order of population density they showed a consistent decline, per 1,000 of population, from the least dense to the most dense, from the most rural to the most urban, from nearly 14 per cent for Hereford Diocese to just over 2 per cent of the population for London Diocese for Easter communicants and from about 9 per cent to 2 per cent for the same dioceses for average Sunday attendances. And differentials of this magnitude seemed to occur whatever pastoral result one was looking for, even recruitment to the ministry. It was as stark a revelation as could be of the lost battle of the cities.

Such figures show only the situation at a given moment of time. What are significant too are the trend lines and these show a slow decline at every point:

Confirmations 1957–70
(Provinces of Canterbury and York)

Year	Confirmations (all ages)	Estimated populations aged 12–20 inclusive	No. of confirmations per 1,000 population aged 12–20
1957	172,288	4,997,000	34·5
1958	173,177	5,092,000	34·0
1959	182,721	5,382,000	34·0
1960	190,713	5.587,000	34·1
1961	191,042	5.756,000	33·2
1962	180,284	5.914,000	30·5
1963	162,728	6.036,000	27·0
1964	156,265	6.038,000	25·9
1968	125,294	5,849,000	21·4
1969	116,631	5,757,000	20·3
1970	113,005	5,748,000	19·7

The Church is losing slowly all along the line: its losses can be paralleled by all other English churches except the Roman Catholics and Pentecostalists. Such a general loss cannot be reasonably attributed to a rise in immigrant population or in the number of Roman Catholics—these are still local factors—but to something more profound, something universal in the mood of the nation. But it accords with the theme that urbanization is necessarily on the increase as the population grows. The young who are born today are not country children who will move into

Deacons Ordained 1960-70
(Numbers)

1	2 Canterbury province	3 York province	4 Total C. of E.	5 Number who were graduates
1960	403	195	598	
1961	394	212	606	
1962	413	220	633	270
1963	434	202	636	304
1964	407	198	605	230
1965	388	204	592	249
1966	398	178	576	197
1967	339	157	496	190
1968	342	136	478	181
1969	313	123	436	161
1970	288	149	437	185
1972	247	114	361*	149

* Provisional figures: includes 21 ordained to the Pastoral Auxiliary ministry.

Marriages 1844-1967
(Proportions per 1,000 total marriages)

Year	C. of E. and Wales	R.C.	Other Christian denominations	Jews	Civil ceremonies
1844	907	17	49	1	26
1899	698	42	116	4	140
1919	597	52	115	5	231
1957	496	115	104	5	280
1962	474	123	102	5	296
1967	449	112	94	4	341

the town. They are babies born in the town and *for* the town. Logic would suggest that if urbanization is a factor in alienation from the Church, an increase in urbanization will increase that alienation. Urbanization in contemporary society is not organic, piecemeal, absorbed by living communities, but so often wholesale, destructive, creative of social deserts. Even where its purpose is good and the housing estate or casual assemblies of tower blocks replace the slum, the transition is from something on a human scale to the sterile and inhuman. It is the fact that many Churches and priests of many denominations struggle heroically to create a community in such conditions and sometimes succeed. But the social trend not only makes this task more and more difficult but renders it often impossible. A community as a delicate creation of trust, tension and understanding cannot survive the loss of those face-to-face relations which are often the first casualty of the contemporary urban process. The tendency in the urban scene is to retreat from what community there is into the privacy of the nuclear family—neither to know what community there is nor to appreciate the need for it. It is a tendency aggravated in the United States by the violence in the streets.

The contrast between the life of the nuclear family and the extended family helps us a little to understand the retreat from community. The extended family included grandmothers and grandfathers—always about the place, living with one branch of relatives or another—aunts and great aunts, uncles and great uncles, all to some extent watching over and helping each other, particularly in times of sickness or trouble, and gathering formidably at weddings, funerals, or moments of success: in the middle class terms of the Forsyte Saga, seeking to avert disaster and to protect the family name. The extended family, so typical of Victorian times, lives on despite the Welfare State, but much attenuated. Perhaps it is most alive in Jewish communities. It was always a bridge into the wider community, exercising its influence on behalf of its weaker members.

The nuclear family is very much the biological family of two generations—parents and children. In the West it tends to be middle class and small, pre-packaged for the suburban semi-detached house and the family car, and isolated from intimate contact with the extended family, partly because mobility in society scatters families more than it did in the past but also because shrinking housing accommodation denies room for elderly guests. So even grandmother and grandfather are banished, sometimes to a home. They can't live on a sofa.

The nuclear family is bracketed off, as it were, within the extended family and because of this the lives of the very elderly tend to become lonely and impoverished. Some times they are just forgotten, packed off to a geriatric ward, for the participation in the life of the wider family is one option the nuclear family can take up or chop at will. Or almost at will, for the married girl tends to cling tenaciously to continued close contact with mother and to be within visiting distance of 'mum' may be very important to her psychological health. Nevertheless, the nuclear family is a unit presented with a few basic obligations but many voluntary opportunities. The necessities present themselves—to house the family, clothe, feed and bring up the children, all falling mostly on the mother, and for the father to earn the wage or salary which makes the rest possible at the level of the family ambition or status. Status, of course, adds to the list of necessities—the car, the TV set, the washing-machine become necessities. But these are strippable, the basic obligations are not, short of complete dependence on the Welfare State. But the options I meant were not so much in the field of possessions as of activity. Beyond the life of obligation what does the family do? Well, it may please itself. A vast field opens out for leisure in sports and recreation alone, in how and where holidays are spent, and leisure time includes the week-ends when the voluntary activity of the family explodes and a trip in the car to the sea, a visit to the caravan are probably more popular than going to church or looking up grannie.

The options in leisure time during the week are great enough. Does one—or do all— go to the cinema or the theatre, does father go to professional or trade union meetings, or political rallies, to clubs, societies, the library, or evening institutes, or stay at home supine before TV or paint the bathroom, do the crossword, assist the boy with homework, or service his car? Almost everything here is subject to decision or non-decision. The urban community offers little or no compulsion: it does not as a community would in a village, or market town, pattern the life of the family. Just as it is possible for an old person in an urban situation to be unknown to her neighbours, even unseen except to postman or milkman, so it is possible for a nuclear family to live a life of near anonymity in a city, despite the man's daily work and the children's life in school. It goes without saying that *the Church* is one of the urban options one might or might not take up and that if one did it would be unlikely to be on grounds of community obligation—as it might very well be still in the countryside.

Then, when options are taken up they are seldom limited by the invisible frontiers of the urban parish—the cinema is in one place, the library in another, the welfare services elsewhere, the school a bus ride, the workplace a train ride away. The family scatters over a *zone humaine* in pursuit of obligations and pleasures Familial or individual isolation, loss of community, the meaningless multiplication of options, cultural vacuity, fragmentation of lives over a wide area—these constitute the urban scene. Even this misses out the dimension of adolescence. .Life in the nuclear nest may be cosy and charming for the young child— television, trips in the car, holidays far away, a school life which encourages creativity, make it all seem a paradise compared with the child life of Victorian times when death and family disaster were often just round the corner. It is upon the adolescent that the blow falls when he discovers, escaping the cushioning, the great emptiness which is our contemporary society beyond its material successes. If he has attended that tenth urban option, the Church, he may not have learnt from it anything which would appear to him relevant to the life which is waiting for him. The youth culture and the counter-culture testify to his efforts to find his own way, testing himself only against his peers. One may speak of the strident, secular life of the great cities as inimical to the cultivation of religious experience and Christian devotion. And so, one lets the Church off the hook. On the other hand, and as expressed by its deployment system, one might speak of the Church as a whole, as *unable to pay attention to, incapable of focusing upon*, the urban scene because of the impediment of its historical forms. If that also is the case then Battersea Deanery is its proper reward.

THREE

'The Vision which rises before us...'

THE road to unity of the Churches is a very hard one if only for the reason that differences of doctrine and order express themselves in opposing institutional forms. Disunity has everywhere become institutionalized. Its scandal presents itself to the world as the norm and so, down the centuries, the abnormal becomes the normal. The Christian becomes reconciled to his sin, parades it as virtue and cannot live without it. The fury with which many Anglicans greeted the movement towards religious toleration in the last century reveals the extent to which Christians can build themselves an idiosyncratic world, as tight and exclusive as a caste system, and convince themselves that nothing entitled to be called Christianity exists beyond it.

To be locked within one's cultural milieu is not the privilege of Anglicans only. In 1837, a certain Robert Curzon visited the Ecumenical Patriarch in Constantinople, and presented him with a letter of introduction from the Archbishop of Canterbury.

' "And who," quoth the Patriarch of Constantinople, the supreme head and primate of the Greek Church of Asia, "who is the Archbishop of Canterbury?"

"What?" said I, a little astonished at the question.

"Who," said he, "is this Archbishop?"

"Why, the Archbishop of Canterbury."

"Archbishop of *what?*" said the Patriarch.

"*Canterbury,*" said I.

"Oh," said the Patriarch, "Ah yes! And who is he?" '

'And so on, *da capo,*' remarks Henry Brandreth, who quotes the passage.[1] One is reminded of the tactically useful difficulty the Communist world had in distinguishing between the Dean of Canterbury and the Archbishop in the days of the famous Red Dean, Dr Hewlett Johnson.

---

[1] In 'The Church of England and the Orthodox Churches in the nineteenth and twentieth centuries', Henry R. T. Brandreth, *Anglican Initiatives in Christian Unity*, edited by E. G. W. Bill, SPCK, London 1967. The dialogue itself comes from Curzon's *Visits to Monasteries in the Levant*, 1955 edn., pp. 175–6.

The symposium in which Henry Brandreth's essay appears reminds us that the search for better ecumenical relations has a long Anglican history. It can be said that even in the latter part of the seventeenth century there was a kind of effort at *rapprochement* between the studious on both sides of the Catholic fence, which, had the institutions not been coldly hostile, might have borne better fruit.[2] And there was even a young man, William Wake, destined to be Archbishop of Canterbury, who in Paris as a chaplain in 1682, engaged the great Bossuet in a controversy in which he scored all the points, asserting, nevertheless, despite his strong criticism of Roman doctrine, 'the desire of Anglicans for reunion, emphasizing the beliefs held in common by Canterbury and Rome and suggesting that these would afford a basis for at least peaceful coexistence whilst debate towards some agreement on points of difference went on'.[3] It seems naïve when seen against the religious enmities of the day, but it showed that tolerance, even understanding, were not total casualties. Ecumenical relations with other Churches—if they can be called such—were as difficult, down the centuries, to initiate and sustain as those with Rome. Motives, in any case, were not always of the best, as Steven Runciman explains:

'It is, in truth, impossible to give the epithet of *ecumenical* to these early [eighteenth century] negotiations between the Orthodox and the Anglicans. There was much good will on both sides and a real desire for a closer connection, but there was not yet sufficient tolerance. The Orthodox with their notion of economy could tolerate much; but they would tolerate neither *Filioque* nor the degradation, as they thought, of the Ecumenical Councils, nor blasphemous attacks on the Mother of God and the Saints. They might tolerate the usages of others, but they were not going to tolerate any criticism of their own usages. The Anglicans for their part had not discarded the superstitions of Rome to unite themselves with a Church whose doctrines, especially over the saints and the sacraments, seemed to be quite as superstitious. The goodwill did not stretch as far as sympathetic understanding. The real trouble was that it was not based on a truly ecumenical and irenical desire, but on the opposite. It was based on a mutual fear and hatred of Rome. It was a movement of self-defence...'[4]

---

[2] 'Even the Whiggish Bishop Burnet expressed in 1683 his admiration for French Catholic patristic studies and publications, whilst the great Maurist Benedictine, Mabillon, recommended the works of the Anglican divines, Bule, Pearson, Ussher, and Hammond, for monastic libraries' from T. M. Parker, 'The Church of England and the Church of Rome from the sixteenth to the eighteenth century', *Anglican Initiatives in Christian Unity*, p. 67. Cf. Norman Sykes, *From Sheldon to Secker*, Ford Lectures 1958, Oxford 1959, p. 115 et seq.

[3] T. M. Parker, ibid. p. 68.

[4] Steven Runciman, 'The Church of England and the Orthodox Churches in the seventeenth and eighteenth centuries', *Anglican Initiatives*, etc. pp. 17–18.

And there was always the question of *orders*. The older a Church, the more unbroken its tradition, the more difficult it was to challenge the validity of its orders. So the orders of the Orthodox and of Rome were safe from challenge unless one took the extreme step of denying them a Christian identity at all. But the Church of England? Ancient indeed, nevertheless it was exposed to the rejection of older Churches because it had broken its tradition. This did not prevent Newman, in Tract I, from declaring, 'All we who have been ordained clergy, in the very form of our ordination acknowledged the doctrine of the *apostolical succession*. And for the same reason we must necessarily consider none to be *really* ordained who have not *thus* been ordained.' Charles Gore crossed the t's and dotted the i's of this declaration when he said that Presbyterians and other Protestants needed an ordination which corresponded to 'the Catholic requirement'. He paid a verbal compliment to their 'spiritual grace' but obviously thought it small beer beside the laying-on of hands. One may look at this sociologically, rather than doctrinally. An exclusive institution needs to define its exclusiveness by drawing up the terms upon which its élite may take office or hold power. The terms will naturally oppose a claim of equality made by those in institutions of which it disapproves but must be couched in such a way as to claim the authority of those institutions which it has usurped. It was not possible for the King to become Supreme Head of the Church of England on terms which made Anglican clergy inferior to those of Rome. And orders, as we shall see, are still a stumbling block whether the Church of England aspires towards Rome or towards the Free Churches.

It is only in this century that the ecumenical theorizing of the Church of England has developed into an official search for union with other Churches. Perhaps we may date this from 1920, when the Lambeth Conference, hard upon the First World War and conscious of the gravity of the human situation, issued an 'Appeal to all Christian People' which owed much to the idealism and initiatives of young American and colonial Bishops.

'The vision which rises before us is that of a Church, genuinely Catholic, loyal to all Truth, and gathering into its fellowship all 'who profess and call themselves Christians', within whose visible unity all the treasures of faith and order, bequeathed as a heritage by the past to the present, shall be possessed in common, and made serviceable to the whole Body in Christ. Within this unity Christian Communions now separated from one another would retain much that has long been distinctive in their methods of worship and service. It is through a rich diversity of life and devotion that the unity of the whole fellowship will be fulfilled.'[5]

---

[5] *The Church of England, 1815–1948*, A Documentary History, R. P. Flindall, SPCK, London 1972, p. 361.

The Lambeth Quadrilateral had fastened upon the Church of England at home and abroad the four bases upon which it must stand—the Bible, the Nicene Creed, the two Gospel sacraments (eucharist and baptism) and the Historic Episcopate. The Appeal virtually repeated this but tempered the episcopal wind to the shorn non-conformist lamb by speaking of 'a ministry acknowledged by every part of the Church as possessing not only the inward call of the Spirit, but also the commission of Christ and the authority of the whole body'. All the same, the Appeal pressed the case for the episcopate and went on to say that 'we eagerly look forward to the day when through its acceptance in a united Church we may all share in that grace which is pledged to the members of the whole body in the apostolic rite of the laying-on of hands. . . .' Even so courteously put, it was a rebuke to those Churches which did not give a fig for the historic episcopate.

Some discussions did develop from the Appeal, but it took a Second World War, in which the challenges to Christianity from atheism, paganism and political terror were seen in all their fury for the very first time, to prod the Church of England to move a little farther. The establishment of a British Council of Churches in 1942, of a World Council of Churches in 1948, tested the ecumenical temper of the Church in earnest.

And so the Lambeth Conference of 1958 was much more passionate and anguished in its concern for unity.

'Conscious of the calling of the Church to be one family in Christ and to make known to the whole world in word and deed his Gospel of the Kingdom, we declare our ardent longing for the healing of our divisions, and for the recovery and manifestation to the world of that unity of the Body of Christ for which he prayed and continues to make intercession. . . . We believe in One, Holy, Catholic, and Apostolic Church, which takes its origin not in the will of man but in the will of our Lord Jesus Christ. *All those who believe in our Lord Jesus Christ and have been baptized in the name of the Holy Trinity are incorporated into the Body of Christ and are members of the Church. Here is a unity already given.*'[6]

Differences appeared to be swept away in the professed desire to unite all Christians to minister to a world 'divided by strife and fear'. There were tangible results to encourage an unctuous optimism.

'The Church of India, Pakistan, Burma and Ceylon asked that the Lambeth Conference should give advice upon three further schemes for united Churches in Ceylon, North India and Pakistan. We examined these schemes with the greatest care, and we would express our gratitude to God for the clear evidence of the guidance of his Holy Spirit in the negotiations, which have led to schemes of union which

---

[6] *The Lambeth Conference, 1958*, SPCK and Seabury Press, 1958, 2.21. Italics mine.

we believe to mark a great and significant step towards the recovery of the visible unity of the Church Universal. We believe that it will be possible for the Church of Lanka to be from the outset in full communion with Churches and provinces of the Anglican Communion. With some modification, the Churches of North India and Pakistan could have the same expectation.'[7]

But the Holy Spirit was not in step with the Anglican Communion over the Church of South India, the pioneer reunion scheme. In an unhappy sentence the Encyclical Letter says, 'We record with thankfulness that many of our Provinces have been able to establish *limited* intercommunion with that Church *on which the grace of God has been so abundantly and manifestly bestowed.*'[8] The Committee on Church Unity and the Church Universal reported that while a majority held that the bishops, presbyters and deacons of the Church of South India should be acknowledged as true bishops, presbyters, and deacons in the Church of Christ, a substantial minority held that it was not yet possible to pass any definite judgment on their precise status (despite the 'abundant grace'). This situation has not changed yet. The Church of South India is still on probation over the validity of its orders; the Holy Spirit is still on trial, though General Synod has laboured hard and sometimes confusedly to right an obvious wrong. For Synod managed to recognize the Church of North India and Pakistan, which also had its problems, and expressed its guilt over South India in a resolution it passed in July 1972:

'That this Synod recognizing that the Church of South India is an episcopally ordered Church and believing it to hold all the essentials of the Christian faith requests the House of Bishops to consider how the Church of England and the Church of South India can now be joined in a relationship of full communion.'

The bishops' considerations came to the Synod in February 1973. The bishops fell over themselves to meet the will of Synod, but were baffled to describe what 'full communion' really meant: there were fifty-seven varieties.[9] They took note of the fact that 'the Church of England might be held by other Churches to be in an anomalous situation in that the Act of Uniformity restricts the Church's freedom to define its relations with other Churches'. In particular they pointed out, the same Act, and canon law, 'restrict the celebration of Holy Communion to those who have been episcopally ordained'. And, of course, some priests of the Church of South India have not been episcopally ordained. What would happen, the bishops wondered, if the Church granted South India full communion and one of its priests, not episcopally ordained, came over

---

[7] Ibid. 1.24.

[8] *The Lambeth Conference, 1958*, SPCK and Seabury Press, 1958. Encyclical Letter, L. 24. Italics mine.

[9] GS 134, *The Church of South India*, a Report from the House of Bishops, January 1973.

here and—as full communion permitted—wanted to celebrate an Anglican eucharist at an Anglican altar?

Generous resolutions came before Synod proclaiming 'that this Synod is satisfied that the Church of South India is a true part of the Church Universal, holding the Catholic faith and possessed of the apostolic ministry of bishops, priests and deacons' and that 'this Synod resolves to enter into communion with the Church of South India *subject to regulations...*'. Alas, one regulation was to be—'ministers of the Church of South India not episcopally ordained are prevented by canon law and the law of England from celebrating the Holy Communion in the Church of England.'

Synod would have none of this final regulation. After a long debate it determined that the resolution of which it was part should not be put to the vote: now the bishops, and Synod, have to decide to leave things as they are, which is intolerable, or to consider the amendment of the Act of Uniformity, which internally and externally could prove politically dangerous. Perhaps the impending repeal will save the day.

In *Religion in Secular Society*[10] the eminent sociologist Bryan Wilson, has some pertinent things to say about what he calls 'ecumenicalism'. Ecumenism or 'ecumenicalism' has become a new faith, he thinks, at a time when no one believes in much else. There has been a mass conversion of the clergy to it.[11] His own hypothesis is that organizations amalgamate when they are weak rather than when they are strong and that ecumenism is a sign of their weakness at a critical time of falling membership, declining faith and secular pressures. Bryan Wilson therefore sees ecumenism as at least in part a professional rescue operation by the ministries of divided churches. 'The sense of being an inferior professional because of one's profession must be harrowing.' If the religious decline continues the sense of failure must grow, the economic rewards decline, status depreciate. Ecumenism alone, under the guise of a compromise with fellow Christians, could justify the process of coming to terms with secular society in order to save the professional and economic status of the ministries. Then, too, clergy self-interest in ecumenism is affected by increasing lay self-assertion, he argues.

'Although religion has not evolved the technical expertise which has occurred among many professional groups, and although the secular trend of Protestantism was distinctly towards laicization of the Church, none the less the inevitable tendencies by which a profession seeks to enhance its status, cultivate its own universe of discourse, and claim its own field of special competence has affected religious functionaries

---

[10] Watt & Co. 1966.
[11] Anyone who has listened to clergy speeches against reunion with the Methodists at Diocesan Synods and General Synod must find this hard to swallow.

hardly less than others...[12] Even among dissenters there has been a reassertion of ministerial authority and an enlargement of the differences between priest and people.'[13]

All this casts an odd light on ecumenism. It is, without doubt, part of the sociological story: Churches *are* coming together in protectiveness faced with a stony secular world in which their influence diminishes. But there are other elements in an ecumenism which extends right across the board. One is certainly the exhaustion of Protestantism as an historical force: the other the collapse of Fortress Rome as a monolithic unity. Fortress Rome, within whose walls the faith was maintained in its purity under an infallible general against the corruptions of an aggressive Protestantism was the answer to, the product of, Protestantism. But Protestantism in its old militancy, the foe of the Scarlet Woman, is dead. When there is no enemy at the gates one has no need to man the walls. In a word, all that convulsed Christendom in the days of Erasmus, Calvin, Luther and More is a spent force. Even if the doctrines which then divided Christians are still believed in, they are no longer aggressively asserted, militantly (or militarily) protested, with power as the reward for the successful and the fires of Smithfield for the defeated. No one will ever go through that again for Christ or pope or king. What *has* been discovered is that what the divided Christians collectively believe is far more important than what separates them. That this is in part the product of their defeats at the hands of the world is true: it is also in part the product of their defeats at the hands of each other in Western and in missionary situations. The great cities of Britain bristle with the religious towers and spires of churches which are tombstones to their own emptiness. The historic conflicts of Lutherans, Catholics, Methodists, Anglicans, Baptists, Seventh-Day Adventists vanished in a colonial bush where the devil gave you leprosy and yellow fever before he gave you heresy. It is no dishonour, but a mark of earnestness that the lesson of this historical tragedy is now being learnt.

It is not precisely the case that a ministerial self-interest has dictated contemporary ecumenical approaches. The initiatives at the Edinburgh Conference of 1910 were lay in character; many of the laity show impatience with those clerical pedantries which impede union. But they have to be non-party laity. Party laity are as fixed in their views as party clergy— perhaps more! The principal opposition to, or suspicion of, reunion in the Church of England has come from the two principal church parties. It was neither specifically ministerial nor lay, though the leadership was clerical. Something of the distribution of opinion in General Synod on reunion is shown by the following table on the voting

---

[12] Op. cit. 131.
[13] Op. cit. 133.

on 3 May, 1972. The motion for reunion was passed but not by the required 75 per cent.

	Ayes	Noes	Percentage
House of Bishops	34	6	85
House of Clergy	152	80	65·52
House of Laity	147	87	62·82
	Overall percentage—65·81		

Certainly many clergy and still more laity at that debate showed *fear* of reunion. Bryan Wilson's case must be held to be not proven.

But his point about the professionalization of the ministry over against a laity apt to be religiously ill-disciplined is curiously made for him in *Growing into Union* by C. O. Buchanan, E. L. Mascall, J. I. Packer, and the Bishop of Willesden.[14] The authors mount a defence of the ministry as a necessary élite in control of discipline and doctrine because the Church is constantly 'under pressure from the world to be conformed to its thought and judgement'. This has two consequences—one, 'a narrow concentration on historical events to the exclusion of the living Christ', and on the other hand (quoting Sir Edwyn Hoskyns) the growth of a 'mystery religion based upon spiritual experience uncontrolled by the death of Jesus and by his teaching and action'—on the lines of the Corinthian heresy denounced by St Paul. In our present age, when 'any idea of religion is alien to the majority of people, it results in . . . a temporal Gospel'.

The teaching of St Paul and St John in the face of these problems is that the function of the ministry is to exercise a pastoral care in the name and power of Christ by which the obedience of the Church to the living Christ is controlled and disciplined by the events which brought it into being. In other words, it is in the ministry of the Church that the two directions in which the Church must look are focused. It is the duty of those called to oversight to minister in Christ's name for the edification of the Church. It is equally their duty to witness to the apostolic faith and to secure 'that the life of the Church is firmly rooted in the events of our redemption' (p. 70). I am not sure that I understand the theology of this argument but I do understand the prefectorial view of the ministry embodied in such concepts as 'obedience', 'control', 'discipline', 'oversight', 'edification'. (Yet it is not from the laity but from the ministry itself that most modern theological heresies emanate! *Quis custodiet ipsos custodes?*)

It is because in part of what they believe to be a 'deficient' view of the ministry that high and low Church parties mounted opposition to the

---

[14] SPCK, 1970, p. 69 et seq. The Rt. Rev. Douglas Leonard is now Bishop of Truro.

scheme of reunion between the Methodist Church and the Church of England, a scheme which was embodied finally in two documents—*Anglican–Methodist Unity: 1. The Ordinal; Anglican–Methodist Unity: 2. The Scheme*[15] and debated by the Methodist conference and Church Assembly in 1969. The Methodist Conference accepted the scheme and so did Church Assembly but with a percentage (69) insufficient to secure approval. In extraordinary deference to the minority, a seventy-five per cent vote of approval had been insisted on from the outset.

The Scheme accepted that there were divergent views on the priesthood in the Church of England. The first, the traditional high church view, is that ordination by the laying-on of hands within the episcopal succession impresses an indelible character on the recipient, who has a priestly role 'in offering to God the eucharist in which Christ's offering is made present'. Non-episcopal ordination, as in Methodism, conveys no such character. The second, the low church view, does not deny episcopacy or that ordination is for life, but denies 'that any part of the presbyter's ministry of Word and Sacrament is priestly in any sense beyond that in which the whole Church's worship is priestly'. The sacerdotal sense of the priesthood is rejected. Therefore, doctrines of the priesthood, and it follows of the eucharist too, sorely divide the two wings of the Church.

The Methodists asked and were conceded the right to have their views of the episcopacy and the ministry judged by no stricter view than that accorded to Anglicans themselves. They themselves say: 'Christ's ministers in the Church are stewards in the household of God and shepherds of his flock. . . . The Methodist Church holds the doctrine of the priesthood of all believers' and rejects the notion of an exclusive priestly class or order. Nevertheless it clearly maintains a separate and even sacramental function for all those members of the priesthood of all believers *ordained to the ministry*. The scheme accepted this as within the breadth of interpretation permitted already to Anglicans and it proposed, as the basis of the theology of ministry for the new church, the priesthood of all believers, but with differences in the forms of its exercise. It saw in this doctrine the common ground between the Methodist Church and the Church of England. In all that followed, the Scheme bent over backwards to reconcile all views of the episcopacy—high, low and hostile—while nevertheless proposing to restore episcopacy to the Methodists, as they themselves desired and desire.

All such conciliatoriness failed to satisfy the two extreme Church parties. The book quoted, *Growing into Union*, is perhaps the most remarkable and thorough of all theological critiques of the scheme. It illustrates that historical oddity noted earlier—the coming together of

---

[15] Both constituting the Report of the Anglican–Methodist Unity Commission, SPCK and Epworth Press, 1968.

representatives of the two extreme Anglican wings in joint theological objections! In general, the opposition in the Church of England based itself upon four points—the nature of the Methodist ministry; the Services of Reconciliation; the rejection of *two* stages in the process of reunion; the lack of a confessional statement.

In the most extreme high church view the Methodist ministry is not validly ordained because not episcopally ordained. In the past this has been so sufficiently the view of Anglican Church order that Methodist ministers entering the Church of England had to be re-ordained into the Anglican ministry as a matter of course. Yet it is the Methodist doctrine that a man is ordained into their ministry once only, and for life. Re-ordination of their own clergy is the custom in the Church of England, however, because it possesses a threefold ministry, of deacons, priests, bishops, and ordination is necessary for entry into each of its forms. But a *second* ordination into any *one* form is inconceivable. Therefore in principle Anglicans and Methodists have the same attitude to double ordination. But if the high Church view that Methodist orders are invalid is maintained, while to regard their ministers as laymen is humiliating, if not insulting, then some form of reordination of Methodist ministers (but not of Anglican ministers) would seem an obligatory step towards union, in the view of the extreme critics. What they asked was capitulation.

Yet the whole Scheme of Reunion involves, as a *sine qua non*, the mutual recognition by the divided Churches of the validity of each other's ministerial orders to be proclaimed in special joint ceremonies of reconciliation. The Services of Reconciliation (they are of two kinds, central and local) proposed by the Scheme can be held to involve both Churches in a curious ambiguity over reconciliation all the same. It is this. Each minister, before a service of reconciliation, was to be asked to make a declaration which is virtually an acceptance of recommissioning in the new united Church. 'I submit myself in this Service wholly to God, to receive from him such grace and authority as he may wish to give me for my ministry as a Presbyter in his Church in the coming together of the Methodist Church and the Church of England.' This, a declaration of loyalty to the new Church, is wholly innocuous doctrinally and theologically and might be construed as all the recommissioning held to be necessary, granted prior acceptance of the validity of both sets of orders. But to those who do not want reordination it appears to be just that! To those who do want it, it is too vague and inconclusive to rank as such![16]

The central service itself, to make doubly sure of the mutual acceptance of ministries, invites, at the crucial point, the archbishops and bishops to

---

[16] The Archbishop of Canterbury, in his speech to Synod, 3 May 1972, called the act a 'conditional ordination'. I remain at a loss to know what this means.

kneel before the president and other ministers of the Methodist Church. After calling down the blessings of God for the renewal of the gifts 'already granted to these thy servants whom thou didst call to be Bishops in thy Church' the President and his team proceed to lay hands on the Anglicans and to say, 'We welcome you into the fellowship of the Ministry in the Methodist Church, to preach the word of God and minister the holy Sacraments among us as need shall arise and you shall be requested to do so. We repeat our pledge that we will serve with you as fellow-workers in Christ and that we will never rest until we have found that fuller unity in him which we believe to be God's will.' Then presently the Methodist president and his ministers kneel before the archbishop and his bishops and receive the same welcome. An ordination or re-ordination? A commissioning or re-commissioning? A humbling of each hierarchy before the other that grace may come at either hand? In this third sense the service of Reconciliation is a moving and indeed gracious thing. But *genuinely* an ordination? This does not seem proposed or even possible *since the prayer before the laying-on of hands precisely recognizes the participants as priests, ministers, bishops in their own right, and concedes no deficiency*; and the prayer which accompanies the laying-on of hands is a prayer of welcome and commissioning not of ordination. The word ordination is never used, but then neither is it in the Anglican ordinal or in the proposed new ordination service for the United Church, except as a title to the service. The crucial phrase in the 1662 Anglican ordinal for 'The ordering of a priest' is 'Receive the Holy Ghost for the office and work of a Priest in the Church of God, now committed unto thee by the imposition of our hands': in the proposed new ordinal it is less personal, though still accompanied by the laying-on of hands by the bishop, 'Send down thy Holy Spirit upon thy servant, for the office and work of a Presbyter in thy Church'. Any similar act of *conferral* of priestly or presbyteral status or power is missing from the Service of Reconciliation.

What then even raises the question of re-ordination? Perhaps the episcopal or presidential laying-on of hands? But *really*? If that is so, all who have ever been confirmed by Anglican bishops have been deluding themselves if they imagine that they are still laymen. Perhaps the loose talk of those who hoped that the high church party would be deceived into accepting this as reordination of the Methodist ministers, while the Methodists would not be so deluded, is to be blamed for charges of disingenuousness? Horror of horrors, any high church Anglican priest who *did* see the Service of Reconciliation as a re-ordination was involved in accepting that a high church Anglican priest was going to be ordained or re-ordained by a Methodist president whose own orders were actually invalid!

Simply seen, and without gross clerical prejudice, the Services of Reconciliation would appear at the ministerial level to be the adoption, prayerfully and lovingly, of each ministry into the life and order of the other ministry as a realization of the intercommunion which would precede organic union. It may very well be a mistake that definite steps towards organic union were not proposed in the Scheme, or as the authors of *Growing into Union* have urged that a Confessional statement was not part of it, though all that is understood by the Lambeth Quadrilateral *is* part of the Scheme. It might have been possible to devise a scheme in which union came first and ministerial reconciliation followed. What is certain is that the Church of England could not move straight away into organic union, nor even propose stages for it, without first using oxy-acetylene to cut its way out of its legal and proprietorial prison. It could never achieve *organic* union even with the angels without that step. What is also true is that mutual adoption and intercommunion would be a generous and not a retrograde step. The spirit of the Reconciliation Scheme is good even if details could be improved.

The authors of *Growing Into Union*, those stern critics, though not opponents of reunion, propose simply the adoption of each ministry into the other. After tough chapters in which episcopacy is justified both by tradition and scripture (which are reconciled rather than opposed) and by sacredness and order, during which the mood of their work appears to mount towards total rejection of those who believe that the priesthood is the function of the whole church rather than the property of a sacred order, they precipitately change their mood. They swoon into the sweetness and light of the vision that ministries of Churches which are clearly of God are genuine ministries of the Holy Spirit. They assert that it would be intolerable to fall into the sin against the Holy Spirit and question this, and so their answer is after all that which the Service of Reconciliation appears (to me) to propose—*adoption*, which is the adoption of each ministry into the orders of the other, and no questions asked, the slate wiped clean. But with the exquisite muddleheadedness which distinguishes the Church of England, the quartet of authors reject the scheme because it contains that which they would propose themselves, albeit in a different form. Never was so much wind expended to so little purpose. Oh for Swift again!

Of course, the authors do make their own proposals for a bit-by-bit accession of Methodist and Anglican Churches to a new united Church and the cession of existing properties and rights by the old Churches to the new Church as this happens—a grassroots, piecemeal union indeed. Is it feasible? What would have occurred had the scheme been adopted would have been the birth of a new Church through the erosion of all the older Churches (because the authors hope for a multilateral union not simply an Anglo–Methodist union). As one sees it *practically*, the older Churches would become increasingly fragmented and ungovernable and the new Church starved of authority and resources from the beginning. The legal complications would be past endurance. The proposals of *Growing Into Union* were stillborn from the day of publication. In any case it cannot be argued that the high church or low church authors spoke for the rest of their respective camps. No case for *Growing Into Union* was made at the July 1971 Synod at York, where the official scheme received the support of sixty-five per cent of those present and voting. At that Synod the official disapproval of the Anglo–Catholic party was expressed by the distinguished Dr J. R. H. Moorman, Bishop of Ripon, who said that the union of the ministries of the Church of England and the Methodists would be the union of an episcopally valid ministry with an invalid ministry and would damage the possibility of union with the Roman Catholic Church (which, however, carries on its own explorations round the table with Lutherans and Methodists).

But who validates Anglican orders? At this we have looked. To the Romans, Anglican orders are invalid and the invalidation of Methodist orders by a Church whose own orders have been declared invalid has as much point as a dog chasing its own tail. Great and serious changes have taken place in the Church of Rome since the papacy of John XXIII and the Second Vatican Council. A genuine ecumenicity has grown up and the most profound studies are going on as to the meaning of the priesthood, the nature of the Church, the theology of the Reformed Churches of which the Church of England is naturally regarded as one. But the brutal Papal Bull of 13 September 1896 has not been revoked, 'We pronounce and declare that Ordinations carried out according to the Anglican rite have been and are absolutely null and utterly void.' It comes close to an anathema. Technically, in the light of this, the Archbishop of Canterbury is a layman, though the Pope is too polite to tell him so.

The *Apostolicae Curae* brought to an end the reunion movement which Lord Halifax and l'Abbé Portal had jointly begun with such enthusiasm in the 1890's. In a letter to l'Abbé Portal, after the papal condemnation, Lord Halifax said, 'it was really the love of souls which motivated us, we wanted nothing else. We wanted to do something to put an end to the divisions which keep so many souls from him. ... We have tried to do what God, as I believe, inspired us to do. We have been checked for the moment, but if God wills it, his will will be accomplished; and if he allows us to be broken, it is because he wants to accomplish things himself. It is not a dream. The thing is as certain as ever. There are afflictions which are worth all earthly joys, and it is a thousand times dearer to suffer with you in such a cause than to triumph with the whole world.'[17]

An exquisite humility. But as John Jay Hughes tells the story of the negotiations in *Absolutely Null and Utterly Void* it gathers the air of a

---

[17] Quoted in *Absolutely Null and Utterly Void, an Account of the 1896 Papal Condemnation of Anglican Orders*, by John Jay Hughes, Corpus Books, Washington 1968, p. 199.

diplomatic game—a salad of poker and intrigue. Chancelleries had victories but ecclesiastically the whole thing was a disgrace. Lord Halifax's sincerity was undoubted, but he could not have delivered up the Church of England into union with Rome, or even intercommunion or mutual recognition of orders. The Church of England itself would have broken in two before that. Had he succeeded he would have produced a constitutional crisis. The crown itself is based upon and affirms the Protestant succession, and its pre-eminence has rested in part on the ecclesiastical supremacy. Were both to go in favour of Rome? A Protestant supremacy was just about endurable to the old militant nonconformism, but anything which appeared to threaten a return of papistical power would have swept the authorizing government away in a political storm.

On the Roman side the Halifax-Portal approach was met with the deepest suspicion: the wounds of the seventeenth century seemed to bleed again. The curial investigating commission was not impartial. The evidence before it was mostly determined by Cardinal Vaughan and his closest British advisers who were convinced of the invalidity of Anglican orders, of the need to secure formal condemnation, of the importance of keeping Anglican fingers out of the English Roman Catholic pie. Misguidedly, Vaugham thought that condemnation of Anglican orders would bring mass conversions from the Anglo–Catholics.

Anglicans were not invited to appear before the curial commission. The scholars who defended their case were ignorant of English Reformation history. A hostile member of the Curia, Monsignor Merry del Val, drafted the Bull. Lord Halifax might have foreseen all this and that things could come out disastrously. The Pope himself feared that the British Empire was about to take over Mother Church. The Empire was then at the height of its power and seemed temporarily at a loss as to what to take over next. It had taken over just about everything else takeable. Lord Halifax was a layman, a great aristocrat, a member of the House of Lords of the British Parliament. Rome thought—what did it all portend? Wasn't the Church of England *parliament's* Church? The confusion of the old gentleman in Rome was understandable. And so came the condemnation, which Bishop George Bell called 'one of the sharpest and most public rebuffs that the Church of Rome can ever have administered to a peaceable Christian communion'. When Dr W. J. Bolt interviewed Cardinal Heenan in March 1966 he spoke of the Bull as stigma still in the eyes of both low church and high church Anglican parties. There have not been wanting bishops and theologians who have spoken of it as an insuperable barrier still, and a source of unease which negates the new ecumenical atmosphere.[18] The Malines conversations twenty-five years

---

[18] John Jay Hughes carries on the story he tells in *Absolutely Null and Utterly Void* in *Stewards of the Lord, A Reappraisal of Anglican Orders*, Sheed and Ward, London 1970.

later in which the principal leaders were Lord Halifax and Cardinal Mercier aroused almost as much suspicion in Rome, which placed a ban on all such explorations.

The consequences of those ancient fears are still officially operative. A directive of the Secretariat for Promoting Christian Unity of 5 October 1968, interpreting the Vatican Council Decree *Unitatis Redintegratio No. 8*, specified the circumstances under which an Anglican or Protestant might receive Eucharistic Communion in a Catholic Church. The person must have 'the same faith concerning the eucharist that is professed by the Catholic Church, and be unable to approach a Minister of his own Confession'. It goes on to say that a Catholic in similar circumstances may not ask for the sacraments except from a minister who has been validly ordained. That is clear enough.

The temper of the Roman Church today is not that of 1896. It has moved with astonishing rapidity into a brave new ecumenical temper, despite the obstacle of *Apostolicae Curae*. In 1967 it set up with the Anglicans a Joint Preparatory Commission of high-powered theologians. This has resulted in a permanent Anglican/Roman International Commission which first met at Windsor in January 1970 and divided into three groups to explore Church and Authority, Church and Eucharist, Church and Ministry.[19] I shall speak of this report presently.

There is considerable Roman interest still in the failure of Anglican and Methodist initiatives towards unity. Conversations as important as those with the Anglicans are proceeding with many Churches. The liturgies of such united Churches as the Church of South India, the Church of North India and Pakistan, the Church of Lanka, are examined with meticulous care, even excitement, by Roman liturgiologists for the effort they demonstrate to arrive at the primitive and complete eucharist. The Pope welcomes visiting divines as if, after all, their orders were as valid as his.

Christians generally have become for Rome the 'separated brethren' instead of heretics and iconoclasts. Within the Roman Church reform and reformist pressures grow apace. The Mass is said in the vernacular. God gets addressed in the second person plural. From the magical secrecy of the old Mass with its silent canon and a view of the priest's back as he crouches over the elements like an alchemist over his crucibles, Rome is moving over to the open Mass, with the congregation as participants, and ending the concept of the Mass as a conspiracy between the priest and God. Rather it becomes seen as a communal act, closer to

---

[19] Their findings are published as *The Venice Conversations* in *Theology* February 1971. The Lambeth Conference, 1968 was presented with documents on *Anglican–Roman Catholic Relations* which included the guarded report of the *Anglo–Roman Catholic Joint Preparatory Commission*.

the primitive memorial meal in which the reception of the sacrament was an act of renewal in faith, a source of grace, not a new sacrifice.

The Editor of *Theology*, G. R. Dunstan, analyses, in an editorial which discusses *The Venice Conversations*,[20] the cryptic assurance of the Pope in his allocution at the canonization of the Forty Martyrs in 1970, 'that on the day when—God willing—the unity of the faith and of the Christian life is restored, no offence will be inflicted on the honour and sovereignty of a great country such as England. There will be no seeking to lessen the legitimate prestige and the worthy patrimony of piety and usage proper to the Anglican Church. The Roman Catholic Church— this humble 'Servant of the Servants of God'—is able to embrace her ever beloved Sister in the one authentic communion of the family of Christ.'

In an exercise in Vaticanology and with the aid of the Roman Bishop B. C. Butler, who wrote about the Pope's words in *The Tablet*,[21] Dunstan sees (with Butler) the cheering possibility of an Anglican rite, fully recognized by Rome and in full communion with her, continuing as an autonomous Church for perhaps some centuries side by side with a Latin rite. The editor felt that this was a time scale to which he could warm. But would the world—or the Churches—hold out that long?

Even for this form of union with Rome to be possible there are many bridges to be crossed. Bishop Butler speaks of Lambeth continuing as the head of the 'Anglican rite'. But Lambeth is not the head. The crown— the Queen—is the head: or rather the crown-in-parliament. There is therefore a constitutional bridge to be crossed. The Church of England must decide whether it is a crown 'thing' and a legal 'thing', with legally entrenched proprietorial interests, or an historic, autonomous Church, before it can accept again the primacy of Rome. It must decide about patronage, freehold, establishment, class, privilege.

On the Roman side the struggle to move into another concept of the church is proving traumatic in the extreme. One must instance the role of the pope and the meaning of the papacy. In the formal correctness of the traditional Roman order, the pope is Christ's vicar, in lineal descent from St Peter, and possessed of the magisterial powers of God. As Charles Davis sees him in *A Question of Conscience* he is an imperial figure, monarch of a feudal order, head of a system saturated with the elements of the Constantinian order and so, logically, his role and his power derive far more from the secular order, from the triple crown, than from the authority first entrusted to Christ's fisherman-disciple. Hans Küng's masterly analysis *Infallible?*[22] speaks to the depth of disquiet among Romans about the papal claims.

---

[20] *Theology*, February 1971.
[21] 14 November 1970.
[22] Collins, London and Doubleday, New York 1971.

What is the pope and what ought he to be? An episcopal president, *primus inter pares*, subject to the will of the whole church or a medieval monarch with a divine infallibility? The Anglicans seem themselves to have raised this question at the Venice Conversations, explaining that Anglicans, in the broadest consensus, question both the historical succession of the Bishop of Rome from Peter and the exclusive claims made for his office. 'They believe that the Petrine Office, rather than being limited to Peter himself, was shared by his fellow aspostles, and indeed, in some way, by the whole community, to which power to bind and loose was entrusted by the Lord (in Matt. 18), and that this office is inherited in a general sense by the whole Church, and in a particular sense by every bishop of the *ecclesia catholica*.'[23]

Yet the Anglican theologians raised the other side of the question too, asking whether, after all, modern exegesis does not point to a primacy of responsibility given to Peter, and therefore genuinely to a Petrine office and that this, in the age of the Fathers—and credibly since?—played a providential role in the Church's life. Manifestly on the decision about the Petrine office more turns than just what we are to think of the pope. On it depends the whole orientation of the Roman Church now and in the future—whether it is to go on being a disciplined army of worshippers from whom absolute obedience is demanded (if it is still that) or a participatory brotherhood of the faithful. Whether it is to accept a genuine ecumenism or to search—however benevolently—for the submission of the separated brethren.

It is fair to say that a new conception of the papacy means a new conception of the priesthood and therefore of what the priest does in the Mass. What alienated Protestantism and much of Anglicanism in the past was the Roman secrecy of the canon, the doctrines of transubstantiation and of the sacrifice of the Mass. In whatever other ways Rome horrified them, it horrified them in these last two doctrines because of the literalism with which they were spelt out. There was a medieval legend of two shepherd boys playing at being priests who said the words of consecration over a piece of bread placed on a stone and found themselves staring at a morsel of bloody flesh. The boys were struck down by fire from heaven for their impiety. It was widely believed. The medieval theologian Gabriel Biel[24] gave the legend as the reason why the canon of

---

[23] *Theology*, February 1971, p. 65.

[24] In *Stewards of the Lord*, John Jay Hughes quotes Gabriel Biel as saying that the Mass is, 'not merely the memorial of that great, unique and perfect sacrifice offered once upon the cross, but the very same sacrifice, always the same'. (Though presently Biel contradicts himself.) A contemporary of Biel, Cardinal Cajetan, had a higher moral and theological view of the sacrifice of the mass. 'Cajetan says that the value of the Mass (*ex opere operato*) is unlimited. In the Mass the victim of Calvary is sacramentally present, so that the Mass has the same infinite value as the passion.'

the Mass was said silently. It was unthinkable that the magical power should be let loose among the laity. And that tells us all we need to know of a superstitious medieval literalism. Of course, that literalism is not quite inexplicable. In the ceremonial of the last supper, Jesus says of the wine, 'This is my blood' and of the bread, 'This is my body'. And what Jesus said must be so: to doubt his word would be blasphemy. Yet Jesus said many things which were symbolically, spiritually true but not literally true. He spoke in metaphors. He was the vine, the true shepherd, the light of the world. When Jesus declared to his disciples that the bread was his body, he was standing before them intact in body and mind and for them a *literal* interpretation of his words would have been absurd. What he spoke to them was the poetry, the imagery, the symbolism of religious experience. No one present then could have taken it otherwise.

Yet the sacrificial temper of his words was deeply intended, and the symbolism of the consecration must have made their impact even more profound, even had the occasion not been filled with foreboding. Once a year, and once a year only the high priest entered the Holy of Holies in the Temple of Jerusalem bearing a vessel filled with the blood of sacrifices. Deliberately Jesus picks up the symbolism in the last meal with the disciples. It must have stunned them—the intention to link the blood of Jesus with the blood of the supreme Temple sacrifice and with the blood of the grape. The eucharistic anamnesis must of course be forever linked with the notion of sacrifice. But the memorial of the sacrifice, the sense that the grace which sprang from it is renewed at the eucharist is one thing: the notion that Christ is the victim who is offered up again at every Mass is another. It proved intolerable and the Reformation was precisely a rebellion over that.

'Turning now to the question of the eucharistic sacrifice,' Dom Gregory Dix writes,[25] 'it is right for an Anglican to say bluntly that no theory of the eucharistic sacrifice can be supposed compatible with our own liturgical practice since 1549 except that which sees the proper sacrificial action not in any specific oblation or destruction of the Victim in the course of the rite, but in the fact of the consecration of the sacrament under two kinds separately, as a representative likeness of the death of Christ. This is the sense not only of our "prayer of consecration", but of the statement in our Catechism that the eucharist was ordained for "the continual remembrance (= *anamnesis*) of the sacrifice of the death and of the benefits which we receive thereby". All theories of a fresh destruction or "mactation", or even of a *status*

[25] *The Shape of the Liturgy*, Dacre Press, London 1954, p. 241.

declivior, of Christ in the eucharist are closed to Anglicans by our formularies, and we may be thankful that it is so.'[26]

As the result of a meeting in September 1971 the Anglican–Roman Catholic International Commission produced 'An Agreed Statement on Eucharistic Doctrine',[27] which was widely publicized and hailed as a great breakthrough, the whole intention of which was to bridge the gap between two sorts of interpretations, and to banish superstitions.

'Christ's redeeming death and resurrection took place once for all in history. Christ's death upon the cross, the culmination of his whole life of obedience, was the one perfect and sufficient sacrifice for the sins of the world. There can be no repetition of or addition to what was then accomplished once for all by Christ. Any attempt to express a nexus between the sacrifice of Christ and the eucharist must not obscure this fundamental fact of the Christian faith.'[28]

The analysis does not end there. The eucharist is an event taking place in the present but riveting itself on a sacrificial event in the past.

'The notion of *memorial* as understood in the passover celebration at the time of Christ, i.e. the making effective in the present of an event in the past, has opened the way to a clearer understanding of the relationship between Christ's sacrifice and the eucharist.'[29]

It is not just memorial, but the effective proclamation of 'God's mighty acts', of his 'reconciling action', of his 'true presence', signified by bread and wine 'which, in this mystery, become his body and blood'.

At this point the puzzle of transubstantiation demands solution. A footnote explains that transubstantiation, in contemporary Roman Catholic theology, is seen as affirming the *fact* of Christ's presence; it is not understood as explaining how the change in the elements takes place. But the real presence 'of his body and blood' can be understood only as the redemptive activity, the redemptive offering of the Saviour. 'When this offering is met by faith, a life-giving encounter results.' But lack of that faith does not alter, or determine Christ's objective presence. God is

---

[26] On the once-for-all sacrifice of Jesus the directive of Hebrews 9:24–28, is clear and final, if scriptural authority is needed, rather than simple commonsense: 'For Christ has entered, not that sanctuary made by men's hands which is only a symbol of the reality, but heaven itself, to appear now before God on our behalf. Nor is he there to offer himself again and again, as the high priest enters the sanctuary year by year with blood not his own. If that were so, he would have had to suffer many times since the world was made. But as it is, he has appeared once and for all at the climax of history to abolish sin by the sacrifice of himself. And as it is the lot of men to die once, and after death comes judgement, so Christ was offered once to bear the burden of men's sins, and will appear a second time, sin done away, to bring salvation to those who are watching for him.' (*New English Bible*).

[27] SPCK, 1972.

[28] Ibid. p. 5.

[29] Ibid. p. 6.

there, not simply to faith. 'The elements are not mere signs; Christ's body and blood become really present and are really given.'[30] In communion we eat the flesh of Christ and drink his blood.'[31]

Does this common re-interpretation bridge the gap between the churches? The doctrine of the perpetual re-sacrifice of Christ goes. Transubstantiation is reduced to an historical footnote. The real Presence in the real flesh and blood of Christ remain as common ground. But really common ground? Protestantism, including Anglican Protestantism, has shrunk from the literal interpretation of the real Presence, seeing it instead in terms of symbolism, and as the sacrament conveying the presence rather than *being* it. And surely it has to be asked—*what presence is present*? The presence of the sacrificial Christ on the cross, or that of the risen Lord, present and working as he promised in the world? The first would require the earthly body and blood, at the thought of which the mind falters. The body and blood of the risen Lord would (for this Christian) be his spiritual sustenance offered to the spiritual man.

Gratifying as this great scholarly effort at reconciliation must be for all who long for reunion, the doctrine of the eucharist still seems unsolved by it and remains potentially divisive. But not *the practice*. It would seem that, down the ages, different Christians have seen the eucharist in different lights and drawn from it succour and consolation according to their understandings. The theories divide, the practice unites. To move from the sacrificial Mass to the sacramental Mass with a participating congregation and perhaps from that to a ceremonial *agape* as the nearest we can come to the confrontation of the disciples by Jesus in what was close to a family situation is a consummation devoutly to be wished. This alone might de-fuse the hoary theological debates.

But even this step towards the actuality of the common meal of believers can involve a major dislocation in the relationships of priests and laity and so prove destructive of traditional roles. The sensitive already know this. In *The Death and Resurrection of the Church* I wrote of the new eucharistic meal taking the place of the old Mass among the eager Catholic faithful in Holland and France. The rising demand among priests to be allowed to marry is itself a sign that many priests wish to live as Christian men among Christian men and women—*primus inter pares*, if you will, but not as members of a sacred caste of untouchables. To take this step necessitates a reappraisal of the whole priestly hierarchy as it comes down to Rome from the Middle Ages almost untouched and even strengthened by the modern apparatus of power. Charles Davis made the whole move—out of the priesthood, out of the Church even, and married. There have been so many priests making

---

[30] Ibid. p. 7.
[31] Ibid. p. 8.

this move, though not necessarily leaving the Church, that relief organizations have been set up to render aid to these hapless men. Lenin called this kind of thing—voting with one's feet. It suggests that Rome itself must pass through many more convulsions before she is ready to bring the reconciled Churches of the world into union with her and under her leadership. The same troubled and bitter path ahead can be prophesied for the Church of England in her ecumenical role, if she dares to sustain it.

FOUR

The Malaise of the Ministry

I DREW attention in an earlier chapter (p. 165) to a paragraph in a report from the World Council of Churches Commission on Faith and Order which spoke of a profound crisis in human institutions. 'The values which served as ordering principles for human life in society in the past have lost much of their validity.' But what has been discovered, in the West today, are not just the difficulties which all institutions find in re-orientating themselves to changing societies but the difficulty of legitimizing themselves at all. Formerly institutions acquired a grandeur over and above the individuals who comprised them, serviced them and governed them. They had an existence in time, a substance which survived its accidents, an accepted durability which stabilized society. Thus the monarchy, a parliament, a church, a bank, a college, the apparatus of the law possessed an august status. This aura of sanctity still hangs about institutions we all can name. And in the past when great institutions such as the monarchy were threatened with destruction through revolution, it was only in the hope of replacing them by what were thought by some to be more beautiful, just and enduring institutions—a senate, a congress, a charismatic dictator.

What we have acquired in this century is a sense of the fragility of institutions. The blows of history have taught us that. The settlements of two world wars almost casually rearranged the frontiers of nations, or even abolished them. The history of the Russian revolution shows how, completely cynically, the state institutions were arranged, abolished, reordered, manipulated to give a decent cover to an otherwise naked exercise of revolutionary terror. Institutions, we see with more pragmatism than earlier centuries, have no more vigour and endurance than men devote to them. If men withdraw their support from an institution then it loses its will and easily dies or is pushed over. Deeply concerned people feel that this is true of the institutional Church, that its continued existence is not written on tablets in the sky for all to read, but depends on the devotion of men. Is it good theology as well as good sense? Indeed it is. Even theologians most concerned to show that the Church is a divine instrument would hesitate to commit a Christ at work in the world to the maintenance of a *particular* ecclesiastical form.

This new Christian sense of precariousness in the world manifests itself
in the crisis in Christian ministries—all or nearly all ministries in the
West are affected, though it is with the Church of England ministry
that I am principally concerned. The sense of unwantedness of which I
have spoken which afflicts the Churches today hits especially their
ministries. The sense of frustration emerges from some of the letters they
sent me in connection with the Paul Report.

One surburban incumbent wrote:

'No parish should have less than two clergy. Partnerships—viz.
doctors—prove best. Breakdown. Most clergy have had one, of one
kind or another. Major cause? So grave a responsibility, and the task
so often completely misunderstood by the laity who regard the
Church as their spare-time job . . .'

Clearly that incumbent related breakdown to isolation. A rural parson,
with a population of 220, and resigning because he had too little to do,
said about this:

'It would appear to me that there are a number of priests like myself
in country livings most of whom suffer from a sense of frustration and
do so in isolation. There is, I believe, a great need for such priests to
meet more often than they do, to plan, discuss, pray and study
together. . .'

Another said, 'I must say I am never lonely, but I sometimes wish my
fellow clergy would drop in and have a talk, but this they never do.' And
another, 'It's very easy to find oneself gently rotting away.' Again and
again they turned to this need for support to sustain their morale.

'I think that the clergy would be much more effective if they worked
a lot more closely together and got to know each other better. . .
conferences, meetings are not enough; the clergy need to meet each
other more informally, perhaps more in each other's homes. I suspect
it is unusual for one parson to visit another unless he has some
particular business to deal with and I do not think that many priest's
wives mix more than on M.U., deanery committees—and so many
wives are working that the needful contacts become less . . . real need for
closer contact between parochial clergy who still work in isolation and
even in competition . . .'

For some it was not professional isolation but social isolation which
mattered.

'Most of the congregation come from a distance; there are about
twenty cottage homes and three or four larger houses. There is not
a shop or even street lighting and we are two miles from nearest
transport, i.e. bus.'

Again, 'In a *totally* working-class parish (i.e. no resident teachers,
doctors or graduates at all and no executives) to deal with one's congregation only would give hope . . . but to care for the whole parish sets
problems which can hardly be stated.'

And again, 'A man may easily lose heart when Sunday after Sunday he is ministering to less than six people at any one service.'[1]

Men often said with moving candour, 'I am a prey to despair', or 'I am fighting demons'. One man wrote, 'Mr. Paul, have you ever thought of suicide? I often have,' and went on in some detail to speak of his sheer unwantedness both in his office and his person. At some point in the letter he said that his father had been an Anglican clergyman before him and often said in his last years that if he died no one would notice it until a sanitary inspector was called in.

Only a few were as despairing as this, but many felt isolated and frustrated, though some were exhilarated by the challenge.

'I really wonder how you are going to establish the difference between the many . . . clergy who are depressed and fed up and felt that they were never trained to face a situation like the one which faces them now, and those who feel that there is real relief to be found in so much of the changing things, and that so much of what our fathers took for granted is gone.'

Under conditions of extreme frustration men leave their jobs and seek others. This is more common in secular employment than in the priesthood for obvious reasons—there is a vocational commitment, an emotional and spiritual investment to the priesthood which has few counterparts in the secular world. There is, for many, the indelible stamp. A priest moving into secular employment not only loses sense of that but the sacred life-style which goes with it. It is a loss few men in the past could contemplate except under duress. In literature the ex-priest has always been a humiliated and pathetic figure; even the object of a contempt no one would throw against an ex-bank manager.

In our day the clerical 'drop-out' has become a common figure, often invited to make his case on television. He is a more familiar Roman Catholic phenomenon than Anglican not only because more noticeable in that communion but more frequent there. All communions, however, are faced with the man who drops out completely as well as with the priest or minister who seeks to move out of a parochial ministry which has become meaningless into a more satisfying ministry within the Church. In a very searching American enquiry into why men left the ministry of the United Church of Christ[2] five reasons, out of a total of twenty-four, received the highest poll in an importance/non-importance table compiled from the replies of the ex-pastors about their reasons for resignation.

---

[1] *The Deployment and Payment of the Clergy*, p. 81 et seq.

[2] *Ex Pastors: Why Men leave the Parish Ministry* by Gerald J. Jud Ph.D., Edgar W. Mills, Jr. Ph.D., Genevieve Walters Burch M.A., intro by Earl D. C. Brewer Ph.D., Pilgrim Press, 1970.

I extract this summary from the findings of the survey[3] which covered 370 ex-pastors of whom 241 (65·1%) replied:

	Degree of importance %			
	None	Low	Med.	High
1. Disillusioned with the Church's relevance to problems of the modern world	19·9	13·0	23·7	43·5
2. Opportunity arose to do specialized work or training	45·8	7·6	7·6	38·9
3. Very attractive type of work offered	46·6	9·9	10·7	32·8
4. Uncertain of own vocation to the ministry	44·3	18·3	16·8	20·6
5. Felt personal inadequacy as a church leader	42·8	23·7	14·5	19·1

The results are pretty random after the first three or four scores and this illustrates that reasons for leaving the ministry are many, complex and divergent. All the same loss or change of faith surprisingly received a high importance rating of only 5·3 per cent and *no importance* rating of 60·3 per cent. 'Serious conflict' with colleagues or trouble with parishioners rated low. 'Crisis in personal life' or the prospects of higher salary and benefits did not rate significantly. Certain answers to key questions confirmed that a search for better pay was not the main cause of resignation. Fifty-eight per cent said that money had nothing to do with the decision to leave and to the question, 'I would have stayed if...', the largest score went to, 'If the Church had moved to a new and more relevant ministry'. Whichever way round the evidence is turned, two reasons dominate—a sense of the failure of the Church itself, and a lack of personal fulfilment. Although many confessed to an improved standard of living in secular work circumstantial pressures such as money or family difficulties were dismissed by the respondents as negligible motives.

Dr W. S. F. Pickering and T. L. Blanchard in *Taken for Granted,*[4] a study of the parish clergy of the Anglican Church of Canada—which did not in any way approach ex-pastors—received an overwhelming 'vote' for 'satisfaction with work and satisfaction with ordination'. It was 78 per cent. Nevertheless, there was a substantial degree of dissatisfaction (16 per cent) on one count or another. A quarter of the 16 per cent were dissatisfied with both their work and their ordination. Indeed nearly seven per cent of all respondents decided that they would not be ordained if they had their time over again and another 5·5 per cent expressed themselves undecided. Nearly 50 per cent of suburban clergy and 46 per cent of rural clergy described themselves as lonely. More than a third of city clergy were lonely too, and the tendency was to relate

[3] Op. cit. p. 180.

[4] *Taken for Granted: A survey of the Parish Clergy of the Anglican Church of Canada,* General Synod of the Anglican Church of Canada, 1967.

this loneliness to lack of fellowship with other clergy and to the stand-offishness of the laity. 73 per cent of all respondents wanted to see reforms or changes in the Anglican Church of Canada and 65 per cent wanted diocesan reforms. The two most popular reforms were in 'Church Organization' and 'Prayer Book and Liturgy'. Better use of money and manpower received the third highest vote.

These figures correspond to a recent Survey of my own[5] among the clergy attending St George's House, Windsor, courses. 82 per cent of the respondents wanted some action on the Paul Report for instance and when that verdict was broken down, some 30 per cent said the Church of England greatly needs reform and 57 per cent said it certainly needs some reform. Even 25 per cent of the rural deans said the church greatly needed reform and 65 per cent that it certainly needed some reform. These were the verdicts of the most staid, secure, 'arrived' group of middle-aged clergy. Over 60 per cent of the respondents wanted reforms in Church structures as the following table indicated:

The Church of England	Incumbents (%)	Rural Deans (%)	Aggregate (%)
1. Greatly needs reform	28	25	30
2. Certainly needs some reform	58	65	57
3. Needs little reform	6	8	7
4. Needs no reform	0·6	0	0·3

(St George's House, Windsor, Survey)

In 1971 members of the Industrial Administration Research Unit of the University of Aston in Birmingham undertook a survey of clergy first and laity subsequently in the Diocese of Birmingham to determine some important roles and attitudes. In a preliminary report,[6] 'Lay Perceptions of Church Issues' Alan Bryman and C. R. Hinings produce a table of responses to Church Reform which makes interesting comparison with my Windsor table above.

Per cent clergy and lay responses on the need for reform in the Church of England

Church of England	Laity (%)	Clergy (%)
Needs no reform	2·3	0·5
Needs a little reform	22·3	7·2
Certainly needs some reform	60·9	65·6
Greatly needs reform	14·5	26·8

[5] Unpublished.
[6] *Research Bulletin 1973*, Institute for the Study of Worship and Religious Architecture, Birmingham p. 81–6.

St. George's House Survey

Analysis of replies on the need for Church reform

	Incumbents	· Rural Deans	Aggregates ⊙
The Church greatly needs reform ———	28	25	30
Certainly some reform – – – –	58	65	57
Little reform ·············	6	8	7

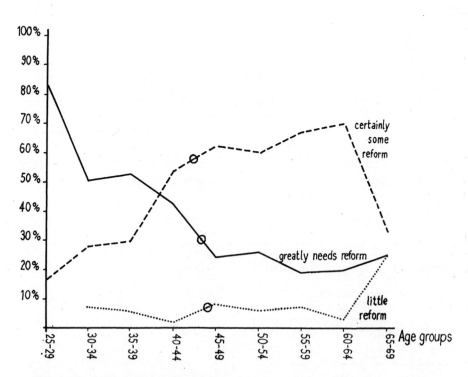

Fig. 5. *The interest of this analysis is the strong vote for 'some reform'. If this is added to the strong vote of young clergy for 'great reform', more than 50 per cent of clergy under 65 would appear to welcome reform.*

The investigation, the authors say, show that the laity 'seem to be generally resistant to change and reform even though they say they are relatively powerless and under-employed' and they produce plenty of evidence for this, which confirms much that has been said in this book about the passivity of the laity.

How does one assess the clergy's more progressive evidence however? Viewed as a whole it would not seem to fault the ordained ministry as such (only 6·5 per cent of the St George's respondents said that if they had their time over again they would not enter the ministry), nor to indicate that there is any loss of personal faith. Rather, the relevance of mission, ministry, and Church life seem put under question, though the dissatisfaction is variously expressed, pointing sometimes to faulty Church organization and parochial structures and at other times to worship and liturgy which are out of date or to poor relationships and communication within the Church. The malaise is unmistakably there. But it is in every ministry, pressing most heavily of all upon the Roman Catholic priesthood because there what is ecclesiastically demanded of it seems now especially ill-related to the patterns of the secular world in which the ministry has to be exercised.

It is even possible that what has been developing for a long time past as a result of the growing difficulty of discovering what the ministry is, and of how it is to be asserted with authority in the modern world, is a retreat into a private holiness and the acceptance of this as authenticating the ministerial role. In 1968 Dr S. H. Mayor[7] dispatched a questionnaire on the Ministry to 957 clergy and ministers in the Counties of Cheshire, Derbyshire, Nottinghamshire, Leicestershire and Lincolnshire. 'The questionnaires went to one third of Anglican clergy, to all Presbyterian, Baptist and Congregational ministers, and to half the Methodists; the Methodists and Anglicans being selected by a random method from official lists.' The questionnaire was an exhaustive one and the detailed findings need not detain us. But Mr Mayor's own summary of the replies to the first section causes one to reflect.

'There are marked differences on the subject of Ordination. Nearly all Free Churchmen and many Anglicans prefer to think of it in terms of the bestowing of authority for certain functions within the life of the Church, all of whose members are in some sense priestly; but a majority of Anglicans believe that in Ordination it is not authority alone, but also the grace necessary for the performance of certain priestly work—representative performance, on behalf of the whole Church—which is given. There is comparatively little variation between the Free Churches, and despite plans of union with Anglicans, Methodists do not differ from other Free Churchmen.

---

[7] His report was privately circulated from Mansfield College, Oxford.

'The minister is almost universally thought of as (a) a pastor, (b) an example of Christian life, and (c) a man of devotion. It is noteworthy that these are all responsibilities which depend largely on the individual rather than on the office and may be carried out behind the scenes.

'Less well-supported are the interpretations of the minister as (a) preacher, (b) evangelist, (c) leader of worship, and (d) pastoral director. No particular pattern of denominational response appears, and it is surprising to find Anglicans stressing evangelism more than Nonconformists and the leading of worship less.

'Least well-supported are the interpretations of the minister as (a) a public figure in the parish, (b) a public spokesman, (c) a scholar, (d) a representative of the Church Catholic. There are no great denominational differences, but there is the surprising revelation that Congregationalists come bottom on the "spokesman" concept, top on the "representative". In no case, except that of Ordination, does a marked Anglican–Free Church division appear.

'Thus it appears to be the "personal" functions which are most favoured, the "representative" and "official" ones least. No clear division of opinion appears except on one issue—the meaning of Ordination: and there the division runs through the middle of the Anglicans.'

If one's personal faith is not in doubt to oneself and one's belief that ordination is the right thing is not in question, but what difference either makes in the contemporary world is the true source of perplexity, then a retreat into quietism is not just possible but necessary. The minister turns to the Lord, who must understand when the world does not. And so the ministry is personalized, even interiorized.

There is another, psychological, sense in which this turning to an introverted Christian life in the ministry may be understood. It is involved in the longing many Roman Catholic priests manifest, and with anguish, to be accepted as men amongst men rather than as those set apart because they can never do wrong. There is a popular mystique about the clergy that they are, or at least must always profess to be, the blameless ones. They are the professional holy men, a role which cuts them off from ordinary sinful men and is one reason, it is said, why a clergyman wearing a dog collar can often get a carriage to himself on the railway. The sinner sees his presence as a reproach and at the same time senses and resents the pharisaism. The pressures of this role of reproachful apartness are felt more strongly by Roman Catholic priests because of their celibacy, which is encountered by their flocks as professional asexuality rather than as a personal discipline. They must not be seen to have, or even be suspected of having, a sexual life. They are expected to be 'above all that' and *in all things* virtuous men. This is not only what the Church of Rome demands of its priests but, *mutatis mutandis*, something close to it is demanded of all ministries by all Churches. To break from this image is to be guilty of moral heresy. Understandably there is a call in some Roman circles for the demystification of the priestly personage and not simply because it would be better to be seen to be as other men are rather than carry a false image but because robed in the role of one who never succumbs to temptation the priest is forced to find false satisfactions which end by corrupting his priestly role, and so in the end the Church too.

'Certains de ces prêtres, en réfléchissant sur leur passé, en font l'aveu: nous avons été trop longtemps plus soucieux de composer notre personnage que de réaliser notre personnalité. Une certaine mentalité ecclésiastique n'aide pas cette personnalisation des jugements et des actions. La conception du témoignage vertueux qui rendra le prêtre admirable en l'Eglise aimable leur paraît dangereuse. *C'est du Christ qu'ils veulent témoigner et non de leur vertu.* Le chrétien, pensent-ils, témoigne pour le Christ autant dans la reconnaissance qu'il est un pécheur que dans la manifestation d'une vertu qui a sa source dans le Christ. Tous les saints ont reconnu qu'ils étaient des pécheurs: la remarque générale ne vaut rien si, dans le concret, ils ne restaient pas disposés à reconnaître leur péché en se référant au Christ. C'est pour eux une exigence spirituelle que de refuser une face de vertu qui ne tendrait qu'à sauvegarder l'extériorité du personnage.'

This judgment, by a Roman priest-sociologist, P. Louis Rétif[8] goes on to say that as a consequence of the false situation in which they find themselves, priests compensate by substituting domination of the flock for service to it, using the sacrament as an instrument of government rather than of sanctification of the faithful. They take refuge in an idealism which only accentuates their inability to attend to the *real*. They find in the trivia of the ecclesiastical round and its little gratifications some sort of substitute for genuine human relations. The result is that a life of the sacristy, in all its pettiness, takes the place of, or is

---

[8] 'Le Prêtre, cette personne et ce personnage' by the Rev. P. Louis Rétif in *Clergy in Church and Society*, Actes de la IX Conférence Internationale de Sociologie Religieuse, Montreal 1967, p. 100.

Translation: 'Some priests, reflecting on their pasts, confess—we have been far too anxious to create a "personage" than to come to terms with our own personality. An ecclesiastical mental attitude of a certain kind does not help one to form personal judgments or to take personal actions. The idea of that chaste witness which makes a priest admired in an easy-going Church appears dangerous to them. It is to Christ they should be witnessing and not to their own moral heroism. The Christian, they think, witnesses as much for Christ in the discovery that he is a sinner as in parading virtues which have their source in Christ. All the saints recognized that they were sinners: that generalization would be valueless were it not for the fact that they did not rest content with discovering their sinfulness but themselves offered it to Christ. It was for them a spiritual necessity to deny themselves an outward show of goodness which had no use except to save the face of the public "personage".'

advanced as, the sacrificial life of Christ. If this is not the whole story it points to an important—for some a major—element in clergy self-consciousness at this moment of re-assessment of clergy roles in a society which does not automatically grant the priest the kind of status his predecessors enjoyed.

Dr Robert Towler has spoken (a little diffidently) of a crisis for ministry which he understands as a problem of the status of the ministry. But first, looking at the Church of England, he grapples with its decline from its peak at the turn of the century.

'The first general problem to be faced is the shrinkage of the ministry. This shrinkage itself has four separate aspects. The absolute numerical strength of the ministry (of the Church of England) has declined by some 20 per cent since the turn of the century. This decline is even greater when compared with a 40 per cent rise in the total population. A third aspect of the shrinkage is seen in the age profile as a whole, which has become progressively more biased towards older men. This is accounted for by an increasing proportion of older men entering the ministry, as well as by the drop in recruitment. This shift in the age profile results in an effective reduction in the number of years of work available from personnel, even when numbers are held constant. Yet a fourth aspect is to be found in the number of the clergy leaving the parochial ministry and this loss is made the more serious by the high proportion of younger men involved, thus biasing the age profile even more.'[9]

This crisis of manpower, or clergy power, was exhaustively studied in the Paul Report.[10] To take the figures at their grossest, there were at the beginning of 1962, 15,488 full-time clergy on the register which gave a ratio of clergy to population of 1:2,838. In the face of rising population, to maintain a ratio of 1:2,500 involved an increase in the number of clergy to nearly 24,000 by the year 2001. By a still more stringent test which would have restricted an incumbent's cure to a maximum of 5,000 souls, and given him a curate at that top level, I estimated that the full-time clergy force needed by December 1971 would be 24,400. It is in fact 17,775. To overcome the shortages this analysis exposed, the average annual ordinations would have needed to be about 1,365. They are in fact running at less than a quarter of that figure. In those Paul Report exercises, conducted at the end of a decade in which recruitment to the ministry had been rising and was expected to average 725 per annum by 1971, it was possible to be moderately optimistic about the future of the ministry even though one foresaw that the ratio of clergy to population was inevitably going to decline and

---

[9] R. Towler, 'The Social Status of the Anglican Minister', in *Sociology of Religion: Selected Readings*, Ed. Roland Robertson, Penguin 1969, p. 443 ff.

[10] *The Deployment and Payment of the Clergy* Chap. IX, 'A Staffing Exercise' p. 160 ff.

that the psychological and spiritual—even physical—burdens imposed on the clergy were going to grow more severe as a consequence. But in the decade since 1961 the Church of England has suffered the severe reverses already discussed; these and the decline in recruitment plus the worsening age-profile caused Dr Trevor Ling to ask[11] whether 'what we are witnessing, therefore, is the gradual disappearance of a once familiar figure, the full-time parochial clergyman'.

It is too early to prophesy this in a world in which the existence of a full-time ministry is common to all Christian communions and in which the psychological and legal barriers against the admission of women to the ministry conceal even from the Churches themselves the full extent of their ministerial 'material'. But already some results are apparent from the decline in recruitment to the ministries and from falling church attendances, even in the countryside. Of the town I have spoken often. But a familiar picture now in the countryside is the parson who has responsibility of several parishes (whether as united benefices or pluralities or both) who cannot serve them all equally or adequately but must motor or cycle round to service them. This all-purposes vicar replaces the peripatetic village vicar walking about his parish and as familiar with the state of the fields of cabbages as the state of the villagers' souls. The new man is assisted, if at all, by lay readers. Presently he will be assisted, as numbers grow, by the auxiliary ministry, which will consist of men in priest's orders who will support themselves in jobs during the working week and serve the Church at week-ends. All this will change the demographic pattern of the ministry, as well as its status. It impoverishes the countryside too which is struggling against so many destructive influences. What we are witnessing already is the laicization of the ministry. Dr Towler does not believe that the ministry is a profession, for no precise occupation can be ascribed to it in the same way that one can say one is a bus driver or a school teacher. The laicization I have described would seem to strengthen this argument.

The important point to notice is that the laicization of the ministry is not the same as the laicization of the Church or the ministry of the laity. If the Church were laicized then the whole Church, the corporate Church, would itself be creating policy, controlling doctrine and liturgy, making and breaking appointments, deciding tenure. These critical decisions would no longer be left in the hands of a privileged élite. Valuable and important as synodical government is, it leaves the clergy strongly entrenched. Episcopacy reinforces their separate, supervisory role. This is not what laicization of the ministry means, nor does it mean that lay people themselves become the senior partner in the Church's mission

---

[11] In *The Modern Churchman*, vol. 10 (1967), 'Religion, society and the teacher'.

(as is certainly the case with many sects).[12] It means that ministry, while remaining an élite, approximates more to lay status than to clergy status—its members earn their keep in secular occupations, enjoy the same standard of living as their secular peers, and the same housing. Only at week-ends and in leisure do they become 'separate persons'.

The Rev. Nicolas Stacey makes a cogent analysis of the process of laicization of the ministry in his account of the work of the team ministry at St Mary's, Woolwich. He had set up there a powerful, even brilliant, ecumenical team ministry but the time came when it could no longer be supported on a full-time basis. There was no more money. He had to explain this to the Parochial Church Council.

'Understandably they were confused. For years it had been drilled into them how important was the parish priest's job, how necessary it was that they should pray for more vocations to the ordained ministry and how, as a congregation, they should be encouraging the best young men in it to consider offering themselves for ordination. Now in effect we were saying the job was something of a waste of time—although we did not put it as crudely as this. I told the PCC that they had a choice between accepting the new plan or reverting to the traditional set-up. This, I explained, would not be a Rector and five assistants such as they had had for the previous five years, but a Rector with possibly one curate.'[13]

It worked well. The team reckoned they were exercising a more effective ministry than they had done when they were full-time priests.

'We discovered that what we thought in theory was in fact true in practice. It was an advance and not a retreat for the clergy to earn their living within secular institutions. We found that we could make a more effective contribution from within them than from the parochial periphery. There was no dearth of openings for us and we actually lived among the people who went to the institutions we were working in. This was unique in our area....'[14]

This is the other side of the medal from the creation of supplementary priests. But note that this laicization of the Woolwich team in no way deprived them of their dominating role in the life of the parish. They

---

[12] George Peabody, an American Episcopalian, said, 'It is staggering that most Episcopalians have believed the ministry of 3 million lay persons to be distinctly less important than that of a handful of about 8,000 clergy. The same confusion exists throughout Christendom. Such confusion is understandable when we remember how narrow our concept of mission has been (only) to involve people within the life of the gathered Church.' I take the quotation from a useful private memorandum, 'The Views and Needs of a Parish and its Parish Priest' by Canon K. W. Jones, a very active parish priest at St John's, Hove.

[13] Who Cares? Nicolas Stacey, Blond, London, 1971. p. 243.

[14] Ibid. p. 247.

remained an élite, and what is insufficiently explored in theories of the ministry is the role of the clergy as a governing élite. Whatever else a ministry is, or is not, it is an élite, maintaining an institution, disseminating a doctrine, dominating a social group and providing a subculture. And of course (as the supplementary or auxiliary ministry is now showing us) one can do this kind of thing without earning a penny from it. The dedicated communist might all his life earn his living from being a pile-driver or miner or trade union district secretary and exercise none the less a profound influence on history. He is a member of an élite serving a cause. The terms 'profession' or 'occupation' seem inadequate here, as they would have been to describe Paul's ministry, but is not the communist a 'professional' in the same way that St Paul was a 'professional'?

For, of course, there is another view of a profession from that which relates it solely to occupation. It is the very ancient one which grants to a profession the guardianship of a corpus of knowledge. Like other free professions, Christian ministries have the power to control entry into their ranks, to determine and preside over training, to regulate ethical practices, and to set up standards. In the case of the Church of England these powers are embodied in statute law, and in courts which enforce it. The élite power of the profession is precisely affirmed by the power of Convocations over the doctrines of the whole church. In the parson's freehold we are faced with a kind of proprietorial entrenchment of the professional independence of the clergyman. The freehold protects him from the encroachments of the laity and other clergy—at least that is one of the justifications advanced for it.

However, there is another sense in which ordination to the ministry is to be understood. A profession like the law or medicine, surgery or military science is its own source of knowledge over which its 'professors' often believe it has a monopoly. It is in a manner an esoteric pursuit served by a private language. Indeed the professionals decide without reference to any external authority what *is* knowledge in the eyes of their profession. To be a layman in these affairs is to be at a disadvantage before the professional experts, to be excluded from their sources of knowledge and techniques for evaluating it. Because of this more and more of society's knowledge becomes, *de facto*, secret knowledge. It would not be regarded as permitted professional etiquette to initiate the laity—as anyone, asking to be told exactly the situation of a relative after an operation soon discovers. Often the technical details would be beyond the layman's understanding.

To a degree this is the clergyman's situation. He is a member of a body which has guardianship of a corpus of knowledge and the insights it gives. It is this which makes him a professional. But unlike many professionals—but rather like teachers and journalists—it is not an occult body of knowledge which he protects. He is in duty bound to communicate his knowledge which then becomes *doctrine* which sustains the *ecclesia* of which he is an élite member. One could say he has an ideological task. The clergy, and the ordination service reminds us of it, are intended to be the transparent instruments of a Power not themselves, the vehicles of the inrush of divine love into the world, of which they are the bearers and evangelists. While this function remains and is recognized the clergy can never become an opaque inward-looking profession, defending itself against the world, and guarding an esoteric revelation. Just professionally it is compelled to be a sacred ministry. To be a member of that professing élite it is necessary to be accepted by its senior members as suitably trained and equipped. But it is not necessary to have a job, or to be paid for it. And in this sense 'the indelible stamp' has a sociological meaning. If they are not happy in this élite professional role today it is in part because they are inhibited in their enjoyment of it. Society has less use for them because Christianity is no longer acceptable as the universal dynamic of the West.

The clergy feel their changing status as a malaise to which their response is to strike out at obvious failures and inconsistencies in Church organization and personnel. In the answers to the open-ended question (Q. 32) of the Main Questionnaire of the Paul Report[15] even those who evinced the greatest satisfaction with their ministry ('nevertheless I would not change my job for the world')—struck out at some aspects of the Church's life. The targets were obvious ones—the bishops, the laity, the 'plant', doctrine/liturgy. Bishops were attacked for being remote, unfeeling 'administrators': the laity for passivity, worldliness, unwillingness to contribute time and money; the 'plant' for its unmanageability; doctrine for lack of relevance to the modern world, liturgy for its opacity. There is a sense in which they are traditional targets of the clergy, for these—authority, congregation, buildings, prayer book—are the basic determinants of every ministry. However much social patterns may vary from parish to parish for each parish these 'targets' form limiting factors. A parson may no more prove able to expand his congregation than to contract his plant: he can influence the degree of episcopal support and interest only as marginally as he can influence doctrine. In times of expansion the basic determinants are seen as beneficent—they set limits to tasks and define activities and render them manageable. In times of contraction they appear maleficent—the too-remote bishop an 'enemy'; the dwindling congregation sadly unrepresentative of the population, a mark of failure; the empty buildings a millstone round the minister's neck. It is for these reasons that the radical wing of the Church of England clergy (that wing most experienced in, or concerned about Church decline in the hard-core industrial zones

---

[15] *The Deployment and Payment of the Clergy.*

and/or most agitated about the new theology) advocates extreme measures—a part-time priesthood (all priests to work at ordinary jobs) or 'non-church' (the scrapping of all ecclesiastical plant and machinery and present liturgical forms).[16]

St. George's House Survey
The Church ; Clergy Dissatisfaction Index

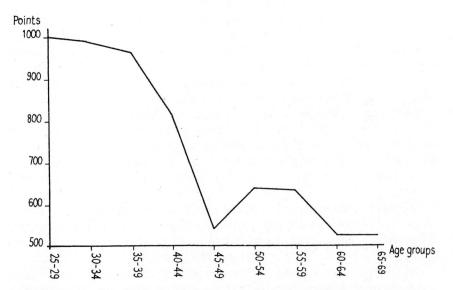

Fig. 6. *The survey showed a high rate of dissatisfaction with all aspects of the ministry among the younger clergy: a not unexpected result. Dissatisfaction is at its lowest among the clergy of the 45–49 age group, men in the prime of life and possibly at the height of their career expectations. The rise in dissatisfaction after 50 could be accounted for by* reflection *on the past and a measure of disillusion, interesting in a sample highly representative of successful clergy.*

The two together would constitute the disappearance of the Church of England as ordinarily understood and its resolution into a Quaker brotherhood (minus Meeting Houses). The impracticality of these propositions (how does one dispose of a paid labour force of 18,000 men, and 14,000 churches, at least a third of which are culturally valuable?) points to the desperation of the more radical clergy-thinking. A viable professional role for the clergy is apparently no longer conceivable to some

---

[16] *The Times*, 19 November 1966: 'Five pointers for the success of the "non-church",' by Rev. Ray Billington. Ray Billington was for a time a member of Nicolas Stacey's ecumenical team at Woolwich.

of the clergy. The malaise easily communicates itself to clergy who are less radical.

The disparity between the (radical) clergy's self-assessment or role-assessment and the public's attitude is striking. In a Television and Religion[17] survey conducted by Gallup Polls, 34 per cent of those interviewed put the 'priest, vicar or minister' as the person with the greatest influence for good in the community. Next in order came doctor (32 per cent), school teacher (19 per cent), local councillor (17 per cent), member of parliament (11 per cent). Moreover, asked the further question as to whether each of these representative figures did what he did for the good of the community or for what he personally could get out of it, the 'good of the community' order produced by respondents was 'vicar, priest or minister' 67 per cent, doctor 55 per cent, school teacher 41 per cent, local councillor 31 per cent, member of parliament 28 per cent. This is a striking compliment to the clergy; the cynicism with which political life is viewed in these responses argues a certain sophistication in those interviewed and makes their idealization of clergy-roles the more remarkable. But perhaps that idealization argues an increasing remoteness of the clergy from social life? Politicians are people we expect to do the right things for us—they seldom do, and so we 'knock' them, but about the parson it could be easier to be pleasant in a disengaged way? This hypothesis might be provisionally supported by the answers interviewers gave to the 1957 Gallup Poll survey on religion where—in answer to a clumsy question—41 per cent gave politics greater influence on life than religion and only 30 per cent gave religion the greater. In any case, 83 per cent say that the clergy do a lot of useful work, 90 per cent say that they are sincere (even 70 per cent of those who have no denomination say that the clergy are sincere). 'Overworked' and 'underpaid' was the general majority verdict on the clergy, and death, loneliness and ill-health topped the list of situations in which people could get help and comfort from the Church. Whatever questions one asks about the methodology of Gallup Polls, these answers constitute a flattering image of the clergyman and a touching concern for him. There is support for the prestige-rating of the clergy in other more rigorous studies of course. 'An Empirical Study of the Prestige of Selected Occupations' by N. D. Richards[18] gave doctor first, lawyer third, clergymen sixth in an analysis from a preliminary frame of ninety occupational titles. The ordinands Anthony Coxon interviewed in one of the small scale studies of his important research put doctor first,

---

[17] *Television and Religion*: A Report prepared by Social Surveys (Gallup Poll) Ltd. on behalf of ABC Television, University of London Press, 1964.

[18] 1962. An unpublished M.A. thesis, University of Nottingham, quoted in *A Sociological Study of the Social Recruitment, Selection, and Professional Socialization of Anglican Ordinands*, 1965 unpublished doctoral thesis by Anthony Coxon, University of Leeds.

lawyer second, clergyman third in terms of difficulty of training. He writes: 'This order is very similar indeed to that given by Richards, although it is difficult ... to decide whether this is because prestige correlates with length of training, or whether it was because prestige was, in fact, being estimated.'[19]

A reasonable hypothesis is that the high ranking which ordinands tend to give the ministry corresponds with a more general public ranking. The ministry is held in esteem prestige-wise and its pastoral function appears to be affectionately (perhaps even sentimentally) regarded. My subjective impression too is that the nineteenth century stereotype of the comic parson or curate has largely disappeared from stage and screen because it no longer corresponds to public experience, which is basically of a serious man. The clerical utopian idiot of the film 'Heavens Above' has no social basis. The sources of the clergy's malaise cannot be wholly in the public image, or even in a sense of declining prestige.

Yet, of course, there is a source of malaise if the clergyman is highly regarded and if at the same time those who so regard him are in retreat from him. I will not enter again into the dilemma, now familiar, of those statistics which show a decline in church-going alongside a stubborn insistence on a religious identity. But a paper by Robert Coles, of York University, read to the Greater London Research and Intelligence Unit Seminar[20] questioned the figures of erosion, asking whether 'declining Church membership is a good indicator of the declining influence of religion, whether the decline in membership of the church indicates the decline in their importance, or merely that the religious community has a different shape; these and many other factors must be settled before secularization is any more than a hypothesis'.

Robert Coles has his own solution to propound (he accepts that it is no more than a generalization). It is that Church membership is a multi-dimensional affair. The different dimensions shift in the course of time: at one time overt membership, church-going and so forth gaining, and at another time subjective membership, private religion growing and overt membership declining. What he calls 'privatized religion' has evolved into an important category in the present social situation.[21] It

---

[19] Op. cit.: 'Roughly 72 per cent of the variance in prestige scores is accounted for by income, and 67 per cent of this variance is accounted for by educational attainment. Hence either income level or educational attainment is a surprisingly good predictor of the "general standing" of an occupation', Albert J. Reiss, *Occupations and Social Status*, Free Press, Glencoe 1961. Quoted by Anthony Coxon, op. cit. p. 197.

[20] January 1969. Privately circulated.

[21] Except among young people where religious communes and other quasi-religious associations spring up completely divorced from traditional religion. See below, the discussion of the Jesus movement, p 335 and the issues of *Community*, the Journal of Christian Renewal, editor Rev. Dr David Clark, 22a Dartmouth Row, London S.E.10.

could be a less secularized faith than that of Church members themselves in that privatized religion relates more to everyday life and to personal moral tensions than does the religion of so many of the regular church-goers. He recognizes this group as unstable, perhaps evanescent. But we can see how perplexing it is for a priest or minister to be faced simultaneously with a dimension of privatized Christianity among the more thoughtful of his parish and a repugnance to its institutionalized forms and to the services of its professional élite.

There is no doubt that there is much confusion in the minds at any rate of Church of England clergy about the roles they should play (the plural is necessary). In older rural England the role of the parish priest was a more settled one. The freehold system—a kind of life-tenure, if he wanted it, gave the parson an inalienable stake in the community. He was the representative there of an estate of the realm, an instrument (inevitably in a society believing itself Christian) of the establishment. He would be the promoter of education locally, the dispenser of charity, the patron of clever boys, the chastizer of morals, the friend and counsellor of the faithful, the mouthpiece of God. He was indeed the *persona* of the community. Even if poor (and many parsons were poor) his role was not in doubt either to himself or to his parishioners.

Historically speaking both the status and the activities described link the Anglican ministry with the gentry. The squire and his lady could do most of those things. To be 'of the gentry' was the necessary qualification for entry to the ministry. And to be a gentleman was not to have to work for a living, but to own enough in land and property to have others work for you, and to send your sons to Oxford or Cambridge. To labour, or to live by trade, was a disqualification for membership of the gentlefolk. And all the original professions, medicine, the law, the military, had this basis too in post-Reformation times. In medieval times the Church was the compendium of all the professions, except soldiering and surgery because they involved shedding blood. This genteel basis Philip Elliott makes clear in *The Sociology of the Professions*[22] where he says that an 'important reason why professions were compatible with the social status of gentlemen was that they allowed their members to lead their lives in the style expected of gentlemen'.[23] Another important reason is that their duties would largely be with other gentlemen. The importance of landed connections and Oxford and Cambridge degrees has already been demonstrated. 'In Halévy's phrase, the clergy were able to enhance the moral influence of their cloth by the social influence of their rank!'[24]

---

[22] Macmillan, London 1972.
[23] Ibid.
[24] E. Halévy, *Imperialism and the Rise of Labour*, London 1951, p. 331.

The sense of social rank adhering to the older professions dies hard as the following illuminating quotation from Philip Elliott shows:

'Church leaders faced with a fall in recruitment in the second half of the nineteenth century resisted attempts to lower entry qualifications and to break the connection with the universities on the grounds that this would threaten the clergy's social position. For example, a speaker at the Church Congress of 1872 claimed that "owing to the union of the character of the clergyman with the social status of gentleman, in fitting him for the latter, they [the universities] have in a manner fitted him for the former. . . ?"'[25]

A sense of the loss of the social status of gentleman among the inferior clergy (social rank still clearly adheres to deans and bishops), or at least of being confused about status in a society socially confusing, may be one important cause of clergy malaise. Added to this, the role-playing of which I spoke has been eroded by five developments—one, the disappearance of natural communities; two, the rise of a national system of education; three, the rise and professionalization of the social services; four, the decline in churchgoing; five, doubt about the divine instrumentality of the Church. The last two of these factors alone would be sufficient to erode ministerial self-confidence. The first raises the question—so acutely felt in the Church of England today but not only there—'with what community am I supposed to be in relation?' If it is a parish sliced out of a score of surburban streets it may be non-identifiable or non-existent. If it is merely the congregation gathered from those streets, this could be a socially withdrawn group, with fractional influence and casualty significance. If it is still a rural parish, this could have been rendered unviable as a natural community by shrinking population or by the influx of commuters or retired persons or the cultural and economic dominance of the nearest conurbation.

As to developments two and three, where these take place in an existent natural community, they have the effect of displacing the parish priest from the centre of the community. The community, in relation to him, ceases to be concentric: he, in relation to the community, becomes eccentric—and perhaps in the popular as well as the strict meaning of the word. Where these developments take place in a parish without identifiable community they limit the empathic alternative role—that of social and welfare worker and (maybe) political spokesman. Development four presents the parish priest with a dwindling care of the faithful and therefore of declining personal influence and five with psychological insecurity—if others no longer believe in him as an instrument of the divine, how can he convince them? Can he any longer believe it himself?

The point is that in the West, with some exceptions, all these developments are reaching their apogee together. The Church of England is

---

[25] *The Sociology of the Professions*, pp. 30–1.

only a special case. It is the confluence of all these social and psychological influences which seems to have produced the Christian secularization movement[26] in Britain and America. The movement would appear to be an answer to the questions—'What kind of a society are the Churches today called to function in? What is it about this society that makes the Churches appear irrelevant?' It is easy to see that one answer brings the Churches under the social judgment that their organizations have failed to adapt themselves to urban and technological society and are structurally more appropriate to rural and small town communities of some generations ago?[27] But this answer raises another question—why did the Churches fail to adapt? This must appear an unnecessary question if one accepts ecclesiastical conservatism as axiomatic. Almost everyone does. The Churches are thought of today as the last places where deep and meaningful organizational changes could occur. If these propositions are true one has to explain, *inter alia*, monasticism, the nineteenth century mission field movements and Methodism, all organizationally ahead of their times.[28] If one does not accept ecclesiastical conservativism as axiomatic one has perhaps to conclude that the Church is backward because the best minds do not enter it today as lay or clerical leaders and organizers. And if they do not enter it, it is not just a matter of careers (labour and nationalist movements the world over have succeeded in securing high quality leadership despite alternative career appeal) but because Christianity as a *Weltanschauung* does not speak convincingly to the problems and insights of the best contemporary minds.

There is a further historical possibility here—if the 'best minds' are hostile to Christian witness, and their satisfaction is important to the 'best *Christian* minds' then the floodgates are open to doctrinal revision which will once again relate doctrine to the 'best minds', however atheistic those minds may be: hence middle of the road revision with Dr John Robinson and the late Professor Ronald Gregor Smith, or extreme revision at the hands of Professor Paul van Buren and the 'death of God' theologians such as Messrs. Altizer and Hamilton. There is a clear sense in which Paul van Buren is directing an argument at Wittgenstein and Ayer, rather than at Aquinas, Augustine and St Paul. The communication problem which all the new theologians recognize is

---

[26] Though a manifesto mostly from the young Episcopalian clergy of the United States, *On the Battle Lines*, ed. by Malcolm Boyd, SCM Press, 1964, does faithfully represent the spectrum of Anglican concern. Its sub-title is significant—'27 Anglican Priests in Rebellion in the United States of America'.

[27] Basically the charge of Gibson Winter, *The Suburban Captivity of The Churches, The New Creation as Metropolis*; Harvey Cox, *The Secular City*; Leslie Paul, *The Deployment and Payment of the Clergy* and many other studies.

[28] Methodism was the first great modern movement in Britain. Democratic, locally based, but efficiently centralized it provided the model for trade unions, co-operatives, political parties, missionary societies and many sects.

then not so much with the masses as with the intellectual élite of Western society—mostly a scientific and humanistic élite. The Churches only feel themselves respectable if they can meet the critiques of that élite.

Certainly no ordinands passing anywhere within reach of a university philosophical department in the heyday of the challenge of logical positivism or during the long dry summer of linguistic analysis could escape the withering judgement of Ayer and others not only on religious statements, characterized mostly as nonsense, but on all metaphysical positions. And the early days of linguistic analysis were hardly more helpful. Oxford theological minds—the late Ian Ramsey, for instance— had perforce to begin to state their theological arguments from a linguistic position. They had no option but discourse at a level which showed that the significance of that position had been understood and absorbed.[29]

One can regard *Honest to God* as an effort to meet, at least in part, the devastating wind which had blown out of Oxford and to produce a restatement of traditional Christian doctrines in language which might pass muster in philosophical quarters, existentialist and positivist, near and far from Oxford. It provoked a typical Oxford response from Alasdair MacIntyre, the philosophy don. Dr Robinson, he said, was doubly an atheist: he demolishes a 'being out there' and he translates religion into non-religious or secular terms.[30] The only remarkable thing about this atheistic stand was that it came from a bishop. So much for trying! One has only to read MacIntyre's essay to understand the rigorous intellectual framework within which the best Christian minds had to operate if they could, or quit. It was no comfort to fall back on existentialism while Sartre held the field! Nor was any comfort to be got by turning from the academics to a world which was increasingly indifferent to religion.

I do not see how this line of theorizing can be resisted. If plausible it lends strength to a theme familiar to students of the sociology of religion— that ideological convulsions in religion have their roots in social and intellectual changes at large, that Christianity has to adapt itself to new and compelling world views (or retreat into rigid sectarianism) of which the non-metaphysical world view is, in the West, the most powerful of contemporary attitudes.

---

[29] Cf. my *Alternatives to Christian Belief*, Chap. 8. 'Positivism and the Negation of Metaphysics'.

[30] Alasdair MacIntyre's essay, from *Encounter*, September 1963, 'God and the Theologians', is reprinted in his *Against the Self-Images of the Age*, Duckworth, London 1971.

PART FOUR

Future World and Future Church

'What a reflection on human perversity, and what a rebuke to the Christian disunion, which we are called upon to repent today. Instead of recognizing the work of God where they saw it, the Pharisees applied the test of formal rules. Christ broke the Sabbath. He was no disciple of Moses in the true succession. What example could apply more exactly to the attitude of Christians to those divided from them by empirical allegiance! He is not sound on Biblical Inspiration. He is incorrect on the doctrine of Justification by faith alone. He is outside legitimate Catholic order. And all these things may have their place; but the first thing is the acknowledgement of the work of Christ, wherever it is manifested, in healing sores and making saints. It is divine, it cannot be gainsaid. What can God himself do with us if we will not love, and welcome, and assist the manifest work of God? We can, in the end, commend the doctrines and institutions of religion by nothing else but this, that they are channels appointed to convey, and actually conveying, the efficacious grace of Christ.'

Austin Farrer in *A Celebration of Faith*

'How to maintain and hand on to the rising generation, and its successors, whatever is true and of abiding value in the religion of the West, hitherto formulated in traditional Christianity, might be considered of greater urgency than finding the formula with which to unite the Christian denominations. From this standpoint the Church has nowhere to go but inwards.'

Dom Aelred Graham in *The Times*, 23 December 1972

ONE

The Several Futures

THERE is now a science of futurology: essentially a series of exercises in prediction. Computerized programmes seek to determine the pattern of a society, an industry or a social service, at a certain date ahead. If the demand for steel or petroleum continues to mount at a curve made predictable by present and past consumption it is feasible to estimate what, in the light of increased population, will be required of it in the year 2000. But an examination of latent resources, including labour, and their relation to other social priorities makes it possible to say whether the requirements could be met and what social and economic effects must follow whichever way the chips fall. Quite inevitably an effort to predict the future of one basic industry involves an assessment about the probable nature of society as a whole, and world society at that. The forecasts are often hair-raising and the projected world one in which it would be better not to have to live.

One is not caught up in these complexities in speaking of the future of the Church, perhaps especially the Church of England, but in others of a still more elusive character. The Church is not an element of the economy. If it vanished men would not lack steel for their cars or shoes for their feet. The economic effects of its disappearance might even be mildly beneficial in releasing labour for more productive purposes and land, buildings, funds for different social needs. Or if Marx is to be believed, it would free men from their other-worldly illusions and compel them to take account of their true material situation. Revolutionaries have rejoiced over the possible disappearance of religion just on that account. The Soviet regime has, as a matter of principle, sought with terror and guile to hasten its demise. And to be honest, a great part of the Western world, a world much the creation of Christianity, does not seem greatly concerned either by its life or its death. Let us be clear then: men might be made spiritually more hungry by the death of the Churches but they might be fractionally better fed and would not necessarily suffer socially or economically. I do not think that the futurologists have to programme the computer with a religious factor X in their predictions about the year 2000 unless they have to grant religion a power in other fields—

national unity, social cohesion, labour-management harmony which are important elements in the viability of a society. We can make a credible prediction of cereal production thirty years ahead and of the world population then and estimate the consequences. We cannot estimate the consequences of the death of religion, or for that matter of its revival. In religion we can never be sure what is positive knowledge.

Of course, some things can be said with safety about the future of religion and they are said statistically from time to time. In the previous chapter I spoke of the statistical probabilities of the ratios of Anglican clergy to population in the years ahead. It is predictably the case for instance that if insufficient younger men are recruited to the ministry to maintain the average age then the average age must rise. It is not an absurd deduction to say that an ageing clergy is going to be socially unrepresentative. A Commission appointed by the Baptist Churches, produced a graph which showed that, in terms of declining attendance, the Baptist Church in England could almost extinguish itself by the year 2001. I reproduced it earlier. It has to be studied in relation to certain Church of England trend lines, pp. 183–5 supra. Exercises of this kind are not only useful but obligatory to an understanding of the future of Churches. They extend our knowledge. They sharpen our wits. But one is in the area of possibilities, not certainties. The future of religion as a whole is unpredictable because of its very nature. This need not exclude us from predicting what in it can be predicted.

Because of its very nature. What is the nature that puts it outside the futurologists' programmes? One might say that its future is unpredictable because it is a cultural element, part therefore of the ground of society, from which society and the economy derive themselves. It is not to be derived from them, but is prior to them, more fundamental. More fundamental because a society and an economy grow out of the way that man looks at himself and his relations to nature, to other men and to God. Religion is in that sense ideological. It is, in the best usage of 'ideological', the ready-made frame of reference one brings to the examination of everything. The critical apparatus one brings to bear upon religion itself could therefore derive from the tools it itself provides. It will be seen that I am taking a Weberian point of view about the cultural and social significance of religion. But it could be also Arnold Toynbee's point of view in *A Study of History*. He sees an interaction between the birth of civilizations and the birth of higher religions. They spring to life together as a consequence of deeper human intuitions about the nature of man. I have been arguing ever since I wrote *The Annihilation of Man*[1] that a society is created and maintained by its doctrine of man: if a society loses its doctrine then it can perish physically or spiritually, or

---

[1] Faber, London, 1944.

in a Hegelian sense turn into its opposite. It is in these terms that a religion can be immeasurable because it is the element in which we swim and even when we disown it we probably continue to live on the mysterious manna it has deposited in our culture. Perhaps we can only discover what it means for a society when all the consequences of its loss have spent themselves. If we are living in a post-Christian society in the West then we are in process of finding this out, but not yet aware of the worst. But we cannot be certain even of this. We know we are not living in a fully Christian society such as the Middle Ages, or even in a Victorian society to which Christianity was indispensable. But there are so many Christian elements, presuppositions, moral values interwoven even with the anti-Christian strands of contemporary Western society that it would be dangerous to assume that as a value system, a moral touchstone, it is dead or dying.

There is another scenario into which we must place Christianity and that is as the rich cultural strand in our civilization I have spoken of and so beyond valuation. W. H. Auden said 'Poetry makes nothing happen'.

> 'For poetry makes nothing happen: it survives
> In the valley of its saying where executives
> Would never want to tamper: it flows south
> From the ranches of isolation and the busy griefs
> Past towns that we believe and die in:
>   it survives,
> A way of happening, a mouth.'[2]

Religion is the poetry of hope and pain, of life and death. Does *religion* make nothing happen? Marx would have said so: at least he would have said that religion was waste, a spiritual opiate, it *produced* nothing, it was the negation of economic activity and Max Weber would have said the opposite, that the protestant ethic was the most powerful dynamic of the Western world which has totally transformed that world, and the non-Christian world too. Yet there is the sense that what one *does* religiously, as what one does poetically, *makes* nothing happen. It belongs to the sphere of art or of music, to that free area of play in which man finds his soul, the area where man is under no compulsions save those of the spirit. In all other areas of his life, food, clothing, shelter, property, sex, family, sickness, death, the pressures are inexorable. If religion is the worship of God and the enjoyment of him forever then consequences do not follow of *necessity*. The whole doctrine of justification by faith moves man into the transcendental realm of the freedom of God. The sense of religion as part of the free play of society in which man moves

---

[2] W. H. Auden, 'In Memory of W. B. Yeats', *Another Time*, 1940. But how untrue this sentiment is of Yeats! His poetry gave birth to that romantic revolutionary republicanism from the blows of which Ireland is still reeling.

away from the iron necessities of everyday into the realm of cultural discovery in which he finds out what he is, and how to shape and reshape what he is, is anticipated for us in the theological insights of St Paul. It makes sense, theological sense, that this is the area in which the Holy Spirit operates, for here man is at his most creative. Of course social consequences follow from religion because acts of religion are acts within society. But they do not have to follow, any more than they must follow from poetry. The necessary connection is not there and religion conducted purely for its social consequences always turns out to be something else, a series of acts of social compassion, admirable in themselves, or, what is far from admirable, the self-justifying ideology of a race or a class. We do not have to look farther than Ulster.

Yet we are talking about the Church of England, which is not a religion in itself but only a certain national variation of Christianity. It would be absurd to assume that the disappearance of the Church of England would involve the disappearance of Christianity. Important though it must be to its members, it is not so important as all that in the perspectives of time and of history. Even in its own time perspective, its role as a national Church or parliament Church (a role now running out for the very good reason that neither nation nor parliament are more than nominally Anglican) has a span of only four hundred years as against a probable span of one thousand four hundred years in the bosom of the mother Church. The disappearance of the Church of England would be only 'a little local difficulty', religiously speaking, for the world.

Need one postulate its disappearance? Indeed one must. It is a necessary hypothesis. How might it disappear? One way would be through the general erosion of religious practice and religious belief which seems part of the Western European, but not yet of the American, scene in this half century. Through failing attendances, falling recruitment to the ministry and mounting financial burdens, declining faith, the Church could crumble away, surviving perhaps here and there as a tourist attraction like the beefeaters and the morris dancers. It might take a century, but the possibility cannot be ruled out. But the other possibility cannot be ruled out either—its revival as a result of an inner transformation in response to the enormity of the challenge of the contemporary world. A Toynbee-like resurrection. The Reformation was just such an inner transformation of Christianity and its Churches in the face of a decline of the Church into the meaninglessness, humbug and hypocrisy Erasmus depicts so savagely in his *Colloquies*. So too was the counter-reformation. The Roman Church at this moment is passing through spiritual convulsions which would have been inconceivable a generation ago in its search for an *aggiornamento*. It is not improper to speak of this as its own reformation and it is not impossible to foresee the staid, pragmatic, conformist Church of England facing a similar crisis and even coming through. Though one is baffled to imagine—in the light of its present retreat—what might spark it off. However, one need not predict a future issuing into, or springing out of, some crisis or calamity. Britain is accustomed to the inevitability of gradualness. A new Church might grow up, as the empire grew up, in a fit of absent-mindedness. Out of a series of local ecumenical decisions, including shared churches and ministries, a new Church might come into existence which was no more than Anglican in name. Indeed, many of those who successfully opposed Anglican–Methodist reunion thought that this was the way unity ought to be achieved. A decision from Rome to recognize Anglican orders and to accept the Church of England as a uniate Church would transform the status, if not the outward appearance, of the Church and lead to some sort of combination with the powerful Roman Church in England. But it could lead to an Evangelical withdrawal too.

This speculation about the future has so far been set within the present institutional frame of the Churches. All Western Churches have a similar institutional pattern—sacred buildings, a full-time minister attached to one or more buildings, voluntary assistants and officers, a congregation gathered in the sacred building, satellite societies in the building or close to it acting as buffers between the Church and the world. The familiar process of religious socialization round a holy edifice seems so inevitable that it is hard to think of its disappearance and the survival of the Church which built it and sustains it. The presence of so many distinctive and culturally valuable religious buildings in Western lands gives us a comforting semantic ambiguity—the church is the building at the corner of the street or in the centre of the village. It is also the society which put it there. And that society is invariably centralized in some way and raises money, no small part of which is devoted to maintaining its scatter of distinctive buildings in which worship according to the cult can be carried on. The buildings are of very first importance whether they are beautiful or not. And buildings—'plant'—are what people think of first when they speak of the Church as an institution.

Dr Kathleen Bliss thought them so central to a faith that she began her *The Future of Religion* with an essay on 'Buildings'.

'A religious building is far more than a place to visit or meet in. It speaks out its meaning to the world and it embodies—shaped as it is by people, living and dead, and their practices—the quintessence of a religious tradition, old or new. It is nonsense to say that buildings do not matter. Why are the early manifestations of outbreaks of anti-semitism almost always attacks on synagogues, if not because the synagogue *represents* the Jewish community? Why does any government repressive of religion or a particular form of it, so often demand that religious buildings should be stripped of anything that identifies them, deprived of access to a road, removed from a street map, if not because the building is the public face of a religious community by which it may be known? The power exerted by buildings and even by sites accounts for the persistence with which new religions build on the top of what they want to change, supplant or destroy.'[3]

One might say that *all* the buildings we encounter have a social significance and that, when we have to, we arrange them in our minds in a hierarchy of meaning and importance. The first—and visually aggressive—way in which a culture reveals itself is through its buildings. And Christian buildings, but especially those in the Catholic tradition, have the added impact that they both house and show forth God himself. A member of a parochial church council objected to a nave altar for Series II parish communion saying, 'Why should we insult God by bringing him down to the altar in the nave? He has always been up there at the high altar and that's where he should be, in the highest place, and that's where we should worship him and the vicar should be. We shouldn't change God's place just because some people somewhere voted something else.' Yet this is not a church in which the sacrament is reserved. The Protestant sense of the chapel as the place where God lives can also give the religious building a sacredness as moving as any Catholic consciousness of it:

> Lone on highway old graves awry in first fall snow
> Under scarlet maples. 1850. Here died simple men.
> *This is God's House* clapboard cabin flatly states . . .[4]

There is a sense then in which a religious future is inconceivable without sacred buildings and sacred sites. Yet the inconceivable may have to be conceived. A Church must *first of all* be its faithful people. Their buildings, their 'public face to the world' must be secondary. One may conceive of a Church without buildings, such as the early Church had of necessity to be, but not of a Church without the faithful. Many secular societies function successfully with little or no investment in buildings. They have a different sort of public face. The Society of Friends has it both ways. Their meeting rooms tend to be so modest and self-effacing as to advertise their humility above all else. Yet they do advertise.

One may speak again, therefore, of several futures. There is a future within the existing Anglican frame and another within a reformed frame and another within a transformed frame. There is more than one ecumenical future. One may be foreseen through union with the non-episcopal Churches and quite another with Rome, or with both. Yet there are futures outside the institutional frame either for a Church which discards

---

[3] *The Future of Religion*, C. A. Watts, The New Thinker's Library, 1969, p.14.

[4] Leslie Paul, 'Letters from the Mississippi', *Mad River Review*, Spring–Summer 1965 issue.

its buildings and seeks an altogether humbler mode or for a Christianity which seeks for a new Christian presence in a world in which the Churches are no longer effective.

I shall look at all the possibilities after first setting the scene.

TWO

The Human Future of the Future World

WE ARE living in an unexpected and unpredicted world in which change of certain kinds is so swift that the bases of prediction vanish as one examines them. Men have always been poor at predicting their own future. The social optimists and utopians at the beginning of the century passionately believed that the advance of science and the spread of rational scientific concepts of man and nature would cause a tolerant understanding between men and societies to burgeon, reduce the influence of religious and other bigotries and so issue in generous, peaceful, democratic societies the world over. They were certain that education and science would produce societies morally superior to those of the past. The new cult of evolution (despite its violent streak) seemed to render cosmic support to man's dream of ascension, even perfection. It must seem to us now (some seventy years after the publication of *A Modern Utopia*) to involve a Nelsonian blindness in both eyes to see man as one who has got rid of evil: it would be closer to the evidence to say that he has increased it. So much has the world scene changed and for the worse since 1905, that the difficulty is not to discover whether the future is going to be utopian or not, but whether there will be one at all. There will be a future world, but whether inhabited by men is open to doubt. The future could foreclose on man. The future of the future world may not include a human future.[1]

The failure to predict belongs to the trivial and the specialized areas too. If the trivial can be borne in this context, one can mention that roller skating and billiards were immensely popular metropolitan recreations about the time of *A Modern Utopia*. A social planner would have covered the suburbs with these amenities. Some suburbs were prodigiously supplied. In the years after the first world war no one knew what to do with the monster roller-skating rinks except to turn them into cinemas. The age of vast investment in super-cinemas could not foresee

---

[1] 'Before the thermonuclear bomb, man had to live with the idea of his death as an individual: from now onward, mankind has to live with the idea of its death as a species.' Arthur Koestler, *The Ghost in the Machine*, Hutchinson, London 1967, p. 322.

home television as the ruin of their dream palaces. Planners of the Hemel Hempstead New Town, the first of the new towns after World War II, estimated they would need to provide for one car to every six families. Now of course cars park on the beautiful green verges and wherever they can. One speaks necessarily of human unpredictability not because of the failure of the quasi-science of futurology, that is to say not for lack of care or accuracy on the part of predictors, but because of human unexpectedness. Man is protean. He is an unfinished creature. A future is not laid out for him as it might be for a bird or a bee. He must make it for himself.[2]

So that the only futures one can speculate about are those already here and making themselves felt, which must expend their considerable energies before they die. Let me give two concrete examples, one economic, one in the sphere of human belief. First, the economics of the motor car. It may be desirable that the motor car should go. But it will not go just because its disadvantages are widely canvassed and accepted, including a rate of casualties which would bring down a government if they occurred in a war or an epidemic. A vast human investment has gone into the car, national economies are constructed round its production and sale and its ubiquity and convenience *create* social structures around it. Both the economic and social factors will have to be worked through to the bitter end before acceptable alternatives can find a foothold. A merely rational judgement of the social consequences of the car cannot be itself a solution of the car problem, any more than it is a solution of the cigarette problem. On the side of beliefs, communism, the political incarnation of Marxism, may be intellectually discredited, shown to be humanly destructive and incapable of existing without political terror. Yet the most devastating moral and intellectual exposures of it do not destroy it: nor do disgraces and defeats. Too vast an emotional and social investment has been made in its creeds and structures for an alternative to be easily credible to those who live under it. Its collapse would produce unimaginable social convulsions. There is a parallel in the history of Christianity itself which effectively disgraced itself with wars, persecution, terror, inquisition in the sixteenth and seventeenth centuries but did not retreat in shame from the scene because of them. This is also to say that man is not the rational-scientific man of a Wellsian utopia. His social structures are only in part susceptible to purely intellectual justifications.

It is with these qualifications in mind that one still seeks to look at our possible (and in some cases our actual) futures. The first concerns the inexorable growth of power.

---

[2] A theme I developed in *Nature into History*, Faber, London 1957, and in *Man's Understanding of Himself*, The Hale Memorial Sermon, Seabury-Western, 1971.

THREE

The Overpowered Future

EVERY schoolboy knows that the Industrial Revolution ended man's immemorial dependence on a few given natural sources of power and bestowed on him new sources, coal, oil, electricity, and that by these instruments his control over nature, over his environment, were increased beyond all the dreams of Leonardo da Vinci or Francis Bacon. To the early list we have in this century added an inexhaustible nuclear fuel. For two centuries mankind has been harvesting power at an accelerating rate to which no end can be foreseen except the exhaustion of the world's resources (impossible anyway for nuclear fuels). Historically speaking mankind finds itself in an unprecedented situation and with few guide rules from the past to help it to understand its future.

Of course the power-explosion created a euphoria, to which the Great Exhibition of 1851 was the first guide, which has been a long time dying. The space break-through may have given it a new lease of life. It is only ten or so years ago that a theology of secularization burst upon the Christian world. Whatever else it hymned, it certainly celebrated the triumph of technology and especially the secular city with its anonymity and mobility which was its creation and broadcast the concept borrowed from Dietrich Bonhoeffer that man had come of age and was now master of his destiny. God, as *deus ex machina*, could be pensioned off. If man did not believe that God was dead he could at least (at last) behave as if he did.

So rapidly do events move that the new thesis (which has not yet found its theology) is of the decay of cities, even their death, of which Geoffrey Moorhouse's immense work on *Calcutta*[1] is almost a text book. With the growth of world population and the increasing influx into cities from the countryside quite apart from that growth, many cities are likely to proliferate until indeed they break down, until it is no longer possible to cope with the elementary services of water, sewage, housing, transport, to say nothing of advanced services such as public health, telephones and

---

[1] London 1971.

popular education. Overcrowding appears to produce of itself a mindless violence and vandalism, often aimed at public property and services, of a degree in some quarters which makes maintenance of vital services difficult. The citizens themselves add to their own burdens by their own protests, blind or articulate, against their living conditions.

It is a vicious circle. The city which was once the creator and guardian of civilization, the home of elegance and wit, of the highest arts and crafts, of splendid architecture and sophisticated worship, tends now (even when these gifts to mankind survive within it) to be a vast dump, a concrete jungle, enemy to the very things it created, the unlivable which nevertheless has to be lived with and lived in. Urban life appears to be the goal towards which the bulk of mankind is heading. If we accept the United Nations definition of an urban place as a town of over 20,000 population, then at present some thirty-five per cent of world population is urbanized. By the year 2000—little more than a generation away—it is predicted that over 50 per cent of the world population will be living in towns, a matter of 3,500,000,000 people. But the situation in developed lands such as Europe, North America and Japan, has already passed the year 2000 point. The United Kingdom, with a present population of 56 million people, concentrates over 80 per cent of them in urban areas and has a present overall density of about 590 per square mile of land 'from which must be subtracted the high hills and bleak uplands and much of Wales and the North. So if the increase in numbers is about 12 million (the official estimate for the next two or three decades), it can exercise formidable pressure, given the island's essentially limited space.'[2]

Living in small towns of 20,000 and upwards, is despite the inexorable build-up of traffic, a bearable, even a pleasant experience. The problem is the great city which swallows up villages, small towns and countryside in rings of concentric growth (often decaying in the centre at the same time) and urbanizes vast areas beyond its boundaries. There could be a catastrophe of cities which would be a world catastrophe. It is not impossible to foresee. The experts predict several Tokyos or Calcuttas to come in the years ahead round the Bay of Bengal or the Yangtse Valley. We have already the spectacle of the population build-up down both the east and west coasts of the United States and the prospect of a continuous conurbation in south-east England from Luton to Dover and one long city of the Lower Rhine. It is a process that does not seem to be able to develop without environmental destruction and the creation of ghettoes, crises of transport and communication, and the inexorable development of new power units which contribute to a further

---

[2] Barbara Ward and Rene Dubos, *Only One Earth, The Care and Maintenance of a Small Planet*, Penguin Books, 1972, p. 172. Cf. also, ibid., 'The Hinge of History'. p. 40 ff.

deterioration of the quality of life. Even inexhaustible nuclear fuel creates indestructible potential pollutants. And these vast urban concentrations have no hope of surviving the exhaustion of the power resources on which they feed at present.

As it is, the industrial and human wastes and poisons pollute the rivers, lakes and estuaries and the shallow seas. The insecticides, pesticides, herbicides of agriculture add to the pollution. An expert has estimated that the oceans of the world could be dead in twenty-five years time through the destruction of the biosphere of plankton. If this plankton is essential to the oxygenization of the atmosphere, then mankind could die too. Here is a future halfway to being realized.

Up to the present the Western world, whether democratic or communist, Christian or humanist, has held a proud consciousness of itself as a society destined to realize certain humane goals—peace, enlightenment, social justice, a continuous mitigation of pain, suffering and deprivation. Viewed along one perspective it could justify that claim. The striving persists and has successes. Viewed along another it has to be seen as the most ferocious society which has ever existed. It is not only a power-generating society, but a self-militarizing society. The world has managed to kill 59 million in wars since 1820. Terrorism under Stalin killed 20 million Russians in less than 20 years. Of course, war has been endemic to human societies, though in some primitive societies it has been ritualized to reduce the damage to the minimum, but the basic change is in the destructive powers of modern war, the harnessing of war to the new power network. Bertrand de Jouvenel developed the theme in *Power, The Natural History of its Growth*[3] where he contrasted what he called the progressive demilitarization of the Roman Empire the longer it lived with opposing modern European tendencies.

He writes:

'The path followed by our own civilization is in the opposite direction; it is leading to a catastrophe just as total [as the decline of Rome] but of a different kind. At Poitiers, which was the decisive battle of the fourteenth century, about 50,000 men were engaged, and about the same number fought at Marignan. Only very few more, some 65,000 it is said fought at Nordlingen, the decisive battle of the Thirty Years' War. But come to Malplaquet in 1709 and Leipzig in 1813: the figures there are 200,000 and 450,000 respectively. In our times we have improved on that. The 1914 war killed or mutilated five times as many men as were under arms in Europe at the end of the Napoleonic Wars. [The war of 1914–18 killed 8,000,000 and mutilated 6,000,000 men. At the end of the Napoleonic Wars there were 3,000,000 men under arms.] And in this present war (1939–45)

---

[3] Hutchinson, London, undated.

there is no counting the men, women and children engaged in the struggle. . . .'[4]

Indeed the number of Russians killed is believed to have exceeded the total killed and mutilated in the First World War. Here then is war advancing in numbers mobilized and destruction achieved by geometrical progression *and as the most powerful characteristic of our civilization.* We have to add one final comment. War power now, though it certainly involves the industrial mobilization of nations, depends less and less on soliders *en masse* and more and more on technicians and their machines. Collectively the great powers have enough overkill to end all civilized life in a day and to make improbable the survival of the human race. This is, according to Bertrand de Jouvenel, our own 'Roman solution' for our civilization, a civilization which, it has to be admitted, was so long and so profoundly Christian. It certainly cannot be said that war has no future. However alarming its consequences may be, nations have not abandoned it as a weapon of last resort. On the contrary they struggle to increase their war-efficiency and war power *vis-à-vis* each other. Two wars have been successfully concluded during the preparation for, or writing of, this book. Another continues[5] into an unimaginable future, having flourished as a way of life for a whole nation since, virtually, the end of World War II. War is indeed an attractive human industry, drawing to itself endless human and material resources. Because it produces political results of a decisiveness few other exercises of power can achieve, it exerts an incredible fascination over power-hungry minds. It is for them a model of how the *internal* conflicts of a nation should be solved. Two civil wars rage as I write, both ideologically provoked. One is in Ulster. Urban guerillas rumbling in the bellies of great cities promise the fulfilment of that extreme Marxist dream—the perpetual revolution, the endless civil war.

---

[4] Op. cit. p. 124.
[5] Mercifully, at the time of revision, a ceasefire has been signed in Vietnam.

FOUR

The Change in Consciousness

ONE OF the most famous and seminal of all interpretations of European consciousness has been Max Weber's theory of the Protestant ethic. Max Weber in *The Protestant Ethic and the Spirit of Capitalism*[1] and Emile Durkheim in *The Elementary Forms of Religious Life*,[2] particularly, develop theses about religion in opposition to the views of such positivist sociologists as Comte or Spencer for whom religion was an archaic survival, not worth attention, something to be got rid of as a hindrance to a scientific age. Weber and Durkheim saw religion as its own thing, not the product of something else (class relations, economic hardship, or social dilemmas) but central to societies and influential, if not decisive, in the outlook and ethics of a society.

Weber's tremendous essay provides the classic interpretation of the centrality of religion in life. He argued that without the spirit generated by the Reformation Western capitalism would never have developed, despite the economic opportunities or the monastic exemplars. Western capitalism is unique in human history not because it is avaricious—men have always been greedy but have not for that reason always been able to create capitalism—but because the motive force was not greed but *dedication to work*. He notes the principal characteristics of the Protestant dynamic as a puritan disapproval of display and indulgence and a spiritual commitment to thrift and frugality, a conviction that work is a necessary physical and spiritual discipline, a good in its own right and not just to be endured for the reward it brings. These beliefs followed naturally from the birth of the individualist Protestant conscience. They involved the rejection of absolute religious authority over economics. Protestant feeling was that economic decisions should be made on the merits of common sense or rationality, rather than by tradition, custom or external fiat. In this the Protestant ethic anticipated that divorce between economic life and social controls characteristic of the

---

[1] First published in Germany, *Die protestantische Ethik und der Geist des Kapitalismus*, 1904–5, in Great Britain in 1930.
[2] First published 1912.

industrial revolution. Nevertheless, in this exercise Weber totally reversed the role usually assigned to religion by positivists. He made it central to the transformation of Europe and so ultimately of the whole world.

Of course, ethical Protestantism, through its work compulsion, infected everything in the end. Every aspect of the competitive struggle in society from progress in schools and universities to triumphs in sport, from social climbing and business promotion to scientific discovery and exploration, seemed justified on the industrious apprentice principle that hard work, endurance and honesty bring success. 'Religion provides the theodicy of good fortune for those who are fortunate', Weber said and this was specially true of Protestantism and Puritanism where a life of self-mortification, early rising and late working almost magically increased one's wealth which appeared a well-deserved reward for godliness. The belief that great wealth and great success are somehow the reward of God for personal qualities still mesmerizes the American business scene. It is so easily translated too into a fundamental doctrine of social Darwinism (one succeeds to survive and society discards failures) that one begins to suspect that evolutionary theory was itself the product of the Protestant ethic, or at least owed to it the terms in which it was formulated.

It was Richard Hoggart who first seized on the idea that we might now be living in the era of the death of the Protestant ethic. His role as a professor at Birmingham University and a participant and mediator in student–staff confrontations seems to have brought him to this point of view. Everyone of an older generation has been amazed by the new student consciousness which emerged in the sixties, by the disappearance of deference, by a new sort of authority in making demands, by a mixture of pity and contempt for the older generation and its career preoccupations. The power of the youth culture, or as some American thinkers already describe it, the counter-culture, is formidable. It already claims the junior and senior members of many university faculties —even in Britain—and reaches down not only to sixth-formers but to pre-pubertal children. 'We could be seeing the beginning of the end of the Protestant ethic in its two mains forms of expression—in its attitudes to competitive work and to the sexual life,' Hoggart wrote in *The Times*.

Dr. Michael Young wrote,

'If people stopped wanting a higher standard of life, that would certainly be revolutionary. Modern society would lose its principal rationale and the common objective which both sustains and binds most of its members. Some people think that this is bound to happen at some point in the future. You probably cannot go on indefinitely loading men, or even women, with personal possessions. Their houses and their psyches will burst. Before that, more and more people will begin to cry off and cease demanding more money because what they can buy with it will no longer be worth having. If as more and more people became rich, they still had plenty of servants, the servants would look after the property, and then there need never be an end to the process. . . . Is there any sign of the limit being reached? Beatniks are still idiosyncratic. So are scientists who cultivate a kind of functional austerity in bare though well-heated sitting rooms. The revival of church-going in the USA has not been accompanied by any of the asceticism with which the Christian Church was once associated. We would be on safer ground in prediction if we understood the reasons for the increase in the birth-rate in many industrial countries in the last quarter of a century. The move towards larger families seems to have been led by richer people. One possible explanation is that they already have so much that income has lost its appeal: it may then be better to have more members of the family to be acquisitive for. The rise in the birth-rate could then represent a last attempt to sustain the rationale, and morale, of society.'[3]

Of course, it is not only the rich in Western society who were affected by the Protestant ethic. The poor and middle income groups felt the drive to work hard as strongly as their hunger for possessions. Duty is also a powerful element in the ethic and one ought to instance down the centuries the readiness of police, soldiers and the law-enforcement officers generally to serve the call of duty for inconsiderable rewards. Until recent times this has been true of teachers too who felt that what they were doing was so important that a poor income from it could be disregarded. In that sense also the Protestant ethic sustained 'the rationale and morale of society'.

If the ethic goes what happens to society? What takes its place if the Western dynamic cannot be sustained? Charles A. Reich, an American scholar, sought to subject the changing consciousness about society to a sociological analysis in *The Greening of America.*[4] His starting point is desperation. 'American history, as it is usually taught, makes today's reality of failure and crisis a mystery and a paradox. After two hundred years of brilliant, unmatched progress, how can it be possible that we are beset by vast problems and desperate impoverishment?'[5] America, he writes, is 'one vast, terrifying anti-community'. The institutions of the USA, the personal lives of its people, even the whole character of the nation seem suddenly to have changed 'beyond recognition'. He is deeply wounded by what he sees as the falsity, the 'false consciousness' of so many lives which is 'a consciousness imposed by the State for its own

---

[3] *The Esso Magazine*, 1966–7, 'Future Social Conditions', p. 36—part of a distinguished symposium on the future of Britain.

[4] Random House, New York, 1970, Penguin, London, 1971.

[5] Op. cit. Penguin edn. p. 29.

purposes'. He instances the lower-middle class family, just beginning to enjoy the material benefits of society, which thereby becomes vulnerable to the seductions of television and all too ready to fall for, 'the expensive home appliances, the new car, the boat, the vicarious world of sports. And this is the family where the "falsity" is most apparent; they "see" the countryside in a speeding car, tear up a fragile lake with a power boat, stand in long lines for "pleasures". It is also the family with the most easily manipulated political consciousness.'[6]

If *The Greening of America* were only a diatribe against the American way of life—and nothing is easier to do—it would be unimportant. It is a diatribe, but it is also a heroic effort at a political analysis and a futurology *which can be applied to all Western societies.*

Reich foresees a revolution coming which 'will not be like revolutions in the past'. It will begin with the individual and his relations with others and in the cultural goals he seeks. It will change the political structure only as a final act. It will not be violent and cannot be stopped by violence because it is the spread of ideas. You cannot arrest ideas or beat them over the head. 'The whole emerging pattern from ideals to campus demonstrations to beads and bell-bottoms to the Woodstock festival, makes sense and is part of a consistent philosophy. It is both necessary and inevitable and in time it will include not only youth but all people in America.'[7] But, to those who know Britain and Europe, the infection has long passed beyond the shores of the USA.

Reich sees three states of consciousness as successive determinants of the American scene. Consciousness I is the Protestant ethic all over again; the traditional ethical outlook of the American pioneers, those planted and colonized under an Old Testament inspiration. It is the creed of the American farmer, small business man and hard-working labourer of the last century and this, who was, and is, trying to get ahead.

Consciousness II is that which belongs to the organization man. Reich sees the individual producer, farmer, small business man as in eclipse since the First World War. America, and Europe too, for that matter, has become the home of the super-organization which like armies and Churches before it, demands quiet, anonymous and even life-long devotion and service. And the life-blood of these super-organizations has been the willingness of men to subordinate all their days to the service of the organizations either because of the rewards (above all in security) such sacrificial service offered, and/or because of the sense that this was a duty demanded of responsible men who achieved a vicarious sense of fulfilment through service to a 'higher cause'. One can see in this a

---

[6] Ibid. p. 73.
[7] Ibid. p. 11.

second phase of the Protestant ethic, since duty, service, self-effacement characterize it. Yet the most striking examples of super-organization are outside the United States. The Soviet Union, Hitler's Germany, and Mussolini's Italy set out to create the organization man and to suppress the individual conscience and private initiatives. They depended upon masses of individuals who accepted that they must obliterate their own feelings and judgments in the interests of the higher purpose of the super-organization, whether state or party, which disciplined them. More, mass parties depraved and exploited them. The crimes against humanity of these powers were committed by moral eunuchs, who were ordinary men and women authorized to act by the organization, to which they had surrendered their moral consciousness. The moral anaesthesia this produced in Germany still leaves one trembling.

Nazi Germany and Mussolini's Italy have vanished into the night, broken by war. The Soviet Union and China remain as great powers totally committed to the most absolute of doctrines of super-organization, dominating the drilled and conscripted masses they have, on the lines of Orwell's *1984*, converted into spiritual puppets.

In Consciousness III—that consciousness which belongs to the contemporary youth culture or the counter-culture—all that belongs to the two previous states of consciousness is rejected. It is not the new cultural will to live a life of endless work and private struggle, nor is it the intention to settle for the anonymity of the faceless servant of the organizational world. If it is true that we are confronted with this double rejection by youth—and ultimately by the whole of society, so Reich argues—the consequences are beyond computing whether for the nation state and its power structure, for commercial super-organizations and their technological bases, *or for Churches of an authoritarian character*. One might see the demand for an end to celibacy as a condition for entry into the Roman priesthood—strong in the USA—as a straw in the wind. One might put it this way, that many who are priests or wish to be priests now question the right of the Roman Church to force an amputation of so significant a part of a man's total being. No institution is held to be entitled to such a right. For the new consciousness the institution *qua* institution is immediately suspect as false and tyrannical.

What emerges from Reich's analysis is the extent of the moral confusion and social unreality of American society. It appears to be a society about to break up. Even when allowance is made for the exaggerations of Reich's eloquence, the indictment is a tremendous one. What also stands out is the fragility of the new consciousness, the hopeless inadequacy of it as the source of a new revolution despite Reich's optimism. Its strength lies in its opposition to much that is socially corrupt in American society, its weakness in its inability to offer more than beautiful thoughts while physically beating a retreat. What the situation demands is much more—intellectual toughness coupled with a religious dynamic. There is no sign yet that they will be forthcoming. Indeed the signs are that the radical movement of the United States, a phenomenon of the sixties, has, in so many of its manifestations extinguished itself. Reich's optimism has come too late. Richard Neuhas, a radical Lutheran pastor in New York, has confessed as much. The radical movement—Reich's new consciousness—was no united and cohesive drive of the politically conscious but the promise of numerous 'revolutions' which would cancel each other out, or produce something altogether monstrous.

'Thus the movement became a zero sum game. It was proclaimed simultaneously and frequently by the same people, as a movement towards unbridled individualism and centrally directed social discipline; toward revolutionary asceticism and the celebration of polymorphous perversity; toward minority separatism and determined universalism. Its symbols were, alternately and sometimes simultaneously, the clenched fist, the clasped hands of different hues, the two-finger peace sign, the one-finger "oneway" sign, the rifle (with or without flower in barrel), a clenched fist inside the circle of the female logogram, a vasectomised (i.e. ecologically innocent) *penis erectus*. All of these represented, presumably, "organized rage against systematic oppression" and were flaunted to the accompaniment of clarion calls for "radical commitment" to "liberation".'[8]

Reich's book belongs precisely to that diffused radical consciousness of the sixties—1967 and 1968 were the peak years—which Neuhas analyses. He takes for permanent that which was fragile and inchoate. There are parallels in the fading of the humanist and Christian radicalism of the sixties in Britain and Europe too—the collapse of the CND and the more revolutionary Committee of 100, the rise of the Angry Brigade and its European nihilist opposite numbers, Ulster terrorism. As to the radical movement on a broad front in Europe generally—the liberal conscience at its most sensitive—it has shown all the confusions of the American.

The dream of the gentle flower people, loving and taking pot and LSD, with Zen as their guide in their search for an exit from the labyrinth of a brutal society, that too would seem to be dead of its own affectlessness. 'Have you seen dozens of hippies watch passively while some burly square beats another hippy to a psychedelic red pulp?'[9] Jeff Nuttall asks in *Bomb Culture*, a stormy, searing autobiographical record of the whole youth counter-culture from 'Ban the Bomb'

---

[8] Richard Neuhas, 'The Loneliness of the Long-Distance Radical', *The Christian Century*, 26 April 1972.

[9] Jeff Nuttall, *Bomb Culture*, Paladin, London 1970, p. 194.

onwards. Unlike Reich's *The Greening of America*, it comes from the inside. It stops the heart dead. 'We were eaten up by repressed violence and we were soured by the constant terror of inconceivable violence being committed on ourselves and the rest of man. From this we had strugglingly produced a culture. It's possible to get hysterical over the obvious connection between that culture, as it stood in 1965, and the Moors murders. I did. It's possible to get carping about it. Pamela Hansford Johnson did. It's possible to pretend there isn't a connection. That's rubbish.'[10] The author goes on to list all the contemporary art movements (including The Royal Shakespeare Company) which had honoured or applauded de Sade. 'To Ian Brady, de Sade was a licence to kill children. We had all, at some time, cried "yes, yes" to Blake's "Sooner murder an infant in its cradle than nurse an unacted desire". Brady did it. . . . Titillatory Nazism was by no means peculiar to Brady and Hindley. We had all applauded and romanticized the American leather-jackets with their swastikas and cheese-cutters.'[11] The self-revelation of the contemporary youth culture may be followed in *Watch Out Kids*.[12] The authors regard the bombs of the Angry Brigade and the Weathermen as a warning to 'the death culture' of older generations and claim that the fact that hundreds of thousands of white kids became social outcasts—and in some cases violent outcasts—rather than accept that culture is the most positive of revolutionary statements. They end with a hysterical call to anarchism. Everything is to be free. All rules are to be demolished. Land, food, shelter, clothing, technology, education, welfare—all are to be free. And this alone will bring the fall of a hated civilization: of course, for who would now work?

In its confessed obsession with violence and lawlessness it all seems a long way from the innocent utopia, 'trailing clouds of glory', of which Reich speaks. And, final irony, Reich does not, in the last resort, rely upon the new consciousness. He needs technology.

'When the new consciousness has achieved its revolution and rescued us from destruction it must go about the task of learning how to live in a new way. This new way of life presupposes all that modern science can offer. It tells us how to make technology and science work for, and not against, the interests of man.' But science and technology already 'work for' the interests of men. That is why they are there at all. But they do not work for all the interests of all men at all times. The interests they do 'work for' and reinforce—the creation of an objective view of the world, separating man from nature that he might successfully manipulate it—are the opposite of the 'interests' the new consciousness

---

[10] Op. cit. p. 127. The connection with the Manson murders is chillingly plain. They occurred after Nuttall's book was written.

[11] Op. cit.

[12] Mick Farren and Edward Barker, Open Gate Books, London 1972.

would seem to want to develop. The new consciousness of Reich is nothing if not warm, close, dionysian, basically poetic. Can it live with technology and science without encouraging and developing the objective, manipulative minds it is absolutely alien to but which are the source of the power and productivity of the hated organizations? These organizations, state or industrial, are not accidental, not importations from a non-human order but the products of a will to exploit the environment, human and non-human, to the maximum in the interests of human power. It is impossible to use *this* drive to stoke a revolution designed to get rid of that very lust for power. It would be fraudulent and end up with the folk hocus-pocus of Fascism as a front for more ruthless policies pursued by anonymous men. Yet if the movement which nourished Charles Reich's optimism appears to have foundered, there is no doubt that there is in Western society a new questioning of social aims and a growing fear about the capacity of civilization to survive the pace of its exploitation of the world's resources. Some of the most gloomy prognostications are being made. The manifesto of scientists, *Blueprint for Survival*,[13] which caused a sensation early in 1972, spoke of the necessity to abandon the modern technological economy and to return to something more primitive. Bishop Hugh Montefiore's *Can Man Survive?*[14] poses the questions and *Only One Earth* by Barbara Ward and René Dubos[15] is even more authoritative. They are but two of a host of doomsday studies.

There is even an historical irony that at the very moment that Consciousness III springs to life the inadequacies of the super-organizations are exposed by something they appear not to have foreseen—the ecological disaster, even the world ecological disaster, and the power explosion. But perhaps it is not so surprising. I wrote briefly, in *The Death and Resurrection of the Church*, about aspects of the industrial super-organization which explain the inadequacies of these single track and inward looking institutions:

'The great plant anywhere is like a closely guarded foreign base. There are high defensive walls, guards and their dogs, warning systems against intruders, services of every kind as well as highly organized administrative and production systems. Citizens who do not work there may live under its walls for a lifetime without ever penetrating within. To get inside, as a stranger, one needs a pass, if not a passport.

'Such productive enclaves are entirely self-regarding. Their disciplines are empirical and pragmatic. They have certain tasks to do

---

[13] *The Ecologist*, January 1972.
[14] Collins, Fontana, London 1972.
[15] André Deutsch and Penguin, London 1972.

—certain commodities to produce—and that is the limit of their corporate vision, apart from the need for political and economic freedom to continue to do so. Within the range of their productive intention they will show endless enterprise and zeal and devote the same ardour to discovering the best name and package for a (worthless) cereal as to producing the latest rocket for a moon probe. The ultimate social or spiritual consequences of their tasks would be mostly beyond their corporate concern.'

Indeed, they would, if they could, work in relative secrecy. Some manage to do so.

'Such plants proliferate in industrial areas. There are hundreds and hundreds of them. They create their own empires of ideas and attitudes, their own authoritarianism. Just their economic activities create a special climate. They demand huge resident populations from which to draw skills and labour, and ultimately to provide the demand for products. They require first class transport facilities to bring in raw materials and take away finished products.... Above all, they demand each other, and this is a snowball process in which they tend to *maximize* everything which comes within their influence—populations, power, urbanization, production—and each other. This is the story of Detroit or Pittsburgh or Chicago, and of Birmingham, Manchester, Liverpool, the Ruhr, Lyons, Milan.'[16]

They also maximize pollution. Such frenzied activities burn up prodigious amounts of energy and create waste not only in the productive process but in the final destination of what is left of the used-up commodity. Hugh Montefiore gives one all the figures in *Can Man Survive?*[17] The manufacturing cost of the product goes always into the price. But the true cost, which includes pollution, environmental destruction, ecological damage—is never computed. Industrial waste or spoil is something to be disposed of quickly and cheaply (and secretly too) outside the enclave—over the end of the garden wall, in fact, into the next chap's yard. It is blown into the sky or pumped into rivers, lakes and the sea, and human society, or other luckless species, have to bear the social and economic cost. Only the *political* power anywhere has sought to stop this and as yet, the world over, not very successfully. Left to themselves the enclaves would never have moved an inch.

It would seem that, beyond a certain critical point only reached as yet in a few industries, the path mapped out for us by the technological organizations and their attendant scientists is closed to humanity. There is an unwilling sentence passed on their expansionist plans. The road ahead is closed, the pop song goes. Yet it is hardly ten years ago since

[16] Op. cit. pp. 25–6.
[17] Collins, Fontana, 1972.

the future of man seemed absolutely assured by his technology. History today presses generations into decades.

The characteristic secrecy and impersonality of the super-organizations has been imitated by the organs of government, even in democracies. Once government departments were small bureaus served by poor industrious clerks. Now they can match in size and complexity —and even in empire building—anything industry can create. To the outsider, industry and government appear to build up similar mega-organizations, impenetrable to the public gaze and indifferent to its emotions. Within them *power* appears to be all, *coûte que coûte*, and anything but a theoretical accountability non-existent. Decisions can be made in such institutions which can nevertheless be final for some or all humans and they may never know of them. It is true that I overstate the impenetrability and strength of institutions in the long run. But in the short run their implacability strikes, particularly, the young and moves them to hate. This is one powerful element in that third consciousness which burns to move away from the forms of contemporary society into one less obsessed with possessions and power, though it cannot really be said that Charles Reich shows us how this is going to come about.

And the outcome of Consciousness III? John Sparrow in *The Times* saw in it the longing for 'the dead level of an impossible Utopia, devoid alike of pain, passion and of nobility. A Utopia, indeed: but we need not look far to see something like such a community in action—or passivity. In the aftermath of a pop festival, when the influence of the hysterical music has abated, or at a love-in, where the air is sweet with cannabis, one may observe the passionless population of a Woodstock world anticipating that Utopian bliss; tender human creatures, tame and same, with the tameness and sameness of a herd of deer, or a school of porpoises, or a gathering of Galapagos lizards—a huddle of bodies snuggling, not struggling, on the smooth firm sand and gently respiring under the warm rays of the broad bland sun.'[18]

Charles Reich has a different vision even for a youth culture which embraces the drug scene: 'It promises a higher reason, a more human community and a new and liberated individual. Its ultimate creation will be a new and enduring wholeness and beauty—a renewed relationship of man to himself, to other men, to society, to nature and to the land.'[19]

Fundamentally the cry of the new consciousness is a religious one. The Jesus freaks who, so far, stand out as the seventies' consciousness, make it a Christian phenomenon. But the longing to reject the con-

---

[18] 'The Blessings of Equality', *The Times*, 23 January 1971, p. 15.
[19] *The Greening of America*, p. 11.

temporary world is as powerful in the Jesus movement as it was in its predecessor. The Christian Churches are not forgiven because the Christ has been rediscovered. Indeed they are in a way accused again—this time of hiding him behind the thick walls of their Churches as though they owned him.

FIVE

The Violent Society

I SPOKE of the great liberal myth which has distinguished the last century or so—the vista of an endless beatific progress towards some final Utopia. Not even Marxism escaped it. The classless society, in which the state had withered away, from which crime and violence were banished, was the apogee of utopianism. All the same Marxism hardly held the liberal view about the slow diminution of violence, for Utopia was to be achieved by the very violence it was hoped ultimately to exorcise from the world. A catastrophic revolution was necessary. Characteristic of revolutionaries of the left and right has been the acceptance of violence as a necessary, salutary thing. Communists, fascists, anarchists have been indistinguishable in their admiration for violence and the contempt they poured on liberal notions of progress by the gradual mitigation of social conflict. Not only does the common ideology of the extreme left and extreme right deny the liberal thesis, but it disputes any notion of a social consensus, either within societies or between them. It does not believe that western nations are making a common movement towards peace and social justice. It declares that this is *a priori* impossible. Societies are irreparably divided into warring groups by their very structures. The state itself, in this view, is violence institutionalized. The generalized Marxist view that *the State* is the instrument by which a ruling class imposes its will on the classes it oppresses and as such is clearly distinguishable from society or nation, runs strongly in the youth culture and the counter-culture. The state is organized violence towards *you*. You are therefore morally justified in any violence you launch against it. This is one influential justification of violence. There is no doubt that it is also a rationalization of a will to violence which has other sources—like the criminal who says he is against *society* because society is against him.

Yet there is a more generalized ethos in the West (and the world) which makes violence, even indiscriminate individual violence more acceptable or at least less easy to condemn. It is hard to define. It may be that a violent century has moved us all to excuse violence, or to delight in it. Revolutionary terror, extermination camps, genocide, mass

257

bombings, Hiroshima, endless war, have persuaded us to take perhaps unconsciously a different view of the capabilities of ourselves and our societies. And the frequent success of violent movements, the notice taken of them, especially by the media, the respect accorded to them, where peaceful protests are so often impotent, have given a new prestige to violence among the angry young. Those same young tend to believe that violence alone can bring the instant, total solutions they demand. And if violence exposes its perpetrators to sacrifice, injury, death, it gathers the aura of heroism which for so long attached itself to the warriors and soldiers of open war. Violence is held to be proof that you really mean what you say, to the death.

In the light of that one can understand a reluctance to ask ethical questions of violence but rather to entertain it as permissible, acceptable. It is by such subtle processes, supported by all the frustrations in personal life and in society which feed our aggression, that society can be moved to violence, that deeply conscientious individuals within it can contemplate violence against their fellows with more and more equanimity. Yet even so a very selective conscience appears to operate. Violence against revolutionaries, terrorism by the democratic state—detention, imprisonment, interrogation, execution—is reprehended by them as a moral outrage, as though the social consensus had ruled out violence: but their own violence is excused, urged, idealized. Equally, while the sporadic violence of the democratic state is abhorred, the permanent terror of the Marxist state is accepted, even approved, as a social norm. If protests are lodged against the singularity of this attitude the reply is that there is no common morality anyway, no consensus binding on everyone. Which effects yet another ideological breach with the past of our civilization. The same, basically Marxist argument about the absence of a civilized consensus is used by those states which, also in the name of a long-dead revolution, wage this endless terror against their own citizens. The mix is the same for Che Guevara's followers, Urban Guerillas, Black Panthers, Minutemen, Angry Brigade, political hi-jackers, IRA, violent student societies, and various regular and irregular groups of Marxist revolutionaries.

Most ordinary citizens, and this would include most Christians, resist these analyses. They do not see society as finally and totally brutal. For them rather, society is beneficent, and if not always just, at least seeking to be just and capable of being made just. They share that sense of the willed direction of Western society of which I have spoken. But into the ordinary events of society the concept that only toughness pays, and conciliation never, 'creeps in this petty pace' more and more. Miners enforce a claim by holding up the whole nation by revolutionary picketing. Other groups practise the same dour brinkmanship. There are social consequences in the brutalization of the relations within society. 'Nobody who looks dispassionately at the contemporary political and social scene can reasonably dispute the validity of the concern which Lord Halifax ... expressed about the temptation to minority interest and opinion groups to try to take under duress what they cannot get by consent, negotiation or legal means. The potential danger in this attitude to the tradition of lawfulness is a very real one. Nevertheless, we are under several inhibitions against recognizing it publicly.[1] Fear, and the wish to 'save face' are the factors which militate against a public outcry. But the danger to civilized consensus in British society is real; silence about it does not make it go away. It does not make the increasing crime rate vanish either. The kind of legal violence against society, which forces society to yield under duress, creates the climate in which crime too demands the right to flourish.

Richard Hoggart saw not only the work-ethic and the duty-ethic of Protestantism as under violent rejection, but the sexual ethic too. Indeed rejection of the sexual ethic is today part of an influential political ideology which preaches the necessity, and heroism, of violence. All sexual restraints have to go, along with political and legal restraints on what one does in society. It is impossible to separate the new sexual ideology from the ideology of violence. They are two sides of the same coin. And by a kind of seepage, acceptable sex is also violent sex, and political violence has the rage and delight of orgasm about it. Anyone who has seen the films *Straw Dogs* or *A Clockwork Orange*, or for that matter read Jean Genet, or Norman Mailer's *An American Dream* will understand the parallel precisely.

The contemporary sexual revolution is to be praised for a new and welcome honesty and candour about sex. It is beyond forgiveness for its readiness to legitimize every perversion, however dehumanizing, and for its complacency in the face of the commercial exploitation of sex by the worst representatives of capitalist enterprise. A trustworthy observer of the contemporary scene, David Holbrook, says:

'As our culture grows more sadistic, violent, and obscene, it becomes thus, increasingly neo-fascist. In breeding hatred of humanness it is fostering the false solutions of hate—and spreading abroad the propaganda that to be strong one should hate and humiliate. In humiliating and degrading women we are symbolically rejecting our humanness and creativity. Audiences in London laugh at violence, on stage and screen. And jolly little tunes in obscene films accompany violence and sex. If we listen closely, can we not hear the laughter of storm-troopers making Jews scrub the pavements? Or making Jewesses dance on the tables at concentration camps? In the indifference of the public to the mounting obscenity and hate do we

---

[1] Ronald Butt, 'A Chance for Real Progress in Wage Bargaining', *The Times*, 27 April 1972.

not experience the same dissociation that made the Germans declare that they "didn't know what was going on"?"[2]

Holbrook felt that it was impossible any longer for the authentic view of man, *Homo humanus*, to get a hearing. In a brutalized British culture one could not speak of genuine love without being greeted by an ironical bitter guffaw. He thought it was time for us to pack our bags and move to some place where we could establish 'a community of belief in man'. 'But where?' he asked.

Perhaps he exaggerates. But then even exaggeration has its point if it bangs our heads against a wall to make us see something we are not willing to see. He certainly points to something real, perhaps decisive, in the changing free world culture. But where to go? Where best to defend man in his wholeness? One would suppose the Christian Churches might have had a place to offer. Since what is being destroyed is the Christian view of the whole man, both sinning and redeemed, it would appear that Christianity has a task here.

[2] 'Cultural violence and the threat of neo-fascism', *The Times*, 6 April 1972.

SIX

The Conflict of Evidence

WE OBSERVE a conflict of evidence. How do the categories of violence tie up with the peaceful herd scene of gently respiring hippies on the beach in the sun, or the new and enduring wholeness and beauty of man which Charles Reich forecasts? Perhaps one should say that there are two possible reactions in the face of what any one fears—flight and aggression. The hippies are in flight from a society which they dread and reject: the angry ones want to fight it. They are the same people from the same monochrome cities, the same monotonous jobs, suffering the same lack of fulfilment in their titanic environments under depersonalized authorities. If their reaction one day could be to escape through drugs and sex, on the next it might be to assert themselves through the bullet.

There is another conflict of evidence. What I have said suggests a tragic, even catastrophic future: not improbable, one might say, in the light of the tragic, catastrophic past. Two things have held more or less firmly along the mysterious dimension of the past—the constant increase in human knowledge and in exploitation of the environment. They have formed the basis of the self-congratulation of our age, and of the euphoria of the theology of secularization. The future is safe—man cannot fail, as Teilhard de Chardin said in *The Phenomenon of Man*. These increases in knowledge and power have been seen by so many for so long as the means by which man guarantees his future. But this optimistic view overlooks certain contingencies. One is that knowledge is being farmed out to machines—the computers—which calculate far faster than battalions of human beings and come up with answers only other computers can check. Without melodrama, one can say that the machines contain knowledge, and the ability to process it, in ways which are beyond the capacities of their creators. Man, in that sense, is in thrall to his machines. The ultimate conseqences of this cannot be foreseen, but one consequence is that new knowledge is created faster and faster and its effects spill out into the technological activities of man before the human mind can absorb what is happening. In any case, the increase in human knowledge is not a general increase. It is the creation of specialist knowledge in technical language to which the masses are not privy. Ironically, it increases their ignorance and helplessness: the knowledge others possess becomes *their* fate. This has always been the human case in some degree, but never so markedly as now.

Every commentator remarks on the speeding-up of events. Alvin Toffler, in *Future Shock*, compares the shock of one future after another crowding upon us, with the effect of culture-shock—moving quickly from one culture to another and becoming disoriented and helpless. He dramatizes the speed of change:

'If the last 50,000 years of man's existence were divided into lifetimes of approximately sixty-two years each, there have been about 800 such lifetimes. Of these 800, fully 650 were spent in caves.

'Only during the last seventy lifetimes has it been possible to communicate effectively from one lifetime to another—as writing made it possible to do. Only during the last six lifetimes did masses of men ever see a printed word. Only during the last four has it been possible to measure time with any precision. Only in the last two has anyone anywhere used an electric motor. And the overwhelming majority of all the material goods we use in daily life today have been developed within the present, the 800th lifetime.'[1]

He goes on to explain that the 800th lifetime is unique because during it man's relationship to his resources has been turned upside down. 'Within a single lifetime, agriculture, the original basis of civilization, has lost its dominance in nation after nation. Today in a dozen major countries agriculture employs fewer than 15 per cent of the economically active population.' And he quotes the dictum of U Thant, when Secretary General of the United Nations, that the central stupendous truth of the shift to super-industrialism is that the developed economies of today can have in the long run the kind and scale of resources they decide to have. 'It is no longer resources that limit decisions. It is the decision that makes the resources.' U Thant thought this the most revolutionary change that man has ever known.

Future Shock is a paean of euphoria, coming like *The Greening of America* from the optimistic climate of the sixties rather than the pessimism of the seventies. It abounds in passages which say of man that 'avoiding future shock as he rides the waves of change, he must master evolution, shaping tomorrow to human need. Instead of rising in revolt against it, he must, from this historic moment on, anticipate and design the future'.[2]

How do you say this to a runaway world? And if men hear, are they even in control? Toffler sees that the first need is even to stop the world, 'to halt the runaway acceleration that is subjecting multitudes to the

---

[1] Op. cit., The Bodley Head, London 1970, p. 15.
[2] Ibid. p. 429.

threat of future shock while, at the very same moment, intensifying all the problems they must deal with—war, ecological incursions, racism, the obscene contrast between rich and poor, the revolt of the young, and the rise of a potentially deadly mass irrationalism'.[3]

'This wild growth', Toffler says, 'this cancer in history!' The rhetoric ends. The future rushing at him appears horrifying. It does not look as though man has mastered his evolution, or could be trusted to.

Dennis Gabor in *Inventing the Future*[4] summarized some of the dangers to which Toffler alludes.

'Our civilization faces three great dangers. The first is destruction by nuclear war, the second is overpopulation, the third is the Age of Leisure. Most of civilization may be destroyed by nuclear war, but not all mankind; for one can perhaps call it an archetypal situation for which man is psychologically well prepared. As a beetle which has dropped into a glass seems to gather new strength everytime that it slips back to the bottom, man will start scrambling vigorously toward what will then appear as a lost paradise. "Some people die easily like rabbits, others die hard like cats"; in the end the "cats" will rebuild civilization. If the world is stricken with overpopulation, people will also know what to do. It will be a harsh world, with little work and strict discipline, and with very little freedom. But though such a crippled life runs contrary to some of men's basic instincts, we know (alas!) that men can survive as slaves. As long as the daily bread is a victory there will be enough incentive left to survive. Only the Age of Leisure will find man psychologically unprepared... the Age of Leisure will be a reality within one generation...'.

And Gabor goes on to say in a chapter 'On Optimism and Pessimism' that the future cannot be predicted, 'but futures can be invented. It was man's ability to invent which has made human society what it is.' Indeed man is 'possessed' by his power to create and build vast civilizations, sciences, cultures, languages, art, music out of nothing given to him in his naked, natural being. But *what* future to invent? One has to insist that no future can be invented off the cuff. It can only be invented under the drive of an imperative which decides to overrule events and trends rather than be ruled by them. Such an imperative—a universal imperative it has to be today—can only capture men's minds and hearts if it arises from a profound religious instinct.

'The crisis which faces *Homo Sapiens* today is fundamentally a spiritual crisis. Until it is faced and met, the future of mankind is in doubt,'

---

[3] Ibid. p. 430. Toffler's euphoria should be measured against his despair in 'The Disposable Society' *Observer Review*, 31 December 1972. Even *society* is being thrown away. 'What we detect in the air is nothing less than the smell of decay that accompanies the end of an era.'

[4] Secker and Warburg, London 1963, p. 11.

Hugh Montefiore wrote.[5] 'Until men come to believe in their hearts that all life is held in trust from God, there can be no valid ethical reason why we should owe a duty to posterity. Once it is believed that men hold their dominion over all nature as stewards and trustees for God, then immediately they are confronted by an inalienable duty towards and concern for their total environment, present and future; and this duty towards environment does not merely include their fellow-men, but all nature and life.'

If it is true that Western civilization is approaching some great divide where it may founder or transform itself, and the world with it, then the future is going to be exciting and dangerous (though it is almost an anti-climax to say so) for man made in the image of God. In it, no institutions are going to be guaranteed, and surely not the Churches which are already suffering from the neglect of their societies and are dark with so many uncertainties of doctrine and faith.

It is possible to contemplate the disappearance of some of the institutional forms of Christianity and the erosion of others. And all world faiths will be affected. Yet the anguish of the crisis in the world must fall on Christianity in which so much of the contemporary world has its origins. Whether it is prepared for them or not, the tests will fall, as they have already fallen on the Russian and South African Churches. They will be of a kind to search out its steel. What is totally impossible to argue is the extinction of religion. Sociologists are no more impressed by theories of the death of religion than theologians have been by the death of God. They uncover in their researches a persistence of untutored religious attitudes. They, and other thinkers, feel the presence, which the drug scene enhances, of a great spiritual hunger for a transforming faith. The famished 'look up, and are not fed'. Then too the crisis itself is a religious one. Behind all the concern for our violence and terror, our prodigal use of resources and piling of pollution, our unique powers of destruction of ourselves and other species lie the unanswered questions about man. Who is he? Why is he here? What are the inward and outward commands laid upon him and made so poignant by his dominating presence, perhaps not in the universe, but certainly upon his own planet?

---

[5] *Can Man Survive?*, Collins Fontana, London 1970, p. 55.

SEVEN

Renewal

FROM time to time, the Anglican Communion has its moments of great-ness, when it is seized of a sense of its international status and that it could be, or ought to be, one of the great Christian Churches of the world with a role to play beyond candles and vestments and the height of the clerical dog-collar. Such a role was approached in the first meeting of the Anglican Consultative Council at Limuru in Kenya in 1971. Its report *The Time is Now* contained two lengthy, broadminded chapters on renewal. One of them inevitably dealt with church order, but the other grappled with racism, power, violence and social change and approved a World Council of Churches Statement[1] on violence which reads as follows.

The 'new stage of the ecumenical debate has been characterized by intensifying support from the Churches for action programmes devoted to building a more just society. It has also shown a growing unwillingness to condemn categorically those groups, including Christians, which resort to violence in the face of situations of massive, entrenched social, racial and economic injustice. Many have spoken of "the violence of the *status quo*"—that is, the suffering and death which result from unjust social structures when they are not effectively challenged. Others have pointed out that "non-violence" (either because it is ineffective in a given situation, or precisely because it *is* effective) may have a more violent long-term impact than some of its advocates recognize. Hence there has been increasing reluctance to pose the issue as "violence" versus "non-violence" and a search for more pertinent Christian criteria for evaluating alternative coercive strategies appropriate to particular situa-tions of social injustice.'[2]

The Council modestly endorsed this, saying it must seek the creation of 'effective courses of action which are alternatives to violence, both in the stage before the situation deteriorates into open violence, and even

---

[1] Statement of the Central Committee of the World Council of Churches meeting in Addis Ababa in January 1971.

[2] Op. cit. p. 23.

in the case of actual armed conflict', and called for 'willingness to stand beside all those who have conscientiously become involved in violence or abstained from it at the cost of moral and physical suffering'. A generous commitment, which frightened the General Synod when it was debated at home.

The same Report takes up 'the fundamental question'—'whether the potentialities of modern science and technology will be used to perpetuate structures of injustice or for mass destruction on an unprecedented scale, or whether these potentialities will bring about prosperity, fellowship, and peace for all the peoples of the earth'—the Charles Reich thesis in fact—and saw with clarity that even if the most ambitious plans of development of underdeveloped nations are fulfilled there will still remain a terrifying burden of poverty, wretchedness and despair. And, of course, not only in the underdeveloped countries.

The generosity and enlightenment of Limuru, precisely because it speaks to the dilemmas of Africa, the East and the United States rather than to those of post-imperial England, become muffled when they reach the General Synod which appears curiously insular and insulated when it comes to great social issues—as though it is unfitted as well as unwilling to deal with them.

The really great contributions to Anglicanism as a *Weltanschauung* and as a social conscience come from independent or semi-independent agencies, as for instance, Christian Action whose defence and support of South African political and racial victims over two decades has been a magnificent enterprise, too little praised, hardly ever even reported. Of course, Christian Action is not wholly Anglican, but its leadership is. Too little regarded has been the work of the official Board for Social Responsibility, with its innumerable thoughtful reports and social initiatives.[3] Here if anywhere the social conscience of the Church finds official expression.

Yet it cannot be said that the Church as a whole is saturated with social awareness, still less filled with an angry zeal for action over social injustices or the moral wreckage of the contemporary world. A group of Californian sociologists[4] once distinguished between the comforting and challenging roles of Churches. For many of the faithful the Church was a place of refuge for the individual from the pressures of the world and the disasters of the psyche. 'Come unto me all ye that are heavy-laden and I will give you rest.' The Church is the place to lay down burdens and to seek that safety in the arms of a loving Saviour which so many hymns celebrate.

---

[3] See, for instance *Man in his Living Environment*, An Ethical Assessment, CIO, 1970, and the monthly journal *Crucible*.

[4] Charles Y. Glock, Benjamin B. Ringer and Earl R. Babbie in *To Comfort and to Challenge*, University of California Press, 1967.

Nothing in my hand I bring,
Simply to thy cross I cling;
Naked, come to thee for dress
Helpless, look to thee for grace.

For others, the Church is nothing if not a challenge to the world for its sin, greed, materialism, corruption, injustice, racism and indifference. The Californian sociologists showed convincingly that the more a Church embarked on the role of challenger, the more those who came to it to be comforted were disturbed if not driven away. The sociologists were studying the whole spectrum of American denominations, but they might have been talking of the Church of England which throws a protective screen of physical beauty and a rapt, somnambulist liturgy round the worshipper, encapsulating him in an ethos from which both thought and care can easily be dismissed. Could he, after that, march on Whitehall and shatter the dream time?

Yet, hard words aside, the Church is not without its inner sense, inner longing for renewal. The forms of that renewal are protean. One can do no more than illustrate the general directions by specific examples: among them the future lies.

If we leave aside the dying struggle of the Church to unite with the Methodists, and its deep reluctance to redeploy its ordained men to meet the new situation in the towns, over which its spiritual failures are painful, we may look at quarters where it has been more courageous. One might instance Canon B15a, overwhelmingly accepted by General Synod in 1971 and 1972, which authorizes the admission to holy communion of others than Anglicans. Those baptized persons in good standing in their own Churches may now come with Anglicans to Church of England communion tables. Some spoke in the Synod debate as though this was the greatest of all ecumenical breakthroughs, which dispensed with the necessity for formal plans of reunion, though in fact its effect on Church practice will be slight. Yet the gesture of welcome to all Christians is there and may help to justify the claim of the Church of England to be a truly national Church. It may make reunion easier. Of course, the gesture costs nothing. Rather more demanding on church order is the learned report *Christian Initiation: Birth and Growth in the Christian Society.*[5]

The report declares, in summary, 'Baptism is the effectual sign of the union of the Church and thereby of the individual with Christ.... This baptismal union with Christ is continually renewed and sustained by Holy Communion to which baptism itself looks forward and for which it is the only sacramental prerequisite.' And so it asks for the Church's

---

[5] Report of the Commission on Christian Initiation, CIO, 1971.

recognition of baptism as the full and complete rite of Christian initiation. It includes infant baptism in its recognition where the parents sincerely desire to bring up the child in the Christian way. Where they do not, they recommend 'a new service of thanksgiving for the birth of a child' which should not be regarded as a substitute for baptism or take place at a font.

What then of confirmation—that most familiar rite of passage by which down the generations, girls and boys at or near puberty became admitted to the eucharist, and by which baptized adults and members of other Churches have always been admitted to the Church of England? Baptism takes its place as the qualifying rite (subject to training of the baptized) and 'The rite of confirmation [should] continue to be administered as a service of commitment and commissioning, but at a suitable stage in adult life, with the laying-on of hands by the bishop or by a priest appointed by the bishop for this purpose'. By the same token, confirmation should cease to be the rite for adult entry. Baptism, or baptism plus training, is to be sufficient—and once baptized, always baptized. A subsequent report, *Baptism, Thanksgiving and Blessing*, by the Archbishops' Commission on Christian Doctrine, October 1971, dotted the i's and crossed the t's of the earlier report.

Even though sociologists and anthropologists are going to say some severe things about the loss of our one formal rite of passage for adolescents[6] a rite which 'in a sort of way' admits a boy or girl to an adult society and adult privileges, the reports advance Christian understanding. If accepted and the recommendations put into practice they would alter profoundly the sense of what it is to be a Christian and an Anglican.

What divided the Churches seemed far more important in the past than what united them. What divided them ritually was adult baptism or infant baptism, confirmation or reception, the Mass or the Lord's Supper, episcopal ordination or congregational commissioning and so forth. What united them was a basic but simple commitment to the lordship of Jesus, Son of God, the affirmation of the Trinity, with baptism and the eucharist as the required sacraments. This was forgotten

---

[6] We have an informal one for those children who do not go on to higher education, and that is leaving school and going to work; the significance of this I discusssed in *The Transition from School to Work*, Industrial Welfare Society, 1962. As fewer children get confirmed, confirmation loses its social importance. The same could be true of baptism of course. The Church sees baptism solely as the rite of Christian initiation, but it has an anthropological or social significance, just as important: at the rite the child is publicly *named* and *socially received* in a short but solemn service. This marks the social recognition of the child and justifies baptism to the non-Christian parent. Similarly marriage in a church is a much more important act of public recognition than a rapid ceremony in a register office. All these rites of passage, which help to integrate a society, are obviously going to fade away.

in the anguished conflicts of religious sub-cultures. Now both reports assert the unity of all Christians in baptism. If this is true then it disposes in a blow of the problem of the divided ministries. *Churches are, by this definition, fellowships of those baptized in the name of the Trinity.* There could be nothing illegitimate about any ministry, no matter how ordained or commissioned, so long as it bore the authority of the baptized, any more than there could be something illegitimate about gatherings and worship of the baptized. Differences of church order cannot disqualify the baptized *or those ministers they commission.* The way is open for a more generous relationship between the ministries of God. Perhaps the Church of England does not yet understand what it has done ecumenically in these two reports.

And also for itself. Anyone who stands close, not just to a parish, but to the whole Church, stands appalled at its legal complexity, that it is in the end a thing of law more than of faith, and the law can always defeat the faith. Nothing is more certain than that it needs a new sense of simplicity about what it is to be a Christian, a new humility about being an Anglican and a new spontaneity and warmth in its worship. A hardworking liturgical Commission has been dragging out of world liturgies and its own insights a series of new, experimental eucharistic services—Series I, II and III. These services advance the understanding and dignity of the eucharist and speak (in II and III) in reasonably contemporary English. Series III even addresses God as 'You'. They involve more 'audience participation'. Yet they will be said in colder, emptier churches from which, on the whole, the Christian fellowship has departed.

One has to ask why this is so. One answer already made would be that congregations no longer reflect the age structure of the population itself. They gather the under-age still, and the faithful over-fifties. The middle groups—the young marrieds and the mature married—are very weakly represented. The congregations tend to have a casualty air and the Church is their ambulance. The young have their own culture outside the Church. The elderly churchgoers, however good their works, cannot be the Christian community outside the Church. In the world outside they are especially isolated and helpless. Age disqualifies them in a society which treats age only at a severe discount. Their witness tends to be solitary.

Then the question really has to be asked—did the Church of England *ever* see itself as the wellspring of Christian *fellowship* in a community? If one thinks of the captive landed-class churches of Jane Austen's England or Parson Woodforde's Diaries or of Parson Kilvert going among his parishioners in English and Welsh villages in Queen Victoria's time, one has to admit that little in those typical situations spoke of a Christian fellowship outside the Church. The barriers between classes were too rigid. What possible fellowship could there be between patrons and patronized? The task inside Church was to go through the immemorial liturgy and to assert Christian duties and social disciplines. The clergy might be kindly, they were always paternal, but were short on *koinonia*. And E. R. Wickham's book shows us that generally speaking the churches in industrial cities were élite churches. The system of pew rents compelled them to be so. The very 'presence' the Church presented to society said 'No' to the poor except as recipients of advice and charity and 'No' to change, if it meant changes in the class structure.

Even today the Church still has a 'No' for society. Its very formality, the *gravitas* of its formality, of its uniforms, processions, procedures, church order, church smells, church bells; the tribute it itself makes in its order to unchangeable hierarchy as the basis of its being; the care with which it distinguishes between the sacred and the secular ends of churches as between sacred and secular persons, all witness to this 'No'. At its worst, Anglicanism is a poor non-Christian thing, a somnambulistic going through the motions, while one's heart is somewhere else. At its best it is a solemn witness to the dimension of the sacred in the midst of the world, productive of awe and majesty and beauty. But never easily a gift of fellowship, and seldom of spontaneity. The professionals hold the field. One would no more wish to shout 'Hallelujah' and dance in joy with the priest up to the altar than a Jew would have processed with the High Priest into the Holy of Holies. So that even Anglican worship at its finest and most traditional emphatically rejects worship as an act of fellowship. Worship is what one 'attends'. The traditional, severely formal Church is magisterial in what it refuses, what it excludes. It is apart. And apartness encourages a sense of rejection in those from whom it is apart. It then becomes the frozen Church of God's frozen people, to quote a popular title.

EIGHT

Community and the Small Group

WHEN the community was Christian and sought in its daily life to be
Christian to the best of its ability (which is something the present age
finds hard to conceive) and in any case *believed* that this was what it was
doing, the gathered congregation on Sunday was the source of renewal
of Christian conviction. Now that this is seldom the case the Sunday
congregation can be a sign, not of the unity of the community, but of
the apartness of the congregation. There is no question of *blaming* the
congregation for this, but only of reassessing the significance of Sunday
worship in church.

All this goes by contraries too. As there is no community necessarily
Christian to be found outside the Church, the Church will have to work
extra-murally to create one or be content to decline. I do not mean by
this the foundation of satellite organizations, from Cub Scouts to Older
Citizens' clubs. These may be important social contributions in themselves but they stratify society. The true community needs to be de-
stratified. In some important senses it needs to feel itself a unity despite
differences of age, sex, occupation, religion. It is the pure *koinonia* of
Christianity to feel that living fellowship before God which transcends
all the natural and social differences of mankind.

To achieve it in our day the Church has to shed much of its formal,
its intramural past. It has to develop a missionary structure in the
parish, or what the Americans would call an outreach, through its quite
ordinary members. And the outreach ought to be at the very beginning
the house Church which Ernest Southcott[1] has spent half a life-time
fighting for. It is a simple thing: the neighbourly eucharist in the living
room of one member of the congregation, with the family and friends
present, and for that reason the Church in the heart of the home and
street situation. This would be the beginning of the Church as mission
as Professor Gordon Davies[2] has expounded it for many years. Here we

---

[1] *The Parish Comes Alive*, Mowbray, London, 1956.
[2] *Dialogue with the World*, 1960, *Worship and Mission* 1966, both SCM Press, London.

271

have the renewal of the Church as diaspora and even as the fellowship of all the baptized, a beginning which does not despise or break with the old but establishes a new growing point.

Fortunately, there are many such Christian enterprises initiated by the Church of England; in this the Church is exemplary; there are many more which half approach it through lay discussion groups, prayer meetings and adult education classes. But neither they, nor the Church as a whole, believe themselves, or feel themselves, to be *the Church*. At the most they see themselves as some temporary contribution to Christian awareness and understanding. Like T. S. Eliot's Mr Prufrock, they would not dare to presume.

John Taylor put his finger on 'the move' that was needed in a pamphlet, *Breaking Down the Parish*.[3] He sums up a great deal of world thinking about the relationship of the parochial structure to the Christian life when he says that, 'if the Church is to engage effectively in its mission in the modern world it must place far more reliance upon smaller units of Christian life and witness than the familiar parish congregation'. He spells out some of them: 'house churches, student groups, Christian cells in office or factory, voluntary "rescue" teams such as Samaritans, and anything else that might be described as a local unit of Christian community'.[4]

He speaks of one formidable problem facing the traditional parochial structure.

'What should a missionary Church be doing in Britain, Sunday by Sunday, for the tens of thousands who stream in their cars to the coast and the countryside? Try to cajole them into postponing their trip till mid-day in order to attend "their parish churches first"? Or try to coax them into a parish church at the other end of the journey? Or try to legislate so that as few amenities as possible will be available to them, in the hope of discouraging the Sunday exodus altogether?

'None of these ideas would ever occur to a missionary Church facing the myriads in a pilgrimage or procession of some great non-Christian culture. How to draw them inside the church buildings would not enter into its reckoning, but rather, how to bring the witness and service of Christians to bear upon the lives of that multitude in a relevant way.'[5]

---

[3] Church Missionary Society, 157 Waterloo Road, London, S.E.1. Undated. The pamphlet is a reprint of *CMS News-Letter* Oct., Nov. and Dec. 1967 with a foreword by Laurence Reading. Cf. also John V. Taylor, *The Go-Between God, The Holy Spirit and Christian Mission*, SCM, London 1972.

[4] Op. cit. p. 2.

[5] Op. cit. p. 3.

His argument begins with all that was said of the parish in a report from the New Delhi World Council of Churches under the title of *The Church for Others* which contrasted the old, traditional parish churches at the heart of small, closely-knit and comparatively isolated communities and the new church situation in fluid, amorphous societies in which the old landmarks are being swept away. In the new situation the local congregations cannot, as congregations, bear the whole missionary task, even if they try. (Many do not try. They are not even aware that there is anything to try about.) There ought therefore to be a complexity of Christian forms serving the area.

They ought not to be, John Taylor argues, a form of sub-church 'through which the uncommitted will eventually be drawn back into our parish churches. Nor are they an interim structure which ought to grow into new parish churches in due course.' They should not be considered subnormal, peripheral, offbeat, *irregular* and therefore developments to be viewed with nervous apprehension, but (quoting George Webber of the East Harlem Protestant Parish) seen 'as an essential structure of congregational life in our days', whatever the status of the 'gathered worship' in an official building.

John Taylor quotes examples from the reports of the group ministry at Notting Hill which has encouraged house meetings.

'Some are devotional and relate to bible study with hymn-singing and free prayer. This is particularly true of West Indian homes, where neighbours and friends crowded into one room join easily together in this relaxed atmosphere. Those in West African households while they often enjoy singing, are more prone to discuss current problems. One house group listened to a tape recording of Nelson Mandela's defence and discussed the situation in South Africa. Another made a study of an Easter Cantata. Some have watched T.V. programmes and discussed them. All the house-churches are directed to think of the life of the neighbourhood around them, and to relate their spiritual exercises to that life.'[6]

John Taylor culls other examples from his world experience of the way in which parish structures can be broken down into face-to-face groups more effective in Christian witness than the impersonal crowd round the altar of a church or scattered in private devotions down the nave.

There is, close by Notting Hill, yet another witness to the Church of the diaspora. It is the West London Chaplaincy. It is Anglican, and the salaries of the priests are paid by the Church. It has no church or chapel and has the air of being *sui generis*. It is university based.

What happens? 'Above all', one Report says, 'people meet in ways that are consciously Christian and which involve their participation.'

---

[6] Op. cit. p. 4.

On Sundays there is a eucharist in the College Block of the Imperial College of Science, attended usually by 130–150 people, on weekdays there are about forty meetings, either at breakfast or lunchtime or in the evenings. Most of these are set within the context of the eucharist, some are meetings for prayer and reflection. At the weekday eucharist over 325 people receive communion and some 600 people are seen by the chaplains at least once every three weeks.

The significance of these meetings, indeed the whole religious life inspired by the chaplaincy, is that they are work-based, not separated from the daily life of the community which is the university. The eucharists take place before breakfast, at lunch, or in the evening in college classrooms. They are intimately part of the college life. Usually they are followed by a communal meal in which the projects of the community are initiated (in the year September 1970 to September 1971 the chaplaincy raised £2220 by collections and other efforts and gave away about £1600 to missionary and social projects). The Christian life is not therefore something put aside until Sunday to take place in buildings insulated from the world but is integral to daily living. The individual and autonomous groups which promote their eucharists whether in the Civil Engineering Dept, the Physics Lab or the Halls of Residence have a continuous life during term time. Lay participation is high. It was commended by John Whitten in a private report on the chaplaincy.[7] The chaplains are praised for a particular skill in finding, training and supporting students and staff who are willing to take a pastoral lead in the halls of residence or the departments where they work.

The eucharists are truly the witness of the group. The group leader is responsible for the arrangements, including the readings, and the intercessions. He will probably give the address, which will be followed by a discussion. The priestly president of the eucharist is not necessarily vested. The informality of the occasion may extend to the prayer of consecration, which might be, not the set prayer of the Book of Common Prayer of 1662, but something quite spontaneous, yet as reverent. The communicants stand, and administer the sacrament to each other. John Gunstone, writing about it in the *Church Times*[8] said, 'These are simple matters, but they symbolize the truth about Christian community—we seek the Word of God together, we are responsible for one another. For those who have never been to these kind of services the difference between them and the ordinary Parish Communion is staggering. Incidentally the development of lay leaders in the chaplaincy has had

---

[7] Discussed by John Gunstone in an article 'Christian Community in the Making', *Church Times*, 3 November 1970.

[8] Op. cit.

another result; in the last twelve years, twenty young men from the chaplaincy have been ordained, and a further five more are at present in training.' Needless to say no ordinary parish achieves such results. Indeed if every parish produced *one ordinand every ten years* there would be no problem about recruitment to the ministry. The theological colleges would be swamped.

It could be said that the chaplaincy is fortunate in its 'captive congregation'. But this is to misunderstand contemporary student life. Students are highly suspicious of establishment religion and as a body most reluctant to be corralled by conventional Christian mission procedures. What does flourish more readily is the unconventional student religion of, for instance, St Francis Hall, Birmingham University, where students appoint and pay their own chaplains and plan their own services. Many conventional university chaplains are haunted by their unwantedness and exist only at the fringes of university life, here (and in the United States) picking up the odd casualty, running an ambulance service, a necessary and a Christian thing but one which ought not to be the limit of university chaplaincy work. The West London Chaplaincy seems exceptional. Its work does not die at the end of every term. It has already drawn together a nucleus of over-25s from staff and local residents to whom the community religious life is more fulfilling than the impersonal Sunday worship at the local parish church.

Of course there is something more profound in this than the novelty of an informal undress eucharist beneath the scrawled blackboards of a dusty university lecture room. There is the philosophy of the small group. The small face-to-face group is one of the casualties of our technological civilization. It exists in the biological or nuclear family, but may be impaired there by uncommunicativeness and by the generation gap: the latter is often the reflection of the former. We live after all in an orally impoverished civilization where eloquent and lyrical speech is associated only with the profitable insincerities of the mass media pressure boys. The noise in the factories, of the streets 'firing on all cylinders', of aircraft overhead, of the television intruders in the home, of the pop record played at maximum decibels—all smother the personal encounters in an impersonal row. The difference between our society and the societies where people stayed in their communities for most of their lives, enjoying the (often argumentative) support of their extended families and the privilege of working closely in small familiar groups, is the difference between two cultures.

There are many who believe that we must recover the intimacy of the small face-to-face group (which is more than the family) if our atomized civilization is not to die through the psychological disaster of impersonality before it collapses from other evils. Christianity, which above all should spell out the loving fellowship, is itself the victim of an impersonality imposed by its structures. I have spoken of how the signifi-

cance of the collective worship of the gathered congregation has changed
with our cultural changes; where in a small community in which everyone
knew everybody else and there was an organic unity of a family, work
and recreation, the pattern of life on the solemn holy day must have
strengthened the community identity and pride. Seldom can it do so
today, even in the villages. What has become more significant in church
life is the anonymous drifting away from the church door at the end of
the service.

The John Gunstone I have quoted in praise of the West London
Chaplaincy wrote *The Dynamics of the Small Group Eucharist*[9] which
discusses the Christian philosophy behind the small group movement.
He speaks in that book of the Christian relevance of much contemporary
thinking in social psychology. The large group, he argues, tends to be
concentrated on one person, who, in the Church at least, is one designated
by higher authority, as well as stamped in his separateness by ordination.
'Studies in the motivation of human behaviour show that large groups
depend on an authoritative leader for their well-being and existence.'
The leader gives them order and a chain of command. He 'personifies
their corporality and aspirations'. Without him, the individual in the
large group is made to feel inferior, threatened, tongue-tied. But the small
group removes these threats, disposes of the dangerous dependence. It
enables each individual to contribute at his level. 'Different kinds of
leadership are performed by different people at different times. ... If a
permanent leader is identifiable, it is usually the one who enables the
individual members of the group to make their fullest contribution to its
corporate life. He is the cohesive personality of the group, a focus rather
than a ruler.'[10]

The social importance of the small group movement is beyond all
question. For community primarily is not the social contract of isolated
individuals embodied in a mass, but rather the interlocking of self-conscious, articulate, face-to-face groups in a larger conscious area group. The
small Christian groups would be a more effective 'leaven in the lump'
in that setting than the formal Sunday church congregations which however generous, even saintly in disposition, are seldom as congregations
activist in the community. (To be active, they must breakdown into small
ad hoc working groups.)

Charles Davis, in his remarkable *A Question of Conscience*, went
baldheaded for the feudalism of Rome. 'The [Roman] Church gives the
impression of wanting to hold men in a state of heteronomy, denying
them their autonomy because this would disturb the *status quo* and call

---

[9] Printed privately by the Societas Liturgica, Document No. 25, 1971. Available from
the Very Rev. Gilbert Mayes, The Deanery, Lismore, Co. Waterford, Ireland.
[10] Op. cit.

into question much that has previously been regarded as unchangeable.'[11] He said harsher things. He protested against the feudal theory of the single supreme, over-arching authority and invoked against it modern theories of organization. 'The typical feature of modern society is the freely created organization. What has now been established is a technological-organizational state of life for man.'[12] Society is highly differentiated and its relationships ever more complex and changing. The organizations which properly correspond to this complexity tend themselves to be *ad hoc* and fluid. They have limited scope, objectifying one set of relations, impersonally, like a motoring organization or a bank, and ignoring all others. The world understands and prefers this clear definition of role and function in organizations. It is part of the 'new consciousness [which] is in fact the death warrant of all fixed hierarchical orders. It has already seen the death of Christendom and is now steadily bringing about the disintegration of the Church in its present form.'

'Men', he says[13] 'must work freely together to create the world of human meaning; organizations are the language they use.' He goes on to argue that men express their 'acknowledgement' of the human community and its demands through three different forms of relationship. First, comes the I–you or limited relationship embodied in particular organizations, such as that illustrated by the motoring association. This is not anti-personal, but usually impersonal and pragmatic. Then comes the personal, unorganized service of one's fellow men wherever one finds them in need or they appeal for help—or, alternatively where one asks for *their* help. These occasions do not commit one to a life-long relationship of friendship, patronage, dependence any more than the acts of the Good Samaritan did or the modern Samaritans do.

The third, which returns us to our small group theme, is the I–Thou relationship, of deep personal commitment and intimate friendship.

'Here men today have the greatest freedom. Modern society, with its general mobility and the limited character of its organizations, leaves men freer than ever before to shape their own individual and social life on the deeply personal level. This in fact makes possible a deeper

---

[11] Op. cit. Hodder & Stoughton, London 1967, p. 197.

[12] Op. cit. p. 199. Note the obeisance to 'the technical-organizational state of life for man'. This is part and parcel of Davis's reading of the process of developing secularization which by producing a 'new consciousness' is proving fatal to the old order and discipline of the feudal Roman Church. But never did social theories fade so fast. The technological organizations which provide the basis of scientific secularization are now seen as just as remote, impersonal, authoritarian and ideological as the Roman Church itself and are attacked with even more bitterness by 'Consciousness III'! See Charles Reich's *The Greening of America* and the discussion of it above, p. 248 et seq. Charles Davis's analysis is not disqualified by the fading of a theological fashion, but needs to be looked at more critically because of that ironic development.

[13] Ibid. p. 205.

because freer personal commitment, as it has, for example, created the partnership marriage in place of the arranged union. I–Thou relationships cannot of their nature be organized. They will be found in intimate personal friendships freely entered into and also give rise to small, inter-personal groups. Such groups will be fluid in form and subject to the vicissitudes of all friendships as persons change and develop or just move away. Attempts to organize them and give them stability usually kill them. Because the principle behind them is free commitment and association it does not mean that they are motivated by selfishness. They require the same kind of unselfish outgoing towards other persons as all friendships.'[14]

These reflections form part of Charles Davis's longing for a new Christian presence in the world, the depth and the anguish of which moves one to shame.

That gadfly of religious and social thinking, Ivan D. Illich, who renounced his priesthood when faced with an inquisition, Roman style, over his *avant garde* ideas (he was formerly Vice-Rector of the Catholic University of Puerto Rico), and who has thrown a time-bomb into the world of compulsory state education, and has been called 'a hero of the reformers of the Catholic left', has said things about the Christian presence which dot the i's and cross the t's of Davis's arguments. Like Davis he writes about the Roman Church but, *mutatis mutandis*, what he says has relevance elsewhere.

He describes the Roman Church as the world's largest non-governmental bureaucracy, employing 1·8 million full-time workers (priests, brothers, sisters, laymen) and rating as one of 'the most efficiently operated organizations in the world' on a par with General Motors and the Chase Manhattan Bank. Nevertheless, he says, the machine-like smoothness is suspect. Men fear it may have lost its relevance to the Gospel and the world. Confusion reigns behind the scenes. 'The giant begins to totter before it collapses.'

He goes on: 'The institutional Church is in trouble. The very persons on whose loyalty and obedience the efficiency structure depends increasingly abandon it. Until the early sixties, the "defections" were relatively rare. Now they are common. Tomorrow they may be the pattern.'[15]

He believes that the problem lies not with the secular world spirit, but the church structures themselves. He looks sourly not only on the self-preserving ecclesiastical bureaucracy, but on the lives and roles of a feather-bedded priesthood, comfortably housed, assured preferential treatment and superior status from the moment they begin training

---

[14] Op. cit. p. 207.
[15] *Celebration of Awareness*, Ivan D. Illich, Calder and Boyars, London 1971, p. 72.

until after death. 'Laymen who work in the ecclesiastical structure are recognized as possessing some few "civil rights", but their careers depend principally on their ability to play the role of Uncle Tom.'[16] On the other hand the clergy survive because 'priestly service at the altar is united with clerical power and privilege'.

All this, Illich prophesies, will have to go. The pressures of the world, the defections from the priesthood, will compel this solution. The Church will be re-made.

'An adult layman, ordained to the ministry, will preside over the "normal" Christian community of the future. The ministry will be an exercise of leisure rather than a job. The "diaconia" will supplant the parish as the fundamental institutional unit in the Church. The periodic meeting of friends will replace the Sunday assembly of strangers. A self-supporting dentist, factory worker, professor, rather than a church-employed scribe or functionary, will preside over the meeting . . . I forsee the face-to-face meeting of families around a table, rather than the impersonal attendance of a crowd around an altar. Celebration will sanctify the dining room, rather than consecrated buildings the ceremony.'[17] As to the priesthood, today 'a man supports himself by working at a job in the world, not by performing a role in a hierarchy'.

Such are some of the ruthless prognostications of this radical Roman. It has to be admitted that though all ecclesiastical structures are under critical analysis the world over, the Church of England is not passing through the same anguished re-assessment as the Church of Rome. It is not suffering from endless defections in the same way and its processes of self-government, from the parish upwards, have long surpassed anything that Rome has conceded to the faithful. They provide the instruments of a consensus. Nevertheless, in the Church of England too, as we have seen, the future of the ministry is in question, and the Church has begun to ordain its dentists and factory workers to the unpaid auxiliary or supplementary ministry! They are in a sense already the ordained laity.

One can understand the chagrin and anger of the average Roman or Anglican priest when faced with a succession of arguments such as those of Illich. They appear to relegate most priestly works to futility. He may question the whole basis of the argument on the grounds of immemorial experience. For most of the two thousand years of Christian history there have always been unique holy buildings, gathered congregations and a paid professional priesthood. There is no instant reason to suppose that the latter should go because attendances decline or societies change. God is still present in the eucharist. Acts of worship are not less significant

---

[16] Ibid. p. 74.
[17] Ibid. p. 82.

to God or man because fewer worshippers attend. In any case there are still churches which overflow with worshippers. Failure can be made to appear a local difficulty and success to appear the local reflection of a universal expectation of a triumph guaranteed by God.

There is not only naïveté but sometimes even cruelty when radical reformers would appear to anticipate (even gleefully) the winding-up of the institutional apparatuses of world churches and the ensuing redundancy of their immense clerical staffs, as though all that effort and devotion counted for nothing and one had no need for gratitude to history. I accept what is quoted on page 1 that the situation, as it is, is the starting point. One builds on the historic legacy and carries forward as much of it as is significant and serviceable. In *any* enterprise one does that. In the Church universal it is obligatory, for it is itself a cultural mnemonic looking back to, and basing itself squarely on, unique and holy moments of a time which it daily, hourly celebrates and ritually recalls.

Therefore one seeks bridges from present structures into the mists of the future. One finds them in ecumenical parishes, in team ministries which keep the parochial charge but restore the small group pattern to the life and work of the clergy themselves, and in the growth of the specialist ministries—prisons, hospitals, universities, industry—in which by 1980, it is officially assumed, no less than twenty-five per cent of the Anglican clergy will be engaged. It is sensible to look at examples.

A fascinating example of adaptation and renewal is to be found in St Philip and St James, the 'multipurpose' church at Hodge Hill, Birmingham. It broke new ground in the concept of what a church could and should be and it came into existence as the result of a series of happy coincidences. In 1962 the University of Birmingham established the Institute for the Study of Worship and Religious Architecture, under the directorship of Professor J. G. Davies, which first concerned itself with the appearance and liturgical suitability of church buildings, then more and more with the theology of churches—asking what these special buildings were supposed to do, and to be, as part of the mission of the whole Church. In general its answer was that a church ought not to be a building which separated the worshipping faithful from the community, silent and inoperative for most of the time apart from its few services every week, but a centre of Christian and community enterprise, used to its maximum, a powerhouse rather than a memorial. J. G. Davies developed this theology in *The Secular Use of Church Buildings*[18] through a wealth of historical examples and social and ecclesiastical considerations. He concluded:

'How then is a consecrated building to be defined? Negatively, it is

---

[18] SCM Press, London 1968.

not to be defined as a habitation of God nor as a shrine of the divine presence; it is not the modern counterpart of the Jerusalem Temple. Nor is it a holy place, in the sense that it has a character of "wholly otherness" set apart from the world. There is then no depersonalization of the Holy. In so far as the term "holy" can be used at all, this must be understood functionally to mean "God-relatedness". A consecrated building is therefore one in which the secular is God-related explicitly and the unity of life thereby shown forth. In emphasizing this functional aspect we are not proposing any startling innovation. For the past a church has always been understood functionally, but this function has been restricted to worship conceived solely as a cultic activity. Our argument leads to the affirmation that either it is wrong to limit the meaning of worship in this way or that it is necessary to acknowledge that the function of a church building is more complex than has previously been conceived. Its function is to serve the Mission of God; it is to be an instrument of his outgoing in concern to the world; it must therefore minister to human need and at the same time its explicit God-relatedness declares the unity of all life in Christ.'[19]

The Institute Davies directs was invited in 1963 by the diocese of Birmingham to plan a Hodge Hill church and vicarage in place of the existing dual purpose hall erected in 1937. Their plans were almost complete when a fire destroyed the pre-war church and everything had to be rethought and redesigned in a three-way discussion between diocese, parish and institute.

'There was almost immediate agreement that if a new church was to be designed at all, "its use should not be restricted to Sunday worship". But what sort of building should it then be—a "proper church" used almost exclusively for worship on Sundays or a "multipurpose church" designed to accommodate a full week-day use for many other activities as well? It was felt that the expenditure of £40,000 might be justified if such a building could be designed to serve the discovered needs of the people in the area as a whole, irrespective of whether or not they chose to call themselves Christians'.[20]

A start was made on a bold plan in 1967. The result is 'a multipurpose church'. Dr Gilbert Cope has divided modern churches into three categories. They are, first, those which acknowledge new building techniques but accept the traditional medieval or Gothic form (Coventry Cathedral is a special example of this); two, those based on the gathered concept of the Liturgical Movement (such as the many new round churches in which the altar is moved to the centre of the congregation),

---

[19] Op. cit. pp. 263–4.
[20] *The Multi-Purpose Church: Hodge Hill—St Philip and St James*: Institute for the Study of Worship and Religious Architecture, Birmingham, 1971. J. G. Davies, p. 9.

and three, those designed for a wider multipurpose use, in which 'secular' activities are allowed to invade even 'sacred' areas.[21] Hodge Hill belongs to the third group.

The building does not resemble any traditional church, certainly not the Gothic cruciform type. From the exterior it might be a pleasant modern school. The church hall, church, parsonage are integral under a low profile roof and without a spire or other vertical element. Inside the main hall there are a few ecclesiastical sheet anchors—a baptistry with a pool, a sanctuary on a dais in the congregational space and, behind the sanctuary, a quiet room or chapel looking out on to a dignified garden of rest. But the congregational space, which is used for games, meetings and dances, is flanked by a fully-equipped stage and a lounge area where one can take coffee and this ramifies away into reading rooms, activities and gymnasium areas, study and reading rooms, coffee bar, foyer, showers, toilets. The resemblance to a community centre is strong. Indeed, one member of the staff is a professional youth warden.

The activities are vigorous and prolific. By the most recent report supplied to me,[22] there are three clergy, the full-time youth warden, a part-time secretary, three paid cleaners and a handyman on the staff. But the bulk of the work falls upon voluntary workers. The electoral roll stands at 320, the parochial council has 56 members and it works through 6 committees. The regular activities at the church during the week are: the pre-school play group (8 voluntary helpers): the day centre for old people (55 voluntary helpers on a rota); centre for autistic and mentally handicapped children; mother and baby club; visiting service for old people; coffee bar (60 helpers on a rota); junior, middle and senior open youth clubs and a small church youth club—these cater between them for over six hundred young people and involve nearly thirty helpers. Then there are the familiar self-governing societies for Badminton, Drama, Opera, Women's Fellowship, Mothers' Union, uniformed organizations, and a Saturday club for adults for music, poetry, dancing. There are perhaps 150 weekly communicants and attendance at all services appears to be in the range of at least 360. There are over 30 in the choir.

The many rooms and halls permit many and varied activities to be going on simultaneously: hence the long list of them. The deliberate intention is to keep going all day with the consequence that (by my arithmetic) at least 1,500 people, old, young, handicapped, hearty must be using the church each week, a remarkable result by any standards and so the 'God-relatedness' and the 'world-relatedness' of the Church in Hodge Hill would seem to fulfill J. G. Davies' expectations magnificently. As a result, it draws its pilgrims from far and near.

---

[21] Cf. G. Cope 'Church Building in the Twentieth Century', *Research Bulletin 1967*, Institute for the Study of Worship and Architecture, pp. 9–14.

[22] I am most grateful to Mr Charles Dixon, Churchwarden, for supplying it.

Its very success raises problems. One cannot plant down a Hodge Hill everywhere and it would be cruel to expect every parish priest to be the dynamic extrovert a community centre needs: though, after all, most of the day-to-day work at Hodge Hill *is* done by volunteers. It is impossible to say that the social activity of Hodge Hill has extinguished the worshipping community; on the contrary it appears to have strengthened it. There are too many churches which have neither strong social activities nor a strong worshipping community—both have irreparably faded. But there is the question as to how far the Church can go in the promotion of these necessary social activities in pursuit of the loving, serving community. So far, no limit has been reached.

Seemingly light-years away from the pragmatic Anglican parochial solution to the dying parish applied at Hodge Hill is the community at Taizé, which has become world-famous.

Taizé, on the hills of Burgundy, come straight out of the monastic tradition of chastity, poverty and obedience and renews that tradition with an impressive sanctity and yet with differences which symbolize an ecumenical healing. For differences of denomination are no barrier to membership, so long as the mother-denomination consents. There is a high degree of informality in the dress of the members of the community (a dog-collar is seen, Canon Peter Moore says, only when an English Anglican happens to be there) and only for the required saying of the appropriate daily offices is a special tunic worn. Members go out to work. They pool their earnings and property. They live simply and are open to the world. At the same time they reject imitators, daughter communities. They reject overloading with their own history and traditions and burn their correspondence every month. Their single Council is left flexible and free. Members may be celibate or married, both states have equal regard. But there is no great refectory such as graces every other monastery. And there is no cloister.

'The Community . . . is divided up into small groups called "foyers" of six or seven members who share a common room where they eat and enjoy a social life of family proportions. The novice who joins Taizé becomes a member of the foyer in charge of the Novice Master. In this way there is an attempt to guard against the danger of the Community becoming a large amorphous group of people, too big to know each other well. . . .'[23]

'Furthermore, worship at Taizé is truly ecumenical. It cuts across the boundaries of denominational allegiance without requiring any-one to be disloyal. Twice daily Calvinists, Presbyterians, Baptists, Roman Catholics and Orthodox worship together without reserve. Yet what a contrast our parish churches and dissenting chapels afford,

---

[23] *Tomorrow is Too Late*, Peter Moore, Mowbray, 1970, p. 98.

each going their own way, in thousands of towns and villages more than half empty and sometimes with a mere handful unable to support each other let alone inspire those outside. The tradition of utterly separate worship on all occasions by all denominations is no longer tenable on any ground whatever, and where it continues it is generally rather from prejudice than any laudable motive. Eucharistic worship is a different matter, and in this the Taizé practice of an open table welcoming any who wish to come could not be wholeheartedly accepted by many christians. Having said that, it leaves a vast area of potentially common ground which would afford, at parochial level, a valuable opportunity of meeting and getting to know each other which Taizé offers in its special way...'[24]

Speaking of the First Rule of the Community, the rule of prayer, the Prior, Roger Schultz, significantly underlines what I have said of baptism. 'Let us begin with ourselves daily recalling the unity in and between us so that we dare summon all the baptized into visible unity. To reverse this order is to put the cart before the horse.'[25]

As important as the visible unity of all the baptized is the second act of community at Taizé—that every meal should be an *agape*, a love feast. If every meal is eaten under the shadow of the eucharist it becomes a source of grace. As Canon Peter Moore says, the common meal was the means by which the Risen Christ made himself known to his disciples, and this can still be the experience of his faithful today. This is the meaning of the grace said before meals by Christians down the ages, but now dying out in the hurly-burly of our age when few home meals have the dignity which once they had. To restore the *agape* is also to help to restore the family and the small group to their proper place as the heart of a Christian life and of church activism. A family in which no common Christian act ever takes place during the week is one which has accomplished the separation of Christianity from the common life. Maybe it can never be restored by the Victorian customs of grace and family prayers: their solemnity could be crushing. The happy, relaxed, yet sacramental nature of the *agape* would seem more appropriate to this century.

Bishop Robinson writes in *The New Reformation?*[26] of one special meal a week, usually supper on Saturday, with his wife and children. It arose from 'dissatisfaction with family prayers, with Communion preparation, with grace before meals'. 'It is not a Eucharist, but rather a special meal to which we all look forward, which includes a bottle of wine... we normally begin (in winter) by lighting the table candles and

---

[24] Ibid. p. 148.

[25] *Unanimité dans le pluralisme*, Taizé Press, p. 28.

[26] SCM Press, 1965, pp. 84–5.

singing the very early Christian hymn, "Hail, gladdening light".' Prayers follow from all and at the close there is a version of another eucharistic hymn. 'I then cut a slice from the loaf and pour out a glass of wine, both of which we pass round, ending with a salutation, or the grace, and a joining of hands.'

If this festive *agape* approaches the eucharist, there have been eucharists (particularly in the Roman Church in Holland and France) which approach the *agape*. I reported on some of these in *The Death and Resurrection of the Church*,[27] particularly on a Mass celebrated in Holland as though it were the Last Supper with a priest without liturgical garments at a table with some sixteen grammar school boys. The priest blessed the wine and bread and himself communicated. The elements were passed round as in John Robinson's family circle. Then, after last prayers, a meal was eaten in all the noise and good fellowship of an ordinary repast. I spoke there of a Mass celebrated by six young men seated round a table covered with a grey blanket—a full sung liturgy conducted in the utmost simplicity in the vernacular. The worshippers communicated themselves. The consecrated bread was flat bread or girdle cake which they broke themselves, not the conventional imprinted wafer which reminds one of nothing so much as Orwell's foodless food.

An example of the new Christian community which all these things foreshadow has come into existence at Llanerchwen near the Brecon Beacons in South Wales. It is not precisely the British Taizé but it has a similar ecumenical approach prompted by what it believes is the most radical upheaval in the church's history.

'It began simply as an Abrahamic going forth into the unknown. There were no blue prints, nothing; only an awareness of this time of great change and crisis facing mankind and of the need for radical reformation within the Christian Church and the Christian tradition to meet it ... The shape [of the venture] is a "parish" one but parish with a difference. Its base is not geographical but personal. It has no boundaries, no borders, no regulations, no closed membership. There are priests and there are people, but they are more concerned with their common Christian ministry than their particular Christian callings. The people who live "in" this parish live up and down the country. They are of very different backgrounds, temperaments and callings, they have both different understandings of Christianity and different responses to it.'[28]

In a deeply mystical Llanerchwen Paper, 'Towards an Unknown Church' the 'community' describes its work negatively. There is no distinction between Christians, no denominational dividing lines, no

---

[27] Hodder, 1968, pp. 105 et seq.
[28] 'One New Bottle?' a memorandum from the Llanerchwen Trust.

division between Christians and non-Christians; no barriers between the secular and the sacred spheres of life, little traditional religious practice, no customs or common rules. It is therefore as unlike the traditional religious community as it could possibly be, except that certain like-minded people do live together in cottages and Colt bungalows on a hillside: it disclaims, however, any intention of creating an 'empire' out of them. It has a mission intention—perhaps of example rather than teaching—for it intends to open an urban centre. How to describe something so frankly nebulous? The paper itself says, 'perhaps most important of all though it can only be said with whatever humility we can muster— we have been brought to a deeper nothingness in ourselves. The stripping away of outward and recognized roles and status has assisted our own journey into the interior, into that reality of inner silence and solitude, that awareness of the mystery both in us and beyond us'—with Thomas Merton as their mentor.

What most painfully afflicts them is a sense of the spiritual dryness of the world which their own thirst mirrors. They are, like many hippy or beat religious communes or Jesus groups, so private and so unknown up and down the country, a commune of expectation which might one day hope to be a community of the annunciation.

What does it all amount to, this search for a new sort of Christian group and a more primitive and direct eucharistic experience? In one sense it comes out of many of the insights I have discussed in this book— the reaction of the sensitive and reflective to the drab impersonality of the modern world, with its powerful uncommunicative super-organizations which control our destinies and are responsible to no one, but are themselves prisoners of their own mindless momentum. Charles Reich is at least right that we are to be rescued from that only by new personal relations, a new social and cultural creativity; a third consciousness. Then there is the sad fact that to those who think this, *the great Churches appear to belong to the super-organizations*—they impose their clumsy super-structures, their cold and formal procedures, their fixed liturgies between the worshipper or the seeker and the direct religious experience. The bill may not be a true one. But it is widely accepted by many, especially by young people, who are often repelled. In any case, there is that sad falling-off in the religious life, that withering of the religious spirit—at least as it has been traditionally expressed in Western lands— of which Llanerchwen is most deeply sensitive. It is not alone.

NINE

New Pastoral Forms

POYNTON is a village of less than four thousand inhabitants in Cheshire. It has an enterprising Council of Churches which has established fourteen—the number tends to fluctuate—'neighbourhood churches'. They cover two-thirds of the households of Poynton, about 2,300 people. Presumably the writ of the Council of Churches does not run over the entire village. Four and a half per cent of those adults living within the areas of the neighbourhood churches are *actively* associated with them. Very few neighbourhood church members (4 per cent) are not already associated in some way with existing churches, but, alas, less than twenty per cent of existing church congregations attend the neighbourhood churches. This suggests that they recruit their membership mainly from Christians who do *not* worship formally in church. Since few young persons are associated with them but all groups over 25 are well represented there would seem to be a certain appeal to established young married people, those least well represented in ordinary congregations. There is a carefully thought out theology, which owes much to Charles Davis and to what he said about the importance of primary groups in *God's Grace in History*. Necessarily it draws inspiration from primitive Christianity.

'The first Christians knew that the Church was a body of people, a dynamic *organic* entity, which had a cellular structure. Often when Christians meet today, it is as organizations within the Parish Church (e.g. Ladies' or Men's Fellowship, Badminton Club, etc.). These are sectional groupings, based on some limiting factor such as age, sex, or shared interest. Clearly, such groups are not representative of a Church. A Neighbourhood Church, on the other hand, is the Parish Church, the Christian congregation of a given place, in miniature. As a small, cell-like unit, it shares the same constituents as the larger body. Today, we have grown accustomed to thinking in terms of isolated fragments, divided into insular, neatly labelled compartments, with little or no connection between each one. This is an outrage to the insights of the New Testament.'[1]

---

[1] From Appendix 2, 'The Theology of the House-Church', in *Report on the Neighbourhood Churches*, Poynton Council of Churches. 1971. This, by a working party, is quite a professional analysis of the scheme.

The theological analysis recognizes that 'until the organic unity of Christians in and through Baptism is *explicitly* acknowledged' the life of the neighbourhood churches is itself impeded: the small group experience of the eucharist is, perhaps because of disunion, reported to be the most rare event compared with fellowship, study, prayer and care of neighbours.

The interesting point about the Poynton neighbourhood churches is that support from the *established* congregations is small. It must mean that those who do not use them feel no need for them: they must deem their traditional worship sufficient. But some eighty per cent of those who *do* use them, though claiming church connections, clearly do not worship regularly on Sundays. The Council of Churches organizes systematic oversight of the neighbourhood churches and does a great deal of planning and programming and some direct publicity for them. What has grown up is a well-defined grass-roots movement which may prove to be a permanent part of the infra-structure of the local churches, but has not yet broken down divisions.

An interesting confirmation of the need for a firm structure such as Poynton possesses comes from the Roman Catholic Parish of Abbey Wood where a house group system has been inaugurated by a team ministry. There, 'the parish was divided into twelve sections and a layman was carefully selected from each area to have the responsibility for that section. Meetings and discussions were held in the parish to explain to a wider audience the purpose of the sections. The section leaders were also given more specific information and instructions.'[2] They then invited interested Catholics into their homes and from these meetings came the Mass-in-the-home, linked with special teaching in the church on Sundays. 'The idea of having Mass at home was met with a good deal of uneasiness at first, yet tension was usually dispelled once the idea had become a reality. It would then be left to the parishioner in whose house the Mass was being offered to invite those living nearby. Whenever possible the priest tried to involve the whole family—even the non-catholic partner—for example, getting the children to write their own bidding prayers. Tea and biscuits would follow the Mass.'[3]

Incidentally, the parish team is taking part in an ecumenical group which is seeking to serve not only the parishes of the co-operating churches but the new Thamesmead community to which Nicolas Stacey refers in his autobiography *Who Cares?* . . .

The vicar of St Peter's, Bushey Heath—an Anglican parish of over 10,000 with an estimated turnover of population of fifteen per cent per annum—wrote to me to say that they had developed house groups out

---

[2] *Report of Summer Vacation Work in the Parish of Abbey Wood, Summer 1970*, by three Franciscan students, The Presbytery, 31 Abbey Grove, London SE12, p. 3.
[3] Ibid.

of a stewardship renewal campaign. The number of groups has grown from seven to eleven in two years.

'The groups begin with only a few guide lines: they were to be fellowship groups whereby a large Sunday congregation (average communicants, 170 plus) might be able through smaller units to get to know itself better; they were to be eucharistic in the sense that at some point during the meeting there would be an informal celebration of holy communion. The fact of having a eucharist means that one of the clergy attends, but he attends as a member of the group and not as an outside importation—and it is a parish where it is the custom to call clergy by their Christian names and this helps. We sit for the service, except the actual communion, which is passed round, each member communicating the next one along and using the Christian name: "The Body of Christ is given for you, John".'

The impulse in the Church of England (and not only there) to find an *ecumenical* basis for new and imaginative ventures is very strong indeed. From correspondence and from the priests and congregations one meets it is clear that the bolder spirits are reluctant to go it alone and establish new ecclesiastical empires or monopolies. They would prefer to move forward with their colleagues, and the faithful, of other communions. This is certainly the case in Swindon Old Town where three churches, Christ Church (the parish church), St Mary's Methodist Church and Immanuel Congregational Church covenanted together in January 1969 to form the Ecumenical Parish of Swindon Old Town. 'In practice this means doing everything together except those things which may be described as limitations imposed by the "Established" position of the Church of England.'[4]

One of the first acts was to create a Parish Synod, consisting of the Senior Clergy and Ministers and lay representatives from each church, to govern all the activities of the Parish from its bi-monthly meetings. The Synod has not taken—and could not legally—take over the role of the Parochial Church Council and similar bodies, but it has assumed 'an ever greater role, whilst the bodies which normally have governed every aspect of the local church's life have played a lesser role. This being so, in 1971, after the Synod had held a full-day meeting at Malmesbury, it was decided to increase the representation from each by appointing a further four members, making ten from each church with the Senior Ministers.'[5]

One must speak of worship. The churches of the parish do not worship together regularly. They are convinced that unity does not mean uniformity and that the wide varieties of liturgy and worship for which

---

[4] Rev. N. Charlton, *The Ecumenical Parish of Old Swindon*, published by The Ecumenical Parish, 71 Bath Road, Swindon 1971.

[5] Ibid. p. 1.

they respectively stand should be retained and even encouraged. Practically, in any case, they could not gather all their congregations into one building for regular worship. Nevertheless, the separation this implies is not quite absolute. 'We do worship together whenever it is the natural and logical thing to do. As for example in the anniversary service of the founding of the Parish, or in the open-air at Whitsuntide, during holiday periods and so on. We have had to approach the question of joint worship in other ways. Thus, there is a regular exchange of pulpits with inter-communion.'[6] Upon the foundation of the Parish a Maundy *agape* was celebrated, based on the liturgy of the Church of South India, with the *agape* meal added. Some three hundred people attended, but they had to be seated in three separate halls. There was no one hall large enough for all of them.

The parish has organized a network of lay stewards who, once merely postmen, now form the basis of 'a pastoral community-care network'. The parish is divided into three districts, each in the charge of a clergyman of the team, and each district has some eight areas, each in the charge of an Area-Steward who has the oversight of Parish Stewards, one for each road or street. But this care and information network is part, too, of a House Group system called into existence every Lent for training. There are about 40 groups. As they are convened by Area Stewards, who are automatically members of the Parish Pastoral Committee, which has oversight of 'care', a permanent role may descend on them. In any case, 'local groups are discovering new and exciting ways of what it means to be "The Church" in a particular road, or small area, and they are being encouraged to develop their own initiatives'. The parallels with Poynton and Abbey Wood schemes are obvious. Yet the difficulties remain: 'There are some issues which will only finally be settled when there is union at a national level between our respective churches, for example a common membership. It was recognized that to create, as it were, a common membership of the "Church of the Ecumenical Parish of Swindon Old Town" even were it to be recognized by anyone other than ourselves, would only have the effect of turning us into yet another denomination. In the interim period in which we find ourselves we believe we must behave more and more as if we were within one Church.'[7]

---

[6] Ibid. p. 5.

[7] Ibid. p. 6. The Ecumenical Parish of Swindon Old Town and the East Swindon Group of Churches combined to send a strongly worded letter to all members of General Synod on the occasion of the final vote on reunion with the Methodists. It said, among other things, 'if on May 3rd you do not achieve a 75% vote in favour we, and the hundreds of other similar areas all over the country, are going to be placed in an intolerable position. This will either dishearten people so much that they will withdraw from organized religion, or they will rebel against their parent bodies which seem so insensitive to their children's needs. ... If our parents do not now get married what will this make us?'

One speaks of Swindon Old Town at length because the care and detail with which the covenant between the Churches has been worked out and the evidence it shows of an ecumenical passion not to be observed everywhere. But there are many other interesting examples. At Milborne Port in Somerset there is an *ad hoc* group ministry (which includes the Roman Catholics) brought together by World Refugee Year, one consequence of which is that the Roman Catholics now hold their weekly Mass in the parish church instead of in 'a rather dull room in the local Town Hall'. Similar arrangements have been made in other parishes—St Chad's in Walsall is an example, where the effort to put a trial scheme on a permanent basis is, ominously, 'still in the hands of the lawyers'.

When it comes to new towns what is the Anglican witness to be? Another costly, laboriously built, semi-gothic memorial to be used for only a few hours a week and set in some place where it can outstare its denominational rivals? Or some building which makes sense in the way it plans and uses its expensive space, as Hodge Hill has done, but is if possible ecumenical rather than denominational? At Killingworth, a new town six miles north-east of Newcastle upon Tyne, there is such an adventure in Christian and social planning. The town is not broken into neighbourhoods, but is strongly centralized. From individual family homes on the periphery it builds up to 'high density access houses' and then to a concentrated town centre. Pedestrian access has been so carefully planned that people can walk from their homes to any part of the town without crossing a road: yet there is free traffic movement and parking spaces close to all homes.

At the beginning of the building of the town the neighbourhood churches set up an 'Open House' in the town centre where all questions could be answered and help given to those who asked for it. Presently, the Killingworth Christian Council was established by the Anglican, Methodist, Presbyterian and Roman Catholic Churches. A priest was appointed Warden of the Communicare Team Ministry. He declared that, 'our main task must be to try and create a caring community rather than to rely on one little Communicare House'. And indeed the brochure[8] which describes all this defines Communicare as 'the total care of the whole community in all its aspects by everyone. In earlier times and in smaller communities it would have evolved automatically but in a complex new society it has to be organized.'

The local authorities, building on what the Churches pioneered, have begun the construction of Communicare complex in the town centre which when finished will include a health centre, library, sports hall,

---

[8] *For Heaven's Sake We Need Space*, Killingworth Christian Council Communicare Appeal.

youth and community centre, swimming baths—and a church and pastoral centre which is the responsibility of the Christian Council. The Council's accommodation will consist of a worship area which will seat 250 people, a sacristy and a vestry large enough for committees and for a secretary, several staff studies available for classes and interviews, a foyer which is also a common room, together with a kitchen to serve it, and a three bedroom flat, the permanent residence of the Warden. The church building will carry its own distinguished witness with a small tower with cross and bell on the skyline of the town.

The cost of the ecumenical slice of the whole project will fall upon the Christian Council, which is appealing for funds. Hence the need to keep the centre busy and its spaces used as fully as possible all the week. And so something in the nature of the policy of Hodge Hill—the maximum economic use of every space, including the worship space, for all sorts of activities during the week—has to be applied.

The architects who designed Hodge Hill, Peter Bridges and Martin Purdy, have also designed the Skelmersdale Ecumenical Centre in Lancashire. Skelmersdale is a new town situated close to the M6 motorway and about 18 miles from Liverpool. From a population of 8,000 before the new town was planned the area is expected to house 80,000 people by the 1980s. The old village areas are well served by churches, and so too are some of the new neighbourhoods where Romans and Anglicans have been building. But the central area which includes the town centre, and is intended to house 25,000 people, is without provision. It is for this area that the ecumenical centre is to be built. The sponsoring Churches are the Church of England, the Methodist, Baptist, Presbyterian and Congregational Churches. The Romans and the Skelmersdale Development Corporation are also represented on the Committee. By letter from the hon. secretary I am told that 'a five-man Ecumenical Team Ministry is working to build up a wholly integrated united congregation which will worship in and serve through the Ecumenical Centre at present being built in the Town Centre'.

The centre is as ambitious as the Killingworth complex. In addition to a main space for large congregational worship and other gatherings of citizens it is served by a teenage coffee bar, dining lounge, a library, seminar rooms, special lecture theatre (part of the 'lay academy') a small, ever-open chapel, exhibition gallery and even a crèche. As there is to be a day centre and lunch club for the elderly, and provision for the disabled, 'a bathroom with a bath specially designed for the infirm has been included' in the part of the building intended for them. Every detail has been thought out.

Here then is yet another Christian centre most conscientiously promoted by an ecumenical team in which the centre of worship is at the same time the heart of the Christian service to the community, a local powerhouse in fact. We know that such powerhouses also flourish on a denominational basis and in old-fashioned plant. From all that I have learnt of it, the parish church of St John the Baptist, Hove, with its intense educational and mission work through house groups and conferences and its enthusiastic lay participation, is an example. And the way in which old plant can be adapted is demonstrated by the conversion of St Matthew's, next door to the old parish church in Cheltenham, into a church shared with the Methodists, who sold their chapel and contributed the proceeds towards the transformation. The vast empty spaces of the Victorian church have been recreated into a worship area, classrooms, social lounge area, cafeteria and are thrown open to the town for social and cultural use. However, churches recreated in this way, as well as ecumenical centres specially designed for maximum daily Christian service, are still all too few. What they point to is the form that renewal must take. Here the future is actually with us.

The Skelmersdale and Killingworth type of centre, with its flexible worship area, does not only pose problems of design and usage, but of the relationship between the sacred and secular, which Hodge Hill too has encountered. And it compels one to ask just what is the 'worship area', for important periods of the week a sacred area, meant to convey? A thoughtful memorandum of the Killingworth Christian Council, concerned with the theology and the liturgiology of their worship area notes this.

'Today's liturgical insights seem to envisage the gathering of the people round the Lord's table for a Fellowship Meal. This is in almost complete contrast to the mediaeval concept which has prevailed till recently (in which the people focus their devotion on a point at, or beyond, the far East wall of the building, via Priest at altar or Methodist in pulpit, according to tradition).

'The Fellowship Meal is, however, not just a human-level event. Host at every Eucharist is Jesus Christ. The glory and beauty for which mediaeval (and mediaeval-type) Churches strove was an attempt to state that the human spirit has ambitions that are more than merely material and mundane. If the architecture even of a "meeting-place" type Church is to attempt to convey anything at all, if, in other words, architecture in this context is an art at least as much as a science, it must have the same ambition.

'Not only an act of adoration and thanksgiving (expressed, however symbolically, in the close connection between the Eucharist and the Cross, between the Supper on the evening of the Thursday and the events that followed that night and the next morning) but also a fellowship meal. To hold these two aspects of the central act of Christian worship perfectly in balance has proved beyond the ability of the Church all down the ages, whether in the words and actions or in the architectural setting of its liturgy. Nevertheless a solution that comes down too firmly on one side of this fence will for ever fail to present the whole Gospel.'

It is important to quote this to illustrate the serious and reverential approach of this ecumenical team to its difficult but exciting tasks. As the Vicar of Killingworth wrote to me to say, the Gospel has to be demonstrated today, not just spoken about, and this means that there is room everywhere in, or beside, the official welfare network for a body of dedicated Christians who have a deeper understanding of man, of his dignity and permanence as a being in the image of God, than that which popularly prevails and who derive from that a greater compassion.

What I have had occasion to describe here as examples of renewal would appear to be no more than the tip of an iceberg. Far fuller information of what is going on than ever I could have recourse to is to be found in *Ecumenical Experiments, a Handbook*[9] and *Case Studies in Unity*[10] both by R. M. C. Jeffery, who was for four years Secretary of the Department of Mission and Unity of the British Council of Churches. The detail of constitutions and structures in *Ecumenical Experiments* is especially valuable.

We see in fact how renewal is bound to go where it can be related to parish structures. It will be demonstrated by denominational and ecumenical team ministries, ecumenical parishes, often with new shared places of worship and pastoral centres, and all going along with parish stewards, section leaders, street wardens, house groups and house communions, and perhaps all calling into existence, as the work of the Institute for the Study of Worship and Architecture has shown, entirely new forms of religious building. But what about that which is needed, and in some places is developing, *outside* the parochial system?

It has been the contention of some that the place where a man works and where he will spend a third of his life in his most productive years is the place where Christian mission should begin. Here man is at his most meaningful, and what goes on in workplaces is of profoundest importance for the economic, moral and social life of mankind. Others have said that the vertical or specialist ministry to industry and commerce must grow while the parochial ministry to suburbs, emptied of their menfold for eight or so hours a day, should wither away. In any case the parochial ministry is a ministry which is thrown out of true because it misses the men and catches only the women, the aged and the little children during the day and tends to build its worshipping congregation around them. And even this aspect of the parochial set-up can be eroded where employment of women is high in local industry.

There is an argument against a ministry which is totally parochial in the narrow sense, but it does not entirely make the case for the vertical

[9] The British Council of Churches, 10 Eaton Gate, London SW1 1971.
[10] SCM Centre Book, 1972.

mission. There is the psychological fact that most jobs are tedious and devoid of satisfactions other than those provided by comradeship and/or money. For many millions of workers, alas, daily work is a void, and if repetitious a dream time, a necessary but despised chore through which to earn the money to continue the true life lived outside work to which the worker returns, and longs to return, every evening, every week-end. There, with wife and family, garden, car, telly, the pools, the pub, Saturday football, he is his own man at last. That freed life could include church and chapel. It often did for his forefathers who worked even harder. It certainly could include interest in the Christian activities in which the rest of his family are caught up. The Church which catches a man at his home finds a man liberated from the subservience which is the plight of most in industry: they find him the independent house-holder, the dignified president of a family. Therefore, however difficult it may turn out in application, the psychology of the parochial ministry is correct as well as important, though the parochial ministry need not have the special shape given to it in the Church of England by history and inertia.

When this has been said the issue is far from closed, as so many cosy clergymen would like it to be, in favour of the (existing) parochial system. The simple, aching fact is that the Church of England—the Churches generally—just cannot grasp the nature of contemporary society. The industrial sector which the worker despises and from which he seeks to escape is nevertheless the sector *no one* escapes from in the long run—the area of endless, dour, brutal struggles between employees and managements, workers and capitalists, as devastating as the battles of medieval barons; of agitation and unrest, of ferocious social energies bound in the end to turn society upside down; of endless technical resource and the world-transforming energies from which come not only our houses, food and clothing but all those surpluses on which our education, culture and religion ultimately depend. To ignore that *practically* (however much we may write or preach about it!) is to bury one's head in an industrial slagheap which in the nature of things will presently cover the rest of the body too. The Marxist thesis of the centrality of the economic life cannot be ignored.

How does the Church separately, or the Churches together, carry mission to the economic life of the country? And without patronage? The Industrial Missions made a fine beginning but their work in working-hours is limited by the disciplines of industry itself and, outside, to forms of dialogue. The worker-priest movement, killed in France by the hierarchy, barely survives in the Anglican Church. To be effective as a witness of total identification with workers in industry there would need to be one or more worker-priests in every great plant, totally economically dependent on their wages and equally independent of their hierarchies. One simply cannot see the men coming forward or the parochially-rooted hierarchies sustaining this. Fear and jealousy would prevent it. An order of industrial 'Jesuits' or 'Franciscans' might succeed, no matter from what 'Church' they derived. It would need men of great courage but also of deep understanding of Marxist and similar movements of social revolution and of the factions they spawn even more rapidly than Protestants fling up sects. Most Christian action, and thinking too, in this field, is generally distinguished by naïveté and need not be attended to.[11]

In any case, the mission cannot be tolerated just as a mission to 'factories' where 'workers' congregate. This is unconsciously to sustain the snobbery of the two worlds the Victorians accepted as providential. The 'Industrial' Mission needs to be retooled to become a mission to all large, separated communities and needs to be grafted on to the team ministries of major parishes wherever possible. What are these separated communities? Some name themselves—schools, colleges, universities, army camps, hospitals, prisons, as well as enormous industrial plants, ICI, BLMC, Fords, the various steelworks and so on, endlessly. The schools and colleges, the industrial plants, are 'separated' during working-hours only and can be served by ministers and laity who keep similar hours. The others are residential and in that sense 'lifted out' of the normal community, even, where hospitals and prisons are concerned, living in a social quarantine. Such enclaves need mission service as residential and as full-time as the rest of the professional staff rather than something added as a bonus to a parochial post. And so we must contemplate the growth of a professional corps energetically enrolled for an extra-parochial ministry. It need not be entirely ministerially recruited of course, but those of its members who are ordained ought not to be excluded from the processes of synodical government. At present in the Church of England they are second class citizens. Yet soon these 'special ministers' will form twenty-five per cent of the entire clergy force.[12] This understandably irritates men in the parochial ministry. They are sure that men moving into these non-parochial posts are deserting a 'tougher' job for easier options and higher pay. In some cases this could be true, in others men move because they have come to find the parish round futile and meaningless. The strength of the movement out certainly says something about negative parochial job satisfaction. A priest wrote to me to say that the Church had tried to develop 'a non-parochial specialist ministry' in recent years, 'while declaring that it supports the parish as well. But in fact the number of clergy is so limited that the parishes have

---

[11] But cf. R. C. Zaehner, *Dialectical Christianity and Christian Materialism*, OUP, Oxford 1971. Professor Zaehner knows his Marxism.

[12] Cf. for a full survey, *Specialised Ministries*: The Report of a Working Party of the Ministry Committee of the Advisory Council for the Church's Ministry on priests in specialized work, CIO, London 1971.

been grievously weakened by this provision of non-parish specialists.' His was a parish of 33,000 plus a prison, and his team consisted of two priests-in-charge, two curates and a parish visitor.

The nature of the new mega-organizations our society is throwing-up almost casually, and which can never be served by any imaginable parochial system, and about which nobody originally gave much pastoral thought, is exhibited by Heathrow Airport. It is not like any *sea*port one ever knew with its slum streets, its bars and pubs, rows of cheap lodgings and brothels where a sailor on the loose could be conned of his pay by all the pimps of the world, and dockers' and seamens' missions and hostels and Flying Angel centres came into existence to serve him and the Salvation Army had a field day saving him. At Heathrow all this is as unimaginable as a Salvation Army band and mission service on the tarmac.

All the same, what is Heathrow? It is a city of 50,045 people, smaller than Basingstoke, bigger than Hereford, but a city without homes, houses, churches, gardens, schools, through which pass 17 million passengers a year, while each passenger is seen off by one to two persons! If we include the visitors, then a population equivalent to that of a major country uses Heathrow each year. It has the highest crime rate in the land. It is almost impossible to imagine the human problems it conjures up in terms of parting and union, hope and despair, crime and personal loss, illness and death, the fright of the elderly, among passengers who can hardly be reached by any Christian or other agency. And what of the employees who often work under unremitting pressures, what of hapless immigrants, strikes, hijackings, crashes, fog? 'All we can do here is to keep the Chapel open and advertised,' the Chaplain writes about travellers, 'and hope those with time will use it. Actually they do. Rather more than anyone imagined. We are busy at present setting up a small organization called "Travellers Help", which has come into existence as a result of the quantities of girls last year looking for abortions. At the height, 75 per day.'

The Church is not idle. The Anglican chaplain is part of the wide-ranging London Industrial Chaplaincy. He shares his work at Heathrow with a Free Church and a Roman Catholic chaplain, using one office, 'one altar, with—simply basic!—one set of bank accounts. None of this would make any difference unless we liked each other as men. We do.... From the diagram of the Chapel...you will see that there are three altars. One for each of us. The central one is being brought forward to the edge of the bay, and the other two are being disposed of. Triumph! Unanimously too, by both Chapel Committee and trustees....'

A Heathrow Counselling Service has been set up (independently of the Chaplaincy of course) by Heathrow Airport with a trained social worker always at hand to listen, help and advise on personal problems with complete confidentiality. 'The major work of the Industrial Committee,' the Chaplain reports—he serves on it—'was to give this the needed impetus.'

The Anglican Chaplain speaks modestly of his work and life. 'I say Matins and Evensong in my office. The Chapel is used by visiting R.C. priests and various groups. I have a strong feeling that we have to build a worshipping body of Christians actually where we happen to be, and not see the parish as the norm. I believe this to be sound on grounds of creation and incarnation, and—blessed word—sociologically. I do not see myself as a so-called specialist, swanning around outside the parish net, but a priest like all the rest, in an area which is no more or less important than all the rest. We have to minister where people are in ways which suit that particular crowd.'[13]

Heathrow points to the shape of the technological future. Side by side with the growth of cities and their productive enclaves will cluster the affluent transport bases, which dwarf anything in the past, and display under our noses the purely functional and quite impersonal super-nexus of passenger and freight reception and dispatch. We hardly knew what we had got until it was there and booming, and as Christians hardly an idea of how it could be humanized. As the chaplains would be the first to admit, we are still groping. Yet society the world over will press more and more of such complexes, such enclaves, upon us. One lesson has to be learnt—whatever we may conclude about church structures, enclaves such as Heathrow can only be served by a strong institution standing outside and able to send in its trained men to establish a base. Hence the importance of all schemes to train men for the *urban* ministry.

---

[13] I am indebted to the Anglican Chaplain, the Rev. B. H. Lewers, for writing to me so fully and frankly. Perhaps the really blessed word, instead of parochial or specialist, would be pastoral, if only it did not make one so sheepish.

TEN
New Shapes for Old Institutions
I.

WHEN I began this study I thought I saw clearly how I might discuss the Church's future. I saw a dichotomy between the Church as static and the Church as reformed or reorganized. Then I saw a second dichotomy between the institutional Church, reformed or unreformed, and a Christian future outside the Churches altogether, a non-institutional Christianity or Christianity of the diaspora to which the institutional Church said nothing, but which had affiliation to that private Christianity which, for many today, has replaced denominational allegiance. So that I envisaged three possible futures. A dying fall for a sleeping Church, for Eliot's 'True Church ... wrapt in the old miasmal mist', the Church which 'can sleep and feed at once', which 'need never stir / to gather in its dividends'. (I confess it was a Church expiring while sleeping I had conjured up) as opposed, and this was my second future, to a Church reformed not least by the measures of the Paul and Morley Reports and, militant at last, doing battle for the souls of the massified cities of the land. And the third future I conceived of was the impotence and eventual death of the institutionalized Churches, reformed or unreformed, united or impenitently isolated, and the growth of a non-dogmatic Christian renewal which owed little or nothing to the ecclesiastical institutional tradition. The Jesus freak-out of the hippies and the growth of Jesus communes serve as warning notice of this possible future.

I grow convinced that this was altogether a simplistic view. Futures do not run together on parallel lines till one or other reaches a terminus and expires. They collide and alter course into something unpredictable. They debate, they battle. They may even turn back. So at the best we grapple with events which may never happen or may have consequences opposite to those we suppose ought to ensue. In all reverence one understands that the Church is a mystery and that the future is a mystery. One is conjoining a holy mystery and a secular mystery. It demands a humility not easy to come by to make predictions about it.

The first thing to be said is that the static Church, Eliot's old hippopotamus resting on the mud, is now a fiction. Even of the Church of Rome, it is no longer true. The Church of England may have resisted

299

formal reform, but the pressures on it are inexorable and they are felt first and most at micro-level. The best analogy is with church buildings. The tourist comes and exclaims with wonder at the antiquity of so many cathedrals and venerable churches. The past seems truly present. But it is only present because of continuous care. Cracks come, 'the years enfilade', stone rots, roofs leak, pillars sink, dry rot and the death watch beetle sneak in, fires burn! Only watchfulness prevents the death of the fabric and in time so much of it can be renewed or replaced that it is no longer the old building but a replica which will itself decay.

One sees the same inexorable pressures on church order and organization. Names may remain the same but roles, functions, status change. Even the sense of the nature and duty of the Church—the world Church—subtly alters in the Kremlins of church power. The old triumphalism is now gone or subdued, for instance. There is a renewal of the doctrine of the serving Church, even the *servant* Church which implies a deeper humility when to be a servant is what nobody wants, yet a servant Church which has to be distinguished from the *servile* Church.

David Edwards put his finger on some of the shifts when he asked in the remarkable swathe he cut through Christian dilemmas in *Religion and Change*[1] 'can Christianity be a community not a code?'

'We do not observe in many now the mood which made Dietrich Bonhoeffer defend the "Confessing" Church against the "German" Christians who compromised with Hitler: "Whoever knowingly cuts himself off from the Confessing Church in Germany cuts himself off from salvation." Even in Roman Catholicism there has been a profound change of tone between the defiant wartime Encyclical on the Church of Pius XII, *Corpus Christi Mysticum* (1943), and the Pastoral Constitution on the Church which was the central achievement of the Second Vatican Council. The Encyclical called Catholics to their own discipline ... and it called the world to a sanity which could be restored only by embracing the true Church; the Constitution, while abandoning no Roman Catholic claim, saw the Church as the fraternity of the faithful, almost all lay and including (in an ill-defined sense) even Christians who had not submitted to the Pope. The Constitution saw Christians, including ecclesiastical officers, as "holy" in the sense that they had been accepted by God; but they were sinners needing constant forgiveness and renewal. It saw the whole Church as "apostolic", for the whole Church was sent into the whole world to demonstrate the Gospel of love. What has survived the rebirth of the corporate emphasis has been the conviction that the Church is more than a voluntary association, for in its spirit-empowered fellowship it was intended by Jesus as the prolongation

---

[1] Hodder, London 1969, p. 282.

of his work. The Church which wrote the New Testament felt the power of its living Lord in its own life—and if Christianity is not to be reduced to rootless, shapeless democracy, the Lordship of Christ over the Church must be recovered for our time.'

'The power of the living Lord in its own life' is an eloquent tribute to that which moved the *early* Church. It was nothing if not charismatic, prophetic. It was not the legal embodiment of a tightly-hammered code. It worked spontaneously in an organization which was makeshift, improvised. It gave no thought to the difficulties it was piling up for future churchmen by failing to record precisely how it *did* work. In its view, in the shadow of the Second Coming, there were not going to be any future churchmen.

Every one contrasting that early Church of a reckless simplicity and freedom with the elaborate institutional frames of contemporary Churches is struck by the sheer institutional weight the latter carry. And the questions are asked—is not this weight smothering the mission of the Churches? And for me it raises the further questions—what does it mean for the Church to be an institution? and, what do institutions mean to culture? For there is the most damaging confusion here, which I have in the past made many efforts to expose.[2] I do not wish to traverse all that ground again but I must at least summarize the argument.

Cultures build themselves upon, incarnate themselves through, institutions. Man's supreme cultural problem is how to give form and permanence to his deepest insights and understandings. The poet knows full well that the line of a poem which flashes into his mind while waking at night will be lost to him unless presently written down. Only its fragrance will remain. The political theorist knows that unless his ideas can be given institutional shape they could be lost to posterity. The text-book example is the constitution of the United States which sets out to enshrine the theories of Locke, as expressed in the American Declaration of Independence, in the permanent legal structure of a state. Religions incarnate their divine commands and human insights in institutions— sacred scriptures, sacred liturgies, creeds and confessions, holy buildings, priests and teachers, forms of order, oversight, mission and all the paraphernalia of discipline, as well as the collection and trusteeship of funds and property. The institutional forms are protean. The institution is, or is intended to be, an instrument of the ideas which prevail in it.

---

[2] I gave an address on 'The Church as an Institution' to a World Council of Churches' Consultation on 'The Christian attitude to Money' at Bossey, Switzerland 1965. It was subsequently published in *Laity* and *The Journal of Ecumenical Studies* and appeared as a Prism Pamphlet, *The Church as an Institution*, 1967. Revised, it formed Chapter 6 of *The Death and Resurrection of the Church*, 'The Institutional and the Charismatic Church', Hodder, 1968. To this the reader is referred for a fuller exposition.

Because of that the institution is *present* to the world, it can usually be seen, or heard or felt. It communicates. The Church is present through its buildings, its services, literature and the labours of its officers. Some of its acts and artefacts become deeply symbolic. They communicate all that it stands for without words—the cross, the peal of church bells, the fume of incense. To assume that man can live without institutions to give substance to his insights and means to make them operable is to misunderstand both the institution and society. Think of Britain without parliament, a cash economy without banks, education without schools and universities and one sees de-institutionalization for the nonsense it is.

This does not mean that institutions are some sort of sacred perfection. For precisely their importance exposes them to misuse—idolization, exploitation, delusions of inviolability and so on. Then, institutions are power and power tends to corrupt and the ambitious tend to gravitate to where the power is. Everyone understands this as the cause of the loss of charisma in the second and third generations of a powerful new movement. But before one deals with that, it is necessary to comment on the misunderstanding of 'institution' in a semantic sense. Almost all the pejorative discussion of institutions centres round *big* institutions—Fords, or Unilever, the Trades Union Congress, the Roman Catholic Church, or the Communist Party of the USSR. But institutions do not have to be mega-organizations. They come in every size or shape. A good sociological definition would be any form of behaviour with a degree of permanence in society. So there is an institutional spectrum ranging from, say, Guy Fawkes' Day on the one hand through the six o'clock news on the BBC, and the morning paper, grace at meals, until finally we come to the monarchy and parliament at the other, the heavy, end. Society needs institutions. Christianity needs institutions. But they do not necessarily need the institutions they have got, in the shape that they have got them. Institutions are fragile. They can be changed. They can be abandoned.

Contemporary society, including the Churches, suffers from an institutional overload. Our contemporary society, because of the scientific and rational concepts which form its *Weltanschauung*, is peculiarly favourable to the rational, impersonal, objectivizing institution, and the more massive it is the more it seems to succeed: and the more it succeeds, the more it alienates. It is unfavourable to the small, local, intimate, spontaneous, ephemeral institution. The large organizations—Charles Reich is illuminating here—recruit and develop an élite and the élite identifies itself with the institution in which it has invested its future. What is best for the power and prestige, and perhaps wealth, of the élite is automatically assumed to be best for the institution's purposes. The élite then appears to outsiders, though never to itself, as manipulating the structures of the institution in its own interests. One might use the patronage system in the politics of the United States as an example. Or the pocket boroughs of British parliamentary history. Or the freehold and patronage system of the Church of England. Or the role of the Communist Party in Russia—an élite which totally excludes all others from power. But history is rife with examples of self-protecting élites and of blind and entrenched ones too, such as collapsing aristocracies.

In no case do we find a mega-institution without a professional servicing élite. Religions and armies down the millennia of human history and up to the present are the classical examples and Lewis Mumford in *The Myth of the Machine*[3] dealt mercilessly with some of the consequences of their effectiveness in the mechanization of man before the machine came long. However, what one is speaking about is not the institution as unserviceable to man, or as an enemy to humanity (which is often the case with military and politico-economic élites) but rather, as with the churches, suffering from organizational senility and proving incapable of the adaptations necessary in times of great change to restore the original serviceability. The fault may not be with the élite itself. Recruited to serve the institution one way, it may not be able to conceive of running it in another. The élite, with the institution, may be trapped in a situation it is incapable of changing. The legal situation of the Church of England is that incumbents are appointed only to legal parishes: they cannot be deployed according to mission or pastoral needs but only according to the legal grid. The consequences have already been described. Continued unaltered, the final consequence would be the total alienation of the Church from the forms and structures of society (parishes without population, populations without priests). When radical reforms are proposed one plea against them is that priests were ordained to serve a particular pattern of institution and it is not fair—a breach of contract!—to ask them to serve a quite different pattern. This illustrates the institutional dilemmas. They are peculiar to the Church of England but not dissimilar from those of the Church of Rome. A third dilemma, common to all Churches, remains. In a way it is the whole point of Bryan Wilson's *Religion in a Secular Society*. Societies discard institutions for which they have no further use, not usually by a death warrant, but by abandoning them. The élites resist this and find new justifications for the existence of the institution they serve or else retreat and themselves abandon the institution. Roman Catholic priestly 'dropouts' represent the latter process; arguments for secular Christianity, the former.

To sum up, institutions are humanly indispensable but contain no *human* guarantees of permanence. They are corruptible and constantly

---

[3] Secker and Warburg, London 1967.

in need of reform or adaptation. They come in every shape and form and are not to be defined solely as the heavy, over-built mega-organizations. What is imperative always is that one begins with the institution one has.

II.

In the last chapter I described Christian enterprises of an impressive freshness and spontaneity. But the point was made that they sprang from traditional church structures. The West London Chaplaincy produced new and flexible forms of Christian commitment, of ecumenical relations, liturgical experiment, and lay leadership in an extra-parochial situation, and independent of special buildings. The responsibility lay, nevertheless, with the Church of England.

The Taizé Community gave birth to a new form of monasticism, the vows and the style of which came straight from historic monasticism. Yet the community is turned to the world and works in the world and is an example of Christian devotion which has moved all Christianity. Its inspiration and leadership came from the French Reformed Church, traditionally anti-monastic.

Alongside these and similar enterprises lie the severely traditional forms of church order, ministerial deployment and parochial structures which have remained virtually unchanged down the centuries in the great world Churches in the West. It is upon these that the pressures grow inexorably. As far as the Church of England is concerned what I said about all this in *The Deployment and Payment of the Clergy* is still quite relevant.

I propose to show now, how these pressures are silently reshaping the Church and presenting us with alternative futures. I am concerned at this point with structures. But there are other pressures of as great importance—theological, philosophical, doctrinal, ecumenical, secular —which cannot for the moment be considered.[4] However, what has been said about institutions has taught us not to despise structures.

The principal pressures are, for the ministry, those deriving from falling recruitment, rising average age, potential decline in numbers through wastage, inadequate pay structure: for the dioceses and parishes, rising overall population, declining downtown and rural population, mobility and resettlement, falling church attendance, sharply rising diocesan and parochial costs, stationary or falling revenue, or revenue out of step with inflation.

Many of the consequences of these pressures have been described in earlier chapters, others I have not space to develop. What I want to do

---

[4] Cf. below 'The Lost Charisma'. I tried also to consider them in *Alternatives to Christian Belief*, Hodder, 1967.

is to show the effect of these pressures upon two contrasting dioceses, Hereford, the most rural in England, and Southwark, one of the most urban (and secular) and to draw conclusions for the future.

Some of the dilemmas of Southwark have already been analysed. A few points need to be made in contrast to Hereford. At the time of the Paul Report, Hereford diocese appeared to be in an ideal situation. Three-quarters of its newly-born infants were being baptized into the Church of England: in Southwark the rate was less than half. On Sunday attendances, confirmations, Easter communicants, expressed as a percentage of the population, Hereford topped all tables. Southwark was near the bottom. The impact of social change and urbanization on Hereford was slight. Southwark's population was declining, Hereford's was rising gradually. Hereford had one parish with over 10,000 population, Southwark had 71. In Hereford I discovered three parishes suffering traumatic change, and one I registered as decaying: Southwark had, respectively, 17 and 11. Hereford ordinations could just about meet its demands for parochial clergy; Southwark's were grossly deficient. Yet the problem is the same for both: how to reorganize pastorally to provide an adequate load and an adequate stipend for each parochial clergyman; how best to serve the changing society pastorally; how to provide for the growth of the extra-parochial ministry. In some cases, it goes even deeper—how to enable the Church to survive. The Battersea Deanery, already studied, provides an example.

Up to the Pastoral Measure, 1967, the Church of England was limited in the way it could adjust its parochial grid to the available men. A diocese could hold a living in suspension, it could subdivide a parish and so create new parishes; it could unite parishes or it could ask an incumbent to hold two or more parishes in plurality. The pastoral Measure, (see p. 111) provides more sweeping powers to reorganize by, for instance, suspending patronage and freehold, and creating team and group ministries. We are only at the beginning of the usefulness of the powers of this measure, for schemes take long to work out, consultation and legal procedures take even longer, and there are many casualties on the way. The Measure will not change the general directions of redeployment. It may simply mean that here and there individual incumbencies will be replaced by team ministries or reinforced by group ministries: in effect that the parishes will be larger in one way or another. Predictions, therefore, could be outstripped or surpassed. There will be many differences in reorganization between dioceses, for the wealth of the diocese rather than its actual mission need is often the final arbiter of the number of full-time clergy a diocese can sustain. It is a case of the devil take the hindmost. Nevertheless the repatterning I shall now try to show will be increasingly common to all dioceses.

The example I choose is a group of 22 livings in the Wye Valley which for fifty years of the last hundred formed the Hereford South

Deanery in which I myself have worked. The livings are still there though reduced to 19 but the deanery is extinct—the diocese has been reorganized. The group is entirely rural, stretching in a great arc of country along the Wye, approaching Hereford at one point, Ross-on-Wye, at another, and the Black Mountains and the Welsh Border at other places—and vast, over 60,000 acres or 100 square miles in area. Indeed, it is one of the most rural places in England, without a major town, a collection therefore of villages and hamlets linked by good roads. In Francis Kilvert's day—he lived higher up the river valley, at Clyro and Bredwardine—the area was well served by railways. For the rest private coaches, farmers' traps, village carriers and the horse had to serve. Now the railways are gone, the County buses are thinner on the roads than they used to be and cars are everywhere. Villages close to Hereford have swollen a little as dormitories: those more remote have suffered a decline. The area presents a picture of extraordinary stability compared, say, with Battersea Deanery. In 1873 there was only one parish with over 1,000 population, and three with populations of under 100 (70, 68, 45 respectively): in 1972 there were three parishes with 1,000 or over population and two parishes of under 100. The overall population 10,669 in 1873, has scarcely changed; in a century it has risen by under 2,000 (1972, 12,000 odd). It may rise another 2,000 by 1980 (my estimate). Hence one is not dealing with an area which has gone through traumatic social and environmental change. There are no motorways, no new towns, no vast industrial complexes, no parishes which untouched since Doomsday blossomed into 10,000 population overnight! The industry is still farming, some of the best in England.

In 1873 the deanery area (the deanery itself was not formed until 1923) provided a livelihood for 26 parochial clergy of whom four were curates. The figures had barely altered fifty years later. Fig. 7 opposite tells the story. There is a long period of clergy stability, from 1873 to 1937. The livings remain almost unchanged. What happens mostly is that the curates go. By 1937 few could afford them any more, and the smallest livings have been amalgamated or suspended, a process which continues to 1972. The ratio of clergy to population is 1:410 in 1873 and 1:800 in 1972—not a very significant change in all that time.

The rub comes with the forward projection. The diocese is acutely aware of two things, first the necessity to increase clergy stipends annually by at least the amount of the rise in the cost of living, and, second, the expected fall in the number of clergy from 1980 onwards. The latest figure for the number of full-time parochial clergy in the diocese is 166, which is about 75 per cent of the 1965 strength. On the basis of an annual inflationary rate in income of 5 per cent and in housing costs of 10 per cent, the parish quota will have to rise substantially each quinquennium to maintain even a slightly reduced clergy force (147) on fair pay. The 1972 Quota and Working Parish Expenses' of £52,500 would have to

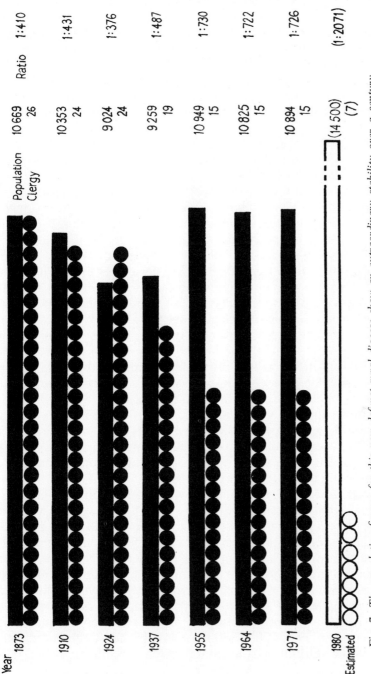

Year		Population Clergy	Ratio
1873		10 669 26	1:410
1910		10 353 24	1:431
1924		9 024 24	1:376
1937		9 259 19	1:487
1955		10 949 15	1:730
1964		10 825 15	1:722
1971		10 894 15	1:726
1980 Estimated		(14 500) (7)	(1:2071)

Clergy : Population ratio in the former South Hereford Deanery

Fig. 7. The population figures for this now defunct rural diocese show an extraordinary stability over a century. For 64 years of that 100, the ministerial pattern hardly alters. Even the diminished post-war pattern was unchanged for over 20 years. The problem comes with the rationalisation of the ministry the diocese must plan for the future. That will leave the area less than a third of its 1873 figure to serve an expanding population and so compels consideration of new forms of Christian ministry. The forward estimate of population for 1980 is my own, and conservative.

rise to £75,000 by 1975 if the diocese retained 167 clergy. To maintain the reduced figure (147) it would have to yield £108,000 in 1980 and £196,000 by 1985. Just these formidable obstacles have led in 1973 to a dialogue between the diocese and the parishes about the future shape of a rationalized ministry. The diocese has before it three schemes; the first would require the maintenance of a clergy force of 147, the second its reduction to 136, the third, the most severe, to 104.[5] Even the second scheme, the one more generally preferred by the knowledgeable, will cost the quota £81,000 in 1980 and £162,000 in 1985. If the parishes want to maintain the present distribution of clergy the financial challenge to them is enormous and probably insuperable.

In the area of the defunct deanery just described the number of clergy will be reduced to 7 by the second scheme, 5 or 6 by the most stringent. There will be a resident priest in each of the major villages and no priest at all in any of the minor villages. The case will certainly be argued for building up church life in every major village so that it can pull in the faithful from all the outlying places even if it means organizing parish cars or buses. It will mean more intensive Christian activity and less sleepy traditionalism about worship. The major villages will have to seek to become church strongholds. But what of the minor ones? Quite a few churches will eventually close. Others will limp along with the occasional services. The loss of a priest or of a church must certainly mean a further falling-off in the number of the faithful. The presence of a supplementary or non-stipendiary priest or of a retired man or lay readers might ease the transition. Best of all, with or without a priest, would be the presence of an active lay house group resolved to keep the church (as a brotherhood of the faithful, not necessarily as a building) alive by meeting and communion in each deprived area. Whether Anglicans of the countryside are yet ready for this break with a long tradition of passivity remains to be seen.

If Hereford Diocese has its problems, what then of Southwark? Again the problem is how to provide for enough men and women who are properly paid for a population of over two million. In 1971 the strength of the full time parochial staff of the Diocese was 289 Incumbents and 196 curates and lay workers: a total of 485 against a requirement of 525. In round figures the cost of these men and women and a handful of diocesan officials was £560,000. The Church Commissioners provided under half that sum, leaving the rest to be raised by parishes with the slender help of a few trusts. But the projection just for 1972 showed a remarkable jump. The cost rose to £675,000, a further £54,000 had to be raised from the parishes, in addition to the quota which was already high. The

---

[5] In 1873 the number of parochial clergy alone was 429: in addition there seem to have been 20 full time clergy on the Cathedral Staff. *The Hereford Diocesan Church Calendar and Clergy List*, 1873, Hereford, E. K. Jakeman, pp. 51 ff.

dilemma was clear—either increase the cost by about 7 per cent and increase the burden already placed on the parishes or deny the diocese the staff it needs or the clergy and lay workers the stipends they ought to receive. This was the dilemma for 1972: by extrapolation from the Hereford situation it requires little imagination to see what the situation could be in 1975 or 1980. In these examples is the point of the argument. Inexorable pressures can force upon a diocese the most stringent re-organization. In Hereford and Southwark the finances of parish, diocese and Church Commissioners determine the frame. Southwark is conscious that it is understaffed, Hereford is moved by the consideration that it must offer men a full time ministry. In times of threatened clergy shortage and when there is that great disparity between rural and urban deploy-ment of clergy which I have already discussed it cannot excuse the under-employment of priests.

Even faced with the facts about the future assembled in the many reports before General Synod, a diocese need not respond in the manner of Hereford (unless General Synod comes across with a national plan) until it faces the pinch.[6]

Of course the retrenchment of which the Hereford South Deanery is an example has been challenged. Colin O. Buchanan has argued in *The Job Prospects of the Anglican Clergy*[7] that the findings of the Archbishops' Advisors on the Church's needs and resources about the potential wastage of clergy are hopelessly at sea.[8] The effect of this official expecta-tion of shortage of clergy has been to hasten schemes of reorganization (and the suspension of livings which is a necessary preliminary) and so to produce an actual shortage of jobs in the period up to 1982. One effect, he thinks, is that curacies, which up to the present have been running at about four years will then run to seven or eight years to the psychological distress of the men concerned. The whole campaign to train supplemen-tary priests (Auxiliary Pastoral Ministry) is a mistake. So would be the ordination of women on *pragmatic* grounds. He would limit the annual intake of ordinands and raise the standards of entry. His main point is that incumbents will not move out of the ministry fast enough to enable the curates to be promoted to their livings. There will be a block. Colin Buchanan is possibly right in supposing that the wastage will be rather

---

[6] Nicolas Stacey would not necessarily have us admire Hereford for its courage, however. 'The Diocese of Hereford', he writes (in *Who Cares?*, p. 256) 'had a population that was smaller than the Deanery of Greenwich but which had two bishops, two archdeacons, a dean of the Cathedral, three full-time canons and 218 full-time clergy. As most of the money for the stipends of the clergy comes from the Church Commissioners, the financial subsidy from headquarters to Hereford would have been about four times as great as that received by Greenwich with only sixty clergy.' His figures are a little out of date but he makes his point.

[7] Grove Books, Bramcote, Notts., 1972.

[8] Cf. *The Church's Needs and Resources*, Sixth Report, CIO 1972.

more slow than we supposed. But come the wastage must. After a battle, the statisticians may get the figures right. On a different view there is a genuine shortage of another kind. Upon the basis of a statistical exercise[9] made by Dr Leonard Wilson when he was Bishop of Birmingham, a rational deployment of clergy according to population, brought up to date, of which the broad principal was one parochial clergyman for every 5,000 population shows a deficiency (1969) of 3,088 clergy![10] On the basis of the *existing* deployment of clergy a questionnaire sent by Colin Buchanan to 24 diocesan bishops revealed that only seven bishops expected a shortage within the next decade. The remainder expected a sufficiency or an abundance. But it is one thing to make forecasts on the basis of the present distribution of clergy and quite another to make them on the basis of demographic priorities.

The governing factor in these matters will certainly be financial stringency which may create in Buchanan's words 'only very slender job prospects'; nevertheless reorganization could come for sociological or ecumenical reasons and be planned in advance of any crisis or irrespective of it.

The Rev. Leslie Harman, when responsible for the sociological department of the diocese of Southwark, foresaw the inevitable contraction in the number of church buildings the diocese could sustain, and in the clergy force, and himself devised a scheme for a more effective pastoral strategy in the light of this.

His study, *The Church in Greater London*,[11] begins with a very proper, today even orthodox, sociological analysis of the urban scene.

He explains what London is in a statutory sense—an area of some 616 square miles with a population of about eight million, administered by the Greater London Council, The Corporation of the City of London and thirty-two London Boroughs with an average population of 250,000 each. But he says this is not the way to understand London which has to be seen socially and humanly as cast into other less formal groupings, which he calls environmental areas.

The largest of these is a natural grouping (which the French sociologist, Fernand Boulard, called a *zone humaine*) 'a cluster of smaller units, usually contained within natural or artificial barriers like rivers and railways ... oriented towards a major centre' and the area in which most of the people live, work, go to school, shop and find their recreational and cultural interests. Below the *natural groupings* he speaks first of localities which should be 'areas of belonging', distinct and indivisible population clusters, with which the citizen identifies. The *locality*, in the London scene, can be of any size, from 6,000 to 25,000. Below the locality

---

[9] *The Deployment and Payment of the Clergy*, pp. 272–4.
[10] *The Church of England Year Book, 1971–72*, CIO, 1971.
[11] Southwark Diocesan Department of Religious Sociology, 1968.

is the *neighbourhood*—something of the size of three-hundred families or 1,000 persons (the village within the town, in fact). These, he argues, are the true social units of municipal structure to which the Church should relate its own pastoral (parochial) organization for greater effectiveness. 'In the average parish of around 10,000 assorted souls, the total population is too large and the worshipping congregation is too small for there ever to be, in any real sense, "a synthesis of the great functions of the Church", worship, mission and social action.'

Taking and adapting terms from Dr Gilbert Cope of the Institute for the Study of Worship and Architecture, Leslie Harman speaks of the ministry of the diocese functioning through specific 'church stations':

1. *The Christian Centre*—which serves the borough with which the deanery should be co-extensive. The Christian centre should be if possible a church of historic interest, making an architectural statement of divine existence and action, at the heart of the borough—of course near the Town Hall. It should be the Church's civic presence and combine such necessities as an office, an information bureau, bookstall, exhibition space, coffee bar and so forth.

2. *The Worship Centre*—should be the church and information centre plus activity centre of the *natural grouping*. Again, if possible, a good building, symbolic of the Church's presence. It would be primarily a place of worship but also the centre of the team or group ministry serving the *natural grouping*. Leslie Harman speaks of it as 'the central church of the New Parish'—a term he prefers to major parish. 'All the inhabitants of the New Parish would normally come here for the occasions of baptism, confirmation, marriage and burial.'

3. *Parochial Units*—'The other churches operating within the structure would be scheduled as parochial units. Normally there would be one to each locality. Each parochial unit should, in its own manner, be the Christian presence in its own locality. Whereas, however, the central church (Worship Centre) should assemble and present a comprehensive Christian programme, the parochial units should diversify and, as the Pastoral Measure has it, "have regard to the traditions, needs and characteristics of individual (localities)". The staff would "live out" in these units and each member of the staff, whatever his speciality or function in the structure, would have his own "cure" and be pastorally responsible for his own people.'[12] The Parochial Units could be of four types: (i) pastoral units, (ii) specialist and sectional units, (iii) house units, (iv) associated units. In other words, they would not function just as parish churches.

---

[12] Op. cit. p. 44.

Leslie Harman finally sees the whole structure as a molecular pattern of pastoral care as the diagram opposite shows very plainly.[13]

Of course, the scheme is purely ideal and will never be applied as it is to Southwark Diocese or any other. It is very schematic, and Leslie Harman is now working it out practically and flexibly in Peterborough Diocese in terms of ecumenical team and group ministries. Then it is open to criticism on the grounds that it is not at all certain what the *parochial unit* is supposed to be. If it is intended to be the Anglican presence in the locality from which the resident priest exercises a personal ministry, then it would turn out to be the existing parish church with some higher liturgical functions (e.g. marriage) taken from it. One definition of a parochial unit as a pastoral unit (p. 45) makes it just that. If, on the other hand it was a youth centre, a geriatric unit, a prison or an armed forces chaplaincy, the carrying-on of a local pastoral ministry from that base has an air of improbability. But when Leslie Harman says about the parochial unit that 'what is wanted today is a personal ministry unencumbered with maintenance problems, building projects and mortgages, being entirely free and flexible to serve the people where they are and as they need', he clearly intends the dismantling of much of the heavy 'plant' in the shape of traditional under-used parish churches, parsonages, church halls, and the substitution of something much smaller and less expensive such as a flat for a priest, a small multi-purpose meeting room shared with other denominations, the use of an office. It is only *this* sense of the parochial unit that gives his plan significance if it is to be part of a team ministry running a major parish based on a definable community. And it must be said too that this molecular structure, going down to house units, is the type which the many new town ministries seem to propose. Depending on the size of the town, they aim at no more than one or two symbolic buildings where the full traditional liturgical glory may be displayed while for the work in the localities and neigh- bourhoods, the small, intimate pastoral centre (or 'unit') is preferred. It could be, or should be, a room or hall for worship shared with other denominations, together with a counselling room, an office, perhaps space for a bookstand and a display. It could be associated with a group of ecumenical flats. It could, at a pinch, be no more than a 'house unit'— in less formal terms, a room occasionally available in someone's house or flat.

Planning authorities are not merely helpful, they are usually enthusiastic about church provision. Access to worship is one of the social amenities they are bound to provide to humanize their brick and mortar wastes. Their traditional procedure though has been to offer denominations a choice of sites and to leave it to them as to what they

---

[13] Diagram from *The Church in Greater London*, Leslie Harman, Southwark Diocesan Department of Religious Sociology, 1968.

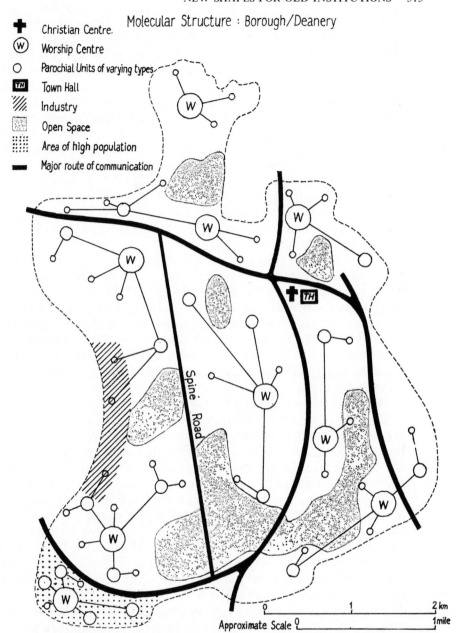

Molecular Structure : Borough/Deanery

✝ Christian Centre.
Ⓦ Worship Centre
◯ Parochial Units of varying types
🔳 Town Hall
▨ Industry
▦ Open Space
⋮⋮ Area of high population
▬ Major route of communication

Spine Road

Approximate Scale

Fig. 8. *This is adapted from Leslie Harman's diagram, Fig. 1, in* The Church in Greater London *(1968). Its strength is that it shows, albeit idealistically, how the Church's institutions could be adapted to serve and strengthen real communities. Its weakness lies in the ambiguities attaching to parochial units. Are they churches or something altogether less ambitious? The development of Harman's ideas is to be found in* The Church and Planning, *an exploratory essay, The Diocesan Development Unit, Hardingstone, Northampton, 1973.*

do. What every new town needs is an *ecumenical* building committee for the shared pastoral units to become the standard provision. The practice in the past in new building areas, it hardly needs to be said, has been for denominations to build where they wanted or were offered sites, and in independence of each other's needs, and sometimes it has seemed almost at random: a senseless, expensive proliferation! Harlow New Town is a conspicuous victim. It has 32 churches chasing 80,000 people and new ones are being built. A report, *Evangelical Strategy in the New Towns*[14] described the results of all that building in spiritual and pastoral terms as disappointing and argued that the Church of England, with its rigid, throttling framework of state law, its parochial system involving a multiplicity of legal rights, its endowments, benefices, and freehold ministries, was not well suited to develop the flexible pattern of church life demanded by new town development. Dr Gilbert Cope writes this about the possibilities:

'A New Town Development Corporation accepts a wide-ranging responsibility for "social amenities" in the new population zone which it brings into existence. The degree of responsibility varies in much the same way as that which operates under existing local authorities, but in a New Town, as is evidenced by the appointment of a Social Development Officer (SDO), there is a much more positive approach to the total social provision. Of this total amenity the churches form a significant part—whatever may be their additional significance in other dimensions of experience they have a contribution to make in the related fields of culture, welfare and recreation.

'Development Corporations do not, of course, make direct financial grants to churches, nor do they undertake the building of ecclesiastical premises, but they do offer sites at a fraction of the commercial value and in general they are prepared to make available some of their community buildings for church use—especially in the early stages of development. The churches are also justified in approaching a corporation concerning the possibility of modifying one or more of their houses for use not only as a residence for a "minister" but, also, for counselling and small meetings etc. (e.g. Communicare House at Killingworth).

'Church authorities which contemplate the provision of any kind of community centre (e.g. pre-school nursery, youth centre, old peoples' club, etc.) would be well-advised to consult the SDO about the discretionary funds which might be made available to assist such a project. In such circumstances, too, the Corporation's planning and design teams might be willing to co-operate without making professional charges.'[15]

---

[14] Evangelical Alliance, London 1971.

[15] *Christian Ministry in the New Towns*, Edited by Gilbert Cope, Institute for the Study of Worship and Religious Architecture, Birmingham University, 1967. Appendix, pages unnumbered.

By 1990 the new towns will house three million people. The presence of a more flexible, less legally ossified type of ministry in these important new urban centres would constitute a breakthrough which would have exemplary influence elsewhere. It is important therefore, that it be known what kind of help would be available from Development Corporations and other official sources to achieve it. It has to be seen as a considerable economy if it reduces the number of heavy buildings and upper middle class parsonages which would otherwise have to be built. The Church of England at present spends annually about £17 millions on old and new ecclesiastical buildings.[16] These are costs most subject to inflationary pressures and it needs no prophet to say that they will mount sharply. Economic pressure alone will compel the Church to rationalize its building programme in new areas and to close down redundant churches and dispose of the sites in older areas, town or country.

All that I have said about the small group church and the house church now becomes relevant. These may bring the Church alive at the grass roots where it has never been alive. Equally, they may keep the Church alive and provide a platform for renewal where the Church has had to withdraw its formal presence, and can offer the community only an occasional visit and occasional service from a multi-church priest. Further, what seemed to be defeat may lead to a more real and more local Christianity. Anglican life never seems so dead as when the priest and his few surviving faithful in a fading church go somnambulistically through the liturgical motions. Yet I spoke only of the loss of a *stipendiary* priest. The new provisions for the training of men for the auxiliary ministry can mean that any small Anglican community can have its resident priest among them. He would be fully ordained, but he would not be paid and on weekdays would work at his job, be it farmer, teacher, delivery man or civil servant.

Let us be clear as to what it all adds up to. A future of retrenchment is already developing for the Church of England (and for almost all other Churches too). It is dictated by social and economic realities beyond the Church's control. But this very stream-lining, rationalizing process could be the basis of renewal if it led also to a revival of small group and house unit worship and a localized Christian fellowship in the development of which the auxiliary ministry could play an important part. The small, face-to-face group is as theologically as it is socio-psychologically sound in relation to impersonal Churches in an impersonal society. The retrenchment is bound to come. But the small group Christianity—the

---

[16] 'At a time when the total annual cost of keeping the Church's buildings going is of the order of £17 million and represents such a high fraction of annual parochial expenditure, there would seem to be every reason to scrutinize the use made of these buildings and resolutely to shed those that are redundant.' *The Church's Needs and Resources*, Sixth Report, 1972, CIO, p. 23.

new Christian presence of which Charles Davis conceived over against the monolithic feudal Roman Church—is *not* bound to come, or if it does come need not have any Anglican associations at all and be no worse for that. The small group Christianity is simply an option open to the Church of England in a future already developing in a way which can only encourage it; it is the response the challenge demands. It does not follow that the Church will accept this opportunity to remake itself at grass roots. It is heavily clergy-dominated and may prefer never to risk that clerical primacy by encouraging a Christian spontaneity of the kind that would involve a new life style for the clergy themselves. Clergy who *patronise* the laity, whose approach is *de haut en bas*, can only succeed in smothering initiatives with a treacle of unctuousness. This does not mean that the laity are theologically informed: even their scriptural knowledge is shaky. Nothing can be taken for granted. Any flowering of the small group life ought to go along with social and theological training. And with clergy re-training too, for the new kind of world their theological colleges never told them about.

III.

There is one more point to be made about the possible futures. It is that other future, not as yet seriously regarded by the Church of England, in which it disappears. Of course that disappearance is always possible sociologically speaking. The slow processes of erosion have been visible for a long time, but it would be melodramatic to speak of them as disastrous. But slow processes have a way of turning into fast ones quite suddenly, they show an exponential curve. The Church of England, just able to adapt itself to the present rate of change, would be deeply shaken by a much faster one. All its institutions, from Parochial Church Councils to General Synod, from curacies to archbishoprics, are based on expectations of stability—that the Church more or less as known will always be there, that there will always be valuable jobs to do and worship to conduct, children to confirm, collections to count. But what does it imply if we take seriously what Dennis Ede, Rector of the successful Hodge Hill multipurpose church, threw off almost casually in his account of his church's work?[17] 'It is quite obvious that the types of service which are dispensed at present will fade out with the departure of the 1970 congregation. By 2000 AD what we understand as worship will surely have disappeared.' And with it the parochial clergyman's *raison d'être*—that above all which he is paid to do?

This possibility must always be before us if we take seriously the pace of change in life styles and human consciousness in the contemporary

---

[17] *Hodge Hill—St Philip and St James's: The Multipurpose Church*, op. cit., p. 48.

world: and if we in fact face the growth of a non-institutional Christianity which turns its back on establishment churches.

We have to consider 'disappearance' in another, ecumenical, sense as the voluntary melting of the Church of England into the larger Christian fellowship of the whole world, which would mean the surrender of its insularity, nationalism and all those idiosyncrasies which, for so many of its officers and members, are upheld as the beginning and end of the Christian faith. On the world scene, the Church of England can be counted both a minority church and a provincial church: its rise to be a world church is the accident of the paths the empire builders trod and the heterogeneous territories they annexed. It will bear the marks of that curious imperial development to the end. There are 65·4 million Anglicans in the world. Just under half of them (28 million) are in England and these are mostly 'affiliated Anglicans' of whom one in three are confirmed: there are only 100,000 Anglicans of any sort on the Continent of Europe, the nearest land mass![18] The overwhelming majority of the rest are in ex-imperial territories. Even in the United States with whom historic relations, language and culture are close, and the Episcopal Church at 6,450,000 adherents is the largest Anglican Church outside England, the Episcopal allegiance is far below that of Protestant denominations generally.

On the world scene Christians constitute the dominant religion, mustering remarkably more than 1,000 million souls. Nearly sixty per cent of them (581,000,000) are Roman Catholic: Protestants (316,000,000) make up about thirty per cent. So that about one in five Protestants, and one in sixteen Christians of all kinds is an Anglican.[19]

The peculiar world virtue of Anglicanism is not in its members but in the bridge it maintains between Catholic and Protestant practices and doctrines, which may decide its future. In ancient dominions such as India, Pakistan and Ceylon, Anglicanism has already been superseded by indigenous, united churches. And this may be, and ought to be its fate elsewhere, Bishop Bayne argues:

'The vocation of Anglicanism is, ultimately, to disappear. That is its vocation precisely because Anglicanism does not believe in itself but it believes only in the Catholic Church of Christ; therefore it is for ever restless until it finds its place in that one Body.'[20]

---

[18] *Membership, Manpower and Money in the Anglican Communion*; a Survey of 27 Churches and 360 Dioceses, Anglican Consultative Council, 21 Chester Street, London, S.W.1.

[19] Professor Geoffrey Parrinder's revised figures for the 1972 edition of *Great World Atlas* (Reader's Digest). These figures show Islam, 515 million, Hinduism 420 million and Buddhism 230 million, as runners-up. Confucianism and Taoism have not been given a value.

[20] From David Edwards, '107 Years of the Lambeth Conference', Church Quarterly, July 1968.

Michael Hurley, S. J. quotes this in *Irish Anglicanism 1869–1969*[21] and follows it with a passage from a former Church of Ireland Primate, Dr McCann, who said in a Presidential Address to General Synod in 1966 that:

'Denominationalism is out-moded. Sectarianism is no longer relevant. The major issues of evangelization in a secular and largely non-Christian world completely eclipse the relatively minor subjects debated by our forefathers.'

Michael Hurley goes on to make the interesting point that the Church of Ireland somehow fails to understand its limitations in Ireland as a minority denomination, because it is still psychologically and spiritually overshadowed by the Church of England from which it was broken in 1869. This makes it inward-looking in Ireland, and content to follow in its own development the initiatives of England.

One wonders whether something like this has not happened to the Church of England. Ever since the break of the sixteenth century the Church of England has had to face the immensity of the Church of Rome. She could never hope, except in the lands controlled by the English crown, to challenge that formidable rival, nor hope to extinguish her power even in the homeland. Neither was she able to shut out continental reformed Christianity from her shores. But Anglicanism had no corresponding hold on the continent of Europe: assailed by continental religious forces, she was never able to reply. No state in Europe was ever prepared to adopt Anglicanism even for purposes of diplomatic war on Rome. Much of the spread overseas was less by the will and spirit of the Church than because settlers took their religion with them. A Church doubly assailed, and always in danger of being penetrated by what it conceived to be alien religious ideologies was bound to grow defensive walls and to accustom itself to looking inwards. The very legality of the Church of England becomes explicable in the light of this. The law is the court of last resort to prevent the Church of England being torn in two by the continental tug-of-war. In another way the high defensive walls, though they did not prevent it, were a discouragement to looking much beyond it. The future of world Christianity, the role of the world Church, was something which, *de facto*, had to be left to Rome. The crown supremacy was the mark of abdication from the European and international roles of Christianity. The Christianity of a pope was capable of confronting the world: the Christianity of a king of England was by definition prohibited from doing so. It was too much the sign of nationalism. It could be propagated within its own *imperium*, or to new

---

[21] Essays on the role of Anglicanism in Irish life presented to the Church of Ireland on the occasion of the centenary of its Disestablishment by a group of Methodist, Presbyterian, Quaker and Roman Catholic scholars. Ed. Michael Hurley, S.J. 'The Future' p. 211, et seq.

continents such as Africa where there were as yet no indigenous nations in the European sense. Its dilemma as an imperial export is shown most clearly in Ireland and the tragic consequences of this are still with us—a politically 'dominant' Church of Ireland was seen simply as an instrument of oppression by the native Irish; its alien presence increased their devotion to an older, richer Catholic culture. The importation of Protestant settlers to the northern counties which constitute Ulster made the religio-national rift irreparable.

Some similar problems befell many of the continental reformed Churches: like the Church of England, they were nationalized. They depended on the favour of princes. But there always was a continental reformed Christianity which recognized itself but did not easily see Anglicanism as part of itself after the breach between the Church of England and the more radical protestants and puritans. One can, however, speak of times when the presence of the Church of England within the larger Catholic Church would have had a decisive influence historically. Over the development of North America and Africa: over against the rise of a communism of civil and religious terror in Russia for example; against pagan National Socialism in Germany: in the prevention of the genocide of the Jews during the Second World War, over which the (Italianate) Roman Church has an unhappy record; in Ulster where, since 1969, the Anglican record has been one of impotence. It is also true to say that Anglicanism is quite impervious to any sense of guilt here.

'Another sequel to the rise of English Protestantism,' A. G. Dickens writes,[22] 'was its capacity for expansion, both in territories mainly populated by Britons and among hitherto non-Christian peoples. The English and Scottish Reformations came to resemble an intense source of light projected across time and falling upon great screens of space. From one viewpoint this process can be regarded as an ideological function of imperialism, yet it could also display in abundance the finest Christian missionary qualities....'

After speaking of the social failures of British Protestantism—particularly over slavery and the sub-human conditions of the industrial revolution—A. G. Dickens says that, despite them, 'Anglicanism and the major Nonconformist churches assumed the status of world-religions. For better or worse, British Protestantism placed its ineradicable stamp upon the image of Britain throughout the world. Most strikingly it showed its capacity to give birth to self-governing Churches, even as secular imperialism created self-governing dominions.' And he pays particular tribute to Thomas Cranmer's Prayer Book as a cultural unifier. He could have added King James's Bible.

---

[22] *The English Reformation*, p. 336.

'The intense light' fell most powerfully on the United States where the Nonconforming Protestants of Britain swept the board. Baptists and Methodists left the Episcopalians trailing. The religious freedom which was so strongly its ethos entered so fully into American life that it was recently discovered to be unconstitutional for the children in public schools to say the Lord's Prayer together. Protestant world status finally found expression in the World Council of Churches, but in this too the British initiatives, from the 1910 Edinburgh Conference on, were important and American pressures and resources irresistible. Much of the British and American search for unity stemmed from the vigour of Protestant missionary enterprise the world over, a transforming agency which among other successes woke nascent nationalisms.

So, the Anglicanism we have studied is far from being solely an insular phenomenon and in its world dimension must be seen as one element in a spreading global Protestantism which has curiously parcelled out the planet into religious spheres of influence. The death of Anglicanism? It is easy to speak of the death of Anglicanism, of the necessity for its death, that it might be resurrected in the life of the larger Church. But lip-service does not accomplish the act, and religio-cultural phenomena do not just lie down and die. They are extraordinarily tough: they have a high survival value. Even if it is important that the Church of England should die to bring to birth a greater Church, it will be necessary to unravel a whole complex of law first, and here it has no courage at all. One reason why full and immediate unity with Methodism was not proposed, but unity in two stages was favoured—though even that failed—was that it was impossible to unite legally and ministerially the two separate institutions without considerable changes in the protective laws. What, for instance, of patronage, freehold?

Finally, what is this tough, legal, historical, organizational muddle about? It is not worth keeping alive, not worth all the cost of doing so, just for the picturesque thing it is. It is only what it is, and worth saving, for what it stands for: for that tremendous and humbling assertion that it is the vehicle of God's mercy and redemption into the world.

It would be impious to prescribe a future for it if it no longer believed in that. One ought to pray for its swift dissolution.

So there is, after all, the matter of faith.

PART FIVE

The Lost Charisma

'We have ecclesiastized the Deity.'
> The Archbishop of York to General Synod,
> February 1973

'Certainly for Christians to be concerned with how God confers grace, that is how He rescues, replenishes and recreates, is a worthwhile interest; but is it conceivable that in this saving activity He conforms to the niceties of formal logic? Too much discussion between Christian denominations smacks of an introversion which clouds rather than illuminates the really important issues which confront them all. When the house is burning one does not waste precious water revivifying the aspidistra.'
> Archdeacon Edward Carpenter, in a letter on the validity of orders, *The Times*, 19 January 1973

'You came upon the followers of Jesus on the first Whit Sunday and swept them off their feet, so that.they found themselves doing what they thought they never had it in them to do.'
> *Contemporary Prayers for Public Worship*

ONE

Lord or Saviour?

A WORK on *The Future of the Christian Church*[1] by two great Christian leaders who are also theologians, Arthur Michael Ramsey and Léon-Joseph Suenens, is an event with significance for the theme of this book. At the present time, Cardinal Suenens writes, 'the Church is like a ship exposed to every wind and battling through a sort of Bay of Biscay. One reason for this situation has nothing to do with the ship—it is caused by the condition of the sea. The Church exists in and for the world and as such lies open to the influence of the unprecedented changes which the world is experiencing. But there is also another reason, which belongs to the condition of the ship itself, not in some dry-dock but out in the open sea.'[2] (We might add, with some passengers having refused the voyage as unnecessary and others daily jumping overboard!)

In a compelling opening speech to the debate of the General Synod on Union with the Methodists, on 3 May 1972, Michael Ramsey spoke of the fading credibility of the Church of England and of the period of darkness it would enter if it could not consummate a marriage it itself had proposed. The period of darkness has come upon it and reunion movements of national significance are dead in England for a decade or two,[3] for the Church of England no longer dares advance them, and no other communions would feel confident enough to initiate them to a Church unable to deliver its seventy-five per cent on the appointed day. 'The fact remains that the Church of England still ministers in a variety of ways to more than two-thirds of the English people, and it is therefore quite unrealistic to speak of Christian unity in such a situation if Anglicans decline commitment.'[4]

---

[1] SCM Press, London 1971.

[2] Prologue, p. 1.

[3] The Union of the Congregational Church in England and Wales and the Presbyterian Church of England to make the United Reformed Church was inaugurated in Westminster Abbey on 5 October 1972. Apart from the role of the Abbey this was not an enterprise in which the Church of England had any standing.

[4] Trevor Beeson, 'Anglicans Now Face Stormy Seas', *The Christian Century*, 24 May 1972.

Yet this shabby setback is only one element in the greater incredibility of the Church—the whole Church—in the modern world with which in a way it was the task of the joint authors of *The Future of the Christian Church* to deal.

They certainly seek to do so, yet as their lectures were to a conference of Episcopal bishops in New York, their hearers were predisposed to accept, even to be comforted by, the special ecclesiastical language they spoke. Cardinal Suenens, in a lecture entitled, 'Christ, the Church, and the World' defined the relation in this way, 'Christ is in and for the world; Christ is against the world: and Christ is beyond the world.' Theologically, this is unexceptionable—Christ incarnate and immanent, in particular through his Church; Christ as judging the world; Christ, in the Godhead as transcending the world. Are they *credible* statements to the modern world? Both divines agree that the Gospel must be preached to the modern world and at the same time they make their preaching more difficult by speaking of the faith as an encounter with the living God and not a matter of theologizing, philosophizing or publicizing. (Though these aids are not altogether to be despised.) Just what does *encounter* with the living God mean to the world?

Suenens goes on, 'Christ is in and for the world; the living, life-centre which gives reality its subsistence and direction. In the letter to the Colossians, St Paul, quoting an ancient hymn, speaks of Christ as the "Image of the unseen God, the first-born of all creation; for in him were created all things in heaven and on earth ... all things were created through him and for him. Before anything was created, he existed and he holds all things in unity".'[5] This is the Logos doctrine of St John's Gospel which Suenens naturally also quotes. His vision proclaims Christ *Pantokrator*, realizing the vocation of Adam—'Man crowned with glory and honour and ruling the whole world.' Thus, the Cardinal says, 'Christ is present in the world outside the physical limits of the Church ... But I would go a step further: Christ is presiding at creation, but creation is not a static thing accomplished once and for all; it is a dynamic process still on the way to completion'[6] ... in which man in his bodily and social reality and his every act modifies the reality experienced by himself and his fellows. God (and God now replaces Christ as the term for the creator) is not just creator, *he is creating*. The creative process is continuous. 'I have always found very attractive that phrase of Gabriel Marcel in which he says that: "Human life is like a sentence which cannot be understood until the final word is spoken". The creation of man in the image of God means that man is himself a creator. He collaborates in creation: it is in him but not without him that God's

---

[5] Ibid. p. 64.
[6] Ibid. p. 65.

intentions become fully realized within creation . . . But I would go even further: in Christ the world has not only been created but recreated.'[7]

This is fine Pauline theologizing and I will say in a moment in what sense I interpret it. But it is not credible theologizing for the modern world. It is not credible theologizing within the Church; it does not speak for the Church's view of itself or of its Christology at congregational level. It is itself part of the credibility gap. Some intimations of this Christology move parts of the Roman Church, and the followers of Teilhard de Chardin in all Churches are excited by it. Anglican theologizing moves at a more pedestrian pace.

But first the incredibility to the modern world. It does not, intellectually and at most articulate levels, conceive of the universe as the product of some vast, unseen platonic demiurge, functioning as its original creator and continuous promotor. It would return an agnostic answer to the *origins* of the universe, which would still be agnostic even if it spoke of 'steady state' and 'big bang' theories. As to the progress of the universe and in particular the evolution of living forms on this planet it would not concede a concerted plan or teleological intention but rather, in all probability, the gigantic lottery or game of bingo which is the serious theorem of Jacques Monod's *Chance and Necessity*.[8] From the sheer, blind operation of chance came, in time, all that we have, this theory runs. It is an intellectual doctrine which dismisses the glorious divine drama of which Suenens writes. The world simply is not seen that way. If a purpose is admitted it is more likely to be spoken of as Bergson's *élan vital* or Bernard Shaw's life-force (Colin Wilson is a modern proponent of this). Even Teilhard de Chardin's evolution is expressed in terms which suggest evolution proceeding by an inner will rather than through the operations of a Platonic demiurge. As Charles Raven used rather to suppose, the birth of Christ was a moment, a dramatic leap, in that human evolution. If a deist position *is* accepted then, of course, it is *God* who is the creator *ex nihil* and not Christ. The stern monotheism of the Old Testament knows nothing of Christ in a Christian sense, though it anticipates a messiah in a Jewish sense. A messiah is not God.

A certain precision attaches to the life and passion of Jesus. The Gospels, despite accretions, pin down his life for us with more than general statements. He is the fearless prophet, born at such and such a time and done to death, who attracts and repels men. Recognition of his divinity comes very slowly and triumphs perhaps only in the post-Resurrection Church. It is still debated. It is no denial of his divinity to insist upon the encounter with Jesus as an encounter with a real historical

---

[7] Ibid. p. 66.

[8] Collins, London, 1972. It is important to read R. C. Zaehner on Jacques Monod and Teilhard de Chardin, in *Drugs, Mysticism and Make-Believe* (Collins, London 1972) particularly in Chaps. 1 and 2.

figure. Everything begins there. The more we insist upon the historicity of Jesus, seeing him as a man of his time, the harder it is to stand upon his divinity. *It is still harder psychologically to project him backwards in time as the Logos, the creator.* It is not just that even the theologians continue to dispute about the nature of the Christ, and what we mean by his dual nature.[9] It is that the roles we are asked to accept are so different that the imagination boggles. The creator looked upon his handiwork and saw that it was good. We are not told that the Incarnate Son came to earth to endorse that commendation, rather the contrary—he sought to wean men from their idolatry of the creation. Only God was good. Everything else failed man. The Son who seeks to overcome the world, and especially the death that had plagued it from the beginning, hardly fits the role of the Great Architect of creation. The creator is better conceived of as the transcendent God than the living Christ.

So Christ the eternal creator, *Pantokrator*, from beyond all time and to the end of all time is not, in these direct terms, the archetypal figure who commends himself to the modern world or is even understood by it as a sufficient first cause. Nor to that world is he lord of human history. Human history predates him, perhaps by two and a half million years. And if human history is along one dimension magical, revealing a splendour of enterprise and culture, it is by another, brutal and bestial. There is no end to man's inhumanity to man. It does not decrease, doctrines of progress, including Teilhard de Chardin's, notwithstanding.

As Suenens points out Christ is *against the world.* He appears in the New Testament as condemning the world, judging the world, calling his followers from the world, ordering them not to be conformed to the world. He came to his own, but his own received him not. He is cruelly destroyed by the world. It is not by the world he is resurrected but by God. The Second Coming promised to the disciples will be to overcome the world. This is not the behaviour of the lord of history and creation in the triumphalist way Suenens speaks of him, but rather the opposite, that Jesus found the world too much for him. A terrible sense of the helplessness of God sweeps over one from the gospels. Pilate is stronger.

The elevation of Jesus into the lord of creation and history darkens the earthly story. It raises the question of why the crucifixion was necessary and even whether it was intended in the primeval plan. It really is

---

[9] 'But suppose the whole notion of "a God" who "visits" the earth in the person of "his Son" is as mythical as the prince (disguised as a beggar) in the fairy story? Suppose there is no realm "out there" from which the "Man from heaven" arrives? Suppose the Christmas myth (the invasion of "this side" by "the other side") —as opposed to the Christmas history (the birth of the man Jesus of Nazareth) —has to go? Are we prepared for that?' etc., etc, J. A. T. Robinson, *Honest to God*, SCM Press, London 1963, p. 67. At a more profound level, cf. *The Edges of Language*, Paul M. Van Buren, SCM Press, London 1972.

something morally dubious when God plans to make men kill God. If God can do that then every other evil can be laid at his feet and Job's protests are justified.

I have spoken in praise of Suenen's theology. All the same it has to be rescued from the traps the historical Jesus has laid for it before it can be acceptable. In the first place, though we may speak of the cosmos as God's creation, it is impossible to understand it. It is ultimately ineffable, like God himself. We do not know how it originated, what it portends, what its end or resolution will be, if it has one. We do not even know, pace Whitehead, why it is this universe and not another. We have simply to accept that it is what it is and not another thing. Equally, the long evolutionary ascension, fascinating though it is, only acquires significance for man as heralding his coming and preparing the stage for him, as the five days of creation in Genesis are crowned by the sixth day. And then we note one supreme thing. Man when he appears and can speak down the corridors of time, is no longer contented with his natural self, or his lot. However that comes about is not at this moment material, but man arrives at human stature not only as Pascal's thinking reed but as a creative but suffering moral being; a tragic figure. Lewis Mumford speaks of him as in his earliest millennia preoccupied above all with the exploration of his mysterious psyche—more concerned about the satisfaction of his psychical or spiritual hungers than his material condition. And from that psyche, rather than from anything else in his natural condition, he throws up again and again languages, cultures, societies, art, magic, religion, industry. He is incredibly, inexhaustibly creative and purposeful, seeking equally command over, and fulfilment of, himself as of his natural and created environment.

If we, Christianly, insist that there is a transcendent God, that man is somehow in his image, that Christ antecedes his earthly life and is Lord of creation—and if we mean all three—then it is there within the cultural explosion which began when man emerged from his confining natural state that we shall find the primal revelation. There we might expect the God–man dialogue. If we do not see the God–word there we have no chance at all of hearing it spoken in any earlier God–universe relationship in which not even a bird sings. But in all that has happened since man arrived on the scene, and on that human stage which is also God's theatre of action, God must have used a host of institutions—religious and secular—and a myriad men to whom to speak, through whom to act. To speak of those ages as godless, if anyone does, because Jesus was not there is a cosmic impiety. To project Jesus backward into those ages somehow impairs both the historicity of his mission and its redemptive significance. Why redeem man from that which God has created?

At the same time we have no right to saddle God (and certainly not Jesus) with all history, as if it were all part of a providential plan and man had no freedom. Nor can we simply say that God was—is—responsible for the good and the devil, or man who so often deputizes for him, for the evil. There cannot be any part of God's creation which is not God's creation unless God subsequently withdraws and grants the creation freedom, abstracting himself in so doing, as Kierkegaard pointed out, to free the debtor from obligation. In the end we can only say that God must have been responsible for man's freedom and that God's work with man continues not by *fiat*, but by dialogue as one man's influence over another when it is not despotic is by dialogue. I will accept that the dialogue surfaces under a thousand names; one name is conscience, another is sacrifice, another is the search for truth: none is a product purely of the Christian era.

The 1968 Lambeth Conference threw up a phrase which chimed with the theology of Suenens, 'Christ, the agent of all creation'. *The Conference Report, 1968*[10] said 'A theology of creation needs to be worked out which sees Christ, the agent of all creation, as inaugurating a cosmic redemption'. John Habgood picks up this point in an essay, 'The Theology of Creation'.[11]

'On the face of it such a phrase sounds nonsensical. Without having the space to argue a whole theological position, I would wish to interpret it by claiming that for Christians the paradigm of God's activity is Christ; and this is no less true for the doctrine of creation than for any other doctrine. If the clue to creation is Christ, then the God we call Creator is not one who stands apart from his creation to make it what it is by acts of arbitrary power, he is himself involved and hidden. His involvement is of such a kind as to allow maximum freedom to his creatures, even the freedom to reject him and push him out of his own world. His power is the power of love which expresses itself most characteristically in bringing good out of evil, and life out of death.'

And John Habgood goes on to speak of Christ as the 'representative' of God's presence in the world and as 'the pointer to the world's consummation beyond itself'. These are important insights into the theology of revelation. But Christ the paradigm, the exemplar of God's work, is not to be confused with the God he shows forth. He flashes a brilliant illumination through creation—'I am the light of the world'—but this does not make him creation or creator. Yet he continues God's creative work. The paradigmatic Christ is also the redemptive Jesus.

It is only in some such sense that I am able to understand Cardinal Suenen's—and Paul's—theology. I find it more defensible to cast God

---

[10] SPCK, London, p. 75.
[11] *Christianity and Change*, Ed. Norman Autton, SPCK, London 1971, p. 49 ff.

than Christ for the role of creator, liberator, co-creator with man in the setting I have described. That is because the obdurate historicity of Jesus, together with his own reverent, worshipful relation to his Father in heaven, creates a barrier to the notion of him as in a platonic sense a transcendental demiurge. Yet, if Jesus is Incarnate Son, second person of the Trinity, it must seem impertinent to allot roles. Equally, it is theologically foolish to *substitute* Jesus for the Godhead, for roles were allotted.

Is all this important? Indeed it is. It is in this way that we can speak of God, and indeed of Christ, not only as beyond in the transcendent sense but as beyond in the sense of being *outside* the Church. 'Christ is not only the life of the soul; he is the life of man,' Suenens writes. And this too must mean, in his theology, the life of man and the soul of man before Christ makes his earthly appearance. And Suenens rubs this in, saying that the Church has always had difficulty in living with the richness of concrete life in all its creative reality. We might add that it has sought to *reduce* that reality to what its nerves would take, what its hard and fast dogmas would tolerate. 'The Church must confront living man where he is and, in the power of the spirit who is moving towards the Father, bringing man to encounter with the living God. This mandate implies a great openness on the part of the Christian community to all that takes place on this globe. *The church must never again appear as an isolated block of humanity preoccupied with its own internal affairs.*'[12]

But that is how it has appeared: and still appears to many. We have to ask how the Church relates to the *cosmic* Christ before one can make a judgment of that last sentence. One must speak of the Church as deriving from the encounter with the living Jesus and not from any theory or theology about him. It was out of this encounter, charismatic and shattering, and imperfectly comprehended, that a community was born seeking to adore, and to live in disciplined devotion to that Person. The community comes down to us in the form of our Churches. No matter in what ways they have failed, they have, through all those generations since Jesus died, provided the gracious means by which individual lives were transformed and enriched and men and women brought to a goodness they had not thought it possible to know. But in the sense that the Christians clung together in communities of faith and drew away from those who rejected Jesus, they tended to be the peculiar people, the separate people, tempted to become the isolated blocks of humanity they are bidden not to be. That has always been the Christian dilemma. Christians, called out of the world by Jesus, were impelled to live their lives as the fellowship commanded, and not as the world commanded. Yet it was the role of the fellowship not just to be separate

---

[12] Ibid. p. 71. My italics.

but to preach the Gospel to the whole world and to baptize in the name of Christ. Clearly the effectiveness of the life of the brotherhood was central to the effectiveness of its mission, a mission which called men to repentance as the price of their redemption. It was the Christ of the synoptic Gospels rather than the Christ of the Logos which gave the Churches their dynamism and their power to transform history.

Without the Churches the Gospel message would never have survived at all. But Christians did not see the Church as their human work, but, with scriptural authority, as the Body of Christ in the world, a body of which they were members. In fact, they saw the Church as the indestructible instrument of the purposes of Jesus and it was this vision which gave it stature and power down the centuries and set it apart in the minds of men from wholly worldly authorities which could not be said to enjoy the unique commission of Christ.

How then do we make reconciliation of the cosmic Christ with the Christ of the *ecclesia*, a reconciliation which concedes the special role of the Church? It is not easy except in a paradigmatic sense. We have argued that if Christ was at work before his incarnation then what he sought to accomplish through it was something not to be found before or there would have been no point in that grave intervention in history which brought his crucifixion. There would seem to be three elements: first the need for God to identify himself with man in the depth of human suffering and iniquity; second, for God to be reunited with man as was the father of the prodigal with his son; third for man to be offered the redemption and renewal he craved. All three can be seen as something new, even astonishing, in the world. Pagans had thought of gods as unpredictable, malicious. Jews saw God as revengeful. Now —God expresses his *love* for man! Man is implored to love his heavenly Father even more than his earthly one. The reward of this new union of God and man is to be man's deathlessness. The previously given natural order in which death was inescapable, was to be overcome. Here, clearly is the Christ role. All the more reason then for Christians to turn to Genesis, where Jesus does not appear, for the Creator role of God.

Yet Paul found no difficulty in reconciling the redemptive and the cosmic roles. He sweeps them together in one eloquent passage:

'He (God) rescued us from the domain of darkness and brought us away into the kingdom of his dear Son, in whom our release is secured and our sins forgiven. He is the image of the invisible God: his is the primacy over all created things. In him everything in heaven and on earth was created, not only things visible but also the invisible orders of thrones, sovereignties, authorities and powers: the whole universe has been created through him and for him. And he exists before everything, and all things are held together in him. He is, moreover, the head of the body, the church. He is its origin, the first to return from the dead, to be in all things alone supreme. For in him the complete being of God, by God's own choice, came to dwell. Through him God chose to reconcile the whole universe to himself . . .' (Col. 1:13–20). And without equivocation he declares later, 'Every power in the universe is subject to him as Head'. The Christ of Paul's Christology swallows up the God of Paul's theology. Yet there is no mistaking Paul's passionate sense that the incarnation marked a turning-point in cosmic as well as human history.

We see more clearly the dilemma. If Christ was the lord of *all* history, what was this special thing, the Church, which claimed to be his chosen instrument, his Body, in the world? As *the Body* of Christ the Church could hardly have been more possessive about Christ, even though it proclaimed him for all men, for in a way it was saying that it *was* Christ. It was not a proprietorship expressed in sermons and creeds only. They were damned or even destroyed who did not accept Christ on the terms the Church offered him. We have looked at parts of this unpleasant story. If on the other hand it is more and more the cosmic Christ who demands our worship then the role of the church changes. It must justify itself in its integrity *in the world* and before God. It is out in the open where nothing is excused. A human institution, it may be the vehicle of the special grace of God, but it cannot pre-empt all grace.

Before we look again at the dilemma we have to underscore again what happens to a Church which is closed in the contemplation of itself, which holds proprietorially to Jesus. We get what many critics in our day have called 'religion' as against a living faith. They have sometimes been so incensed by Christian religiosity and inflamed by the need to get rid of it that they have denied altogether that Christianity is a 'religion'. It is a faith, they say, and by its nature 'against religion'. There is some semantic cheating here by accepted definitions of religion and it would be a nonsense to suppose either that Christianity is not a religion or that the Christian religion buries the Christian faith. It could mean though that 'religion' coupled with religiosity muffles and perverts the faith it is intending to transmit. Religion as religiosity, as a culture or sub-culture, drawing people together, putting a stamp upon them through regular cultic practices which proclaim their status within society, their 'possession' of certain truths or privileges, this is a phenomenon of all religions, and very far from the earth-shaking faith of early Christians. 'The mistake,' Michael Ramsey wrote,[13] of ecclesiasticism through the ages has been to believe in the Church as a kind of thing-in-itself. The apostles never regarded the Church as a thing-in-itself.' Their faith was in God who had raised Jesus from the dead and,

---

[13] 'Death and Resurrection', *The Future of the Christian Church*, op. cit. p. 22.

despite their unworthiness, they knew that the power of the Resurrection was at work in them. So that the true nature of the Church was to lay hold on 'the power of the Resurrection. And because it is that, it is always on the converse side *death*: death to self; death to worldly hopes; death to self-sufficiency; death to any kind of security for the church or for Christianity, other than the security of God and the Resurrection.'[14] It was indeed the community of saints waiting to die.

Dr Ramsey goes on to speak of the continuous effort to find a human security for the Church—to make it credible on grounds other than those of the passion. So,

> 'there is the false security of religion. We have had in the West much "religious prosperity": large congregations, devotional fervour, lovely music, the enjoyment of a genuine religious culture. This may be a true and authentic outcome of the gospel. Yet it may become a self-contained realm and with it there may be the tacit acceptance of assumptions about human society which are not those of the New Testament. So secure may religion feel itself that it may run on for long periods without criticizing itself, without submitting itself to the judgement of the Gospel. And the genuine Christian virtues it produces may make it the more blind in its security. Then the drought comes. It came in England several decades ago. It is perhaps beginning to come in America today. When it comes, our religious security begins to fail us. We discover what F. D. Maurice meant when he said "We have been dosing our people with religion, when what they want is not that but the living God".'[15]

Or, of course, what they do *not* want. Religion as the cultural thing-in-itself is more comfortable.

Where does this leave the Church of England? It hardly needs to be said now that it is a religious thing-in-itself in the pejorative sense of the Archbishop's definitions. It is a national version of a world religion, identified with establishment values in war and peace, very much in thrall therefore to the outlook of middle and upper classes and dominated by them, practising a prim and formal worship, legally tied up in all sorts of preposterous ways which protect especially a priesthood enjoying the Church as a property. But the sad human contradictions of the Church of England are not uncommon in human institutions. They are a challenge to reform but not a total disqualification, for the saintliness which the Archbishop implied does have refuge there, and

---

[14] 'Wherever we go we carry death with us in our body, the death that Jesus died, that in this body also life may reveal itself, the life that Jesus lives. For continually, while still alive, we are being surrendered into the hands of death, for Jesus' sake.... Thus death is at work in us and life in you' (2 Cor. 4:10–12). 'For we have been saved, though only in hope' (Romans 8:24).

[15] Ibid. p. 22.

holiness, like someone else's cheerfulness, keeps breaking in, because some windows remain open in an otherwise inward-looking *ecclesia*.

It might very well be that the Church of England would prefer to die rather than to change. It throws itself into an anguish of nostalgia when serious proposals of reform disturb it. Perhaps quietly to fade away is within its decent ethos. Its decline is statistically predictable but may never happen: if it does happen it may never be noticed. On the other hand it changes all the time despite itself. In an anti-institutional mood the parishes throw up their own new forms, including liturgical forms, and find themselves with strange new bedfellows. Once they would not even have raised their hats to them.

TWO

The Gale of the Spirit

DR HUGH SCHONFIELD wrote an article in *The Times*[1] bearing the title, 'The Revival of the Messianic Vision'. Short though it was it bore a peculiar challenge to the Churches, arguing that the Churches had no exclusive right to represent Jesus, who was not in himself the conformist who expected conformism in others. 'In his public life Jesus was noted for his sturdy independence. He outraged the religious authorities by his nonconformity and by the kind of company he kept. He quietly put the apostles in their place when they showed a disposition to proprietorship, to acting as if they were the Messiah's manager, objecting to others speaking in his name, deciding his engagements and policies and who was to be given access to him. Jesus reminded them that it was he who had chosen them, and not they him.'

And Schonfield goes on to speak of an extra-Christian interest in Jesus. Anyone can study him, read the Gospels and commentaries and form a judgment about him, and so the services of the Church as an interpreter, as the public relations officer, are superfluous. Schonfield was not thinking only of the privatized Christianity of which I spoke earlier but of the very public Jesus movement which has found its way into the drug and hippie scene and produced the astonishing musicals, *Godspell* and *Jesus Christ, Superstar* (which earned a public rebuke from a Cardinal[2]) but rather, of what lies behind this movement of youth, and he understands it as stemming from the confusion and despair of modern man because of the perils he faces in 'the absence of any commanding exemplification of the brotherhood of man'. Only in Jesus do they find

---

[1] 8 January 1972.

[2] 'Rejecting the standards offered by their elders, they (the young) are ready to revolt against anyone in authority—civic, academic, or religious. They are still only at the protesting stage. They will repudiate existing authority but have not yet found a satisfying solution. That is where the Church can help them. They must be directed not to Jesus Christ, Superstar, but to Jesus Christ, Son of God. Jesus, the gentle, bewildered leader persecuted by priests and politicians may serve as a hero in a stage musical but he cannot become the centre of their spiritual lives.' Cardinal Heenan in a pastoral letter to all churches, Trinity Sunday, 28 May 1972.

a King of mankind 'whose universal sympathies and penetrating insight can be requisitioned to aid the world in the quest for solutions to the problems of conflict and disharmony'. It is Christ as Messiah in the full prophetic sense of promoting the coming of the Kingdom of God on earth that Schonfield demands to be preached again, and by the churches if they can rise to it, though it is precisely this role of Christ that has been muted, he thinks, by them. He is, however, doubtful whether they will give up their proprietorship and go along with the Jesus of an independent spirit and an unpredictable behaviour. If they cannot, the implication is, they had better shut up shop for there has come 'the point in the Drama of Ages where the directions read, exit the Man of Sorrows and enter Christ the King. Has the Church still the will to respond with "*Maranatha*. Come, Lord Jesus"?'

The quirks of fortune are hard to bear. It does not seem long since the modernists thought that the Church was too wrapped up in the divine, charismatic Christ whom no one could understand in a scientific age except as a good man and a zealous social worker (or more dubiously a political agitator). Nor is it long since, in the wave of Bultmannism, that the historical Christ was rejected altogether in favour of an existential encounter with a myth, or under the mantle of secularism it was argued that the dechristianization of the world was something that God, if he existed, intended and Jesus would have welcomed. It is not long either since I read an article, 'Living without an Overlord' by Ray Billington, who was 'expelled by the Methodist Church' for the unorthodoxy of his *The Christian Outsider*,[3] and who was once a member of Nicolas Stacey's team at St Mary's, Woolwich. The article celebrated his relief at living under the tyranny of God no longer, free at last from the humiliation of subservience to a Being for whom there is no evidence 'other than that which is self-induced or instilled by others'. Belief in him was unhealthy because it allowed 'men to pass the buck, to shirk responsibility, to leave decisions to the overlord who holds the whole world in his hands'.[4]

A certain kind of theologizing was bound to reach that atheist conclusion in the long run.

Now there is a movement away from theologizing about Christ, and it is not an academic movement but a popular one, and it is towards the discovery or rediscovery of Jesus. To some extent Schonfield spoke for it. It is in its way the search for the living encounter of which Suenens and Ramsey also speak. It demands Jesus simple, and shrinks from the institutional wrappings in which he has been hidden, believing that anyway he is misrepresented by the Churches and that instant and overwhelming personal access to him is possible: a doctrine not far short

[3] London, 1972.
[4] *The Guardian*, 17 November 1972.

of the conversion principle of evangelicalism right across the board from John Wesley to Billy Graham. But the accent is not so much on conviction of sin and total unworthiness but of joy and release of the spirit at the discovery of a loving Jesus with whom the young can identify as another misunderstood, persecuted youth, alienated from his authoritarian elders, and done to death. 'Jesus is God' the lapel buttons say, and *The Jesus Trip*,[5] the title of a book, tells all about the expectations of the Jesus movements. Jesus provides his own 'freak out' for believers into a realm of transcendent mystical experience, into an aesthetic and physical hypersensitivity, more lasting and spiritually exalting than drugs because other-related, not simply self-related. Sin-conviction is a small part of this and certainly not cast in what the Jesus freaks would regard as the cold moral orthodoxy of the traditional churches. From Jesus they take the primary injunction to love and would by no means translate this into indiscriminate or promiscuous sex—rather the contrary.

The United States is above all the promoter of eccentric religion and, despite the fervour of its mass conversion rallies, much the land of private enterprise in this and other things. And so it is difficult to generalize about the Jesus movement, even to know how deeply it will influence young people in Britain or how permanent will be its effects. However, it is there, and it is easy to see how by the contagion of a new life style it can touch millions without resort to a single theologian or any ministers save those who jump on the band wagon (and they abound: America is also a land of religious opportunism).

As the charisma grows a little cold, it gets 'routinized' in Weber's phrase, and the critics assemble. In the opinion of one, Richard Gelwick,[6] the insistence of the Jesus Revolution that its beliefs constitute the only religious truth fosters 'a twofold attitude toward non-Christians: missionary zeal and hostility'. What alarms Richard Gelwick most is that the insistence of the revolution that Jesus is God revives all the horror of deicide, the source of antisemitism. He traces a possible causal relation[7] between 'a bad theology, Jesus is God', and a social pattern that discriminates against Jews, the 'killers of God'.[8] He attacks the

---

[5] Lowell Streiker, Abingdon Press, New York 1971.

[6] 'Will the Jesus Revolution Revive Anti-Semitism?' *Christian Century*, 10 May 1972.

[7] With the aid of *Christian Beliefs and Anti-Semitism*, Charles Glock and Rodney Stark, Harper and Row, New York 1966.

[8] 'Nowhere in the New Testament', Gelwick says, 'was the claim advanced that Jesus is God'. It is rather hard to saddle the Jesus freaks with this heresy, if heresy it is, unless one is to count Cardinal Heenan among them. In the Trinity Pastoral letter to which I have referred he writes, 'Those who say that Jesus neither claimed to be God nor knew that he was God make mockery of the Christian religion.' Indeed one might say that the Christian Church has spent two thousand years convincing the world of the divinity of Jesus. The best that can be said, on Gelwick's side, by orthodox theology is that the statement, 'Jesus is God', does not exhaust the definition of the godhead.

movement for its anti-intellectualism, its fundamentalism and 'its naïve assumption that a personalistic religion can solve the world's complex social problems'.

Primitivism in theology need not disqualify a grassroots religious movement: the history of the Church from primitive times is full of of examples such as those through which men—and the Church—groped painfully towards a fuller understanding of God and his demands upon them. Heresies are not new and never all loss. What stands out in the Jesus revolution is the charisma the tidy traditional Churches have long lost. The Jesus revolution is a charismatic explosion owing nothing (to my knowledge) to one or another eloquent religious revivalist but all to a spontaneous movement of discovery. If we relate it to the third consciousness, we see that its emergence has special point. For many generations no ordinary traditional Christians thought that this kind of conduct was possible in our rational-scientific world and they looked down their noses at it as the eighteenth century intellectuals did at *enthusiasm*. However, the new consciousness is far from being rational-scientific. It *is* enthusiastic.

The Jesus revolution is not alone in its charismatic authority. An Anglican rector wrote to me of his experiences with the 'Assemblies of God' in South America and elsewhere. Though he approached them critically, he was convinced that,

'the movement gripped the multitudes like a mighty fire of God, full of love and compassion. In the Latin Americas and in other parts of the world the pastors often had the privilege of witnessing to multitudes ranging up to one million or more (especially in Indonesia). The Evangelist I observed in action was undoubtedly a magnificent "unfolder" of the New Testament especially in declaring the power and compassion of our Lord in healing in the past and present. So vast were the crowds that services were always in the open air, usually in the evenings under sunny skies and to look down into the faces of up to 100,000 people absorbing the message and results made me realize what Christianity is meant to be, most likely.

'The personal simplicity and charm of the evangelist I observed was striking. He was so absolutely natural in spite of the fact that he was favoured with such fantastic results. He had no room for things extraneous to the proclamation and carrying out of the Gospel. He did not wear a clerical collar and I remember him saying that to be an evangelist one did not necessarily have to be trained in college, etc. The results of invitations to be divinely healed were undoubted by all who were present to see the blind restored, the deaf healed and Christian hope instilled throughout the vast throng of people.'

The charisma is that of a healing ministry and published photographs of vast gatherings show its explosive power. Its theology is abysmally White Anglo-Saxon Protestant. The evangelist, Pastor T. L. Osborn, from Tulsa, Oklahoma, from *inter alia*, 'the front-line trenches of the great Java campaign' presents his reports[9] to ministers and laymen so as to encourage them in 'the task of evangelizing a billion heathen souls'. The cover of one bears as slogan, 'And the heathen shall know that I am the Lord'. The superiority is insufferable, especially when the pastor boasts that his mission has convinced 'the Catholics and Mohammedans by the thousands to believe the Gospel of Jesus Christ'.

However spellbinding the evangelist, one is appalled at the possible impact of a naïve and conceited Bible-belt theology upon Osborn's heathens. But the charisma was there, the impact of the word on millions of those craving for healing and comfort. It cannot be gainsaid. Of course we have grown used to the idea that personal revival campaigns promising individual salvation pass over us like 'the wind in dry grass'. Perhaps indeed they are on the way out and if it comforts us, we can dismiss them.

This cannot possibly be said of Pentecostalism or of the charismatic movement which has sprung from pentecostal theology. One may speak speak of pentecostal theology as seeking to bring back to theology generally and to Christian practice especially a wholeness it once possessed and has since lost. What has happened to the gifts of the Holy Spirit? Why has the gift of healing vanished from the Christian agenda? How long since men were 'filled with the Lord', 'seized by the Spirit'? One knows that a spontaneity, a rapture, rushes through pentecostal congregations in a worship which is both open and impulsive.

The charismatic movement in Britain with the aid and direction of the Fountain Trust (which was Michael Harper's brain-child) seeks constantly for the warmth and excitement, characteristic of the Pentecostalist churches, but free from the sectarian emphasis they give it and their fundamentalist theology. The fact that it gains much Roman Catholic support is a tribute to its theological orthodoxy—up to a point. It is international too, strong in America and Europe, and its claim to be ecumenical is a genuine one, but it is ecumenical with a difference, exploding churches from within rather than uniting them organically.

In 1971 the Fountain Trust held an international conference at Guildford and claimed representatives from twenty nations and most major churches and confessions including over forty Lutherans and over thirty Roman Catholics. It expressed its concern 'not to minimize actual sources of division between churches, but to rejoice in the matters that unite us'. Above all to display 'a constant concern to be filled with the

---

[9] Evangelist T. L. Osborn. *Frontier Evangelism, with Miracles of Healing,* and *Healing the Sick and Casting out Devils.* T. L. Osborn Evangelistic Corporation, Tulsa, Oklahoma 1955.

Holy Spirit',[10] and to be led by him into every kind of ministry. A highlight of charismatic worship is the 'extended communion service' when a formal liturgy and spontaneous worship flow freely together. One Pentecostal leader from Europe described the Guildford gathering as the greatest Pentecostal conference he had ever attended. Guildford Cathedral was packed every night for worship and people stood on tiptoe waiting to see what the Lord would do next. 'But we must not dawdle or bask in the wonder and glory of this experience at Guildford. The Lord is drawing us all onwards to the final goal—His glorious return', Michael Harper wrote. So the charismatic movement is adventist too.

Michael Harper is a key to the understanding of the charismatic movement in Britain. He would disdain to be called its leader, since that role is reserved to the Holy Spirit. He has told his story in *None Can Guess*.[11] A Cambridge law student, who hardly knew whether he belonged to a church or not, he was converted by attending a King's College Chapel communion service and after taking his degree went to the evangelical Ridley Hall, Cambridge, from which theological college he was in due course ordained. He served in Battersea and then at the famous All Saints', Langham Place, under John Stott. An address he had to make on *Ephesians* filled him with an elating sense of what Paul was really preaching. The week-end at the conference where this happened changed his life. 'The crowning miracle of all was the new relationship that was forged with the Lord Jesus Christ. I remember the sense of gratitude I felt when I first turned to Him at university. But this was nothing in comparison with what I now felt.'[12]

Both he and his wife from then on began to perceive a supernatural presence in their lives, transforming them. Harper is introduced to 'speaking in tongues'. Interested, but prejudiced against it, he found himself led towards it. Exasperated, he waited for the gift, but it did not come. At least *speak*, a friend urged him and let the Holy Spirit do the rest.

'Around the middle of the night I remembered all that Larry [Christenson] had said to me. "Try it; begin to speak; don't speak English," and so on. So I tried. Maybe for a split second there were some man-made sounds. I forget. But almost instantly I was speaking a new language. As I did so, two wonderful things happened all at once. The Lord seemed to take two steps forward. He had seemed a little out of touch. Now He was really close. And secondly those worries and fears evaporated. And here I was, not in any state of ecstasy (I defy anyone to feel ecstatic lying on a hard floor!) but

---

[10] *Renewal*, September 1971.
[11] Hodder and Stoughton, London 1971.
[12] Ibid. pp. 29–30.

speaking to God with a freedom and joy I had always wanted to, and never quite found possible. My mind was unclouded, and fully aware of what was going on. It was a most glorious sensation of perfect communication between God and man.'[13]

I quote this passage from an honest autobiography because it reveals the core of the charismatic movement—the baptism into the spirit. Those who have received it claim to be able to recognize others who have, even if they do not hear them speak with tongues, and the worshippers at charismatic services wait 'on tiptoe' for the rolling cadences which say nothing except to God whose language it is. There is an extraordinary release about it all into the hands of the Spirit, from whom too comes the power of healing.

These two experiences, healing and speaking in tongues are at the heart of pentecostalism. 'In Christendom it is perhaps the major grass-roots religious revolution of our time. Born in this century, raised largely among the poor, at mid-century entering the middle class, it is reputedly growing faster than any other modern Christian movement and is increasingly pressing its existence upon the attention of the church and the world.'

That is the judgement, which Michael Harper quotes, of Frederick Dale Bruner in *A Theology of the Holy Spirit*.[14] Of course there are immediate theological questions, of which the most important are those which raise the relationship of baptism by the Spirit to baptism by water. For me, in the charismatic literature, what sharply posed itself was the sense that those baptized by the Spirit, as they understood it and Michael Harper describes it, felt themselves for all their humility a new élite, nearer to God and specially to be cared for. The charismatic movement could be argued therefore to be re-drafting the terms of member-ship of the Christian way and perhaps dangerously, since those most in need of that membership would probably be those least likely to acquire the special baptismal technique. In that sense the charismatic movement could be seen as sectarian, like the Pentecostal Churches themselves. However, as it crosses denominational lines and does not aim at a confessional basis it is more like the early evangelical movement. Indeed it closely resembles it in its ecstatic conversion experiences and, one suspects, its theology too.

This part has dealt with some of the dangers of the proprietorship of Jesus by the Churches. The charge of proprietorship of the Holy Spirit can be levelled against the charismatics. It is embarrassing to read how readily the Holy Spirit was to hand from the time Michael Harper estab-lished the Fountain Trust onward, always acceding to prayer for that extra £200 that was needed, to deal with housing problems, or even to

[13] London, 1971.
[14] Hodder and Stoughton, 1971.

sort out the confusion of tangled air tickets. The Holy Spirit was like a retriever ready to run for the catch whenever unleashed. It seemed shameful that the Holy Spirit was engaged, not in the vital elements of personal spiritual struggle, but in domestic errands when so much of terror and suffering in the world appeared God forsaken.

Well, proprietorship of that stamp is not new to the Christian faith and few of us are guiltless of asking for favours which must appear trivial against a world canvas. We cannot for that reason dismiss a Christian movement which has administered an electric shock to the various communions and extended the sense of what is spiritually possible. What at least it has done is to reintroduce joy and rapture into worship, haunted by the sense that the Pentecost of the Apostles ought to be the norm.

THREE
'Take the gentle path'

IN THE first chapter of this part I posed the problem of the nature of Christ and the nature of the Church. How were they related? How could the temporal Church preach and represent the timeless Christ of its theology? If Christ was the creator from before all time then that seemed to weaken if not to dispose of the special relationship of the Church with Christ, of its unique function as the instrument of Christ. If on the other hand Jesus begins a mission at a precise moment in time, a mission which cannot move backward in time, and commissions the Church as his redemptive hand, his role before the incarnation grows obscure and uncertain. If the Church asserts both Christ roles with equal force (which it seldom does) then it must somehow assume the overlordship of history which mystically it might claim but practically it is not competent to achieve even over present and future history. We reach an antinomy.

As all theology claims that Christ in the godhead shares in the trinitarian creation and as Christ, as the Son incarnate in man, sets in motion a redemptive mission for which the Church he founded is the proper means, the antinomy must be lived with. If there is a lesson in it, it is that the Church must lay hold of Christ in faith at the same time that it leaves hold of Christ proprietorially. The historical Church cannot be the only instrument open to Christ-creator, Christ *pantokrator*. The spirit of Christ, too, must be allowed 'to blow where it listeth'. It cannot be bound or compelled. The history of the Church is full of human disasters in which it sought to use Christ as an instrument of power and the justification of every terror. Even the promises of Christ that the gates of hell would not prevail against the Church were contingent ones: it goes without saying that the Church had to remain the Church as Christ conceived it, and not become something else—which is its continual fate by reason of human fallibility. We recall that one accusation against Rome during the Reformation was that it had become antichrist. There is nothing in history or doctrine to compel us to accept the temporal Church as immortal, imperishable. We have not to confuse the heavenly city, *civitas dei*, with a heavenly *Church* despite the hymn

342

books. A heavenly Church is a logical improbability: an earthly Church is expendable. It could already have pronounced sentence upon itself.

What then is the stance of the Church to be, if once we say goodbye to its triumphalism? That it must die, or die to the world, to be born anew, that it cannot be assured exemption from the death and resurrection of its Saviour? It was something like this that Charles Davis meant when he wrote in *A Question of Conscience* of the importance of a new Christian presence. It was certainly to be a humbler one. The combination of humility and charisma would seem to be the proper stance. The Church must show Christ, the paradigm, forth to the world and let *him* speak at the same time that it bends the knee and accepts him as Lord. There are Renaissance representations of the Virgin and Child and Orthodox icons which show Mary holding in her arms the infant who nevertheless sits bravely upright and blesses the world. The infant is giving himself to the world, Mary is holding him out to the world. In Andrea Mantegna's 'The Virgin and Child with St John the Baptist and Mary Magdalene' (in the National Gallery), Mary has her head bowed with love and submission and hardly dares touch the Child she is nevertheless supporting. He stands upright, bold, naked, with a lively, determined face, blessing the world. He is his own man. Nevertheless the saints who flank him look not at him or the Virgin but appear transfixed, raptly intent on events in heaven. Christ faces the world, the Virgin sustains him, but does not possess him. In herself she communicates his charisma, which illuminates her being and her bearing. Or there is another Christ, in a great altar piece by Parmigiano called 'The Vision of St Jerome' in the National Gallery. Here Christ is not an infant but a rosy boy with a calm, radiant face and confident but eager eyes. He rests against his mother's knee as a small boy would and she is relaxed and fulfilled. She does not touch him. He is to make his own way. He leans forward, one foot seeming to step already into a world of which he is not afraid. It is in that sense that the antinomy of church-Christ and creator-Christ can be held in tension. The Church has to be the self-effacing vehicle of that charisma which at the same time suffuses it.[1] The paradigm of Christ, as Christ is the Paradigm of the Creator.

We dare not idealize it into a picture dreaming on the walls of a silent gallery. The Church is, whatever else it also is, an institution run by men battling with their own and others' inadequacies. The preaching, teaching, 'holding' role of the Church necessitates an institution which does these things, trains people for these duties, seeks constantly to understand what it is doing *sub specie aeternitatis*. But the Church which recognizes that the Christ role goes far beyond anything which the Church can master will accept too the painful consequences of its

---

[1] Cf. *Andrea Mantegna*, P. Kristaller, 1907.

work in a world (of which it is part) which Christ incarnate rebuked even as he loved it. And recognizes too, if it cannot rejoice in, the fact that Christ working within its institutions may be as implosive there as Christianity once was explosive in the world, and still may be again.

A Church which accepts its preaching, teaching sacramental role—and what Church does not?—has to decide in what spirit it is commissioned to do these things. It has necessarily preservative, conservative tasks. Charisma 'routinized' is not to be despised. An institution is itself an historical mnemonic. But the spirit even of conserving, safeguarding has to be charismatic, at once the proffered love of God and the grace of transformation, or it is worthless.

We return to ask what the charisma of the Church of England is, or can be expected to be, in the royal flush of futures opening out to it. At once it must be said that charisma is not going to be promoted by a campaign. It may be prayed for, but not established by diploma in the theological department of a university. Like longed-for love itself it may come of hope and expectation and waiting. And of course, like love, it can be counterfeited. It is often—again like love—present and active and we do not recognize it, and so it is lost to many of us. 'How can I describe this generation? They are like children sitting in the market-place and shouting at each other:

'We piped for you and you would not dance.
We wept and wailed, and you would not mourn.'

Then, there are different charismatic gifts. We must speak of the little charisma and the great charisma. The little charisma is that everyday Christian awareness of grace, seeing it suddenly and unexpectedly in lives lived uncomplainingly and sacrificially, or receiving it as help or love or understanding from others. It can indeed be found in the work-life and prayer-life of the parish priest and though this certainly could not be guaranteed this is where many would look for it. It could be in the experience of communion in a house group when what has become a formality made meaningless by repetition blossoms into a new sense of the Presence and of commitment to the Lord. For me, time and time again, the awful encounter with the Presence, the *mysterium tremendum*, has been through the music and the glowing inner architecture of great churches and in all that Christian art conveys. Then too, the poetry of the charisma is felt in the poetry of poets. And so, endlessly. In a church sense it all has meaning in terms of what I pointed out—much earlier— that the real seminal work of the Christian Church is manifested in the daily work, teaching and example in parishes, homes, schools and other Christian points and centres.

But the *great charisma*, what is that? How hard it is to describe. Without it, the little charisma has a hard time, sometimes even appears hypocrisy. It has to be felt, D. H. Lawrence might have said, in the solar plexus. It is felt when a great statesman resigns on some profound point of principle, gives up office and profit perhaps to go into obscurity because he will not go along with what is being done. Then we are thrilled to see that honour is alive, and integrity can be tested. Or we see it in a Solzhenitsyn who will write what he sees and believes and will not fudge his moral standards, though they kill him for it. Or in a Martin Luther King who was assassinated. There are many such events in the world. In the Church nothing surpasses the charisma of Pope John. 'I remember,' Cardinal Suenens wrote,[2] 'a few days after the death of Pope John, an agnostic was speaking to me and said these words, which I will never forget: "Pope John has made my unbelief uncomfortable." Well, that is what we have to do for the world today.' The charismatic John changed the world.

The Church of England has produced its charismatic figures. One may instance John Collins who from St Paul's created the Campaign for Nuclear Disarmament, which had and still has an astonishing world impact, and who founded the African Defence Fund which was far more than a defence and aid fund. It became an international forum through which the persecution of Africans could be exposed and publicized and even prevented. Through these things alone Christian Action justified itself. Yet it had a curious, even negative, effect on the parishes. They remained locked in a passionless ennui, suspicious of anything pacifist or left. Collins received far more support from radical humanists. He himself was never promoted. Or there is Trevor Huddleston with his sacrificial African experiences, who moves Anglican hearts because he speaks more closely from familiar parochial and missionary situations. One recalls the selfless labours of Guy and Molly Clutton-Brock in Rhodesia. One cannot forget Leonard Wilson suffering for, and maintaining, the faith in Singapore in the last war. One remembers John Groser in the East End in the war. It is often exposures to peril and trial which reveal the charisma: one pays tribute to Ambrose Reeves, Alan Paton, and the Dean of Johannesburg, the Very Rev. Gonville ffrench-Beytagh, all of whom mounted the world stage for adherence to their faith, which was offensive to the South African Government. Conditions of trial are not everything: one recalls the two speeches of Michael Ramsey at the Church's General Synod, 3 May 1972, which were those of a saintly statesmanship and revealed the grace the man himself usually hid behind a decent scholarly reticence. It is invidious to go on mentioning the names of living men—if only because one must miss out so many—and it would be bad form were one not dealing with a Church of the future which can only emerge from the Church and leadership of the present. Yet, though (as we have seen) there is lively enterprise and leadership at the parochial and ecumenical level and though strong individuals emerge and make their mark, happy

---

[2] *The Future of the Christian Church*, p. 76.

to use the structures of the Church as a platform while showing some contempt for them, the great figures which move the Church by their passion and faith are thin on the ground. David Edwards, in his *Leaders of the Church of England, 1828–1944*[3] appears to feel that the Church was far better served by outstanding men in the Victorian age than it is today. One has only to mention some of his subjects, the Arnolds, Newman, Keble, Pusey, Wilberforce, Tait, Gladstone, Lightfoot, Westcott, F. D. Maurice, to see that these are often more effective moulders of the ethos of the contemporary Church than most of those who have succeeded them, with the possible exception of William Temple and George Bell. It could be, as I have already explored, that outstanding minds do not enter a Church the social and intellectual roles of which have lost so much credibility. It could be that an establishment more prim and humdrum, but not less powerful than in the past, works to discourage the rise and influence of charismatic men who might prove uncomfortable and cause trouble.

In the Epilogue to his book David Edwards was not very optimistic. 'All that could be said in 1970 was that the Church of England was humbler than it had been since the beginning of the nineteenth century. It was less insistant on old formularies; the Athanasian Creed was almost never heard, and it seemed probable that the terms of the clergy's assent to the Thirty-nine articles would soon be relaxed still farther. It was more convinced that a love of living people was true religion. It was more ready to listen to contemporary critics who might convey the voice of God. It was more concerned to support "secular" causes which might reflect the will of God. Its own membership was consulted more patiently, and it was more ready to accept other churches as fully Christian and to work with them. Groups or parties within it were far less rude to each other, and its parishes were less exclusively parochial. There was widespread support for the revision and modernisation of its Prayer Book through experiments. Those were signs of hope in a generally discouraging situation.'[4]
But what it lacked was fire in its belly.

Edwards speaks of a loss of nerve in potential leaders, and of how, once more, echoing Thomas Arnold in the 1830s, no human power seemed likely to save the Church of England as it stood. 'Once more it needed courage to wait for the revival of the tradition: for the heavenly spark and the kindly light, leading perhaps into a new period of widespread religion, or at least into a reaction against the dominance of cynicism and sensuality.'[5]

---

[3] Oxford University Press, 1971.
[4] Op. cit. p. 347.
[5] Op. cit. p. 348.

There are theological difficulties in the way of recovery of nerve. Belief in the transcendence of God the Father whom Christ worshipped and who was the the God of *our* Fathers needs to be recovered—whatever the terminological or semantic difficulties and the need for restatement— or we shall limp amputated through a non-Christian future. The need is plain for a recovery of the charismatic spirit—which must suffuse the whole Church and be seen by the nation to do so. But like the rich of the Magnificat, the Church will be sent empty away unless it can stand more loosely to the properties to which it ties its priests, and less proprietorially to the Christ it exists only to serve. A man moving into a new life has to abandon the old, as Jesus abandoned the security of boyhood Nazareth and threw himself into an unknown world. A sensible man doing so disposes of unwanted things and the Church can do likewise. It can do the same over the inhibiting social ideas which tie it to worn-out apron strings; in the case of the Church of England, to the apron strings of an Establishment which no longer carries the prestige and credibility it once had and now, though the Church is far from accepting this, is like Sinbad's old man of the sea enthroned on its shoulders.

The Church cries out for simplicity, for the charisma of preaching with lives and deeds that the special grace may be spread abroad. Pope John said, 'Some people always want to complicate simple matters; I wish to simplify complicated matters.' It is this simplification of complicated matters that the Church of England needs if a future of something more than the tying and untying of legal knots is to open up to it. It has to give up its special privileges and cushioning safeguards. It has to forget its proprietorship even of the apostolic succession and accept itself (in more than words) as part of a Christian universalism to which all those baptised in the name of the Trinity equally belong.

If only some of these hopes were to be fulfilled, the words of Paul to the Colossians would have relevance to it too. 'May he strengthen you, in his glorious might, with ample power to meet whatever comes with fortitude, patience, and joy; and to give thanks to the Father who has made you fit to share the heritage of God's people in the realm of light.'

Select Bibliography

Adamson, J. W., *English Education 1789–1902*, 1930.
Addleshaw, G. W. O., *The Beginnings of the Parochial System* (St Anthony's Hall Publications No. 3), 1953; *The Development of the Parochial System from Charlemagne (768–814) to Urban II (1088–1099)* (St Anthony's Hall Publications No. 6), 1954; *Rectors, Vicars and Patrons in the Twelfth and early Thirteenth Century Canon Law* (St Anthony's Hall Publications No. 9), 1956.
Armytage, W. H. G., *The Rise of the Technocrats*, 1965.
Arnold, A. J., *The History of the Evangelical Alliance*, 1897.
Arnold, Thomas, *Principles of Church Reform*, 2nd edn., 1833.
Arnott, Anne, *The Brethren*, 1969; *Journey into Understanding*, 1971.
Aubrey, John (ed. A. Clark), *Brief Lives*, 2 vols. 1890.
Auden, W. H., *Another Time*, 1940.
Autton, Norman (ed.), *Christianity and Change*, 1971.
Baldwin, James and Mead, Margaret, *A Rap on Race*, 1971.
Banton, Michael, *Roles*, 1965.
Baring-Gould, S., *The Church Revival*, 1914.
Barry, F. R., *Asking the Right Questions*, 1960; *Vocation and Ministry*, 1963.
Bedouelle, Guy, *L'Eglise d'Angleterre et la Société Politique Contemporaine*, 1968.
Beer, M., *A History of British Socialism*, vol. I, 1919; vol. II, 1921.
Beeson, Trevor, *The Church of England in Crisis*, 1973.
Beeson, Trevor (ed.), *Partnership in Ministry*, 1964.
Bellah, R. N., 'Civil Religion in America', *Daedalus*, Winter, 1967.
Bentham, Jeremy, *Church of Englandism and its Catechism examined*, 1818.
Bernanos, George, *Un Mauvais Rêve*, 1961.
Berger, Peter L., *The Noise of Solemn Assemblies*, 1961; *The Social Reality of Religion*, 1969.
Berton, Pierre, *The Comfortable Pew*, 1965.
Bettenson, Henry, *Documents of the Christian Church*, 1943.
Bicknell, E. J., *A Theological Introduction to the Thirty-Nine Articles*, 1944.
Bill, E. G. W. (ed.), *Anglican Initiatives in Christian Unity*, 1967.
Billington, Ray, *The Christian Outsider*, 1972.
The Black Book, or Corruption Unmasked, 1820–23.
The Extraordinary Black Book, 1831.
Bland, A. E., Brown, D. A. and Tawney, R. H., *English Economic History, Select Documents*, 1933.
Bliss, Kathleen, *We the People*, 1963; *The Future of Religion*, 1969.
Blizzard, Samuel W., 'The Minister's Dilemma', *Christian Century*, LXXIII, pp. 508–10, 25 April 1956.
Booth, Charles, *Life and Labour of People in London*, 1892–7.
Bottomore, J. B., *Elites and Society*, 1964; *Classes in Modern Society*, 1965.

Boulard, F., *An Introduction to Religious Sociology*, 1960.

Bowers, K., *Conflicts of the Clergy*, 1963.

Boyd, Malcolm (ed.), *On the Battle Lines: 27 Anglican Priests in Rebellion in the U.S.A.*, 1964.

Bricknell, W. S., *The Judgment of the Bishops on Tractarian Theology*, 1845.

Brose, Olive J., *Church and Parliament, the re-shaping of the Church of England 1828–60*, 1959.

Brothers, J. B., 'Social Change and the Role of the Priest', *Social Compass*, vol. X, No. 6, 1963.

Brown, C. K. F., *A History of the English Clergy*, 1954.

Bruner, Frederick Dale, *A Theology of the Holy Spirit*, 1971.

Bryant, Arthur, *The Story of England: Makers of the Realm*, 1953; *The Age of Chivalry*, 1963.

Buchanan, C. O., *The Job Prospects of the Anglican Clergy*, 1972.

Buchanan, C. O., Mascall, E. L., Packer, J. I. and Graham D. Leonard, *Growing into Union*, 1970.

Burke, Edmund, *Reflexions on the Revolution in France*, 1791.

Burton, J. H. (ed.), *Life and Correspondence of David Hume*, 1846.

Butler, Joseph, *Analogy of Religion*, 1736.

Butterfield, Herbert, *Christianity in European History*, 1952.

The Canons of the Church of England: Canons Ecclesiastical promulged by the Convocations of Canterbury and York in 1964 and 1969, 1969.

Carlyle, Thomas, *Cromwell's Letters and Speeches*, 2nd edn., 1846.

Carpenter, Edward, *The Service of a Parson*, 1965; *Cantaur*: the Archbishops in their Office, 1971.

Cecil, Lord David, *The Stricken Deer*, 1929.

Chadwick, Owen, *The Mind of the Oxford Movement*, 1960; *The Reformation*, 1964; *The Victorian Church*, 2 vols., 1966.

Chambers, R. W., *Thomas More*, 1935.

Chardin, Teilhard de, *The Phenomenon of Man*, 1959.

Chesterton, G. K., *Autobiography*, 1936.

Christmas, F. E., *The Parson in English Literature*, 1950.

The Church of England Year Book, 1971–72.

The Church of England Year Book, 1973.

Church, R. W., *The Oxford Movement 1833–45*, 1891.

Clark, Sir Kenneth, *Civilisation, a personal view*, 1969.

Clark, G. Kitson, *Churchmen and the Condition of England, 1832–1885*, 1973.

Clarke, W. K. Lowther, *Eighteenth Century Piety*, 1944.

Collins, L. John, *A Theology of Christian Action*, 1949; *Faith under Fire*, 1966.

Congar, Yves M., *Lay People in the Church*, 1957.

Contemporary Prayers for Public Worship.

Coombs, H. and Bax, A. N., *Journal of a Somerset Rector*, 1930.

Cope, Gilbert (ed.), *Christian Ministry in the New Towns*, 1967; *Cathedral and Mission* (Institute for the Study of Worship and Religious Architecture), 1970; *Problem Churches* (Institute for the Study of Worship and Religious Architecture), 1972.

Cosin, John, *Works*, 5 vols, 1843–55.

Cox, Harvey, *The Secular City*, 1965.

Coxon, Anthony M., 'A Sociological Study of the Social Recruitment, Selection and Professional Socialization of Anglican Ordinands.' Unpublished doctoral thesis, University of Leeds, 1965.

Cruikshank, M., *Church and State in English Education: 1870 to present day*, 1963.

Currie, Robert, *Methodism Divided*, 1968.

Curzon, Robert, *Visits to Monasteries in the Levant*, 1955 edn.

Darwin, Charles, *The Origin of Species*, 1859; *The Descent of Man*, 1871.

Davidson, Randall Thomas, *The Five Lambeth Conferences*, 1920.

Davies, J. G., *Dialogue with the World*, 1960; *Worship and Mission*, 1966; *The Secular Use of Church Buildings*, 1968; *Everyday God*, 1973.

Davies, J. G. (ed.), *The Multi-Purpose Church*: Hodge Hill, St Philip and St James, 1971; *Research Bulletin*, Institute for the Study of Religious Worship and Architecture, 1972.

Davis, Charles, *God's Grace in History*, 1966; *A Question of Conscience*, 1967.

Dickens, A. G., *Thomas Cromwell and the English Reformation*, 1959; *The English Reformation*, 1964; *Reformation and Society in 16th Century Europe*, 1966.

Dillistone, F. W., *The Structure of the Divine Society*, 1951; *The Christian Faith*, 1964; *The Christian Understanding of Atonement*, 1968.

Dix, Gregory, *The Shape of the Liturgy*, 1954.

Dugmore, C. W., *The Mass and the English Reformers*, 1958.

Duncan, D., *The Life and Letters of Herbert Spencer*, 1908.

Durkheim, Emile, *The Elementary Forms of Religious Life*, 1912.

Earle, Nick, *What's Wrong with the Church of England?*, 1961.

Edwards, David L., *This Church of England*, 1962; *Religion and Change*, 1969; *Leaders of the Church of England, 1828–1944*, 1971.

Edwards, David L. (ed.), *Preparing for the Ministry of the 1970s*, 1964.

Eliot, T. S., *Murder in the Cathedral*, 1935; *Little Gidding*, 1942.

Elliott, Philip, *The Sociology of the Professions*, 1972.

Elliott-Binns, L. E., *English Thought 1860–1900: the Theological Aspect*, 1956.

Elton, G. R., *Policy and Police in the Time of Thomas Cromwell*, 1972.

Engels, Friedrich, *The Condition of the Working Class in England in 1844*.

Erasmus, *Colloquies*, Edn. 1680.

Facts and Figures about the Church of England No. 3, 1967.

Farren, Mick and Barker, Edward, *Watch out Kids!*, 1972.

Farrer, Austin, *A Celebration of Faith*, 1970.

Fay, C. R., *Life and Labour in the Nineteenth Century*, 1920.

Ferris, Paul, *The Church of England*, 1962.

Filmer, Sir Robert, *Patriarcha*, 1680.

Fisher, Geoffrey Francis, *A Step Forward in Church Relations*, 1946.

Flindall, R. P., *The Church of England, 1815–1948*, 1972.

Fox, Adam, *Dean Inge*, 1960.

Fuller, T., *The Church History of Britain*, 3 vols., ed. J. Nichols, 1868.

Gabor, Dennis, *Inventing the Future*, 1963.

Gay, John D., *The Geography of Religion in England*, 1971.

Gee, H. and Hardy, W., *Documents Illustrative of English Church History*, 1921.

Gibbs, Mark and Morton, T. Ralph, *God's Frozen People*, 1964.

Glasse, James D., *Profession: Minister*, 1968.

Glock, Charles Y., Ringer, Benjamin B. and Babbie, Earl R., *To Comfort and to Challenge*, 1967.

Glock, Charles Y. and Stark, Rodney, *Religion and Society in Tension*, 1965; *Christian Beliefs and Anti-Semitism*, 1966.

Gore, Charles and others, *Lux Mundi*, 1889.

Green, J. R., *A Short History of the English People*, 1874.

Gunstone, John, *The Dynamics of the Small Group Eucharist* (Societas Liturgica), 1971.

Halévy, E., *A History of the English People*, 2nd edn., 6 vols. in 7, 1949–52; *Imperialism and the Rise of Labour*, 1951.

Hall, Edward, *Chronicles*, 1548.

Hamilton, William, *The New Essence of Christianity*, 1961.

Hammond, J. R. and Barbara, *The Town Labourer, 1760–1832*, 1917; *The Skilled Labourer, 1760–1832*, 1919; *The Village Labourer, 1760–1832*, 1920.

Harman, Leslie, *The Church in Greater London*, 1968; *The Church and Planning*, 1973.

Harper, Michael, *None Can Guess*, 1971.

Harrison, B., *Drink and The Victorians: The Temperance Question in England 1815–1872*, 1971.

Hart, A. Tindal, *The Eighteenth Century Country Parson*, 1955; *Clergy and Society 1600–1800*, 1968.

Haw, G. (ed.), *Christianity and the Working Class*, 1906.

Hebert, A. G., *Liturgy and Society*, 1961.

Henry VIII, *A Necessary Doctrine and Erudition for any Christian Man*, 1543; *The Letters and Papers of Henry VIII*.

The Hereford Diocesan Church Calendar and Clergy List, 1873.

Higham, F., *Catholic and Reformed*, 1962.

Hinchliff, Peter, *The One-Sided Reciprocity*, 1966.

Hill, Christopher, *God's Englishman: Oliver Cromwell and the English Revolution*, 1970.

Hill, Michael, *A Sociology of Religion*, 1973.

Hoggart, Richard, *The Uses of Literacy*, 1957; *Speaking to Each Other*, 2 vols., 1970.

Holmes, Ann, *Church, Property and People*, the results of a survey in Bradford, Derby and Lambeth, British Council of Churches, 1973.

Hooker, Richard, *Ecclesiastical Polity*, bks. I–IV, 1593, bk. V, 1597.

Hughes, John Jay, *Absolutely Null and Utterly Void*: an Account of the 1896 Condemnation of Anglican Orders, 1968; *Stewards of the Lord*, 1970.

Hume, David, *Treatise of Human Nature*, 1739–40.

Hunter, Leslie S. (ed.), *The English Church: a New Look*, 1966.

Hurley, Michael (ed.), *Irish Anglicanism, 1869–1969*, 1969.

Illich, Ivan D., *The Celebration of Awareness*, 1971.

Inglis, K. S., *Churches and the Working Class in Victorian England*, 1963.

Iremonger, F. A., *On the need for a G.H.Q. for the Church of England*, 1945; *William Temple, Archbishop of Canterbury, his Life and Letters*, 1948.

James, Eric, *Odd Man Out?*, 1962.

Jeffery, R. M. C., *Ecumenical Experiments*, a Handbook, 1971; *Case Studies in Unity*, 1972.

Johnson, Howard A., *Global Odyssey*: an Episcopalian's Encounter with the Anglican Communion in 80 countries, 1963.

Johnson, Robert Clyde (ed.), *The Church and its Changing Ministry* (The United Presbyterian Church of U.S.A.), 1961.

Jones, K. W., 'The Views and Needs of a Parish and its Parish Priest': a private memorandum, 1971.

Jones, P. D. A., *The Christian Socialist Revival, 1877–1914*.

Jouvenel, Bertrand de, *Power. The Natural History of its Growth*, undated.

Jud, Gerald J., Mills, Edgar W., and Burch, Genevieve Walters, *Ex-Pastors: Why Men Leave the Parish Ministry*, 1970.

Judy, Marvin T., *The Larger Parish and Group Ministry*, 1959.

Kent, J. H. S., *From Darwin to Blatchford: the role of Darwinism in Christian apologetics, 1875–1910*, 1966.

Kenrick, Bruce, *Come out the Wilderness*, 1963.

Kilvert's Diary (ed. W. Plomer), 2nd edn., 3 vols., 1961.

King, John, *The Evangelicals*, 1969.

Knowles, David, *Archbishop Thomas Becket*: A character study (Proceedings of the British Academy, vol. XXXV), 1949; *Thomas Becket*, 1970.

Koestler, Arthur, *The Ghost in the Machine*, 1967.

Kraemer, Hendrik, *A Theology of the Laity*, 1958.

Kristaller, P., *Andrea Mantegna*, 1907.

Küng, Hans, *Infallible?* 1971.

Lamont, W., *Godly Rule*, 1969.

Langland, William, *Piers Plowman*, c. 1381.

Lansbury, George, *My Life*, 1928.

Law, William, *A Serious Call to a Devout and Holy Life*, 1728.

Lenski, Gerhard, *The Religious Factor*, 1963.

Lloyd, Roger, *The Church of England in the Twentieth Century*, 2 vols., 1946.

Locke, John, *Essay on Toleration*, 1689; *Two Treatises on Civil Government*, 1690; *Essay Concerning Human Understanding*, 1690; *The Reasonableness of Christianity*, 1694.

Lovell, George, *The Church and Community Development*, 1971.

McBrien, Richard P., *Do we need the Church?*, 1969.

McCulloch, Joseph, *Parson in Revolt*, 1952.

MacFarlane, K. B., *John Wycliffe and the Beginnings of English Nonconformity*, 1952.

McGrath, P., *Papists and Puritans under Elizabeth I*, 1967.

MacIntyre, Alasdair, *Secularisation and Moral Change*, 1967; *Against the Self-Images of the Age*, 1971.

MacKinnon, Donald, *The Stripping of the Altars*, 1969.

McLuhan, Marshall, *The Gutenberg Galaxy*, 1962.

Mailer, Norman, *An American Dream*, 1965.

Mann, Horace, *Religious Worship in England and Wales* (census of Great Britain, 1851), 1854.

Mann, Peter H., *An Approach to Urban Sociology*, 1965.

Manning, B. L., *The Making of Modern English Religion*, 1929.

Marsh, P. T., *The Victorian Church in Decline*, 1969.

Marson, Charles L., *God's Cooperative Society*, 1914.

Martin, David, *A Sociology of English Religion*, 1967.

Marx, Karl and Engels, Friedrich, *The Communist Manifesto*, 1848.

Mascall, E. L., *The Secularisation of Christianity*, 1965.

Masterman, N. C., *John Malcolm Ludlow*, 1963.

Mathieson, W. L., *English Church Reform, 1815–40*, 1923.

Matthews, Walter, *The Thirty-Nine Articles*, 1961; *Memoirs and Meanings*, 1969.

Maurice, Frederick Denison, *The Kingdom of Christ*, 1838.

Maurice, J. F., *The Life of Frederick Denison Maurice*, 2 vols., 1884.

Maycock, A. L., *Nicholas Ferrar of Little Gidding*, 1938.

Mayfield, Guy, *The Church of England: its members and its business*, 1958; *Like Nothing on Earth*, 1965.

Mayor, Stephen, *The Churches and the Labour Movement*, 1967.

Milton, John, *Areopagitica*, 1644.

Mitton, C. L. (ed.), *The Social Sciences and The Churches*, 1972.

Monod, Jacques, *Chance and Necessity*, 1972.

Montefiore, Hugh, *Doom or Deliverance?* The dogmas and duties of a technological age, 1972; *Can Man Survive?*, 1972.

Moore, Peter, *Tomorrow is Too Late*, 1970.

Moorhouse, Geoffrey, *Calcutta*, 1971.

Moorman, J. R. H., *A History of the Church in England*, 1954.

More, Thomas, *Four Last Things*, 1522; *A Dialogue of Comfort*, 1534.

Morgan, David H. T., 'The Social and Educational Backgrounds of English Diocesan Bishops, 1860–1960.' Unpublished M.A. Thesis of Nottingham University.

Mumford, Lewis, *The Myth of the Machine*, 1967; *The City in History*, 1961; *The Condition of Man*, 1944.

Neil, William, *The Truth about the Early Church*, 1970.

Neill, Stephen, *Anglicanism*, Revised edn., 1960; *Men of Unity*, 1960; *A History of Christian Missions*, 1964.

Neill, Stephen and Weber, Hans-Ruedi, *The Layman in Christian History*, 1963.

Nelson, Geoffrey K. and Clews, Rosemary A., *Mobility and Religious Commitment*, 1971.

New English Bible, 1961, 1970.

Newman, John Henry, *Apologia Pro Vita Sua*, 1864.

Nuttall, G. F. and Chadwick, Owen, *From Uniformity to Unity*, 1962.

Nuttall, Jeff, *The Bomb Culture*, 1970.

Occam, William of, *Quodlibeta Septem.*

Ogden, Schubert M., *Philosophers speak of God,* 1953; *The Reality of God,* 1967.

Opinions of the Legal Board, 1973.

Osborn, T. L., *Frontier Evangelism, with Miracles of Healing,* 1955; *Healing the Sick and Casting Out Devils,* 1955.

O'Sullivan, Richard, *The King's Good Servant:* Papers read to the Thomas More Society of London, 1948.

Overton, J. H., *The Non-Jurors,* 1902.

Paley, William, *Evidences of Christianity,* 1794.

Parker, G. N. H., *Morning Star,* 1965.

Parsons, Talcott, *The Structure of Social Action:* vol. I, Marshall, Pareto, Durkheim; vol. II, Weber, 1937.

Paul, Leslie, *The English Philosophers,* 1953; *Nature into History,* 1957; *Persons and Perception,* 1961; *Deployment and Payment of the Clergy,* 1964; *The Church as an Institution,* 1966; *Alternatives to Christian Belief,* 1967; *Death and Resurrection of the Church,* 1968; *Sir Thomas More,* 1953; *Studies in the Sociology of Religion,* 1970; *Man's Understanding of Himself,* 1971.

Payne, E. A., *The Baptist Union: a Short History,* 1959.

Pearsall, Ronald, *The Worm in the Bud:* the World of Victorian Sexuality, 1969.

Perkins, Harold, *The Origins of Modern English Society,* 1969.

Perrin, Henri, *Priest and Worker,* 1964.

Pickering, W. S. F. (ed.), *Anglo–Methodist relations,* some institutional factors, 1961.

Pickering, W. S. F. and Blanchard, T. L., *Taken for Granted:* a survey of the Parish Clergy of the Anglican Church of Canada, 1967.

Pitt, Valerie, *The Church and Social Revolution* (Prism Pamphlet No. 27), 1966.

Pittenger, Norman, *God in Process,* 1967.

Pius XII, *Corpus Christi Mysticum,* Encyclical of 1943.

Postgate, Raymond, *The Life of George Lansbury,* 1957.

Proctor, F. and Frere, W. H., *A New History of the Book of Common Prayer,* 1908.

Ramsey, Arthur Michael, *From Gore to Temple* (Hale Memorial Lectures, 1959), 1960.

Ramsey, Arthur Michael and Suenens, Léon-Joseph, *The Future of the Christian Church,* 1971.

Rauschenbusch, Walter (ed. Max. L. Stackhaus), *The Righteousness of the Kingdom,* 1968.

Ray, John, *The Wisdom of God in the Works of Creation,* 1691.

Reckitt, Maurice, *As it Happened,* 1941; *Maurice to Temple:* a Century of Social Movement in the Church of England, 1947.

Reckitt, Maurice and Bechhofer, C. E., *The Meaning of National Guilds,* 1918.

Reich, Charles A., *The Greening of America,* 1970.

Reiss, Albert J., *Occupations and Social Status,* 1961.

Research Bulletin 1967, Institute for the Study of Worship and Architecture.

Reynolds, E. E., *Thomas More and Erasmus,* 1965.

Reynolds, J. S., *The Evangelicals at Oxford,* 1953.

Roberts, Ted, *Partners and Ministers:* an experiment in supplementary ministry, 1972.

Robertson, Roland (ed.), *Sociology of Religion: Selected Readings,* 1969.

Robinson, J. A. T., *Honest to God,* 1963; *The New Reformation,* 1965; *Exploration into God,* 1967; *The Human Face of God,* 1973.

Robinson, J. A. T. and others, *Layman's Church,* 1963.

Roszak, Theodore, *The Making of the Counter Culture,* 1969.

Rowe, John, *Priests and Workers,* 1965.

Rowse, A. L., *The Elizabethan Renaissance:* 1. *The Life of the Society,* 1971; 2. *The Cultural Achievement,* 1972.

Rudge, Peter F., *Ministry and Management,* 1968.

Schallert, Eugene J. and Kelley, Jacqueline M., 'Some Factors Associated with Voluntary Withdrawal from the Catholic Priesthood' *Lumen Vitae,* XXV, 1970, No. 3.

Scharf, Betty R., *The Sociological Study of Religion*, 1970.

Schultz, Roger, *Unanimité dans la Pluralisme*, 1970.

Selborne, Lord, *A Defence of the Church of England against Disestablishment*, 1886.

Sheppard, Dick, *The Impatience of a Parson*.

Smethurst, A. F., Wilson, H. R. and Riley, H., *Acts of the Convocation of Canterbury and York*, 1961.

Smith, Arthur C., *Team and Group Ministry*, 1965.

Smith, Ronald Gregor, *Secular Christianity*, 1966.

Smyth, Charles, *Simeon and Church Order*, 1940.

A Sociological Yearbook of Religion, 1968 and subsequent years.

Southcott, Ernest, *The Parish Comes Alive*, 1956.

Spencer, Herbert, *Principles of Biology*, 1864; *The Man versus the State*, 1884.

Stacey, Nicolas, *Who Cares?* 1971.

Stanley, A. P., *The Life of Dr Arnold*, 1858.

Stark, Rodney and Glock, Charles Y., *American Piety: The Nature of Religious Commitment*, 1968.

Stark, Werner, *The Sociology of Religion*: A Study of Christendom, The Macrasociology of Religion in 3 vols. 1. Established Religion, 1966. 2. Sectarian Religion, 3. The Universal Church. 1967.

Streiker, Lowell, *The Jesus Trip*, 1971.

Toffler, Alvin, *Future Shock*, 1970.

Swift, Jonathan, *Gulliver's Travels*, 1726.

Sykes, Norman, *Church and State in England in the Eighteenth Century*, 1934; *Old Priest and New Presbyter*, 1956; *From Sheldon to Secker* (Ford Lectures 1958), 1959; *Man as Churchman*, 1960.

Taine, Hippolyte (Trans. Edward Hyams), *Notes on England*, 1957.

Tait, A. J., *Charles Simeon and his Trust*, 1936.

Tatham, G. B., *The Puritans in Power*, 1913.

Tawney, R. H., *Religion and the Rise of Capitalism*, 1927, Pelican 1938.

Taylor, John V., *Breaking down the Parish*, 1967; *The Go-Between God*, 1972.

Temple, Frederick and others, *Essays and Reviews*, 1860.

Temple, Frederick, *The Relations between Religion and Science*, 1884.

Temple, W., *Life and Liberty*, 1917.

Thompson, A. Hamilton, *The English Clergy*, 1947.

Thompson, Kenneth A., *Bureaucracy and Church Reform*: The Organizational Response of the Church of England to Social Change, 1800–1965. 1970.

Tindal, Matthew, *Christianity as Old as Creation, or the Gospel a Republication of the Religion of Nature*, 1730.

The Tourists' Church Guide, 1902.

Toland, John, *Christianity not Mysterious*, 1696.

Towards the Conversion of England, 1945.

Toynbee, Arnold, *The Industrial Revolution of the Eighteenth Century in England*, 1913; *A Study of History*, vols. I–III, 1934; IV–VI, 1939; VII–X, 1954; XI, 1958; XII, 1961.

Tracts for the Times, Oxford 1833–41.

Traherne, Thomas, *The Centuries of Meditations*, 1908.

Trevelyan, G. M., *English Social History*, 1946.

Van Buren, Paul M., *The Secular Meaning of the Gospel*, 1963; *The Edges of Language*, 1972.

Verney, Stephen, *People and Cities*, 1969.

Vidler, A. R. F. (ed.), *Soundings*, 1962.

Vidler, A. R. F., *Maurice and Others*, 1966.

Waal, Victor de, *What is the Church?*, 1969.

Wakefield, G. E., *Methodist Devotion*, 1791–1945.

Ward, Barbara and Dubos, René, *Only One Earth: The Care and Maintenance of a Small Planet*, 1972.

Ward, C. K., *Priests and People*, 1961.

Weber, Max, *The Protestant Ethic and the Spirit of Capitalism*, 1930.

Wedell, Eberhard, *The Reform of Church Government* (Prism Pamphlet No. 20), 1965.

Wells, H. G., *A Modern Utopia*, 1905.

West, Frank, *Sparrows of the Spirit*, 1961.

Westminster Confession of Faith, The, 1643.

Whale, J. S., *The Protestant Tradition*, 1955.

White, W. Hale, *The Autobiography of Mark Rutherford*, 1881.

Wicker, Brian, *Culture and Theology*, 1966.

Wickham, E. R., *Church and People in an Industrial City*, 1957; *Encounter with Modern Society*, 1964.

Williams, G. H., *The Radical Reformation*, 1962.

Williams, H. A., *The True Wilderness*, 1965.

Wilkinson, Paul, *Social Movement*, 1971.

Williams, Raymond, *Culture and Society, 1780–1950*, 1958.

Wilson, Bryan R., *Religion in Secular Society*, 1966.

Wilson, Bryan R. (ed.), *Patterns of Sectarianism*, 1967.

Winnington-Ingram, A. F., *Work in Great Cities*, 1896.

Wing, Charles, *The Evils of the Factory System*, 1837.

Winter, Gibson, *The Suburban Captivity of the Churches*, 1961; *The New Creation as Metropolis*, 1963.

Wycliffe, John, *De Officio Regis*, Wyclif Society 1887.

Yeo, S. and others, *For Christ and People*: Studies of four socialist priests and prophets of the Church of England between 1870 and 1930, 1951.

Zaehner, R. C., *Dialectical Christianity and Christian Materialism*, 1971; *Drugs, Mysticism and Make-Believe*, 1972.

Reports

An Agreed Statement on Eucharistic Doctrine, Anglican–Roman Catholic International Commission, 1972.

Barnes, Irwin, '*Let my People go!*' A Report on Lay Training prepared for the Selly Oak Colleges, Birmingham, 1970.

Battersea Deanery Survey, Battersea Rural Deanery, 1966.

Battersea Deanery Organisation Committee Report, 1971.

Beeson, Trevor, *The World is the Agenda*, Report of a Conference on The Missionary Structure of the Congregation, Parish and People, 1966.

Bishops and Dioceses, Report of the ACCM Ministry Committee Working Party, CIO, 1971.

Blueprint for Survival (*The Ecologist*) January 1972.

Buildings and Breakthrough: Report of the Buildings Study Group of the Diocese of Chichester: Institute for the Study of Worship and Religious Architecture, Undated.

Christian Initiations, Birth and Growth in the Christian Society, CIO, 1971.

Church Assembly, *Report of Proceedings*, CIO.

Church and State, Report of the Archbishops' Commission, CIO, 1970.

Church and State (Selborne Committee) CIO, 1916.

The Church for Others, World Council of Churches.

The Church, Its Nature, Function and Ordering: Report of a Joint Commission of Congregationalists, Methodists and Presbyterians.

The Church's Needs and Resources, Sixth Report, CIO, 1972.

Clergy in Church and Society, Actes de la IX Conférence Internationale de Sociologie Religieuse, 1967.

Civil Strife, A Report presented by the Board for Social Responsibility, CIO, 1972.

Crown Appointments and the Church, Report of the Archbishops' Commission, CIO, 1964.

Deployment and Payment of the Clergy (The Paul Report), 1964.

Diocesan Boundaries, Report of the Archbishop's Commission on the Organization of the Church by Dioceses in London and the south-east of England, CIO, 1967.

A Diocese Looks Forward, Report of the 1970 Committee to the Bishop of St Alban's, 1967.

Reports of the Archbishop's Committees on Diocesan Reorganization, Diocese of Melbourne, 1969.

The Division of the Diocese, Report of the Bishop of Oxford's Working Party, 1970.

Doctrine in the Church of England, 1938.

Charlton, N., *The Ecumenical Parish of Old Swindon*, The Ecumenical Parish, 71 Bath Road, Swindon, 1971.

Evangelical Strategy in the New Towns, Evangelical Alliance, 1971.

Faith and Order Findings, Report to the Fourth World Conference on Faith and Order (ed. Paul S. Minear) WCC, 1963.

'*For Heaven's Sake We Need Space*'. Killingworth Christian Council, No date.

General Synod. *Reports of Proceedings*, CIO.

Government by Synod, CIO, 1966.

Initiative in History, A Christian–Marxist Exchange between Roger Garaudy and Myron B. Bloy. Church Society for College Work, U.S.A., 1967.

Intercommunion Today, Report of the Archbishops' Commission, CIO, 1968.

The Lambeth Conference, CIO, 1958.

The Lambeth Conference Report, CIO, 1968.

Report of the Bishop's Lay Commission, Diocese of Chelmsford, 1967.

Man in his Living Environment, CIO, 1970.

Membership, Manpower and Money in the Anglican Communion: A Survey of 27 Churches and 300 Dioceses, Anglican Consultative Council, 1973.

Conversations Between the Church of England and the Methodist Church, CIO, 1963.

Towards Reconciliation, the Interim Statement of the Anglican–Methodist Unity Commission, CIO, 1967.

Anglican–Methodist Unity, 1 The Ordinal; 2 The Scheme, CIO, 1968.

Anglican–Methodist Unity, Report of a Joint Working Group, CIO, 1971.

Mayor, S. H., *Ministry in the Midlands*, 1968.

Ministry Tomorrow, Report of the Commission on the Ministry, Baptist Union, London, undated.

The Nature and Function of the Episcopate, CIO, 1967.

Reciprocal Intercommunion, General Synod Commission 1970, CIO, 1973.

Report on the Neighbourhood Churches, Poynton Council of Churches, 1971.

The Ordination of Women to the Priesthood, A Consultative document, by the Advisory Council for the Church's Ministry, CIO, 1972.

Partners in Ministry (The Morley Report), CIO, 1967.

The Paul Report, The Next Steps, CIO, 1964.

A Study of the Paul Report on the Deployment and Payment of the Clergy, CIO, 1964.

The Paul Report, Issues Raised, CIO, 1965.

The Place of Auxiliary Ministry, Ordained and Lay, ACCM, CIO, 1973.

The Position of the Laity in the Church, 2nd edn., 1952.

Prayer and the Departed. Report of the Archbishops' Commission on Christian Doctrine, CIO, 1971.

Advisory Board for Redundant Churches, *Annual Reports*, CIO.

The Archbishops' Commission on Redundant Churches, CIO, 1960.

Redundant Churches Fund, *Second Annual Report*, CIO, 1970.

Sanitary Officer's Second Annual Report for the Strand District of London, 1858.

The Shape of the Ministry, British Council of Churches, Undated.

Sharing of Churches, Report of the Archbishops' Commission, CIO, 1966.

Specialist Ministries, Report of the Working Party of the Ministry Committee of ACCM, CIO, 1971.

'Spirit, Order and Organization' Report of the WCC Study Group *Study Encounter*, Fall 1970.

Report of the Commission on the Staffing of Parishes to the Church Assembly, CIO, 1930.

Report of the Summer Vacation Work in the Parish of Abbey Wood, by three Franciscan Students, The Presbytery, 31 Abbey Grove, London, S.E.12, 1970.

Television and Religion, A Report prepared by Social Surveys (Gallup Poll) Ltd, 1964.

First Report of the Terms of Ministry Committee, CIO, 1972, *Second Report*, CIO, 1973.

The Church of South India, A Report from the House of Bishops, CIO, 1973.

A Supporting Ministry, A Report of the Ministry Committee of ACCM, CIO, 1968.

Theological Colleges for Tomorrow, Report of a Working Party, CIO, 1968.

The Time is Now, Report of the Anglican Consultative Council at Limuru, 1971. CIO, 1971.

Tomorrow's Parish. Introduction by the Bishop of Southwark I.C.F. Press, 1969.

The Transition from School to Work, Industrial Society, 1962.

Unity Begins at Home, A Report from the First British Conference on Faith and Order, 1964.

Women and Holy Orders, Report of the Archbishops' Commission, CIO, 1966.

Index